ECONOMIC TRANSITION IN AFRICA

NORTHWESTERN UNIVERSITY African Studies

Number Twelve

ECONOMIC TRANSITION IN AFRICA

edited by
MELVILLE J. HERSKOVITS
and
MITCHELL HARWITZ

Northwestern University Press

Published 1964 by Northwestern University Press

Library of Congress Catalog Number: 63–13559

This volume was prepared from papers presented at a Conference on Indigenous and Induced Elements in the Economics of Subsaharan Africa held by the Committee on Economic Growth, Social Science Research Council, at Northwestern University, November 16–18, 1961.

Printed in Great Britain

This book is dedicated
to the memory of
Melville J. Herskovits
by his colleagues,
the members of the
Committee on Economic Growth
of the Social Science Research Council

Preface

The Conference on Indigenous and Induced Elements in the Economics of Subsaharan Africa was one of a series held under the auspices of the Committee on Economic Growth of the Social Science Research Council. This was in accordance with its policy, stated in the reports of the Council for 1960–1961, "to stimulate critical examination of the assumptions that underlie analyses of the processes of economic growth and the validity and relevance of available bodies of data."

This policy dictated the selection of the topics treated in the papers of the Conference, revised versions of which constitute the chapters of this book. The uniqueness of this volume, and the essence of its scholarly contribution, arises out of the fact that it takes into full account the sectors of the historical continuum which, in all world areas, order a given process of change and its observed results. It takes on additional importance from the fact that it points towards the welding of the analytical resources of economics to the imperatives of traditional practices in the study of economic growth, especially in economically underdeveloped areas. To give the reader an idea of the interdisciplinary scope of an undertaking of this kind, we have indicated the fields of the participants as well as their institutional affiliations in the list of those who participated in the meetings.

Though originally each of the several chapters carried its own references, we have consolidated these into a single bibliography, to avoid duplication and also to provide a ready compilation of useful works. Names of African countries, in most cases, are those of the period under discussion, a point of some importance in view of the fact that some of the newly independent nations have taken on new designations. At times this can be confusing. Thus the Congo Republic is what, in United Nations parlance, is called Congo (Brazzaville), and was the province of Moyen Congo of French Equatorial Africa. The Republic of the Congo, on the other hand, often termed Congo (Leopoldville), was the Belgian Congo. Names of African ethnic groupings are rendered as the authors of the various chapters indicated. Thus, in some cases the Bantu prefix (as in Baganda, called by some Ganda) is given, elsewhere in others (as in Lega, for Warega) it is not.

Tables and charts are numbered in accordance with the decimal system that is increasingly employed in the behavioral sciences. We have used all diligence in ascertaining the correct reference numbers to United Nations publications. In this we have been greatly helped by the staff of the Documents Room, Deering Library. For the retyping of text and tables we are beholden to the Program of African Studies, particularly to Miss Anne Moneypenny, its Executive Secretary.

MELVILLE J. HERSKOVITS
MITCHELL HARWITZ

Northwestern University
5 September, 1962

The extraordinary editorial burdens caused by the untimely death of Melville J. Herskovits have fallen most heavily upon Mrs. Frances S. Herskovits, Miss Anne Moneypenny, Mrs. Kathleen Ayrton, and Dr. Margaret Katzin. Thanks are owed to them for their invaluable aid.

MITCHELL HARWITZ

Evanston
October, 1963

Contents

PREFACE   *page* vii

PARTICIPANTS AT THE CONFERENCE   xvii

PART ONE: INTRODUCTORY

1. AFRICA AND THE PROBLEMS OF ECONOMIC GROWTH
   Melville J. Herskovits (Northwestern University)   3
2. SUBSAHARAN AFRICA AS A GROWING ECONOMIC SYSTEM
   Mitchell Harwitz (Northwestern University)   15

PART TWO: THE INDIGENOUS PATTERNS

3. ECONOMICS IN EAST AFRICAN ABORIGINAL SOCIETIES
   Harold K. Schneider (Lawrence College)   53
4. WEST AFRICAN ECONOMIC SYSTEMS
   Elliott P. Skinner (New York University)   77
5. LAND HOLDING AND SOCIAL ORGANIZATION
   Daniel Biebuyck (University of Delaware)   99
6. SOCIAL STRATIFICATION AND ECONOMIC PROCESSES
   Lloyd A. Fallers (University of Chicago)   113

PART THREE: INDUCED ECONOMIC PHENOMENA

7. LAND USE, LAND TENURE AND LAND REFORM
   Paul J. Bohannan (Northwestern University)   133
8. CHANGES IN AGRICULTURAL PRODUCTIVITY
   Bruce F. Johnston (Stanford University)   151
9. THE ROLE OF THE SMALL ENTREPRENEUR
   Margaret Katzin (Northwestern University)   179
10. REAL INCOME TRENDS IN WEST AFRICA, 1939–1960
    Elliot J. Berg (Harvard University)   199

PART FOUR: THE CHANGING ECONOMIC SCENE

11. DEMOGRAPHIC FACTORS IN SUBSAHARAN ECONOMIC DEVELOPMENT
    H. W. Singer (United Nations)   241

12. THE DEVELOPMENT OF THE ECONOMIC INFRASTRUCTURE
   A. M. Kamarck (International Bank for Reconstruction
   and Development)   *page* 263
13. THE ADAPTATION OF AFRICAN LABOR SYSTEMS TO SOCIAL CHANGE
   Wilbert E. Moore (Princeton University)   277
14. THE MOVEMENT INTO THE WORLD ECONOMY
   William J. Barber (Wesleyan University)   299

PART FIVE: PROBLEMS OF ECONOMIC GROWTH

15. INDEPENDENCE AND THE PROBLEM OF ECONOMIC GROWTH
   P. N. C. Okigbo (Ministry of Economic Planning, Enugu,
   Nigeria)   323
16. TRENDS IN AFRICAN EXPORTS AND CAPITAL INFLOWS
   Walter A. Chudson (United Nations)   337
17. INTERNATIONAL ORGANIZATION AND AFRICAN ECONOMIC GROWTH
   Lattee A. Fahm (Massachusetts Institute of Technology) 357
18. ECONOMIC GROWTH AND POLITICAL REORIENTATION
   James S. Coleman (University of California, Los Angeles) 377

PART SIX: SOME SUGGESTIONS FOR FUTURE
   RESEARCH

19. THE CONFERENCE DISCUSSIONS
   Melville J. Herskovits (Northwestern University)   399

BIBLIOGRAPHY   409

INDEX OF SUBJECTS   427

INDEX OF NAMES AND PLACES   439

Tables

2.1. Indices of Output of Principal Minerals   *page* 19
2.2. Summary Percentage Table   28
2.3. Territorial Allocation of Subsaharan Export Trade: Percentage
     Shares of Territories in Total Domestic Exports in Selected
     Years   29–30
2.4. Total Overseas Capital per capita in Each African Territory (ca.
     1935)   30
2.5. Total Value of Domestic Exports of each African Territory in
     1907, 1929, 1935   31
2.6. Total Value of Domestic Imports of each African Territory in
     1907, 1929, 1935   32
2.7. Trends in Average Annual Outputs of Major Agricultural
     Export Commodities for Selected Periods between 1920
     and 1958   33–35
2.8. International Seaborne Shipping and Foreign Trade   36
2.9. African Share in World Production and Exports of Selected
     Agricultural Commodities   37
2.10. African Share in World Production and Exports of Selected
     Minerals   37
2.11. Main Flows of African Inter-Territorial Trade, 1957   38
2.12. Value of Trade between Selected African Countries, 1950–1957   39
2.13. Gross Value of Output of Mining and Quarrying   40
2.14. Imports by Category as Percentage of Total Value   41
2.15. Output per Man of Principal Minerals in Selected Countries   42–43
2.16. Major Export Commodities and Percentage of Total Domestic
     Exports Accounted for by Each in Selected Years   44–47
2.17. Industrial Origin of Gross Domestic Product at Current Factor
     Cost, Selected Countries, 1955   48
2.18. Distribution of Economically Active Population by Sex and
     Ethnic Composition, Selected Countries   49
3.1. Relation between Grain Production and the Variables of Manure,
     Acres Cultivated, and Number of Wives in Thirty Farmsteads
     in a Turu Village   58
4.1. Volume, Value, Type, Source, and Destination of Goods in Kano
     Market, 1851   90–91
8.1. Prewar and Postwar Population of Selected Cities of Tropical
     Africa   161
8.2. Percentage of Able-bodied Males Engaged in Wage Employ-
     ment, Prewar and Postwar   162

xi

10.1. Changes in Money Incomes and Prices of Consumer Goods, NIGERIA, 1939–1949   *page* 204
10.2. Indicators of Changes in Real Incomes, NIGERIA, 1939–1949   205
10.3. Changes in Money Incomes and Prices of Consumer Goods, GHANA (GOLD COAST), 1939–1949   206
10.4. Indicators of Changes in Real Incomes, GHANA (GOLD COAST), 1939–1949   207
10.5. Changes in Money Incomes and Prices of Consumer Goods, FRENCH WEST AFRICA, 1938–1949   208
10.6. Indicators of Changes in Real Incomes, FRENCH WEST AFRICA, 1938–1949   209
10.7. Changes in Money Incomes and Prices of Consumer Goods, NIGERIA, 1946–1960   219
10.8. Indicators of Changes in Real Incomes, NIGERIA, 1946–1960   220
10.9. Changes in Money Incomes and Prices of Consumer Goods, GHANA (GOLD COAST), 1946–1960   221
10.10. Indicators of Changes in Real Incomes, GHANA (GOLD COAST), 1946–1960   222
10.11. Changes in Money Incomes and Prices of Consumer Goods, FRENCH WEST AFRICA, 1946–1960   223
10.12. Indicators of Changes in Real Incomes, FRENCH WEST AFRICA, 1946–1960   224
10.13. NIGERIA. Producer Prices, Sales and Aggregate Receipts of Export Crop Growers, and Wage Rates, 1939–1960   231
10.14. GHANA (GOLD COAST). Producer Prices, Sales and Aggregate Receipts of Cocoa Farmers, and Wage Rates, 1939–1960 232
10.15. FRENCH WEST AFRICA. Prices, Sales and Estimated Aggregate Receipts of Export Crop Growers, and Wage Rates, 1938–1960   233
11.1. Estimated Population and Population Density by Total Land Area and Agricultural Land Area for African Countries, and Range of Densities for Administrative Divisions within Countries   253–254
11.2. Africans Employed in Selected Countries, by Country of Origin (Local and Non-Local)   255
11.3. Economically Active Population by Sex in Selected African Countries   256
11.4. Estimated Economically Active Population Classified as Engaged in Agriculture and in Non-agricultural Activities, and Proportions of Wage and Salary Earners in the Total Population for Selected African Countries   257
11.5. Percentage of Population in Selected Countries of Africa Classified as Residing in Urban Areas, in Cities of 20,000 Population and Over, and in Largest Cities   258
11.6. Estimated Dependency Ratios in Selected African Countries   259

11.7. Birth Rates, Death Rates and Natural Increase Rates, 1950–1959, and Rates of Population Growth, 1941–1960, for Selected African Countries *page* 260
12.1. Railways, Subsaharan Africa, 1959 265
12.2. Motor Vehicles in Circulation, 1959 267
12.3. International Port Traffic, 1959 268
12.4. Electric Power Output in African Countries 271
12.5. Percentage of Enrolment to School-Age Population 273
16.1. Subsaharan Africa: Net international Flow of Long-term Capital and official donations, by country, 1951–1955 and 1956–1959 355
17.1. Financing of Development Plans of Selected African Countries— By Source of Funds 361
17.2. Multilateral Assistance to Economically Less Developed Areas in Subsaharan Africa; 1954–1958; 1959–1960 364
17.3. Bilateral Assistance to Less Developed Areas in Subsaharan Africa; 1954–1958; 1959–1960 372
17.4. Gross National Product Projections of African Countries, South of the Sahara, 1961–1971 373
17.5. Foreign Capital Inflow Required for Underdeveloped African Countries, South of the Sahara, 1961–1971 374
17.6. Composition of Foreign Capital Inflow per Annum 375

Charts

3.1. Graph Showing Actual Livestock Wealth (Wealth Index) in Relation to Livestock Held (Implied by Manure Index) and Grain Production in Thirty Farmsteads in a Turu Village   *page* 60

7.1. Relationship of Genealogy to Territory, Tiv Tribe   136

7.2. a. The Kikuyu *mbari*   146

7.2. b. Expansion of the *mbari*   146

8.1. Agricultural Exports of Selected African Countries, 1909–1959   157

    A. Cocoa   157

    B. Coffee   157

    C. Unmanufactured Tobacco   158

    D. Palm Oil   158

    E. Palm Kernels and Palm Kernel Oil   158

    F. Peanuts and Peanut Oil   159

    G. Cotton   159

    H. Sisal   160

    I. Rubber   160

Participants

Daniel Biebuyck (Anthropology), University of Delaware
W. O. Brown (Sociology),[1] Boston University
Paul J. Bohannan (Anthropology), Northwestern University
Elliot Berg (Economics), Harvard University
W. J. Barber (Economics), Wesleyan University
Walter A. Chudson (Economics), United Nations
James S. Coleman (Political Science), University of California, Los Angeles
St. Clair Drake (Sociology),[2] Roosevelt University
Lloyd Fallers (Anthropology), University of Chicago
Lattee Fahm (Economics), Massachusetts Institute of Technology
Melville J. Herskovits (Anthropology),[1,3] Northwestern University
Richard Hartshorne (Geography),[1,3] University of Wisconsin
Bert Hoselitz (Economics),[3] University of Chicago
Mitchell Harwitz (Economics), Northwestern University
Paul Henry (Economics), United Nations
William O. Jones (Economics),[2] Stanford University
Bruce Johnston (Economics),[2] Stanford University
Margaret Katzin (Anthropology), Northwestern University
Simon Kuznets (Economics),[1,3] Harvard University
Andrew Kamarck (Economics), International Bank for Reconstruction and Development
Frank Lorimer (Demography),[1] Princeton University
Wilbert E. Moore (Sociology),[3] Princeton University
Benton F. Massell (Economics), The Rand Corporation
Selby B. Ngcobo (Economics), University College of Rhodesia and Nyasaland
Pius Okigbo (Economics),[4] Ministry of Economic Planning, Enugu, Nigeria
Arnold Rivkin (Economics),[2] Massachusetts Institute of Technology
Jerome Rothenberg (Economics), Northwestern University
Hans Panofsky (Economics), Northwestern University
N. Manfred Shaffer (Geography), Northwestern University
H. W. Singer (Economics), United Nations
Harold K. Schneider (Anthropology), Lawrence College

xvii

Elliott P. Skinner (Anthropology), New York University
Paul Webbink (Economics),[3] Social Science Research Council
Fred Westfield (Economics), Northwestern University
Harold Williamson (Economics),[1] Northwestern University

[1] Chairman of Session.
[2] Discussant.
[3] Member of Social Science Research Council Committee on Economic Development.
[4] Contributed paper, but unable to attend because of official duties.

PART ONE
Introductory

I

Africa and the Problems of Economic Growth

by Melville J. Herskovits
Northwestern University

The questions raised by the papers presented in this volume provide an added dimension to the study of problems of economic growth, as the insights their substantive materials yield are projected on to the complexities of the rapidly changing African scene. These questions, particularly those having to do with method, have wide ramifications. They have to do with the nature of the interdisciplinary approach, the relation of the study of economic growth to area research in general, the kinds of information that are pertinent, the role of the world area as a laboratory where generalizations can be tested, and the place of the scholar in establishing guide-lines for the implementation of practical problems, among others.

While concern with economic development, whether in its theoretical or its practical implications, is not entirely new in the academic repertory, there can be little question that the degree of interest in problems of this order has greatly increased since the second World War. As is so often the case in the human sciences, areas of research that have been given little attention, and some problems whose significance had been accorded recognition, have been moved to the fore by circumstances extraneous to academic considerations. This has been strikingly true of matters having to do with economic growth, particularly in what is called the "underdeveloped" countries, as the desire of their peoples has become more pressing for raised standards of living and enlarged opportunities to participate in the benefits derived from greater technological competence. Concomitant with the break-up of the colonial system, and implemented by the attainment of sovereignty, the claims of these countries were not to be denied. The question of how to

3

determine the relevant facts, and how to mobilize these facts so as to attain desired ends, became paramount.

With the urgency of the problems ever more apparent, appeal was made to the economists and the technicians for guidance. In our present context, we need not be concerned with what the technicians did. Suffice it to say that in too many instances their experience in applying expert knowledge in the areas to which they were sent was not of the happiest. On the strictly technical side, they discovered that procedures which they had successfully used in their home countries would not necessarily work in different ecological and cultural settings. They began to find out for themselves, usually through trial and error, that extensive revisions of their ideas as to the degree to which their scientific techniques could be thought of as universally applicable were very much in order.

This was also true of the economists. On the theoretical side, the principles which they had developed in the study of Euroamerican economic systems, and the mathematical models that were expressions of these principles, were found inadequate when applied to economies in process of rapid change. In large measure, this resulted from the fact that new parameters had to be determined to fit the dynamics of such economies. For here change was not only of the essence, but moved along lines which had historical and cultural roots quite different from those of the pecuniary, industrialized countries of Europe and America.

There was, in addition, another element in this new field that posed difficulties for those who wished to study economic growth, or to operate in its context. This was the lack of empirical quantitative data, either for a given moment, or from which time series could be derived. Records in dependent territories, even toward the end of the colonial system, to say nothing of the case in independent countries where the statistical tradition did not exist, were sparse. Even when figures on such a basic datum as the numbers of people who inhabited a given territory were available, they were too often essentially impressionistic. Statistics of national wealth, national product, national income, were fragmentary. Yet these are the essential materials of economic science; where they were absent, methods of coping with the lack of them had to be improvised until enough information of requisite quality could be obtained.

Gradually, it began to be discerned that factors long taken for granted in drawing up models and developing general principles might be an important cause of the difficulty. For despite the introduction of money and the machine, despite the development of urban centres where industry could be sited and the growth of large-scale, mechanized agriculture, assumptions whose validity had gained general acceptance were found not always to hold. Concepts of value, allocations of wealth, motivations in both the productive and distributive aspects of the economies were seen to differ from those present in the Euroamerican systems from which economists had derived the principles held to govern their functions. Factors deriving from antecedent patterns of kinship, or of prestige, invaded considerations of self-interest in unanticipated ways, which meant that fresh orientations in theory and practice had to be sought.

Students of economic growth were thus faced with a new problem. In essence, this was to account for observed differences and to derive conclusions appropriate to them, in the light of the general principles of economic science. It was apparent that while the conventional approaches, and the theories on which they were based, needed revision to fit the new economic settings, this was more a matter of modifying conventionally accepted concepts and principles than, as some enthusiasts had it, of jettisoning them and beginning anew. Given the differing historical and cultural contexts of economies under rapid change, the problem became one of determining common denominators in observed economies, or, in the case of a particular society, revising models to fit the particularities of its developing economic system.

Here the importance of the cross-cultural factor in the study of the economies of economically developing non-European peoples enters as a significant component. Traditional institutions, systems of value, types of economic motivation, add a new variable, or a series of variables, to every equation. Without taking these into account, the conventional approaches lose much of their worth—lose this to the extent and in the degree that such imponderables of tradition deviate from the norms of the Euroamerican societies in which economic theory and method has been developed.

We may put this in another way. Economic theorists and planners, in this new setting, began to find that their concepts and practices were applicable only to the degree to which the economic and social forms found in a developing society were comparable to those of the one from which they had come. This is why, for example, it has been so much easier to study economic growth in South Africa than in the Sudan, in Southern Rhodesia than in the Gabon. The study of Northern Rhodesian economics by Phyllis Deane bears ample testimony to the difficulties to be encountered by the economist who, taking the aboriginal economic sector of a nonindustrialized country into account, would study its national economy.[1]

[1] Deane, P., 1953, *passim.*

2

This need for what amounted to a cross-disciplinary attack on the problems of economic growth brought about a considerable reorientation in the study of societies undergoing change in their technological and economic modes of life. Yet, as we all know, academic traditions change but reluctantly, even in comparison with the traditions of the most conservative societies. The problem in not inconsiderable measure thus became one of communication between practitioners of different disciplines that had had little contact. Each of the academic disciplines has its own technical language, which for outsiders takes on an esoteric quality not easily comprehended by members of the guild who are trained in its use. Even such a common phrase in the language of economics as "marginal utility" is as beclouded for most anthropologists, as an equally common word in the language of anthropologists, "matrilineal," is for most economists.

This difficulty in communication was brought out clearly in an earlier conference which attempted to assess the problems in the study of economically underdeveloped areas on a multidisciplinary basis. At the Twenty-seventh Norman Wait Harris Institute, held in 1951 at the University of Chicago, economists, anthropologists and political scientists, among others, were brought together to consider "The Progress of Undeveloped Areas." The rationale for holding this cross-disciplinary Institute was summarized in the statement, "The study of economic development not only extends into the fields of history but also embraces areas of anthropology, sociology and politics."[2] Yet those who attended these sessions are not likely to forget the failure in communication that characterized the discussion of points raised by participants who belonged to different disciplines. One recalls how difficult it was for the economists to see the importance of taking aboriginal economic patterns or total cultural context into account—the Hopi Indians were their favorite whipping boy—and how the anthropologists had equal difficulty in grasping the relevance of concepts employed by the economists because their applicability was restricted to the industrialized countries of Europe and America.

Though the societies in which anthropologists traditionally have worked are those which, in the main, are undergoing economic change, the adjustment of an anthropologist to the dynamic character of the new setting also had to be gained through hard-won experience. Committed from the early days of their discipline to the study of "primitive" peoples, their objective was to comprehend the range of human cultural

[2] Hoselitz, B. (ed.), 1952, p. vi.

capacity. To this end, efforts were for many years primarily directed toward recovering the cultures of non-literate peoples as they existed prior to their intensive contact with European or American culture. That they achieved this aim is apparent from the fact that today we possess sound knowledge on which to base our conclusions as to the wide range of variation in socially sanctioned modes of human behavior. Without the intensive studies of "uncontaminated" or "pre-contact" cultures, as they were called, that were made by these earlier students of comparative cultures, we should have little in the way of a baseline for the analysis of cultural dynamics, a range of phenomena that is especially important in understanding the modes and mechanisms of economic development.

It eventually became evident to anthropologists that their conventional objective, however important it might be, was not enough. Hence, as the research interests of economists broadened, so did those of anthropologists. In their case, the influences that made for change in the formulation of their problems moved on two levels. One was the level of scientific method. Anthropologists began to realize that the understanding of process must be based on induction from observed change; that such general principles concerning cultural dynamics as might be advanced must be derived from first-hand field research rather than from inference. This resulted in the rise of the movement toward acculturation studies or studies of culture-contact, as they were also called. As a result, anthropology was brought squarely into the orbit of the same societies that had become the concern of economists studying economic growth. In some cases, they dealt with the same problems.

We must, however, also take account of the second of these influences, which reflected the growing concern of anthropologists with the economic aspects of the cultures they studied.[3] It is not necessary to repeat here the tale of why this interest developed as late as it did. Suffice it to say that, on their part, the anthropologists, not being equipped to grasp the applicability of conventional economic theory and the concepts of economic science to the systems of the societies they studied, retreated from economics to technology or, as it was called, to "material culture." Only slowly did the realization develop that problems of production and distribution, of value and economic motivation, of the allocation of available means for the realization of desired ends, were universals in human experience.

A challenging problem, here as in the study of all aspects of culture, was thus raised. This was to discover just how applicable the concepts

[3] Cf. Malinowski, B., 1926; Firth, R., 1929; Herskovits, M. J., 1940, 1952.

and methods employed by economists in the study of Euroamerican economics might be when considered in the light of cross-cultural analysis. This would achieve two ends. It would put the generalizations of the economists to the test of wider applicability, while broadening conclusions concerning the nature of economic behavior. More particularly, as regards our present concerns, it would reveal the relevance of a cross-cultural approach for the study of the economies of technologically underdeveloped areas, and for indicating the lines along which programs of economic growth should best be planned.

3

We have thus far considered the question of the development of the interdisciplinary attack on economic growth in terms of only two of the disciplines involved, because in this particular context it is these two which represent the polarities of a continuum of commitment to the cross-cultural point of view. The typical orientation of anthropology is toward the intensive study of all aspects of cultural behavior in a particular society having relatively small numbers, even when, as in Africa, the populations involved may mount to the figure of a million or more. In contrast, the characteristic orientation of the economist is toward the broad survey, the nation as a whole, the development of models that look toward universal applicability. His concern is with economic forces having a degree of power, functioning in population aggregates of a size that are nowhere comparable to those that characterize the non-literate peoples outside the industrialized societies of Europe and America, and which we may again recall have been those traditionally studied by anthropologists. If we were to contrast the two disciplines with regard to their approach to economic phenomena, then, we might say that to the extent they have been concerned with the economic aspects of the societies in which they have both worked, anthropologists have devoted themselves to the study of microeconomies, while economists have been oriented toward the study of macroeconomies.

We must not, of course, take this to be the entire story of interdisciplinary concern with economic growth. Merely to say that the two disciplines which we have discussed represent polarities implies that other bodies of knowledge which bear on this phenomenon stand in intermediate positions. This comes out clearly in the chapters in which the resources of other disciplines are brought to bear on the common problem. At the anthropological pole, we have the question raised by Schneider concerning the degree to which cattle may be considered to function as money in the aboriginal economies of eastern and southern

Africa, or Skinner's discussion of markets and other trading activities in the pecuniarily oriented societies of pre-colonial West Africa. At the other extreme are the analyses of the problems of the new African nations in developing their economies, as presented by Fahm and Chudson. In their treatment, these problems are considered in terms that could be applied, in considerable measure, to the study of economic change in any society.

Most of the other papers take an intermediate position, without particular reference to discipline. It is obvious, from Johnston's consideration of the problem of stimulating agricultural production in both the subsistence and export sectors of African economies, that the traditional phase must be taken into account. We can discern an implicit recognition of the need to know as much as we can of pre-colonial economies in Berg's discussion of changes in African standards of living, or an explicit one in Barber's consideration of the continuities, as well as the innovations, in the patterns of African trade. Katzin balances the old and the new in analyzing attitudes in marketing practices, or the way in which the entrepreneurial function is conceived, or the impediments to the establishment of trading interprises by Africans that derive from earlier custom, in all these instances projecting innovation against traditional practices.

Coleman, writing from the point of view of political science, takes a position midway between the polarities we have been considering. In this, he follows the growing tradition of political studies of the new African nations. This has arisen from the fact that the almost axiomatic assumption made during the colonial period, that Euroamerican models would be followed in the political systems of African peoples after they gained their independence had, by force of events, to be revised to take into account the influence of pre-colonial patterns of political institutions and behavior. In the contemporary scene, the importance of the political component in the total picture of growth not only in Africa but elsewhere in the world, is self-evident. This is because there is no escape from the fact that the need for economic aid essential to this development means that decisions on the highest level of governmental policy must be made.

The reciprocal, also, is recognized, though it does not enter in economic surveys to the extent that might be desired, perhaps for reasons of diplomacy. Yet one need only consider the role of the power-dam as a prestige symbol in the newly independent countries of Africa to understand the significance of the play between political and economic forces. As Okigbo puts it, it is essential to seek out and analyze the total range of problems which face the newly independent nations, "which are at once jealous of their independence and anxious to achieve the maximum socially desirable rate of growth of per capita output."

In doing this, however, we only begin to approach our basic problem, which is how to balance continuities and innovations in African economic growth. If we take the role of major technical and economic innovations, again in terms of such a factor as the power-dam, we may consider this as a symbol that invades the political problem of integrating territories with a tradition of tribal fragmentation into nation-states, something that seems to be a prerequisite for the kind of economic growth the new countries of Africa hold as a major *desideratum*. Coleman speaks of the "new imperatives" that have emerged in the post-colonial period, all of which arise from the need to establish national unity and loyalty, a sense of national interest. What has been necessary, we are told, is for the leaders of these states "to create new nations out of the ensemble of disparate cultural groups situated by historical accident within the boundaries of the territories over which they have inherited political power."

More than such generally recognized aspects of historic continuities in the interplay between political and economic factors must, however, be taken into account in probing into African economic growth. Thus Fallers, in treating of the relation between economic differentials and social stratification, speaks of the "peculiar prominence of the political" in African systems of stratification. He finds a tendency for economic structures and processes not only to be "overshadowed by . . . political structures and processes" but to be *"contained within"* them. In this phrasing we have a principle, whose basic significance cannot but grow on us as we ponder its implications. It embodies a point of view that merits being incorporated into the conceptual framework of all who address themselves to the study of African economic growth, or have to do with implementing programs of technical aid.

Other examples of continuities are to be drawn from the papers which deal with the pre-colonial cultures. Bohannan points up the political aspect of African land tenure and land use when he calls it "territorial dimension" of African societies, and contrasts it with the essentially economic nature of the approach toward land in the pecuniary economies of Europe and America. Taken in connection with the position of the agricultural sector in both aboriginal and later economies of Africa, as shown by Johnston, the principle needs only to be stated for its relevance to become apparent. Yet we need only a cursory acquaintance with the literature to make us realize how rarely this insight enters into the work or writings of those who treat of the changing African economic scene. It suggests continuities that go far to explain the disasters that have overtaken most of the "schemes" for agricultural development that marked the post-World War II decades in the African experience.

4

We may at this point consider how the disciplines concerned with the study of economic change in Africa may be placed on our continuum between the polarities we have indicated—that is, between concentration on the aboriginal cultures of pre-colonial days and preoccupation with the later period when Africa came to participate in the world economy. Again, turning to the chapters of this work, we move from anthropology through political science and sociology, the latter represented in the approach indicated by Moore, to demography, as treated by Singer, before reaching the other end of the sequence, where economics is found. The position of geography enters somewhat specially in this context. Its basic data may be thought of as more or less the constant in our equation, since the natural setting it studies provides an ecological frame for the economies of both pre-colonial and post-colonial times.

This statement, of course, must be taken with certain reservations in mind. If we consider the role of the infrastructural factor of communication as presented by Kamarck, we can see how the natural environment can influence economic and technological growth in some of its more critical phases. Where this is the emphasis, and there is manipulation of the habitat, geography may move toward the pole of concern with later development. Resources, understandably, are to be evaluated in terms of environment and technological level. Yet contemporaneous environmental factors can, and must be brought into the picture if we are to understand the setting of the earlier economies. In this sense, we can regard the influence of habitat as a constant, in something of the way that in the broader picture, historical and psychological factors not discussed in this book enter into the list of causal components in the total picture of change.

As we take an overview of the contributions in the pages that follow, it is apparent that the fact of concentration on an area, and on a problem in an area, has come to make for better communication between practitioners of different disciplines. This, as a matter of fact, may be regarded as one of the principal results, on the methodological as against the substantive level, that has been derived from the pursuit of area studies. It has been said that the research value of an area lies in the fact that it affords a *locus* for the study of problems. In somewhat different terms, it is to be thought of as a place which provides those in the behavioral and historical sciences with a laboratory in which they can test their hypotheses. But more than this, it encourages focus on a problem; and there is no problem, in the context of area studies, that does not impel the student to stray outside the bounds of his discipline.

African area studies, in whatever phase, partake of all these characteristics. But research into African problems has had special attractions that go far to explain the enormous increase we have witnessed in the number of scholars who committed themselves to the study of African affairs in the years following the second World War. This attraction has arisen, for one thing, from the variety of situations to be encountered there, something that is a function of the sheer physical size of the continent—or of the sub-continent—if historical rather than geographical convention is followed. Also entering here has been the rapidity of change, something that is particularly apparent in the fields of technology and economics. What this means is that Africa, as an area for study, attracts us because there we find situations wherein the variables can be manipulated with particular effectiveness in assessing the validity of many sorts of hypotheses. There is another reason, too. For in Africa conclusions deriving from scholarly research committed only to extending the boundaries of knowledge may be tested in practice, something that holds a very real appeal to the scientific student of man who approaches a problem with a sense of its implications for the workaday world.

On the substantive level, the materials in these chapters pose questions, both interdisciplinary and lying within disciplines, of far-reaching significance for understanding the processes of African economic growth, as well as for the examination of general theories. Some of these questions recur again and again. The impact on African peoples, both those who had and did not have special pecuniary tokens of value and exchange, of the particular kind of money economy that was imposed on them under colonial controls, is one such point. The importance of this fact is invariably indicated in discussion of African economic change; yet because it is so obvious, it has been largely taken for granted. But how much do we really know of the operation of the mechanisms that underlay this fundamental alteration in African economics? How far have we pressed investigations that will tell us how this aspect of the history of African economic acculturation has affected the functioning of the resulting economic systems of Africa?

Schneider gives us some insights into this process, as he considers the differential exchange values accorded the animals herded by East African peoples, and the translation of these values into European currency. Moore suggests the stages which the process of accommodation took as it moved from emphasis on subsistence through transitional adaptations to a stabilized sector, and indicates some of the means used to effect the change, ranging from forced labor in the earlier colonial period and the requirement to pay taxes in European currency to the operation of the color bar. From a somewhat different point of view, Katzin provides some indications of the effect of the lag between aboriginal convention and later requirements on developing trading enterprises, and on the nature of the problems faced by traders in reinvesting their earnings.

But the basic question remains. In West Africa, it is held that money incentives reinforced by tax liabilities have been effective in encouraging agricultural production for export. Are we dealing with phenomena here that can be explained exclusively in terms of macroscopic economic forces? To what extent has the mode of adjustment of the individual African to a money economy, or to a new kind of medium of exchange, affected the broader social adjustments? The "why" questions continue to nag at us.

It is apparent, from the range of problems of this type, and of numerous other types that might be named, that the kind of cross-disciplinary attack found in the pages that follow offers fresh insights into the questions to be resolved in the study of African economic growth, and new leads toward understanding them. If we compare the breadth of approach found in many of the contributions with other, especially earlier studies, it is apparent that a definite tendency is to be detected in the direction of more inclusive conceptions of the kind of theoretical orientation that must frame investigations of economic and technological growth in underdeveloped countries, and of the methods of study that must be employed. It is to be anticipated that the logic of the area approach will assure the continuation of this tendency, and that in consequence a more realistic grasp of the forces in play, and greater perception in the application of findings, will result.

Subsaharan Africa as a Growing Economic System

by Mitchell Harwitz
Northwestern University

The year that followed the Berlin Conference, 1885, is a good bench-mark for a brief historical survey of the development of the mid-twentieth century African economy. Lord Lugard's dictum as to the importance of transport in the economic development of Africa contains the seed of an analytical understanding of the processes that took place during the decades following the partition of Africa among the colonial powers. As Kamarck shows,[1] the absence of mechanized transportation everywhere in the subcontinent except for a small part of the Republic of South Africa meant that costs of transportation for commodities, other than those that were either self-transporting or relatively very valuable per unit of weight, were prohibitively high in relation to the prices obtainable for these goods. This situation, and the general char-acteristics of the indigenous systems of production, suffice to provide a basic understanding of the patterns of trade and production within the area and between Subsaharan Africa and the rest of the world.

Broadly speaking, African production for sale on world markets con-sisted of certain tropical tree products, such as palm kernels and wild rubber, that were relatively easy to gather without additional cultivation by the indigenous population, precious minerals like gold and diamonds, certain specialty goods like leather work produced in Northern Nigeria, and the remnants of the slave trade.[2] The total value of these exports is not easy to measure, and it is impossible also to give quantitative content to statements about the relative importance of export activity as it related to the total activity of the indigenous populations. An indication of the relatively limited involvement of these populations in such exporting

---

[1] *Infra*, pp. 263–275.
[2] For details, see Frankel, S. H., 1938, Ch. 1.

B   15

activities as were present in most parts of Subsaharan Africa can be obtained from a backward projection of later figures. In 1960, no Sub-saharan country other than South Africa exhibited a proportion greater than one-third of its economically active population engaged in wage-earning activities, and only one country reported that more than ten per cent of the total population was classed as wage-earners.[3] This set of facts can be taken in conjunction with the information contained in Chart 8.1 presented by Johnston, and Table 2.7 of this essay, which indicates that the quantity of almost all agricultural exports, with the notable exception of palm products, increased by a factor of at least ten over the half-century from 1905 to 1955.

Although one must make allowances for increase in population and the labor force through birth and immigration, there can be very little doubt that the magnitude of this increase indicates a very sizeable growth in the proportion of the population engaged in activity oriented toward pecuniary return. It thus remains to establish a presumption that there was no shift of an opposite sort during the period 1885–1905. In the absence of data, one can only argue somewhat circularly, from the logical validity of economic principles whose empirical applicability one is here concerned to examine. However, the following arguments are favorable. First, during this period there was a great deal of railroad building, the net effect of which was to encourage trade rather than destroy it, except in the case of the slave trade, the elimination of which was the proximate cause for the construction of some of the railroads of Subsaharan Africa. Second, and perhaps even more important, is the fact that these two decades constituted an era of steady and appreciable growth of world trade and production.[4] It is not unreasonable to argue that this brought an increased demand for the products of Subsaharan Africa. Thus, it is most likely that the total output of Africa increased over that period, with the possible exceptions of the Belgian Congo, which changed administrations in 1908, and Liberia, which had a very unreliable history of export activity during the period.[5] Finally, then, by a process of reasoning that will be reversed in a later section of this paper and in other papers, such as those of Berg, Johnston, and Singer, it has been established that activity oriented toward export must have been a limited part of the activity of the indigenous population of Africa in the bench year 1885.

It would seem very likely that, in this situation, the economic founda-tions of one of the most noticeable features of the Subsaharan economy,

[3] *Infra*, Table 11. 4.
[4] See Nurkse, R., 1961, pages 16–20.
[5] Johnston, Sir H. H., 1906, Vol. 1, Ch. XVIII.

namely, the very large semi-permanent and seasonal migrations that take place between areas of rapid growth and high employment and those of slow growth and limited opportunities for employment, would have been absent. In addition, the absence of heavy transport would have meant that the production of cocoa, groundnuts, minerals, and other bulky items would have been unprofitable except in areas where there was either easy access to water transportation or low-cost forced labor to gather and transport those commodities. It is furthermore reasonable to suppose that the circulation of food through regions was rather limited, so that even in those areas where market systems were already highly developed, such as those Skinner describes,[6] the zone of supply to any given market center for goods other than luxuries and specialty items was limited to walking distance. Thus, the economies of Subsaharan Africa could be characterized as highly segmented, with only local participation in the markets for many of the commodities that entered the budget of the typical African.[7]

A second period for which some data are available is 1905–1929. Though World War I intervened, and though the great era of railroad building in Africa ended by 1914, it seems convenient to treat these two and a half decades, for which over-all data are available, as a whole. The Great Depression can be taken as the breakoff point.[8] A first index of measurable growth over the period is the increase in the value of exports. For all of Subsaharan Africa, including the Sudan, the recorded value of exports increased about 2.6 times from 1907 to 1929. The absolute physical magnitude is, of course, unclear, in the sense that it is not possible to disentangle the effects of changes in price from those of changes in quantity. Using the figure, however, as a rough index, one observes a rather wide dispersion around this average, ranging from the very small increase in Somaliland, to the very large percentage gains over the period reported for the Sudan, Kenya, Nyasaland, and South West Africa. The following noticeable characteristics are indicative of future developments: South Africa showed the largest absolute gain and one of the lowest percentage gains; Nigeria and French West Africa both manifested large absolute and relative growth; the British territories, including South Africa, while dominating total exports, grew

---

[6] *Infra*, pp. 77–97.
[7] See Hoselitz, B. F., 1960, p. 217, for a formal discussion of this kind of market segmentation.
[8] Frankel, S. H., 1938, provides some information for this period. We shall presume that all his figures are in then current pounds or are converted at then ruling rates of exchange. Comparison between Frankel's data and those compiled by the United Nations for later periods is rendered difficult by uncertainty as to the validity of these assumptions.

somewhat less rapidly as exporters than the non-British colonies.[9] The redistribution of export shares over the period shows the relative positions of the major colonial groupings almost unchanged, with a major internal shift, within the British territories, away from the predominance of South Africa.

The years 1929–1935, which span the major impact of the Great Depression, show a striking cessation of the apparent growth of the export sectors of almost all the economies of Subsaharan Africa. Again, the percentage of total exports forthcoming from the colonies of the major metropolitan powers remained fairly stable. However, the mineral-exporting territories—the Belgian Congo, Northern and Southern Rhodesia, and South Africa—were clearly less affected by the impact of the Depression on their export markets than were the areas specializing in agricultural products. It is, of course, difficult to determine accurately the behavior of prices during these eight years. Index numbers of production computed from United Nations data indicate a rising trend of output for most commodities, and, by implication, a falling trend in prices.

The behavior of exports over the period 1935–1955 can best be understood if we consider the behavior of total value and volume of exports separately. The former is one measure of the growth of African command over imports, while the latter provides an approximation to the growth of resource inputs into export production during the period. The data concerning volume indicate that during these decades, total output of almost all major export commodities, except cocoa in Ghana and palm products in Nigeria, grew significantly.[10] The data also show that in these two products there was an appreciable increase in the relative contribution of non-British territories. The following table shows that the volume of mineral production also grew, with the exception of gold output, and grew more, proportionally, than agricultural output. There is good reason to believe, then, that total inputs in the way of resources—land, labor, and capital—employed in the production of most, if not all, of these commodities expanded significantly during these two decades. This statement does not exclude such occurrences as a decrease in the number of workers employed, which did take place in gold mining in the Gold Coast (Ghana) between 1948 and 1958 as a result of more capital-intensive methods of production. We may exclude, in this crude approximation, drastic changes in overall technology that lead to increases in physical output with fixed or declining levels of all physical inputs. The detailed data presented in Table 4 of the Statistical

[9] Cf. Table 2.3.
[10] Cf. Table 2.7.

Appendix of the first Economic Bulletin for Africa,[11] which are too long to be given here, indicate that the dollar value of all principal export commodities also grew significantly from 1938 to 1958, even including the values of cocoa, palm products, and gold exports.

The pattern of participation in these growing activities exhibited broad territorial trends similar to those noted previously, except that the share of non-Commonwealth countries spurted sharply upward,

TABLE 2.1. *Indices of Output of Principal Minerals* (1948–1950 average = 100)

Product	Production 1937–1938 average	Production 1955–1957 average
Copper	91	155
Manganese	68	136
Iron Ore	96	188
Lead Ore	56	213
Zinc Ore	31	224
Tin Concentrate	91	112
Bauxite Ore	—	404
Chromite	54	145
Cobalt	55	196
Asbestos	29	164
Gold	132	120

Source: United Nations, Department of Economic and Social Affairs, 1959, Table 2–1, p. 115.

mainly as a result of the relative recovery of the French non-mineral exporters in the mid–1930's and the rapid postwar expansion of their exports. The relative position of South Africa continued to decline, and this trend may be expected to extend into the future. The relation between the Federation of Rhodesia and Nyasaland and South Africa is worth examining a little more closely. Available data on inter-African trade indicate that the exchange between these two countries—broadly, export of foodstuffs and light manufactures from South Africa in return for minerals from the Federation—is a dominating element in inter-African trade flows. Indeed, with minor exceptions, trade with other African territories does not exceed 10 per cent of the total trade of any Subsaharan country except for these two. It can be expected that any cessation of preferential tariff arrangements between them will greatly reduce the flow of trade, and thereby lessen the significance of inter-African trade in the total trade of the region.

[11] United Nations, Economic Commission for Africa, 1961, Appendix pages III–V.

2

What have been the connections of this broad historical sweep of increased export earnings with the internal structures of African economies? The papers of Barber, Berg, Johnston and Singer in this volume[12] trace various aspects of these relations. One element is common to almost all of these histories of transformation in the internal economy: the export market is the initial stimulus. There are limited exceptions in certain parts of Commonwealth East Africa, but even here the image seems to be broadly accurate. This does not mean that the pattern of development "surrounding" and "succeeding" this enabling factor, considered in continental scope, is invariant. The United Nations *Economic Survey of Africa Since 1950*[13] suggests two prototypes: 1) a pattern of development by transformation of the indigenous economy, with relatively little large-scale foreign investment and limited outflows of wage labor from the traditional to the non-traditional sector; 2) a pattern in which export development has taken place within a foreign-dominated exchange economy that is based on foreign capital, foreign settlement, or both, and that uses relatively modern productive techniques and relatively large amounts of wage labor flowing from the indigenous population. These prototypes correspond roughly to Barber's distinction between the "trader's frontier" and the "settler's frontier."[14]

For analytical purposes, it is useful to suggest a typology that goes beyond this dual division. The criteria of classification can be summarized in four observable characteristics that can be related meaningfully to an economic analysis of development trends. These characteristics are:

1. the control over non-labor resources in the export and import-competing sectors (private or corporate, domestic or foreign);
2. the technology of these sectors;
3. the sources of capital for infrastructure;
4. the role of import-competing goods in markets for importable commodities.

These categories are not meant to provide a set of variables whose values are functionally related to a measureable property called "economic development." They do suggest, as they were meant to, that there are important distinctions between South Africa, Republic of the Congo, and Kenya, all of which generally correspond to the second prototype of

[12] *Infra,* pp. 299–319, 199–238, 151–178, and 241–261, respectively.
[13] United Nations, Department of Economic and Social Affairs, 1959a, p. 12.
[14] *Infra,* p. 299–319.

the United Nations classification. Similarly, there are distinctions to be made between, say, Nigeria and the countries of former French West Africa, though most of them fit the first prototype of the United Nations classification.

The first category rephrases the essential distinction of the two United Nations prototypes, which is that non-labor resources are commanded in the first instance by the indigenous population, though the concept of control is complex, as Biebuyck and Bohannan point out,[15] and in the second by non-indigenous persons or groups. The second partially parallels the first, but in addition provides for a distinction between foreign-owned plantation agriculture or silviculture on the one hand, and foreign-owned mining or manufacturing on the other. Thus, the distinction already made is further clarified by differentiating agricultural exporters like Ghana, where production is by indigenous small-holders, from those like Liberia and the Belgian Congo, where plantations predominate. The third class is useful in that it distinguishes between economies, such as those of Ghana, the Congo, and South Africa, that have financed significant portions of their infrastructure from self-generated capital, and those that have relied more heavily on public subvention from abroad or have been able to borrow on metropolitan capital markets. Finally, the role of import-competing industry, besides being a general index of the progress of economic growth, is a good measure of the internal complexity or "depth" of the monetized sectors. It should be noted that the United Nations list does not further subdivide the categories listed above.

The later structure of the African economies can also be discussed along these lines. It is the disposition of returns to non-labor resources that has set an upper limit to the size of actual or potential domestic capital accumulation in these countries. As a rule, the relative size of private domestic saving in the national income would be highest where these returns accrued to non-indigenous owners located permanently in Africa, such as settlers in Kenya, and corporations in the ex-Belgian Congo or the Federation of Rhodesia and Nyasaland, and lower where these resources are owned by indigenous groups. Groups that are not permanent and not indigenous, such as foreign corporations, might or might not contribute heavily to private capital accumulation, depending on whether or not their activities were or were not expanding, and also upon the reporting system for the national accounts. Unpublished evidence from Liberia indicates that, while net capital inflows may be high, the totals may consist of the sum of large new inflows and significant repatriation of profits by foreign corporations. For Africa as a

[15] *Infra*, pp. 99–112 and 133–149.

whole, the net effect of this sort of repatriation is apparently small.[16] Leaving it aside, then, it would appear that knowledge about the ownership of non-labor resources is a good means of predicting the rate of domestic saving out of reported national income. This varies from about 2 per cent in Nigeria to about 12 per cent in South Africa. Among African countries for which gross domestic product and gross national product accounts are available, deviations from a positive correlation between per capita product and the rate of savings out of income are generally explicable by an examination of the distribution of income among different sectors of the population. Concentration of income in the hands of non-Africans, which is significant in such territories as Kenya, the Federation of Rhodesia and Nyasaland, South Africa, and the Republic of the Congo, produces a rate of saving for the territory as a whole that may be rather higher than its position in the per-capita income ranking would suggest. The Congo under Belgian rule was a good example, with Nigeria as its converse.[17]

The technology of the exporting sectors had important consequences for the spread of income originating in these sectors into the hands of the indigenous population. A distinction should here be made between indigenous or plantation production of agricultural export commodities, and extractive industries. Although detailed figures are not available, limited data on capital per head and output per head such as those given in Tables 2.13 and 2.15 suggest that extractive industries are more capital intensive than are plantations, and that both are more capital intensive than indigenous agricultural production, whether for export or domestic consumption. As Table 2.15 indicates, there are probably also wide variations within each type. These relations lead to the following conclusion: 1. If extractive industries require large labor forces, and possibly even migration, they will bulk very large in the domestic product of such territories as the Rhodesias, Katanga, and South Africa; 2. If indigenous export production is important in the domestic product, it will require large labor forces, and possibly migration at certain seasons, as has been found essential in Ghana, Nigeria, the Sudan, and former French West Africa.

The final two items in our criteria for classification are more directly concerned with the political economy of Africa. The financing of infrastructure, past and present, is, first of all, a rough indication of future capacity to provide needed facilities out of domestic income, and, secondly, an index of possible trends in capital flows. Broadly, as Kamarck indicates,[18] African infrastructure has been provided either

---

[16] United Nations, Department of Economic and Social Affairs, 1959a, p. 86.
[17] *Ibid.*, p. 90.   [18] *Infra.*, pp. 263–275.

publicly or privately by the metropolitan power or by the colony itself, the former being predominant. This pattern has been changing, one possible replacement being suggested by Fahm.[19]

3

The future of indigenously-controlled industry in Africa is, of course, a central issue in any discussion of trends in African development. Though it is dangerous to generalize too broadly, most evidence in the developed economies and in South Africa suggests that, given sufficient productivity in agriculture, a key element in successful economic development is the establishment of viable import-competing industries. The greater the degree of current indigenous control of these industries, the more likely is it that successful enterprises in these lines will be managed by Africans when markets for their products become large enough for import-competing industries to be economically viable. The degree of "Africanization" or "localization" of management in exporting, import-competing, and infrastructural activity is a useful index of the potential of African economies for rapid capitalization of their opportunities for internal expansion.

Available information on total imports by category into Tropical Africa and into two of its sub-divisions provides rough quantitative indices of the importance of possible import replacement in African economies, and gives a sense of the structure of activity in these economies. Food, textiles, and miscellaneous manufacturing imports that are potential candidates for domestic production apparently constituted about one-third of this total, or about $800,000,000 in value in 1955. In Nigeria the proportion is more on the order of two-thirds, or about $250,000,000 in value, while in Ghana the corresponding figures are something more than two-thirds or $160,000,000. These figures indicate the possibility that import replacement may be worthwhile economically to some degree, even if the new industries have to be subsidized or in terms of a less desirable alternative protected by a tariff. The economic arguments were put many years ago by Alexander Hamilton,[20] and an application of this line of inquiry can be found in W. A. Lewis' *Report on Industrialization and the Gold Coast*.[21] The limited importance of such activity in most African economies, and its disproportionate employment of non-Africans, is made clear by the very limited data in

[19] *Ibid.*, pp. 357–375.
[20] Hamilton, A., "Report on Manufactures, December 5, 1791," in McKeever, S. (ed.), 1934, pp. 175–276.
[21] Lewis, W. A., 1953, *passim*.

Tables 2.17 and 2.18 on the distribution of the active labor force in various countries, and the distribution of gross national or gross domestic product by source. Only the former Belgian Congo, the Federation of Rhodesia and Nyasaland, and the Republic of South Africa show noticeable deviations from the typical pattern in the direction of more complex import-competing sectors and relative concentration of the domestic labor force in non-export activity.

The importance of population in the total picture of economic growth should not be overestimated. It is fairly obvious that population is a "permissive" factor, in the sense that indigenous or immigrant populations provide the labor force requisite to any development. Very high population densities, or a very high proportion of very young in a population, in the presence of unfavorable natural resources and limited technological possibilities, can mean a very small reinvestible surplus available for development. But, as Singer makes clear,[22] both of these problems have been resolved in Africa by a widespread pattern of migrations from areas of relatively high population density to those of either low density or high levels of employment opportunity. The productivity of this kind of migratory labor, and the future trends of population growth, are still too unclear to allow meaningful predictions, but it may be assumed that population as such will not for some time represent a major problem, except in certain very limited areas, such as Rwanda and Burundi, or Kenya, where the limitations of opportunity are mainly political and technological.

As regards their more general characteristics, the economies of Subsaharan Africa present a picture of "island" development, if one seeks areas of relatively high per capita output, per capita trade, and "depth" of import-competing development. These islands are, roughly, the major ones of South Africa and the mining region of Rhodesia-*cum*-Katanga, and the lesser islands of Leopoldville, the West African coast from the Ivory Coast to Nigeria, and the Kenya-Uganda complex. These areas have accounted for major portions of African exports, inter-African trade, and inter-territorial migration. Furthermore, they have been and doubtless will continue to be major recipients of inflows of private investment capital.

The possible spread of development outward from these centers clearly depends on several major economic factors, as well as a host of non-economic ones. One element, commented upon by Kamarck,[23] is the spread of a transport net that makes flows of goods into and out of the "hinterlands" as cheap, relatively, as the flow of people. Another, which both justifies and depends upon the first, is an increase in the total and

[22] *Infra*, pp. 241–261.   [23] *Ibid.*, pp. 263–275.

the per capita productivity of economic activity in these hinterlands; the discussions of agricultural productivity and population trends by Johnston and Singer[24] are supremely relevant in this connection. Something more should be said at this stage about the development of export industries in these hinterland regions. Chudson notes that trends in world markets for exports are of crucial importance for the profitability of such activities.[25] Naturally, the possibilities of increased output and increased transportation of that output to ports must pre-exist sale on any terms, favorable or unfavorable. In this connection, one can quote Dixey:

> "It is necessary to bear in mind that present knowledge of the geology and mineral resources of the Continent is very patchy . . . within almost every territory; nonetheless, on the whole much of Africa is better known than may be supposed by those unfamiliar with its problem."[26]

It is noteworthy that the potential annual output of some minerals in Africa has become larger than the amounts which could possibly be moved to ports by the existing systems of transportation, or sold at 1960 world market prices. A similar marketing situation has apparently come to confront some traditional agricultural export commodities, such as cocoa and palm products. Hence, emphasis on the cultivation of African markets for African production would seem advisable. A third possible source of income, the export of industrial goods, seems less important for African economies than it has been for Japan and India.

This suggestion leads immediately to examination of the problems and possibilities, considered by Johnston and Okigbo,[27] of increases in agricultural output for domestic consumption, and of the possibilities brought to light by consideration of African economies under the fourth item of our typology. The examination of the performance of entrepreneurs in Nigeria by Katzin[28] is suggestive. Equally to the point is a possibility suggested by the importance of trade between South Africa and the Federation of Rhodesia and Nyasaland in the total configuration of inter-African trade. If production develops in Africa on a scale sufficient to make its substitution for importation a long-run gain for Africans, some of the highly segmented markets of Africa will probably combine, so as to provide markets of adequate magnitude. This does not mean that a territory having the vast size and population of Nigeria is already economically integrated, since the concept of size is really a concept of potential expenditure in such markets. In this sense, parts of

[24] *Infra*, pp. 151–178 and 241–261.   [25] *Infra*, p. 340.
[26] United Nations, Economic Commission for Africa, 1956, p. 6.
[27] *Infra*, pp. 151–178 and 323–335.   [28] *Infra*, pp. 179–198.

the ex-Belgian Congo or of Ghana are "larger" than parts of Nigeria having greater area and population. Here the progress of urbanization in various parts of Africa, as noted by Johnston and Singer,[29] is a significant factor, because of the tendency of cities to be importers of both food and people from their hinterlands. Two caveats are necessary in this context, however. The apparent growth of urban unemployment in some African cities indicates that the population of cities can outrun employment opportunities, which are a measure of the city's ability to import both goods and labor services. Again, an inadequate transportation system can mean that it is less costly to bring goods into the city from abroad than from a domestic hinterland; in other words, urban growth can only help the hinterland if transportation is available at sufficiently low rates.

The replacement of non-African with African management and entrepreneurship also enters here. Kamarck and Okigbo[30] both bring up this point in discussing the economic returns to education and training. Though their terminology is different, in essence they are in agreement that the educational system produces a commodity the value of which in the long run is immense, and may in the short run be high enough to make public investment worthwhile even on a "commercial" basis. The length of time that must pass before the full economic benefits of "investment in human capital" can be reaped should not be underestimated, however. Examination of the performance of the foreign trade sectors that have dominated African economies for the past half century, and that will continue to do so for the next decade at least, shows clearly that even their best possible rates of growth cannot finance major transformations in the African economies within the present decade. The capital requirements projected by Rodan[31] indicate that, if current income is to grow at between 3 and 3.5 per cent *per annum* over the next decade, something on the order of one-third of total net investment must come from abroad. If this magnitude of inflow is to be utilized without a simple extension of enclave growth, resources of skills and managerial talent will have to be developed in an efficient and, perhaps, somewhat specialized way, with matching domestic investments.

The importance of a steady and successful increase in the productivity of domestically oriented industry—or in a broader context, African oriented industry—in increasing the capacity of African economies to provide this matching domestic saving has been limited in scope but must increase as limitations of land availability and export markets

[29] *Ibid.*, pp. 151–178 and 241–261.   [30] *Ibid.*, pp. 263–275 and 323–335.
[31] Cf. Table 61.1, *infra.*

necessitate diversion of resources to internal markets. The treatment of this point by Johnston and Chudson makes this clear.[32] That is, one way of looking at the problems of most African economies is to say, perhaps too sweepingly, that they face the twin tasks of educating their populations to changed methods of agricultural production, and to effective methods of establishing and managing new lines of non-agricultural production. Since African economies are, in one sense, the people in them, this is to say that Africans face these problems of self-education as prerequisites to the adoption or adaptation of new productive techniques.

[32] *Infra*, pp. 151–178 and 337–355.

TABLE 2.2. *Summary Percentage Table*

	Capital Invested in each Territory as per cent of Total Capital Invested in Africa (ca. 1935)	Trade of each Territory as per cent of Total African Trade		Domestic Exports of each Territory as per cent of Total Domestic Exports of all Africa	
		1928	1935	1928	1935
All Commonwealth Africa	77.05	83.42	84.76	85.65	85.04
All non-Commonwealth Africa	22.95	16.58	15.24	14.35	14.96
All Commonwealth except South Africa and South West Africa	34.24	34.28	28.83	33.50	28.78
Union of South Africa	42.81	47.38	54.69	50.29	54.87
Southern Rhodesia } Northern Rhodesia } Bechuanaland	8.38	4.81 (c)	6.74 (c)	4.16 (c)	7.15 (c)
British West Africa (a)	9.56	18.08	12.34	18.80	12.53
British East Africa (b)	12.81	11.39	9.66	10.54	9.10
French West Africa	2.49	5.95	5.87	5.22	5.28
French Equatorial Africa	1.74	.87	1.48	.68	1.32
All French Territories	5.76	8.08	8.34	7.01	7.62

Notes to Table:

(a) Gambia, Sierra Leone, Gold Coast, Nigeria.
(b) Nyasaland, Tanganyika, Kenya, Uganda, Anglo-Egyptian Sudan, Somaliland, and Zanzibar.
(c) Southern and Northern Rhodesia only.

Source: Frankel, S. H., 1938, *Capital Investment in Africa*, Table 48, p. 202.

TABLE 2.3. *Territorial Allocation of Subsaharan Export Trade: Percentage Shares of Territories in Total Domestic Exports in Selected Years*

	1907	1928	1935	1938	1948	1958
Gambia	.4	.6	.2	.2	.3	.3
Sierra Leone	1.0	.9	.9	1.2	.8	1.2
Ghana (Gold Coast)	3.8	7.7	5.2	5.6	7.9	6.4
Nigeria	5.4	9.6	6.3	4.8	8.7	8.1
Total, Commonwealth West Africa	10.6	18.8	12.6	11.8	17.7	16.0
Somaliland	.3	.3	.1	.1	.1	.1
Kenya	.2	1.8	1.7			
Uganda	.2	1.9	2.0	6.2	5.9	7.5
Tanganyika	.9	2.2	1.9			
Zanzibar	.8	.6	.4	.4	.3	.3
Total, Commonwealth East Africa	3.2	6.8	6.1	6.7	6.3	7.9
Northern Rhodesia	.1	.4	2.6	5.0	4.0	
Southern Rhodesia	3.5	3.7	4.5	5.8	4.1	8.7
Nyasaland	.1	.4	.4	.5	.7	
Total, Commonwealth Central Africa	3.7	4.5	7.5	11.3	8.8	8.7
French West Africa	4.8	5.2	5.3	4.1	5.4	7.5
French Equatorial Africa	1.1	.7	1.3	.8	1.9	2.1
Togo	.4	.4	.3	.2	.3	.3
Cameroons	1.2	.7	.8	.8	1.3	2.4
Total, French Territories	7.5	7.0	7.7	5.9	8.9	12.3
Angola	1.4	1.3	1.1	1.5	2.1	2.8
Mozambique	1.4	1.8	1.0	.9	1.6	1.5
Guinea	.2	.2	—	.1	.2	.1
Total, Portuguese Africa	3.0	3.3	2.1	2.5	3.9	4.4
Belgian Congo (incl. Ruanda-Urundi)	3.5	4.0	5.2	5.4	8.6	8.9

TABLE 2.3 (continued)

	1907	1928	1935	1938	1948	1958
South Africa (incl. South-West Africa)	68.4	52.1	56.3	52.5	42.1	38.5
Sudan	.7	3.3	2.6	3.0	3.4	2.9
Liberia	—	—	—	.2	.6	.9

Sources: Data for the years 1907, 1928, and 1935 have been adapted from Frankel, S. H., *op. cit.*, Table 48, pp. 202–203. Liberia was not included in his calculations. Data for the remaining years have been calculated from the United Nations, *Yearbooks of International Trade Statistics*. Gold has been treated as a commodity export.

General Notes:
1. Percentages may not add to totals owing to rounding.
2. Exports are valued f.o.b. Re-exports have been excluded wherever possible.

TABLE 2.4. *Total Overseas Capital per capita in each African Territory* (ca. 1935)
(£000; millions of persons)

Territory	Total Capital Invested (a)	Estimated Total Population (b)	Per Capita Investment (a)
South Africa and South- West Africa	554,681	9.9	55.8
Northern Rhodesia⎫ Southern Rhodesia⎬	102,403	2.7	38.4
Nigeria	75,087	19.1	3.9
British West Africa	116,730	24.4	4.8
Anglo-Egyptian Sudan	43,354	5.8	
Kenya and Uganda	46,144	6.7	6.8
Total, Kenya, Uganda, Tanganyika, Nyasaland	110,189	13.5	8.1
French West Africa	30,426	14.7	2.1
French Equatorial Africa, Togo and Cameroons	39,884	6.5	6.1
Total, French Territories	70,310	21.2	3.3
Belgian Congo	143,337	11.0	13.0
Angola and Mozambique	66,732	6.8	9.8

Notes to Table:

(a) Frankel, S. H., *op. cit.*, Table 32, p. 170.
(b) Apparently drawn from R. R. Kuczinski, 1936.

TABLE 2.5. *Total Value of Domestic Exports of each African Territory in 1907,* 1929, 1935
(£000)

	1907	1929	1935
Gambia	280	783	376
Sierra Leone	676	1,319	1,556
Gold Coast (Ghana)	2,502	12,401	9,241
Nigeria	3,612	17,581	11,197
Total, Commonwealth West Africa	7,070	32,084	22,370
Somaliland	212	239	127
Kenya	157	2,746	2,978
Uganda	140	4,275	3,631
Tanganyika	625	3,722	3,445
Zanzibar	548 (a)	1,269	655
Total, Commonwealth East Africa	1,682	12,251	10,836
Northern Rhodesia	96	819	4,668
Southern Rhodesia	2,319	6,609	8,077
Nyasaland	54	589	736
Total, Commonwealth Central Africa	2,469	8,017	13,481
Total, Commonwealth Africa	11,221	52,352	46,687
French West Africa	3,174	9,396	9,432
French Equatorial Africa	739	1,223	2,351
Togo (b)	296	678	487
Cameroons (b)	793	1,370	1,338
Total, French Territories	5,002	12,667	13,608
Angola	961 (c)	2,610	2,018
Mozambique	955	3,089	1,753
Guinea	122 (d)	458	—
Total, Portuguese Africa	2,038	6,157	3,771
Belgian Congo and Ruanda-Urundi	2,340	8,326	9,336
Total, French, Portuguese, Belgian Africa	9,380	27,150	26,715
Union of South Africa and South-West Africa	45,576	92,555	100,404
Sudan	461	6,692	4,684

Source: Frankel, S. H., *op. cit.*, Table 43, facing p. 192.

Notes to Table:
(a) Domestic exports plus total imports (including goods subsequently re-exported).
(b) The post-World-War-I area included here is smaller than the pre-war area.
(c) 1905 figures.
(d) 1906 figures.

TABLE 2.6. *Total Value of Domestic Imports of each AfricanTerritory in* 1907,
1929, 1935
(£000)

	1907	1929	1935
Gambia	285	539	466
Sierra Leone	806	1,558	1,113
Gold Coast (Ghana)	1,917	9,530	7,274
Nigeria	3,587	13,040	7,662
Total, Commonwealth West Africa	6,595	24,667	16,515
Somaliland	262	471	271
Kenya ⎫ Uganda ⎭	897	8,208	4,577
Tanganyika	1,190	4,021	2,711
Zanzibar	1,082	1,138	721
Total, Commonwealth East Africa	3,431	13,838	8,280
Northern Rhodesia	115	3,551	2,854
Southern Rhodesia	1,282	6,783	5,482
Nyasaland	166	735	609
Total, Commonwealth Central Africa	1,563	11,069	8,945
Total, Commonwealth Africa	11,589	49,574	33,740
French West Africa	3,770	10,676	8,946
French Equatorial Africa	606	2,238	2,271
Togo (b)	334	822	481
Cameroons (b)	865	1,565	864
Total, French Territories	5,575	15,301	12,499
Angola	1,366	2,909	1,495
Mozambique	1,514	4,537	2,763
Guinea	187	401	—
Total, Portuguese Africa	3,067	7,847	4,258
Belgian Congo and Ruanda-Urundi	993	11,428	4,204
Total, French, Portuguese, Belgian Africa	9,635	34,576	20,961
Union of South Africa and South-West Africa	27,311	82,035	74,601
Sudan	1,596	6,742	5,074

Source: Frankel, S. H., *op. cit.*, Table 44, pp. 194–195.
Notes to Table: See Notes to Table IV, *supra.*

TABLE 2.7. *Trends in Average Annual Outputs of Major Agricultural Export Commodities for Selected Periods between 1920 and 1958 (Indices shown in parentheses; average annual output 1950–1954=100)*

A. *Cocoa (ooo's of metric tons)*

	Ghana (Gold Coast) (a) Quantity	Nigeria (b) Quantity	French West Africa Quantity	French Cameroons Quantity	French Equatorial Africa Quantity	Togo Quantity	Belgian Congo Quantity
1920–24	173.0 (73)	29.8 (37)	2.6 (4)	3.5 (7)	.3 (12)	3.5 (51)	.7 (32)
1925–29	233.6 (99)	48.9 (45)	NA	7.0 (14)	.2 (8)	5.6 (81)	.9 (41)
1930–34	241.6 (102)	62.6 (57)	NA	14.4 (28)	.4 (16)	6.6 (96)	1.0 (45)
1935–39	277.0 (118)	98.9 (90)	50.0 (86)	26.6 (52)	.6 (24)	NA	1.3 (59)
1950–54	235.7 (100)	109.6 (100)	58.4 (100)	50.8 (100)	2.5 (100)	6.9 (100)	2.2 (100)
1955–58	228.1 (97)	108.8 (99)	66.9 (115)	52.4 (103)	2.7 (108)	7.2 (104)	4.3 (195)

Notes to Table: (a) Includes British Togo. (b) Includes British Cameroons.

B. *Coffee (ooo's of metric tons of green beans)*

	Uganda Quantity	Kenya Quantity	Tanganyika Quantity	Belgian Congo Quantity	Ruanda-Urundi Quantity	Angola Quantity	French West Africa Quantity	French Equatorial Africa Quantity	French Cameroons Quantity
1920–24	2.4 (6)(a)	4.8 (32)(a)	3.6 (20)(a)	.1 (—)(a)	(—)	9.5 (16)(b)			
1925–29	1.9 (5)	8.2 (54)	7.1 (40)	1.0 (4)	(—)	15.2 (26)			
1930–34	3.5 (8)	13.0 (86)	10.9 (62)	6.6 (29)	(—)	11.2 (19)			
1935–39	10.6 (25)	18.2 (120)	14.8 (84)	17.4 (76)	(—)	16.2 (28)			
1950–54	42.6 (100)	15.1 (100)	17.6 (100)	22.8 (100)	12.7 (100)	58.7 (100)	68.7 (100)	4.3 (100)	10.2 (100)
1955–58	71.2 (164)	22.0 (141)	21.6 (123)	41.1 (180)	18.8 (148)	79.5 (135)	122.2 (178)	5.9 (137)	20.2 (198)

Notes to Table: (a) Average of four years. (b) Average of three years.

General Note: (—) Negligible or not recorded.

TABLE 2.7 (continued)

C. *Tea (000's of metric tons of made tea or equivalent)*

	Nyasaland Quantity	Kenya Quantity	Mozambique Quantity	Tanganyika Quantity	Uganda Quantity	Belgian Congo Quantity
1920-24	.3 (4)	(—)	(—)	(—)	(—)	(—)
1925-29	.7 (10)	(—)	(—)	(—)	(—)	(—)
1930-34	1.3 (19)	1.1 (16)	(—)	(—)	(—)	(—)
1935-39	4.5 (64)	4.1 (61) (a)	(—)	(—)	(—)	(—)
1950-54	7.0 (100)	6.7 (100)	3.6 (100)	1.2 (100)	2.1 (100)	.4 (100)
1955-58	9.0 (128)	9.9 (148)	6.6 (183)	2.6 (216)	3.4 (162)	1.9 (475)

Note to Table: (a) Average of three years.

D. *Exports of Palm Products (000's of metric tons of palm oil or equivalent) (a)*

	Nigeria (b) Quantity	Sierra Leone Quantity	French West Africa Quantity	Belgian Congo Quantity	Angola Quantity
1921-24	185.6 (51)	26.9 (82)	45.1 (93)	33.0 (15)	5.4 (33) (d)
1925-29	240.3 (66)	32.1 (98)	54.2 (112)	55.4 (26)	6.8 (42)
1930-34	249.6 (68)	29.6 (90)	48.0 (99)	69.5 (32)	6.8 (42)
1935-39	294.9 (81) (c)	35.9 (109)	59.5 (123) (c)	102.2 (47) (c)	5.2 (32)
1950-54	365.5 (100)	32.9 (100)	48.4 (100)	216.5 (100)	16.2 (100)
1955-58	376.9 (106)	25.5 (78)	52.2 (108)	195.8 (90)	14.0 (86)

Notes to Table: (a) Exports of palm kernels have been converted to oil equivalents at a 45 per cent extraction rate. Only the Belgian Congo processed palm kernels into oil for export.   (b) Includes British Cameroons.   (c) Average of four years.   (d) Average of three years.

E. *Cotton, ginned (ooo's of metric tons)*

	Sudan Quantity	Uganda Quantity	Tanganyika Quantity	French Equatorial Africa Quantity	Belgian Congo Quantity	Nigeria (a) Quantity	Mozambique Quantity
1920–24	6.4 (8)	19.5 (31)	1.7 (14)	(—)	2.1 (4)	4.6 (21)	(—)
1925–29	27.2 (33)	28.5 (45)	4.5 (38)	.5 (2)	6.3 (13)	6.3 (28)	(—)
1930–34	34.2 (41)	44.6 (71)	4.4 (37)	3.1 (10)	15.2 (32)	4.7 (21)	(—)
1935–39	54.3 (65)	59.2 (94)	10.1 (84)	7.3 (24) (b)	30.4 (65)	8.6 (38) (b)	(—)
1950–54	83.6 (100)	63.0 (100)	12.0 (100)	30.6 (100)	46.8 (100)	22.4 (100)	32.0 (100)
1955–58	99.9 (118)	69.0 (109)	27.0 (225)	36.5 (119)	48.8 (104)	31.2 (140)	32.0 (100)

Notes to Table: (a) Includes British Cameroons.   (b) Average of four years.
General Note: (—) Negligible or not recorded.

F. *Tobacco (ooo's of metric tons of dried leaves)*

	Southern Rhodesia Quantity	Nyasaland Quantity	Nigeria Quantity	Tanganyika Quantity
1920–24	1.8 (4)	2.6 (19)	(—)	(—)
1925–29	6.7 (14)	6.0 (44)	(—)	(—)
1930–34	8.3 (17)	6.8 (50)	(—)	(—)
1935–39	11.3 (23)	7.2 (53)	(—)	(—)
1950–54	49.1 (100)	13.7 (100)	11.5 (100)	2.4 (100)
1955–58	71.3 (145)	17.0 (124)	13.1 (114)	2.4 (100)

Note to Table: (—) Negligible or not recorded.
General Note: Data, when reported by crop seasons rather than by calendar years, refer to the years in which the crop season ends.
Sources: League of Nations, *International Statistical Year books*; United Nations, *Statistical Yearbooks*, various years.

TABLE 2.8. *International Seaborne Shipping and Foreign Trade (1955–1957 average)*

Country	Goods Loaded and Unloaded (000 tons)	Foreign Trade		
		Total ($000,000)	As % of Total African	Per Capita ($)
Union of South Africa (b)	12,583	2,577 (c)	29.1	185.1
Central Africa				
Belgian Congo	2,061	898 (d)	10.1	52.1
Federation of Rhodesia and Nyasaland		921 (e, f)	10.4	126.9
East Africa				
Ethiopia	372 (a)	132 (g)	1.5	6.6
Kenya, Uganda, Tanganyika	4,577 (a,h,i)	717 (j)	8.1	35.5
Madagascar	689 (h)	219	2.5	44.5
Mauritius	972 (h)	114	1.3	200.4
Mozambique	5,417	153	1.7	25.3
Reunion	416	82	0.9	277.0
Somaliland (Italian)	114	25	0.3	19.2
Sudan	1,403 (l)	308	3.5	30.1
West Africa				
Angola	2,089 (a)	218	2.5	50.0
Cameroons (French)	703 (a)	183	2.1	57.4
French Equatorial Africa	1,136 (a)	200	2.3	41.0
French West Africa	7,068 (a,m)	719	8.1	38.0
Ghana	3,073 (h)	486	5.5	103.6
Liberia	2,041 (n)	71	0.8	56.8
Nigeria	4,252 (o,p)	778	8.8	24.4
Sierra Leone	1,774 (k)	103	1.2	49.0
Total Africa	50,750 (q)	8,864 (q)	100.0 (q)	

Notes to Table:
(a) Including coastwise shipping.
(b) Including South-West Africa.
(c) Excluding trade between the Union and South-West Africa.
(d) Including Ruanda-Urundi.
(e) Imports f.o.b.
(f) Excluding trade within the Federation.
(g) Twelve months ending 10 September of year stated.
(h) Including bunkers.
(i) Excluding sailing vessels.
(j) Excluding trade between the three countries.
(k) 1955–1956.
(l) Including transhipments; excluding livestock.
(m) Excluding minor ports.
(n) 1955.
(o) Including Cameroons under British administration.
(p) Excluding packing.
(q) Total of countries listed.

Source: United Nations, Department of Economic and Social Affairs, 1959a, Table I–XX, p. 38.

TABLE 2.9. *African Share in World Production* (a) *and Exports* (b) *of Selected Agricultural Commodities* (*Average*, 1934–1938, 1950–1958) (*Percentages*)

Commodity	Production (1934–1938)	Export (1934–1938)	Production (1950–1958)	Export (1950–1958)
Palm kernals	—	91.5	82.9	93.0
Palm oil	—	52.8	81.0	65.3
Sisal	63.6	42.1 (c)	67.5	59.2 (c)
Cocoa beans	66.2	67.2	64.2	67.9
Groundnuts	29.9	43.2	33.8	94.3 (d)
Coffee	5.9	7.9	16.0	19.4
Tobacco	3.6	6.6	5.9	13.1
Natural rubber	1.0	0.7	4.0	3.9

Notes to Table: (a) World excluding Eastern Europe, USSR, and Mainland China. (b) Eastern Europe, USSR, and Mainland China are excluded as sources of exports but included as destinations of exports. (c) Sisal and other agave fibres. (d) 1958.

Source: Production: United Nations, Economic Commission for Africa, 1960: *International Action for Commodity Stabilization and the Role of Africa*, E/CN.14/68 Table 1, pp. 18–19. Exports: *ibid.*, Table 4, p. 20.

TABLE 2.10. *African Share in World Production* (a) *and Exports* (b) *of Selected Minerals* (*Average*, 1936–1938, 1950–1958) (*Percentages*)

Commodity	Production (1936–1938)	Export (1936–1938)	Production (1950–1958)	Export (1950–1958)
Diamonds	97.3	52.6	96.3	51.9
Cobalt Ore	—		72.8	
Gold	47.1		60.0	
Manganese Ore	33.4	46.9	42.2	45.4
Chrome Ore	44.3	43.3	39.3	41.8
Antimony Ore	5.0	3.9	39.0	39.9
Copper Ore	19.8	5.2	24.7	14.2
Copper Metal	17.5		23.8	
Tin Concentrates	11.8	22.4	15.1	25.3
Lead Ore	3.9	35.6	11.9	48.0
Iron Ore	5.0	19.6	4.8	31.6
Bauxite	—	—	3.5	4.6
Lead Metal	1.7	—	2.4	—
Tin Metal	1.3	—	2.4	—
Silver	—	—	4.5	—

Notes to Table: (a) World excluding Eastern Europe, USSR, and Mainland China. (b) Eastern Europe, USSR and Mainland China are excluded from world as origins of exports but included as destinations of exports.

Source: United Nations, Economic Commission for Africa, 1960: *International Action for Commodity Stabilization and the Role of Africa*, E/CN.14/58. For Production Table 2, p. 20; for Exports, Table 5, p. 23.

TABLE 2.11. *Main Flows of African Inter-territorial Trade, 1957 ($000,000)*

Exporting Country or Area	Country or Area of Destination											Total
	South Africa (a)	North Africa (b)	Mozambique	French West Africa	French Equatorial Africa	Federation of Rhodesia and Nyasaland	Ghana and British West Africa (c)	British East Africa	Belgian Congo	Angola	Other African Countries	
South Africa (b,d)	—	0.2	18.1	0.4	0.3	188.8	6.1	13.5	11.5	0.7	4.1	243.7
North Africa	..	—	..	18.4	1.1	..	0.2	..	..	..	4.8	24.5
Mozambique	3.3	..	—	—	..	..	..	..	..	..	—	3.3
French West Africa	..	26.7	..	..	2.3	..	6.7	..	..	..	3.5	39.2
French Equatorial Africa	0.8	2.2	..	0.6	—	..	2.4	..	1.1	..	1.7	8.8
Federation of Rhodesia and Nyasaland	46.8	..	1.5	..	..	—	1.3	0.6	6.0	..	—	56.2
Ghana and British West Africa (c,d)	3.4	..	..	0.3	..	..	—	..	..	..	2.3	6.0
British East Africa (d)	8.3	..	0.3	..	..	1.8	..	—	6.6	..	13.4	30.4
Belgian Congo	5.3	1.5	..	0.5	4.6	4.7	0.1	0.3	—	1.2	3.0	21.2
Angola	1.3	..	..	..	..	..	..	..	2.1	—	4.1	7.5

Source: United Nations, Department of Economic and Social Affairs, 1959a, Table 3–xv, p. 183.

Notes to Table:
   (a) Including exports from South-West Africa, but excluding trade between South Africa and South-West Africa.
   (b) Algeria, Morocco, and Tunisia.
   (c) "British West Africa" here refers to Nigeria and Sierra Leone.
   (d) Excluding trade among countries comprising the area.

TABLE 2.12. *Value of Import, Export and Total Trade between Selected African Countries (1950–1957)*
($000,000; percentage)

Country	Aggregate Trade with African Countries A			Aggregate Trade with all Countries B			A as Percentage of B		
	I	E	T	I	E	T	I	E	T
Angola	15	59	74	733	836	1,569	2.0	7.0	4.7
Belgian Congo (a)	221	152	373	2,863	3,279	6,142	7.7	4.6	6.1
Cameroons (French)	49	42	91	734	591	1,325	6.7	7.1	6.9
French Equatorial Africa	73	59	132	839	523	1,362	8.7	11.3	9.7
French West Africa	246	277	523	2,819	2,202	5,021	8.7	12.6	10.4
Ghana	102	47	149	1,672	1,885	3,557	6.1	2.5	4.2
Kenya, Uganda, Tanganyika (b)	116	203	319	2,754	2,536	5,290	4.2	8.0	6.0
Madagascar	51	66	117	1,016	649	1,665	5.0	10.2	7.0
Mozambique	84	56	140	661	409	1,070	12.7	13.7	13.1
Nigeria	20	36	56	2,582	2,819	5,401	0.8	1.3	1.0
Federation of Rhodesia and Nyasaland (c)	1,121	604	1,725	3,077	3,331	6,408	36.4	18.1	26.9
Sierra Leone	10	3	13	330	262	592	3.0	1.1	2.2
Union of South Africa (d)	832	1,683	2,515	10,017	7,456	17,473	8.3	22.6	14.4
Total (e)	2,940	3,287	6,227	30,097	26,778	56,875	9.8	12.3	10.9

Notes to Table:

(a) Including Ruanda-Urundi.
(b) Including trade between these countries.
(c) Including trade between members of the Federation prior to 1954.
(d) Including South-West Africa from 1955.
(e) Total of figures shown. "African countries" as defined in heading of table includes North Africa.

Source: United Nations, Department of Economic and Social Affairs, 1958, Table 3–3, p. 152.

TABLE 2.13. *Gross Value of Output of Mining and Quarrying*

Country	Year	Total (000,000 currency units)		Per Capita (dollars)
		Local Currency	Dollars	
Total, Tropical Africa			933.5	
Total, West Africa			159.6	
Angola	1955–57	481.0	16.7	3.83
Cameroons (French)	1958	86.0	0.2	0.06
French Equatorial Africa	1958	4,106.0	8.3	1.70
French West Africa	1958	2,471.0	5.0	0.26
Ghana	1955–57	24.5	68.7	14.65
Liberia	1955–57	9.2	9.2 (*a*)	7.36
Nigeria	1954/55–1956/57	11.9	33.5	0.95
Sierra Leone	1955–57	7.9	22.3	10.62
Total, Central Africa			748.1	
Belgian Congo	1955–57	17,555.0	351.1	27.41
Ruanda-Urundi	1955–57	334.0	6.7	1.51
Federation of Rhodesia and Nyasaland	1955–57	139.0	390.3	53.76
Northern Rhodesia	1955–57	116.0	325.4	149.27
Southern Rhodesia	1955–57	23.0	64.9	26.17
Total, East Africa			25.8	
Kenya	1955–57	2.2	6.2	1.01
Madagascar	1958	622.0	1.3	0.26
Mozambique	1955–56	34.0	1.2	0.20
Tanganyika	1955–57	5.5	15.3	1.81
Uganda	1955–57	0.7	2.0	0.36
Total, South Africa			1,035.7	
Bechuanaland	1955–57	0.2	0.6	2.02
South-West Africa	1955–57	30.3	84.8 (*b*)	165.95
Swaziland	1956–57	2.4	6.8	28.69
Union of South Africa	1955–57	337.0	943.5 (*b*)	65.80

Notes to Table:

(*a*) Exports of iron ore and diamonds. Diamond exports include re-exports.

(*b*) Local sales and exports.

Source: United Nations, Department of Economic and Social Affairs, 1959a, Table I–XXXV, p. 64.

TABLE 2.14. *Imports by Category as Percentage of Total Value*

	Value ($000,000)	Percent
I. Tropical Africa (a) 1955		
Category		
Food, Beverages, and Tobacco	261.4	10.6
Basic Materials	32.2	1.3
Mineral Fuels	173.0	7.0
Chemicals	139.0	5.7
Machinery and Transport Equipment	779.6	31.7
Textiles	365.4	14.9
Metals and Metal Manufactures	277.8	11.3
Other Manufactures	345.1	14.0
Miscellaneous	85.4	3.5
Total	2,458.9	100.0
II. Gold Coast (Ghana) 1955		
Category		
Food, Beverages, and Tobacco		20
Basic Materials and Mineral Fuels		7
Chemicals		6
Textiles		22
Machinery and Transport Equipment		17
Other Manufactures		26
Miscellaneous		2
Total Imports	246	100
III. Nigeria 1955		
Category		
Food, Beverages and Tobacco		13
Basic Materials and Mineral Fuels		6
Chemicals		5
Textiles		25
Machinery and Transport Equipment		21
Other Manufactures		28
Miscellaneous		2
Total Imports	381	100

Notes to Table:

(a) Tropical Africa for this purpose, apparently includes all of Subsaharan Africa except the Union of South Africa and the Federation of Rhodesia and Nyasaland.

Sources: I. United Nations, Department of Economic and Social Affairs, 1959a, Table 3–XI, p. 180. II and III. United Nations, Economic Commission for Africa, 1961, Vol. I, No. 1, p. 28.

TABLE 2.15. *Output per Man of Principal Minerals in Selected Countries*

Mineral and Country	Year	Number Employed			Output (000 tons)	Output per Man (tons)
		African	Non-African	Total		
Coal						
Nigeria	1955/1956			7,900	761.0	96.3
Southern Rhodesia	1956	8,592			3,544.0	413.6 (a)
Union of South Africa	1957	56,519	5,768	62,287	34,769.0	558.2
Copper						
Belgian Congo	1956				250.0	
Northern Rhodesia	1957	38,763	7,304	46,067	389.6	8.5
Union of South Africa	1957	7,508	1,405	8,913	43.9	4.9
Diamonds						
Belgian Congo	1956				14,010.0 (b)	
Ghana	1957/1958					
Companies		5,101	109	5,210	1,457.2 (b)	279.7 (c)
African Enterprizes		12,100		12,100	1,694.9 (b)	140.1 (c)
Union of South Africa	1957					
Mines		8,003	1,818	9,821	2,246.7 (b)	228.8 (c)
Alluvial Workings		4,901	1,451	6,352	332.2 (b)	52.3 (c)
Gold						
Belgian Congo	1956				11.6 (d)	1.1 (e)
Ghana	1957/1958	21,350	685	22,035	24.6 (d)	0.8 (a,e)
Southern Rhodesia	1956	19,894			16.7 (d)	
Union of South Africa	1957	353,845	49,732	403,577	529.7 (d)	1.3 (e)

TABLE 2.15 (continued)

Mineral and Country	Year	Number Employed African	Non-African	Total	Output (000 tons)	Output per Man (tons)
Iron Ore						
Sierra Leone	1956			2,960	823.0	278.0
Union of South Africa	1957	2,850	503	3,353	1,316.0	392.5
Manganese						
Belgian Congo	1956				164.8	
Ghana	1957/1958	4,593	40	4,633	309.0	66.7
Union of South Africa	1957	7,286	395	7,681	252.8	32.9
Tin						
Belgian Congo	1956	36,811	572	37,383	15.1	0.4
Nigeria	1956/1957	50,566	322	50,888	9.3	0.2
Union of South Africa	1957	2,798	206	3,004	1.5	0.5

Notes to Table:
(a) Output per African employee.
(b) Thousands of metric carats.
(c) Metric carats.
(d) Tons.
(e) Kilograms.

Source: United Nations, Department of Economic and Social Affairs, 1959a, *op. cit.*, Table I-XXXVIII, p. 68.

TABLE 2.16. *Major Export Commodities and Percentage of Total Domestic Exports Accounted for by Each in Selected Years*

	1928		1938		1948		1958	
I. Commonwealth West Africa								
1. Ghana (Gold Coast)	1. Cocoa	82.4	1. Gold	42.6	1. Cocoa	75.5	1. Cocoa	60.0
	2. Gold	5.0	2. Cocoa	40.0	2. Gold	9.7	2. Wood, timber, lumber	10.5
	3. Diamonds	4.0	3. Manganese	8.0	3. Manganese	4.8	3. Gold	10.1
			4. Diamonds	4.8	4. Wood, timber, lumber	4.4	4. Diamonds	8.3
					5. Diamonds	1.8	5. Manganese	8.3
Total		91.4		95.4		96.2		97.2
2. Nigeria	1. Palm Products	48.3	1. Palm Products	33.9	1. Palm Products	33.5	1. Palm Products	24.9
	2. Cocoa	14.3	2. Cocoa	16.9	2. Cocoa	29.2	2. Groundnuts	20.3
	3. Tin	13.1	3. Tin	15.5	3. Groundnuts	16.0	3. Cocoa	20.2
	4. Groundnuts	10.9	4. Groundnuts	14.1	4. Tin	7.2	4. Cotton	5.9
							5. Tin	3.0
Total		86.6		80.4		85.9		74.3
3. Sierra Leone	1. Palm Products	71.5	1. Diamonds	40.2	1. Palm Products	41.4	1. Diamonds	42.8
	2. Kola Nuts	17.5	2. Iron ore and Concentrates	30.2	2. Diamonds	21.9	2. Iron ore and Concentrates	29.2
			3. Palm Products	21.4	3. Iron ore and Concentrates	20.6	3. Palm Products	15.0
			4. Kola Nuts	1.4	4. Kola Nuts	4.0	4. Coffee	6.0
							5. Cocoa	2.6
Total		89.0		93.2		87.9		95.6
4. Gambia	Groundnuts over 90 per cent of domestic exports in all years							

	1928		1938		1948		1958	
II. French Territories								
1. French West Africa	1. Groundnuts	52.7	1. Groundnuts and Products	45.2	1. Groundnuts and Products	44.2	1. Groundnuts and Products	37.9
	2. Palm Products	13.3	2. Cocoa	13.3	2. Coffee	13.8	2. Coffee	28.1
	3. Cocoa	9.2	3. Palm Products	8.1	3. Cocoa	8.3	3. Cocoa	8.7
	4. Wood and Timber	7.5	4. Coffee	6.0	4. Palm Products	6.0	4. Wood	4.5
							5. Palm Products	3.5
Total		82.7		76.6		72.3		82.7
2. French Equatorial Africa	NA		1. Wood and Products	43.4	1. Cotton	52.2	1. Wood and Products	39.3
			2. Cotton	23.5	2. Wood and Products	22.1	2. Cotton	30.1
			3. Coffee	4.6	3. Coffee	2.0	3. Coffee	4.6
Total				71.5		76.3		74.0
III. British Central Africa								
1. Southern Rhodesia	1. Gold	36.8	1. Gold	53.3	1. Tobacco	43.7	1. Copper	47.5
	2. Tobacco	12.7	2. Asbestos	12.0	. Gold	17.4	2. Tobacco	19.4
	3. Asbestos	11.1	3. Tobacco	11.9	3. Asbestos	11.4	3. Asbestos	5.2
	4. Chrome	6.0	4. Chrome	4.9	4. Chrome	4.4	4. Gold	4.8
							5. Tea	2.1
Total		66.6		82.6		76.9		
2. Northern Rhodesia	1. Copper	30.6	1. Copper	87.8	1. Copper	84.5	} 79.0
3. Nyasaland	1. Tobacco	73.5	1. Tea	46.7	1. Tobacco	53.9	
	2. Tea	10.9	2. Tobacco	41.0	2. Tea	32.4	
	3. Cotton	8.6	3. Cotton	10.4	3. Cotton	8.9	
Total		93.0		98.1		95.2		

TABLE 2.16 (continued)

IV. British East Africa

1. Tanganyika

	1928		1938		1948		1958	
1.	Sisal	28.7	Sisal	38.6	Sisal	55.0	Coffee	31.8
2.	Coffee	19.1	Gold	16.0	Cotton	8.2	Cotton	21.2
3.	Cotton	12.8	Cotton	9.7	Diamonds	6.4	Sisal	10.6
4.			Coffee	8.5	Coffee	5.5	Tea	3.9
5.							Diamonds	3.6
Total		60.6		72.8		75.1		71.1

2. Kenya–Uganda

	1928		1938		1948		1958	
1.	Cotton	37.3	Cotton	41.5	Cotton	29.2		
2.	Coffee	19.3	Coffee	12.9	Coffee	20.2		
3.	Sisal	7.4	Gold	7.9	Sisal	9.5		
4.	Cotton-seed	4.8	Sisal	5.4				
Total		68.8		67.7		58.9		

V. Portuguese Africa

1. Angola

	1928		1938		1948		1958	
1.	Coffee	22.7	Diamonds	29.4	Coffee	30.9	Coffee	41.7
2.	Diamonds	19.6	Maize	20.2	French Beans	11.8	Diamonds	14.9
3.	Maize	18.4	Sugar	11.0	Diamonds	10.7	Fish Meal for Cattle	7.5
4.			Coffee	10.9	Sisal	8.0	Maize	5.9
5.					Sugar	4.5	Sisal	5.8
Total		60.7		71.5		65.9		75.8

2. Mozambique

	1928		1938		1948		1958	
1.	NA		Sugar	30.5	Cotton	23.2	Cotton	27.0
2.			Cotton	15.7	Copra	21.6	Sugar	16.6
3.			Sisal	15.2	Sisal	12.0	Cashew Nuts	12.5
4.			Copra	14.7	Sugar	7.4	Copra	9.3
5.					Cashew Nuts	5.5	Sisal	6.2
Total				76.1		69.7		71.6

TABLE 2.16 (continued)

	1928		1938		1948		1958	
VI. *Belgian Congo*	1. Copper	44.0	1. Copper	33.2	1. Copper	29.2	1. Copper	27.0
	2. Palm Products	19.1	2. Cotton	14.6	2. Cotton	14.3	2. Coffee	14.1
	3. Diamonds	8.4	3. Palm Products	11.7	3. Palm Products	11.7	3. Diamonds	8.4
	4. Cotton	8.3	4. Tin	11.2	4. Tin	10.1	4. Palm Products	7.2
			5. Diamonds	8.2	5. Diamonds	4.7	5. Cobalt	5.5
Total		79.8		78.9		70.0		62.2
VII. *Union of South Africa*	1. Gold	48.1	1. Gold	69.3	1. Gold	54.2	1. Gold	36.2
	2. Wool	18.9	2. Wool	8.5	2. Wool	10.6	2. Fissionable Materials	8.7
	3. Diamonds	10.0					3. Wool	6.9
							4. Diamonds	5.0
Total		77.0		77.3		64.8		56.8

Sources: For 1928, calculations are based on territorial trade statistics reported by Frankel, 1938. For the remaining years, calculations have been drawn from the United Nations, *Yearbooks of International Trade Statistics.*

TABLE 2.17. *Industrial Origin of Gross Domestic Product at Current Factor Cost, Selected Countries, 1955*

Country	Currency and Unit	Total	Agriculture, Forestry, and Fishing	Mining	Manufacturing	Construction	Transportation and Commerce	Trade	Public Administration and Defense	Other Services
Belgian Congo (a)	Billions of Belgian francs	56.1	15.6	13.4	6.7 (b)	3.9 (c)	5.4	4.4	5.6	5.8
Kenya	Millions of pounds Sterling	159.3	62.8	1.7	20.6 (e,f)	9.1	11.3	23.6	20.0	10.2
Nigeria (i)	Millions of pounds Sterling	806.9	506.9	9.7	19.5 (b)	89.4	——— 109.1 ———		46.0	26.3
Rhodesia and Nyasaland	Millions of pounds Sterling	335.3	53.8	116.2	——— ———		——— 165.3 ———			
Tanganyika	Millions of pounds Sterling	130.2	84.5	5.1	4.1	4.2	9.2	7.6	8.7	6.7
Uganda (d)	Millions of pounds Sterling	118.0	76.2	—	——— ———		41.8			
Union of South Africa (d,g)	Millions of South African pounds	1,796.6	253.7	237.2	— 428.5 (h) —		144.8	233.9	168.5	330.0

Source: United Nations, Department of Economic and Social Affairs, 1959a, Table I–IV, p. 16.

Notes to Table: (a) Individual items include imported raw materials, and therefore their totals exceed the recorded totals in the years 1950 to 1957, in 1955 by 4.6 billion francs. (b) Including utilities (electricity and gas). (c) Including construction materials. (d) Net domestic product at factor cost. (e) Including some processing in agriculture. (f) Comprising wages, salaries, profits, and surpluses. (g) 12 months beginning July 1 of year stated. (h) Private enterprises only. (i) 1956.

TABLE 2.18. *Distribution of Economically Active Population by Sex and Ethnic Composition, Selected Countries*
(*Percentage, unless otherwise stated.*)

Country, Year and Item	Total Active Population ('000 persons)	Source of Employment								
		Agri-culture	Mining	Manu-facturing	Con-struction	Elec-tricity, etc.	Trade	Trans-port	Services	Other
Union of South Africa (1951)										
Male: Europeans	768.6	18.4	7.1	18.6	8.6	0.9	14.2	13.3	16.1	2.7
Other (a)	2,915.5	43.4	15.5	9.8	5.9	0.6	4.9	3.1	5.4	11.4
Female: Europeans	214.8	1.8	1.0	18.4	0.6	0.2	32.5	4.9	37.4	3.2
Other (a)	693.1	14.3	0.2	4.9	0.1	—	0.7	0.1	77.5	2.3
Belgian Congo (1955 est.)										
Male: Non-Africans (b)	33.4									
Africans	3,042.0	69.8	2.9	5.7	4.3	—	3.0	3.0	1.2	10.1
Female: Africans	3,156.9									
Federation of Rhodesia and Nyasaland (1956)										
Europeans	110.5	8.6	8.4	12.1	12.6	1.3	21.4	9.4	25.2	1.0
Asians and Coloured	9.3	3.2	1.1	14.4	6.9	0.5	56.0	3.7	10.4	3.7
Africans (wage and salary earners only)	1,037.3	34.5	9.5	11.4	14.2	0.9	5.4	2.5	21.6	—
French Equatorial Africa (c,d) (1951)										
Male: Non-Africans	10.2	5.4	4.8	5.7	10.3	0.9	16.8	10.5	54.6	—
Africans (e)	1,166.3									
Female: Non-Africans	1.9	1.9	3.0	5.8	5.1	1.6	32.7	6.4	44.1	—

Source: United Nations, Department of Economic and Social Affairs, 1959a, Table I–XXXII, pp. 45-46.

Notes to Table: (a) Asians, coloured persons and natives of 15 years and over. (b) Government employees (7,219) and company employees (15,953). (c) Persons reporting a classifiable occupation. (d) Persons employed in petroleum and natural gas industries included under electricity, etc., rather than under mining; those employed in domestic service included under electricity rather than under services. (e) Excluding government employees.

PART TWO

The
Indigenous
Patterns

3

Economics in East African Aboriginal Societies

by Harold K. Schneider*
Lawrence College

"The distinctions to be drawn between literate and non-
literate economies are . . . those of degree rather than kind."[1]

Scarcely anyone who has ever had contact with the so-called cattle-
keeping peoples of East Africa has failed to comment on their admira-
tion for cattle, and the prestige that possession of them gives their
holders. They seem to be principally stores of value outside normal
market processes. To those concerned with the economic future of
Africa, this matter naturally requires attention because of its implications for economic development, since a very considerable number of
people, from the Sudan to South Africa, in what I shall call East Africa,
possess great numbers of these animals.

I have placed the quotation from Herskovits at the head of the paper
to set the mood, because the attempt will be made here to show that the
function of cattle as a symbol of status is dependent on their economic
use. It will be shown that the Wanyaturu, whose economy will be most
extensively discussed, have a market or money economy, or something
very like a market economy in which livestock, not just cattle, are the
items most frequently traded, so that they are more or less standardized
media of exchange. It will be further shown that livestock seem to be
used in the same general way over most of East Africa and that this fact,
contradicting the impression that they are merely stores of value,
explains to a large extent the comparatively unusual attitude toward and
use of cattle in this part of the world.

* I wish to express gratitude to the National Science Foundation for a grant which
made possible field work among the Wanyaturu in 1959–1960.
[1] Herskovits, M. J., 1952, p. 488.

It is not intended here to describe the actual working of these economies, except incidentally, for though this would be ideal, the recognition that they are pecuniary type economies has only just begun to bear fruit. The paper will merely support my assertion while all the multitude of questions that are fostered about the operation of the systems will have to wait for future investigation.

We shall begin with some relevant aspects of Turu (or Wanyaturu) economics, follow with a discussion of the concepts of money as applied to this area, and conclude with a comparative discussion of the phenomenon in other East African societies.

2

Cattle in Turu economics play three roles: they are *real capital, money* and, at times, *consumption goods.* In contrast it will be recognized that cattle in Euroamerican economies are principally real capital, as in the case of milk production, and consumption goods, as with beef and hides. The failure to see this distinction has been at the core of a great deal of misunderstanding of East African people by outsiders.

The most obvious role of cattle is that of capital. Among the Turu and other people of the Turu cluster, return on this capital is predominantly found in the production of manure. While milk is a fundamental element of subsistence in the Nilotic societies to the North, such as the Masai, Suk, Turkana and Nandi, the Turu use it only to feed children and as a luxury for adults. Among the Turu, production of an adequate supply of grain is normally impossible without manure to fertilize the crops. This means that all people who start independent homesteads must have cattle, and the economy is "arranged" to see that they get them through the cattle loaning system called *uriha* if they are not otherwise available. One way or another Turu have much meat to eat—all animals that die are eaten unless contaminated—but purposeful slaughter of livestock for food is avoided except for various sacrificial rites; thus livestock are only incidentally to be regarded as a consumption good.

Whether cattle are money is a subject of much debate. In Turu, cattle, together with small stock, are media of exchange and standards of value as well as stores of value, and they can be converted into wives, grain, honey, iron goods, land, services and many other less important items. But cattle are the "big notes" of the system, and since in themselves they lack divisibility, small stock rest in a standardized ratio to them, so that three smaller animals always equal a young bull or steer, or five head of small stock equal a heifer. Because of this it is possible to translate a man's livestock wealth into livestock units, each unit being one small animal. This system of equivalents is overtly known to the people and is so used that, for example, when discussing the inheritance of one heifer by two sons, it will be converted into five small animals. In a similar way, when explaining bridewealth payments a person will speak of having paid an *njiku* (steer) when in fact he actually paid three small animals. Von Sick recorded the prevailing system of equivalents at the time of the German conquest:

1 goat equals an iron hoe, or a spear, or one bow and five arrows, or the *honga* shield.
2 goats equal an ostrich feather headdress.
3 goats equal a Colobus monkey skin.[2]

It seems clear that the equation within the indigenous economy between small stock and cattle was the same as later, so that the last item, the Colobus monkey skin, could be priced at 1 steer, which is the equivalent of 3 goats, the word "goat" being interchangeable with "sheep" since there is no difference in the economic value of these two kinds of animals.

Thus Turu are accustomed to think in terms of standardized values. Von Sick notes that a knife was priced at one hen; for trading grain, not only did they have a standardized ox-hide bag (*musuta*), which holds about 200 pounds of millet, but they had standardized wooden troughs used to measure the contents of the bag so that the *sori ya ngombe* ("cow trough"), three of which filled a musuta, held an amount equivalent in value to a male calf. Even arrows, which are used as a means of payment in some aspects of marriage, are occasionally generalized as a measure of value in relation to other things. Indeed, the term *muyi*, arrow, has come to mean "fee" when the price is very small. It must be noted that the value of cows as capital for producing calves normally outweighs their use as money, such animals never being slaughtered or sold if it is possible to avoid it. Since Von Sick's day, the commodities traded have changed somewhat, but the basic structure of the indigenous economy remains the same. War helmets, spears and shields are now unimportant, and the export of salt to the Iramba or trading beads and cloth from the Gogo for cattle has stopped, while Arab, Indian and other foreign traders have come to be middlemen for the import and export of goods even, in certain cases, between Turu groups themselves.

The first goal of Turu economic activity is, of course, to provide a sufficient supply of food for the family; the ultimate goal is to accumulate as many cattle as possible. The method of achieving this, a norm

[2] Von Sick, E., 1916, pp. 25–26.

followed in some degree by all, is to grow a surplus of grain, the staple food, which can be sold for livestock. In order to do this it is necessary to capitalize production with land on which to grow a crop and graze the livestock, and wives to do the necessary productive work. The system is so composed as to make it possible for individual households to control these variables to a sufficient degree in order to increase their number of livestock.

The Turu live in compact villages composed of homesteads situated on the arable land, each of which is headed by a male, or in rare cases a female, all of whom are related through a common ancestor about five generations removed from the adult men. Though land can be and is sold, its saleability is hedged about by restrictions which serve to preserve it to the occupying lineage. That is, a father must pass on his land to his sons, and all sales are reversible on demand by the seller or his descendants who must, however, pay twice the original selling price. This right, however, weakens with time, so that it is unenforceable in most instances after the original parties and witnesses to the transaction are dead.

Marsh land adjoining the village, crucial for reserve grazing, is more frequently sold than arable land. In fact, such land is valued for the prestige it brings and because it is a good investment, being relatively scarce and in great demand. Those who own it, however, would not normally entirely exclude dependable fellow-members of the village from its use, though grazing fees are often charged. Since sale seldom occurs, it is difficult to obtain a clear picture of its price, but it seems that one heifer will buy about 5 to 10 acres.

Polygyny is possible and desirable. The average initial disbursement for a wife, four or five head of cattle, or about three heifers and one or two steers, seems to be in recompense for the services of the woman, who runs her own house, produces and processes grain and provides firewood, water and the like. Though the husband theoretically has exclusive sexual rights to his wife, he is expected to allow her a lover, from whom he can extract a fine of six goats if he catches the pair *in flagrante delicto*. Her child-bearing function is taken into account in the bridewealth only indirectly; initially bridewealth merely compensates the bride's mother for loss of her services. An extra payment of a heifer for a girl or a steer for a boy, levied at a later date when the woman has borne two children, is determined by the sex of the first child.

Other rights in a woman are retained by her father and brothers. They may fine the husband for badly beating her, or for any act on his part which can be claimed to have shortened her life. Turu bridewealth, indeed, is technically a part of a reciprocal loan, since the father reserves rights in his daughter while the husband reserves rights in the cattle of the bridewealth.

Millet of either of two varieties is the staple food; in "normal" years it is exchangeable for livestock, when a seller can be found, at the rate of four *debes*—that is, four gasoline tins, the unit of measuring grain—for one small animal, twenty debes for a heifer, and twelve debes for a steer. This rate is correlated with sterling, so that one debe is worth five shillings (East African) and one goat shs. 20, with four debes thus equaling one goat. Prices in the European market are similar, a debe of grain in normal times costing four or five shillings, a goat averaging about shs. 17 and a heifer selling for about shs. 105. It is thus evident that the Turu take account of the prices in both indigenous and induced systems, but fix them at standard rates. That is, the sterling equivalents have risen over the years with the inflation of prices in the European economy, but the ratio of value of the goods in the European market is very close to that in the Turu indigenous economy.

It is the exchange of grain for livestock and vice versa that comprises the main sector of the Turu economic system. The prices quoted above for grain are those expected in normally productive years. In a bad year, when production of grain falls off markedly, the price of grain goes up so that in some instances, as in 1937, one could buy a heifer for only three debes, or 120 lbs. of grain. It is for this that the enterprising Turu waits. Normally a Turu who produces an excess of grain stores it in his house sealed with ant-hill clay in bark vats (*kiu*), carefully attended so that it will last two or three years or more. But it has a regular turn-over, achieved by lending it in small quantities to members of the village who run short before the harvest, so that it is returned fresh. No interest is paid on such loans, the freshness of the grain which is returned being regarded as sufficient payment. If the owner can hold on to his stocks, the grain is sold at the optimum time and a large profit made in the acquisition of livestock.

Livestock are essential because of the need for manure. But since many people do not own enough animals to provide sufficient manure, the economy would be seriously imbalanced without the system of loaning cattle. Almost anyone who is not totally unreliable can get someone to provide him with animals on loan, if not from a non-kinsman, then from a relative on whose sense of obligation he can play. The desire always is first for female animals which will produce not only manure but milk for the children, though male animals are acceptable. The care given to the animals is considered to balance the service rendered, but the recipient is usually insecure because the owner can legally remove the animals at any time.

It is important to recognize also that because of the system of loaning cattle, the number of these animals it is theoretically possible for a Turu to own is for all practical purposes unlimited. The number of wives he may have is limited by his ability to cope with them, availability of land,

TABLE 3.1. *Relation between Grain Production and the Variables of Manure, Acres Cultivated and Numbers of Wives in Thirty Farmsteads in a Turu Village*

	1.	2.	3.	4.	5.	6.
Farmstead	Acres	Women	Cattle Present	Manure Index	Wealth Index	Grain Pro-duction
1. Muhomi	4.1	4	34	187	315+	189
2. Sunas	4.7	3	35	177	160	95
3. Nkango	6.4	3	25	148	272	335
4. Kinyisi	5+	3	23	130	336	150
5. Ikoti	4.6	1	22	130	268	57
6. S. Masaka	6.8	5	30	127	188	195
7. Lisu	3.5	2	24	113	156	205
8. Mudemis	5.2	2	16	98	31	72
9. Petero	3.1	3	18	90	28	90
10. Sunja	2.6	1	16	87	57	75
11. Ibi	8.8	4	18	85	92	163
12. S. Mosi	2.6	1	16	82	109	53
13. Chima	2.7	1	20	79	179	96
14. Mtinangi	4.3	2	11	71	66	95
15. Mutinda	2+	3	10	70	28	55
16. Nkuwi	2.6	1	18	69	27	75
17. M. Mpondo	6.7	3	16	69	1	58
18. Mutatuu	2.3	1	9	61	75	36
19. Ghula K.	4.2	1	13	56	17	76
20. Ikita	4.0	1	13	54	2	125
21. Samahii	4.0	1	6	54	40	45
22. Msumari	6.1	3	11	51	45	90
23. Ibunka	2.7	1	9	50	22	37
24. Ntui	2.6	1	10	41	15+	35
25. Nkongolo	4.1	2	6	39	14	41
26. M. Sinda	1.8	1	6	35	8	40
27. Mujou	2.0	2	8	34	33	61
28. Bula	3.0	2	8	34	5	49
29. Ngua	3.3	1	4	17	0	40
30. M. Nkese	1+	0	0	0	0	4

permission of a previous wife to use her cattle for another marriage, and the like, though some men have managed to have more than ten. The amount of grain one can possess is limited by the physical limits to the size of houses, danger of deterioration and the fact that grain can not usually be stored anywhere but in one's home. The amount of land one can get is limited by its availability. But the number of livestock a man may own is limited only by his ability to get them.

Therefore, individual Turu homesteads may be thought of as small firms. The head of the household manages all external buying and selling while the wives exchange goods within the household. Technically the male household head owns none of the wealth of the house which is all in the names of his various wives whose obligation is to increase it and pass it on to their sons, but from the outside he is seen as the owner because it is his prerogative to handle all exchanges or disbursements in the market of the wealth of his wives. Sharing and mutual aid are important among men of the same village, but this does not by any means exclude private enterprise, expressed in wide variations in wealth even among full brothers. This is best shown in Table 3.1 which records the economic positions of most of the homesteads in one village, and in which number five is the younger brother of number twenty-four. In Table 3.1 the households are arranged in terms of the amount of manure produced, a "manure index" being obtained by counting the number of animals actually in the corral and assigning a figure to each in terms of a goat as 1, a calf 2 and each full-grown cow or bull 5 (column 4). The other columns show the amount of land available for production in 1958–1959 (column 1), the number of women heading individual houses in a household, both wives and mothers (column 2), the number of cattle actually held in the corral whether they are owned or borrowed (column 3), the number of livestock actually owned by members of the household expressed in livestock units, i.e., the "wealth index" (column 5), and the number of debes of grain produced in the 1959 harvest (column 6). While the number of livestock units producing manure in the homestead does not represent the "wealth index," which derives from the actual number owned, since most homesteads have loaned some livestock out and borrowed others, actual wealth correlates with the number held in the homestead as may be seen in Chart 3.1, which shows the correlation between the manure index, productivity of grain in debes and the wealth index. The wealth index skews upward away from the manure index at the top and downward and away from the manure index at the bottom as we would expect if the rich loan out excess livestock and the poor borrow these animals.

The graph shows the interplay of the important variables in production and the wide variations in wealth that are possible in the Turu system through the manipulation of the variables. It is generally clear that there is a correlation between the amount of manure available and the amount of grain produced. It is also apparent that productivity is markedly affected by the number of workers available, who are principally the women. The amount of land available, while quite important in a few cases, such as No. 11, where it apparently allows the four women

CHART 3.1.   *Graph showing Actual Livestock Wealth (Wealth Index) in Relation to Livestock Held (Implied by Manure Index) and Grain Production in Thirty Farmsteads in a Turu Village.*

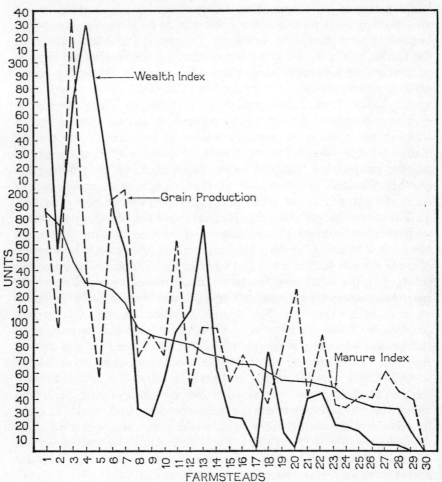

of the homestead wide latitude, on the whole has less significance. Other variables are at work in this system, but cannot be shown in quantitative terms. A very important one is incentive. No. 24, an old man with an old wife, is unwilling to try to excell. Those Turu who work hard to get ahead tend to view those who fall behind as lazy, though they recognize that other factors may enter.

This graph, treating of the main elements of the economy, suggests its dynamics, which may be more explicitly detailed. For one thing, the matter of loaning out cattle creates a network of ties within and without the village that affects almost everyone in some way. The rich men, at the top of the table, have multiple ties. These relations are constantly being reviewed, with cattle passing back and forth. Additionally, when the census on which these data are based was taken, the total cattle population of this village was about 550. During the preceding year about 110 head of cattle were born while about 80 animals died or were disposed of by slaughter. The number of cattle transferred on loan was relatively small; about 40 were sold during the year, most of which were sent to the government livestock markets for a total of about shs. 4100, or $575. This represents a 7 per cent takeoff, which is about average for all of Turu. Thirty-one head of cattle were involved in bridewealth transactions, of which 12 were gained and nineteen lost. But at the core of the dynamics is the fact that in this village, out of a total of about seventy independent productive units—that is, the houses composing each homestead, each of which is autonomous as concerns production and consumption—twenty-nine did not produce enough grain for normative subsistence, which is 18 debes per year per adult. Because of the large degree of unpredictability of success in production, many of the inferior producers own livestock while many of the surplus producers do not. The incentive for the circulation of livestock and grain derives from this fact, though, as has been pointed out, the expectation of periodic droughts and other natural impediments to production also provide an incentive to surplus producers of grain to hold on to it to sell at a high price. Thus while there is a correlation between wealth reckoned in livestock and wealth reckoned in amount of grain stored, there is enough lack of a relationship between the two to keep the economy viable.

When the Germans imposed their rule on Turu country, there was an immediate influx of traders—Arabs, Wanyamwezi and others—who were interested in the surpluses of grain and the large number of livestock. It is noteworthy that the Turu entered the livestock export market almost immediately, showing their familiarity with market processes. Von Sick[3] noted that during the first year of the establishment of a German military post in the area, in 1909, livestock were sold to traders at the post in the amount of 50,000 rupees, or about shs. 100,000.

[3] Von Sick, E., 1916, p. 60.

While the introduction of taxation had something to do with this, it is an undeniable fact that the Turu took immediately to clothing and certain other imported items. This has continued so that clothing is still the most important general item imported. Limitation in the demand for imports, shown by the continued use of indigenously made iron goods, pots, stools and the like, reflects the continued importance of this indigenous economy. That is, the livestock and grain markets introduced by outsiders are a source of cash for items which have come to serve as prestige symbols, but this external economy does not substitute for the indigenous one, because it cannot sufficiently guarantee subsistence security.

In Turu society prestige derives from a number of sources. A *muhomi*, a man who has killed a lion, a woman who has borne twins, a feat considered equal to killing a lion, a *muxai*, or courageous and aggressive person, all receive the deference due them. Skill, intelligence and cleverness of all kinds, especially in human relations, are admired. On this list the possession of wealth in livestock ranks high. In former times men used to keep the especially large and handsome steers out of the market because of the prestige they conferred. Even today a man may acquire prestige by being the keystone in a voluntary herding group which is identified by his name.

It has been suggested above that the prestige associated with cattle, or rather livestock, is a result of the role of livestock as a medium of exchange. That is, the owner of many animals is admired for his control of resources. He may be called *mnyampa*, "sir," and will be offered a stool to sit on when he visits, even if he is a young man. He is given the better beer and otherwise favored, especially if he is not of the particular village in which he is visiting and is thus outside the local system of stratification based on age. If we consider the first three men listed in Table 3.1, the richest in the village, it is significant that all three are strongly disliked. The one thing they all have in common is a callous attitude toward others. In another village, the two richest men were also strongly disliked, and for the same reason. In contrast, Nos. 4 and 5 in Table 3.1 are considered to be "good" men, in that they are quiet and apparently unaggressive. This points to a paradox in Turu economic psychology: to become wealthy necessitates aggressiveness, which brings on dislike while also leading to the deference that derives from wealth in livestock which, as we have seen, more than any other single fact confers prestige. Prestige is thus separable from respect. The envy and hatred generated by the possession of wealth is a normal risk. "It is god's will that a man seek riches," said one old man, "so that a man must try to get it despite its hazards."

3

Dalton, in a recent article on market economies and "primitive" economics[4] asserts that a market economy *is* a money economy. Contrary to Goodfellow's position,[5] he holds that there is no market economy in East African societies. To Dalton a market economy is a specific kind of economy which occurs only in industrialized nations, all other economies being different from it *in kind*. In these terms, Goodfellow is accused of applying market concepts to an area where they are not applicable because there is no money. Yet is it not possible that in East Africa we have something which, while not a market economy in this restricted sense of the term, does not differ from it in kind?

Turu livestock may be considered money because animals are standards of value, media of exchange and stores of value. Livestock are normally used for purchasing goods priced in terms of them, and they are the supreme stores of value, the end of all economic pursuits. Thus, however strange a form of money they may appear to be, they are functionally equivalent to money as defined by economists.

Here another question arises. We have seen that in the Turu system the exchange rate between livestock and grain is usually stable. Why, then, should we not also regard grain as a medium of exchange? It is true that in some instances Turu price commodities other than livestock in terms of the number of debes of grain they are worth. In some instances they may make payments in grain. Von Sick, in 1910, told of a Turu who bought a "cow trough" for the amount of grain it would hold. Yet, significantly enough, the price of the trough could be stated as one calf. Moreover, the deficiencies of grain as a medium of exchange are apparent. Grain, in any appreciable amount of value, has little portability. To carry an amount equivalent in value to a heifer, some twenty containers, would mean that a bridegroom going to claim his bride would in most cases be faced with the problem of transporting grain in the amount of one ton! Again, grain is highly perishable and must be carefully protected, whereas with luck a man can expect his livestock to exist for many years with a minimum of care. Third, livestock retain significantly high value no matter what the condition of an animal may be, short of severe sickness or death, whereas the value of grain fluctuates with the state of the crops in a given year so that at times there is no demand for it. Finally, livestock holdings increase by themselves through natural processes, whereas the amount of grain a man owns can be increased only through the expenditure of labor.

[4] Dalton, George, 1961, p. 10.
[5] Goodfellow, D. M., 1939.

The reason why goats and sheep have become standardized in relation to cattle is perhaps due to the fact that, except in unusual conditions, the ratio of small stock to cattle in a given area and to the human population seems to remain constant. What would kill cattle in exceptional numbers would also kill the small animals, notably severe drought. The tendency for bridewealth to remain relatively constant may also perhaps be explained this way. In 1910 Von Sick's census of the Turu showed about 102,000 human beings and about 173,000 head of cattle.[6] In 1958 there were about 150,000 human beings and slightly over 200,000 head of cattle. The bridewealth has also remained about the same.

The Turu must be thought of as possessing money and a market system which are not different in kind from those of Europe and America, even though limited in terms of the variety of goods exchanged. Differences must be sought in such things as their social orientation and cultural values, which lead to different emphases, and in the differing degrees of technological complexity their culture manifests.

4

When we examine the economic systems of other East African societies, we find that livestock tend to monopolize exchange at all levels above the value of a single goat, and are everywhere used as media of exchange, standards of value and stores of value. It may even be possible to construct a general economic model for these societies showing the interplay of such important variables as women, livestock, grain and land in the socio-cultural setting in which they occur. Such a model would enable us to predict, for example, that bridewealth rates rise with the increase of livestock proportionately with the population, and in relation to other variables, such as the value in terms of potential productivity held to be paid for by the bridewealth. It is not without significance that while no one has suggested a regular system of standards of value in East African economies, almost every observer has recorded some data indicating the existence of such a system. A partial survey of these data may be given, beginning with the Suk of Kenya, among whom I gathered the following information in 1951–1952. Among the *Suk*, bridewealth varies in proportion to the general wealth of the subarea from about one cow in the cattle-poor hills to more than 20 in the cattle-rich plains.[7] Other than this:

[6] Von Sick, E., 1916, p. 4.
[7] Schneider, Harold K., 1953, pp. 272ff.

```
10 goats=1 steer
40 goats=1 camel (hence four steers equal one camel)
 4 bags of grain (100–150 lb.)=1 load of meat (two legs and a few other
   parts)
 1 goat  =2 axes
 1 goat  =1 spear
 1 goat  =a small irrigated plot; 2 goats=a large plot
 1 goat  =1 pot of honey
 1 steer =about shs. 100 (in internal trade)
 1 goat  =about shs. 10 (hence shs. 100=10 goats=1 steer)
```

Grain is also exchanged for live cattle, but the equivalents could not be determined.

According to Wagner,[8] bridewealth in the *Vugusu* cattle-rich area in the region inhabited by the Bantu of North Kavirondo is six head and up, much less in the south. The exchange system is as follows:

```
4 or 5 goats      =1 steer
1 heifer          =25–30 bundles of eleusine grain
1 basket of grain=1 basket of meat
50 lb. of grain   =1 sword or 1 chicken
1 pot             —1 spear head
```

Wagner also refers to grain and hoes as the "currency" of the *Logoli*, the cattle-poor group south of the Vugusu. Otherwise cattle, goats and sheep are exchanged on "an economic basis" for grain, iron work, and other goods and services including payment with steers or heifers, depending on the service, for the work of diviners. Grain is loaned out before harvest at an interest rate of 25–30 per cent for a period of about two months and chickens are sold.

Kikuyu[9] commodity values were traditionally reckoned in goats since they far outnumber cattle, there being only a few of the latter. A rich man might possess only 10–12 head. Beads were once used as "currency" in the regular markets and there was trade with Masai from whom, for swords, tobacco, honey and ochre, they obtained livestock. In times of shortage livestock were exchanged between tribes for grain. Among the *Nandi*,[10] one axe equaled one full bag of honey in 1938 and one arrow head was equal to one gourd of honey. Steers are traded for various commodities; they are also used for bridewealth. There was trade with the Bantu of Kavirondo for grain, while pottery and iron goods were exchanged with the Dorobo for baskets of honey. Land with an unripe crop on it was sold.

[8] Wagner, Günter, 1956, pp. 102, 109, 161, 162, *et al.*
[9] Middleton, J.F.M., 1953, pp. 19, 20.
[10] Huntingford, G. W. B., 1950, pp. 40, 59, 68, 81, 82.

Iteso[11] bridewealth varies from 10–15 head, though after the rinder-pest epidemic of 1890, it fell to 1 cow and 30 goats. The government set the legal rate at five head, but this is systematically violated. Cattle have come to be sold in large numbers, to obtain cash for luxuries, at a legal price for a "cow" of shs. 100. In 1920, except for the final item in the following list, the system of values in exchange was recorded as follows:

      1 basket of millet=a pot, or "iron work," or a plaited door, or a basket, a
                        hoe handle, sandals, a chair, or a mortar
     25 baskets of unthreshed millet=1 heifer
     10 baskets of unthreshed millet=1 bull
    2–3 baskets of unthreshed millet=1 goat or sheep
      1 bull   =1 large drum
      "goats" =1 small drum
      2 goats =1 ostrich-feather headdress
      2 heifers and 1 bull=1 live ostrich
      1 "cow"=1 donkey
      2 hoes =1 heifer
      1 "cow"=shs. 600 (but regularly exchange for bicycles worth shs. 300)

Turkana[12] livestock are used for exchange, particularly with other tribes, but also in internal trading for grain and other goods. It is recorded by Huntingford[13] that the *Masai* trade with the Bantu for grain and other goods, using livestock as "media of exchange." Cattle are regularly sold on the livestock markets in large numbers. *Gusii*[14] bridewealth fluctuates, being equated by the people with change in prices in European market economics. Cattle and goats, equated in set ratio, are used to price other goods. Most valued, in order, are women, cattle, goats, grain.

Duruma[15] are said to "invest" their money in sheep and goats, which are then exchanged for cattle at the following rates:

    8 small animals=1 steer
    4 small animals and 1 steer (or 12 small animals)=1 cow

The main items of exchange are grain and cattle.

As concerns the *Sonjo*,[16] bridewealth varies between sixty and three hundred goats, with an average of 100. Goats are otherwise used as measures of value for honey, grain, beehives, pottery, iron goods and

[11] Lawrence, J. C. D., 1957, pp. 93, 143, 148, 202.
[12] Gulliver, P. H., 1951, p. 164.
[13] Huntingford, G. W. B., 1953, p. 109.
[14] Mayer, Philip, 1950, p. 38.
[15] Prins, A. H. J., 1952, p. 57.
[16] Gray, Robert F., 1960, pp. 37–38.

irrigation rights. Among the *Sukuma*,[17] bridewealth varies across the country from none in districts having no cattle to over 10 in richer areas. Few actual examples of the monetary structure are given, but it is apparent that one exists. Cattle were formerly rare all over the country but have been introduced in most places and now replace hoes, small stock and grain as symbols of wealth. Grain is used to purchase cloth, hoes and the like. Cattle are "capital"; they are seen as grain stored in another form. Land rights were sold in marshes where sorghum was grown, the price being "1 or 2 cattle," while slaughtered cows are used to pay those who work the fields. Grain is customarily exchanged for livestock in good times, the animals being reconverted to grain in bad times.

Data from people living south of central Tanganyika show the same pattern of economic organization that exists in the North. The *Tonga*[18] exchanged livestock for grain; Goodfellow, in discussing the economics of the Bantu of the South, states, "it is still evident that ... cattle are managed on precisely the same lines as grain."[19] The *Sotho* have always recognized the exchange value of one steer for 2 calves or 4 bags of grain. "The esteem in which the Basuto hold cattle is closely related to the superior facilities for storing and investing wealth that cattle provide in such an economy."[20] As concerns the *Tswana*, Schapera tells us that cattle and small animals were and still are the "standard medium of exchange."[21] Other instances could be cited, but these suffice to make the point.

In the facts recorded above we see examples of how values vary, though apparently in terms of similar economic models. There is a noticeable tendency to use grain to pay for small items but grain seems universally to be traded for livestock. It is noteworthy, in this context, that a number of investigators have seen the signs of a market economy, and have referred to cattle and goats as "capital," "investments" and "currency," terms also applied in some cases to hoes and grain. Finally, while valuation between livestock and other goods is usually given as though prices are stabilized, the information generally suggests that the prices fluctuate with market conditions.

With the gradual intrusion of the Euroamerican economy, a shift seems to be occurring all over East Africa to the use of cash as a medium of exchange. The use of cash, however, does not displace cattle, since these continue to be depositories of value which earn superior interest by

[17] Malcolm, D. W., 1953, pp. 44, 50, 70, 81.
[18] Colson, E., 1951, p. 27.
[19] Goodfellow, D. M., 1939, p. 67.
[20] Sheddick, U. G. J., 1953, p. 21.
[21] Schapera, I., 1953, p. 23.

bearing calves and solidify capital. This is additive to the indigenous functions of cattle, making it impossible to dispense with cattle even if money is present. Cash pays taxes, and is convenient for purchasing trade goods; it is even useful within the indigenous systems for some exchanges. But this only masks the continued operation of indigenous economies. In Suk the process takes the form of selling cattle to Somali traders and using the money to buy grain; this renders unnecessary the older system of exchanging cattle for surplus grain directly with hill Suk. Probably a strong reason for the rise of cash dealings is the greater precision in pricing that is made possible, for though differences in the qualities of animals are recognized, it is not always possible to express this in fine terms with indigenous media of exchange.

The relative dependence on grain and livestock is a critical factor in determining the nature of the exchange economy in East Africa. The staple food is ordinarily grain, or milk, or both. Other foods, such as meat, blood and various vegetables, are important to varying degrees, but seldom compete with the two principal items. In general, it seems that all people depend on grain to some extent, the more the better, for milk does not by itself seem to satisfy and meat, though much is consumed, is in most places of limited importance because of prohibitions against slaughter; eating cows is the most inefficient way of economizing them. Turu, Sukuma, Logoli and probably most Bantu have grain as their staple, while milk and meat are of varying but lesser importance. Among the Turu milk is of little importance, but in some of the more arid regions of East Africa it is crucial for subsistence, at least during parts of the year when grain supplies are low. The Nilotics, who are most dependent on milk, seem to try to grow or buy grain to economize their livestock. Among the Nilotic Suk the greatest dependence on milk is during the period of a few months before the harvest, when the only available plant foods are wild, when the rains have freshened the grass and so brought the cattle to their best milk productivity. During this time, however, they also sell meat and livestock for grain and slaughter animals for food. For both groups, Bantu and Nilotics, except for the Turu, milk is therefore important at some time.

Despite the predominant value of grain and milk, one should not underestimate the importance of meat. All these peoples like meat; its nutritional values are everywhere recognized. Under economic acculturation, consumption grows as traders buy cattle to slaughter and sell back to the people, so that the situation arises whereby the Vugusu, because of the meat markets that have grown up in Kenya, may be consuming less meat than their cattle-poor cousins, the Logoli.[22] Con-

22 Wagner, Günter, 1956, p. 61.

trariwise, consumption of meat has fallen among the Turu, since mature steers and smaller animals are no longer so extensively slaughtered, but are sold to other groups.

Throughout East Africa one finds a norm relating to slaughter which may be summed up in the statement, "One should not kill an animal without a good reason." Understandably, this often is taken to mean that killing occurs only at funerals, ancestral sacrifices, and other ritual observances. This interpretation, however, places too much emphasis on ritual as a determinant of economic behavior. The meaning is rather that there is nothing wrong with slaughtering animals if this is the most economic thing to do. This interpretation is supported by the Turu attitude toward eating eggs, which is precisely the same as the reason given for not eating meat. Chickens are almost never used in rituals, but are a supplementary food; what is meant is that it is foolish to eat an egg when it can grow into a chicken.

Land is often a commodity, but as such has a particular character. The sale of rights in land, as among the Turu, Sukuma and Logoli, seems to depend on whether the land has intrinsic worth for production over a significant period of time; in areas where it has no worth beyond the work put into it each year, it has no value. But transfer of land is frequently hedged with restrictions which derive from the feeling that land is essential for the continuation of the social group. A common example is the right of a seller to redeem his land at will. The fact that Suk sell "freeholds" on irrigation plots seems to be a function of the lack of strong, permanently localized kin groups. In general, even when intrinsically valuable, land is too immobile to participate to an appreciable extent in market processes.

5

The relation between grain and livestock is, as we have seen, the central fact in most of the economies of Eastern Africa. There is a general tendency for emphasis to be laid on the production of grain but for this to decline as numbers of livestock rise. The Sukuma offer a test case. Malcolm reports that in South Sukuma there are thirty or forty men who have managed to acquire herds of one thousand head of cattle or more.[23] These men have entirely dispensed with agriculture, depending for subsistence on grain bought with their cattle. The reason for this does not seem to be lack of interest in agriculture but abandonment of one type of productivity for a superior one. Grain can always be purchased; if not, one can live off the cattle.

[23] Malcolm, D. W., 1953, p. 70.

Between north and south North Kavirondo, the amount of grain produced is in inverse ratio to wealth in livestock. This is also true in Suk where there are at least four stages, ranging from the extreme pastoralism of the far plains where no grain is produced, through a second stage of balance between the two forms, to the high hills where few animals are owned and grain is the most important form of wealth, and finally to the irrigated subdistrict of Wei Wei where there are no cattle whatever, and a good surplus of grain is grown.

It is easy to overlook a fact of fundamental importance, that the universal desirability of livestock in East Africa is such that they can be employed for trading both internally and externally. Thus to specialize in cattle it is not necessary for some part of each society to produce a surplus of grain. In general the Turkana produce little grain and internal trade seems weak, as is the case in other Nilotic groups, but they conduct external trade with people who have grain, in contrast to the Turu for whom both internal and external trade flourish. Where in normal times in a Bantu society like the Turu the market consists most importantly of internal redistribution of grain between variably producing units, in times of drought the same process occurs between tribes variously affected by the drought. Indeed, in pre-contact days the surrounding tribes seem to have looked on Turu district as a "bread basket."

It is possible that some misunderstanding about the role of cattle in these economies might derive from the idea that individual freedom in the market is greatly limited. It is true that the systems of reciprocity and joint rights that operate to one degree or another in all areas are factors that must be considered to understand market processes. Among the Turu a younger son's freedom to dispose of his animals is to some degree limited by his subordination to his eldest brother. But despite this, someone always has sufficient rights in livestock to be able to dispose of them if market conditions make this reasonable. If there is one thing East Africanists seem to agree on it is that livestock are individually owned. By the same token, men are everywhere much more interested in livestock than are the women, because only men are allowed to buy and sell them.

This leads us to the factor of profit orientation, a subject on which there is by no means agreement. Gray argues that the Sonjo have no profit orientation at all, which is why he speaks of bridewealth as being so important in stimulating their economy.[24] But his notion of profit orientation, the attempt to buy cheap and sell dear in a dramatic fashion, would seem to be too narrow. The slow, unromantic accumulation of grain and its conversion to livestock when possible is as much profit

[24] Gray, Robert F., 1960, p. 46.

seeking as is long term investment in pecuniary economies. It may be assumed that Wagner's assertion that the Kavirondo Bantu only exceptionally used cattle in economic exchange in precontact days also implies a lack of profit orientation.[25] Huntingford strongly infers a non-profit orientation when he says that Nandi in the past did not engage in trade.[26]

As long as livestock are not perceived as a form of money, the functioning of the profit motive is beclouded. This becomes clear if the thesis of this paper, that everywhere people tend to try to amass livestock in as great an amount as possible, because livestock are money, is kept in mind. We have seen the profit motive at work in Turu. Everywhere manipulations designed to increase livestock are most apparent, including the widespread method of robbing one's neighbors. Except for Audrey Butt in her description of the Nuer,[27] no one has asserted that in East Africa all members of a given society are equally rich or poor. Our information is rather that wealth varies, and that maximization of herds is a central aim.

East Africans seem normally to be oriented toward making profit. In Suk some men express it in a new way by going to a part of the district where goats and sheep are cheap, buying them in large quantities, and taking them to parts of the district where they are scarce to sell them dear for a cash profit.

It is not just in terms of livestock, however, that the profit motive operates. We have seen that the Logoli charge what would elsewhere be considered exorbitant rates of interest for the loan of grain. The fundamental reason for polygyny, besides the desire to perpetuate the family, seems usually to be the desire to increase the surplus production of grain. In short, the assumption of an intimate association of money and profit orientation is, if anything, strengthened in these societies. This does not mean that methods of making a profit do not vary. The custom of selling dear is represented in some places, as among the Suk, in haggling over everything, including bridewealth, while among the Turu prices are simply stated and either accepted or rejected without further discussion.

The prestige that derives from the ownership of cattle is everywhere based on the feeling that a man who has many animals is to be admired for his superior control of resources. While it is not possible to say that the prestige inherent in the possession of cattle is nothing but pecuniary, it does not seem possible any longer to entertain the notion that it is

[25] Wagner, Günter, 1956, p. 104.
[26] Huntingford, G. W. B., 1950, p. 81.
[27] Butt, Audrey, 1952, p. 41.

purely non-economic. And though in accord with Herskovits' discussion of prestige economies,[28] we find that there are various techniques for impressive display of their wealth, the mere marshalling of numbers of cattle is not one of these. The total number of animals a man owns is everywhere concealed, this in the main being based on a desire to avoid the envy of others.

Conspicuous display is, however, not absent. It is seen in the slaughter of numerous head of livestock at the funerals of chiefs and important men, so that we may say that funerals tend to be the occasion for reasserting the status of the family of the deceased. In Turu, normally, two or three cows are slaughtered by the family of a man who has died, while additional animals are killed by his sons-in-law to show their respect. Since status is intimately connected with control of resources, when is the need greater to display wealth and thus assert status than when the head of the house dies?

One of the most impressive kinds of conspicuous display in East Africa, and one of the most misleading, is the singling out of an ox for special attention by each man who can afford it, thereby impressing others while deriving emotional satisfaction himself. This custom seems to have led to the belief that such affectionate attention extends to all livestock; but nothing could be farther from the truth. Even in the case of such prize oxen, we should remember that frequently a most impressive act of conspicuous consumption is to kill one for a feast for members of the community. Among the Turu, the significance of the adulation of the ox is to be seen in a new light; to a great extent, such animals are sold on the induced livestock market to buy the new symbols of status—clothing, bicycles, radios and the like. However, it should be noted that the man working within the strict confines of the indigenous system considers such things useless.

The sacrificial role of cattle varies greatly. In many places men tend to identify cattle with themselves, and show this in sacrifices where the animals act as surrogates for men, as among the Nuer. But the logic behind this for the Nuer is explained in a passage that has an ambiguous meaning, one ritual and the other "economic": "In the time of the ancestor of his clan the 'cow' gave her life for his salvation, and so it is with his descendants today and so it will be with their descendants to-morrow. Whence springs the identification of man with ox, of lineage with herd, and of men with cattle."[29]

It is not necessary to take an exclusive position in the matter of whether cattle are economically valued or ritually valued. They are

[28] Herskovits, M. J., 1952a, p. 461ff.
[29] Evans-Pritchard, E. E., 1953, p. 197.

both. They can be used to gain pecuniary ends while still being "gods with wet noses," as Schapera puts it.[30] The only thing to be insisted on is that for the most part the one objective is integral to the other, ritual status being intimately tied in with economic value, just as pecuniary use is integral with subsistence use.

6

We are thus led to the final segment of this comparative survey. Lest it be thought that in this paper market economics is emphasized at the expense of all else, we may recall the fundamental principle that the working out of any element in a given culture, including the economy, will depend upon the total setting of which it is a part. For example, the degree of individualism permitted is to be associated with the type of society. Among the Turu localized lineages act as corporations, in which oint ownership of livestock and other goods is recognized. Within the corporation, exchange of goods and services is in some respects achieved by reciprocity rather than open trade. Contrariwise, in Suk, the obligations of kin toward each other are greatly lessened and hardly extend outside the group of full brothers. It is possible that in the Kavirondo area the greater part of exchange is also achieved in the localized lineages through the means of mutual obligations and to a much greater degree than among Turu.

It has already been noted that bridewealth seems to be affected by ideas concerning what is being contracted for; it should further be noted that though no mention has been made in this paper of the non-economic aspects of marriage, such as assuaging of the feelings of a mother-in-law for the loss of her daughter or the love that the bride and groom often feel for each other, they nonetheless enter. Furthermore, the values of a people may intrude on the processes of exchange, so that, for example, among the Suk a person who grossly deceives another in a transaction can be made to rectify the wrong. Everywhere a significant number of animals is constantly being drawn off for rituals, gifts, and fines for ritual offenses which are necessary to the mental well-being of the people.

But despite these things, which are normally sufficiently emphasized, the very fact of variations in wealth and the existence of systems of valuation and exchange among people in these different societies proves that nowhere are cultural and social factors so overwhelming as to eliminate market behavior or make impossible economic analysis without taking them fully into account. Herskovits notes,

[30] Schapera, I., 1937, p. 138.

"... it must ... be understood that economic problems may be studied without the need to give a complete account of all the interrelations between an economic system and other aspects of social life, or the need to consider all the sanctions on which a given body of economic custom rests."[31]

With this statement, as a methodological principle, we must agree; this survey suggests that a general theory of economics in East African societies is possible on this basis.

If Gray is right when he comments that anthropologists have over-played their hand with regard to bridewealth by insisting that it is not an economic transaction, presumably because if it were it would be offensive,[32] I suggest further that it is an error to think that social mechanisms must take precedence over or completely negate individual marketing behavior. Too often students have been content with mere assertion as to the economic component in marriage, ritual, exchange, and the like. Yet this is not a matter for assertion but investigation and, in particular, for the collection of statistical, quantitative data. If reciprocity and other comparable methods of exchange are important, it must be shown in what respect, and to what degree. Among the Turu mutual obligations are seldom so diffuse as to be undefinable or make other kinds of exchange unimportant. When a Turu gives his brother a cow for his marriage, this is an obligation so well understood that he can verbalize it and document his statement. And if his brother comes to him for another cow for another marriage, it is as well understood that he has no moral right to the animal and will not get it unless he contracts to pay it back. In fact it may be argued that, as in all human societies, throughout East Africa the social obligations imposed on people are constantly at war with their individual desires.

We have argued that among the cattle-keeping people of East Africa we find market economies in which the main elements of trade are women, grain, land and livestock, the exchange of which is achieved by the use of livestock as money. Livestock are to be thought of as the functional equivalents of money because they have the properties of a standard of value, constitute a medium of exchange and are a store of value. Thus, with some variations, the fundamental orientation of the economic systems is toward maximization of livestock, usually through the conversion of surplus grain to livestock and subsequent promotion of natural increase, with further investment in women and land to increase grain supplies and thus increase wealth in livestock. It was pointed out in the opening paragraphs of this essay that the great value assigned to cattle has been widely interpreted as being a function of their ritual

[31] Herskovits, M. J., 1952a, p. 502.
[32] Gray, Robert, F., 1960, p. 34.

worth, deriving from their role as symbols of status. A more adequate interpretation would seem to be that the prestige of livestock wealth is of the same order as the prestige gained through the control of resources in any market economy.

The recognition of the existence of indigenous market systems gives promise of working out development in the future because we are dealing with peoples who are not unfamiliar with the kind of economic thinking and processes which will be essential to national development. They should be sympathetically consulted when changes are proposed. When destocking was imposed on the Turu, they complained that its effect would simply be to make the rich richer and the poor poorer. While this sounded like merely an emotional reaction, it was in fact a reasonable prediction. By arbitrarily reducing the number of livestock across the board, the currency was in effect inflated in value while the price of grain accordingly fell. The chance for the "poor" to convert their holdings of grain into livestock was thus reduced and market viability reduced as if, in our economy, Federal Reserve interest rates were increased. But the future is not all promising. It will not be easy to find a new focus of economic life which will provide as much productivity and security as livestock. The resistence of many herding peoples to change is based on reluctance to forsake a proven system for others which are less certain.

4

West African Economic Systems

by Elliott P. Skinner
New York University

West Africa was by far the region of greatest indigenous economic development in Subsaharan Africa. In contrast to most parts of central, eastern and southern Africa, the peoples of this part of the continent had economies which made agricultural produce available in amounts large enough to be sold in rural and urban markets; craft specialization often organized along the line of craft guilds, whose members manufactured goods to be sold in these markets; different kinds of currencies which were nearly always convertible one to another and, later, to European denominations of values; and elaborate trading systems, external as well as internal. Goods produced in even the smallest West African societies were circulated in local markets, and from there were funnelled to urban market centers, and ultimately by porters, caravans, and boats, to the large Sudanese emporiums from which they could be shipped to Mediterranean areas in exchange for foreign products.

The economic unity of West Africa has not received the recognition it merits. Scholars have known that such towns as Kano, Timbuktu and others had large markets, but they have too often considered the other areas of West Africa as an economic wasteland. What they have not realized is that the markets of the larger societies could not exist without those of the smaller ones. The economic systems of pre-colonial West Africa must therefore be seen within the context of a West African economic unit, in which the more highly developed economies were intimately tied to the less developed ones.

According to Bovill and Cornevin, the Carthaginians and the Romans had important commercial relations with northern Africa, and knew something about the economic resources of those lands south of the Sahara.[1] Subsaharan produce such as Moroccan leather and Sudanese gold continued to filter into north Africa during the early years of the

[1] Bovill, E. W., 1958, pp. 17ff, 31ff; Cornevin, R., 1956, pp. 64ff.

77

Christian epoch. But it was only with the coming of the Arabs to West Africa in the eighth century that many Mediterranean peoples learned about such cities as Kombi, Mali, Djenne, Timbuktu, Gao, and Kano, the sources of much of their gold, ivory, skins, kola nuts, and slaves. Even then, the Arab merchants who participated in and often controlled this trade zealously barred others from taking part in it. "Consequently, Europe remained in almost complete ignorance of what lay beyond the coastal belt of North Africa. . . . All that Europe knew of the interior of Africa was that it concealed countries of immense wealth."[2] The nature of the wealth of the Sudan at this time can be judged from the story that in the fourteenth century Mansa Musa took thousands of pounds of gold dust with him to Cairo and Mecca, and that in early sixteenth-century Timbuktu "divers manuscripts or written books out of Barbary . . . are sold for more money than other merchandise."[3] With time, many of the trading cities lost a great deal of their influence, and many of the old caravan routes became unknown. Nevertheless, extant sources, used in conjunction with data from the still existing West African traditional economies, provide a good idea of the economic systems of this area just prior to European conquest.

The physical environment of West Africa provided some of the major pre-conditions for the development of a complex of economic systems. West Africa is a well-defined region. The two million or more square miles which make it up are drained by the internal systems of Lake Chad and by the tributaries of such rivers as the Senegal, the Voltas and the Niger, all of which flow into the Atlantic. Because of relatively heavy rainfall, its coastal plain is narrow, heavily forested and swampy. From this plain the land rises gently to a plateau, 500 to 1,000 feet high in places, and extending some 600 to 700 miles inland. Rainfall varies from 180 inches to fifteen and less as we move in a northerly direction. The vegetation reflects this pattern of rainfall, changing successively from evergreen to deciduous forests with grass to Sudanese-type savannas, and fading to scrubby desert.

The nature of the soil has always been influenced by this pattern of rainfall. Lateritic soils, characteristic of the coastal plains, were formed primarily by heavy precipitation and severe climate. The savanna red and red-brown soils are the commonest in West Africa. They are fairly fertile, but have lost most of their lime because of leaching in torrential rains. In the Sudan–Sahel region, soils range from dark brown in regions of heaviest precipitation, to a fairly fertile chestnut brown where it is drier. Mineral deposits are scattered throughout the entire area, and the

[2] Bovill, E. W., *op. cit.*, p. 12.
[3] *Ibid.*, p. 127.

Africans have long exploited deposits of iron, copper, tin, rock salt, saline earths and gold, in addition to panning the rivers for alluvial gold. It has been estimated that about one million square miles of this variegated environment which is West Africa was, and is still, capable of supporting human habitation, and providing the basic conditions for the elaboration of human societies with complex cultures.[4]

2

West African peoples were basically farmers. Agriculture, or more technically horticulture, is old in this area, and at least one scholar has suggested that West Africa was one of the world centers of plant domestication.[5] The shifting cultivators of the rain forest produced such staple root crops as yams, taro or cocoyams, various kinds of cultivated bananas, varieties of both wet rice and dry rice, and such vegetables as okra, peas, gourds, fluted pumpkins, and beans, among other things. In addition, they harvested the products of such cultivated or protected trees and bushes as the kola tree, okee, tamarind, pepper bushes, red sorrel, and oil and raffia palms. With the discovery of the New World, the West Africans in the forest region and, to some extent, those in the savanna region, adopted maize, manioc, peanuts, sweet potatoes, and many other crops.[6] The savanna peoples were also shifting cultivators, but they specialized in the production of cereals. These included varieties of pearl millet, sorghum, fonio, and both wet rice and dry rice. Maize was later introduced in some areas. The savanna peoples also cultivated many varieties of root crops, tubers, vines, gourds, legumes, and leaf and stalk vegetables. In addition, they cultivated cotton and indigo, two crops which played an important role in their specialized economies. They collected the produce of such cultivated and protected trees and bushes as the shea-butter, locust bean, and hemp-leaved hibiscus.[7]

Animal husbandry was very important in the northern parts of West Africa, but it also played a role in the economies of several cultures to the south. Cattle were particularly valued by the Fulani people for their milk and butter, and among the many non-Fulani populations, for their meat and skins. The tsetse fly prevented herding by the West Africans in the forest zones, permitting them to keep only a variety of immune dwarf cattle. Goats and sheep, being more immune to the tsetse, had a wider distribution in West Africa, and were valued by their meat and skins. Chickens, ducks, bees, and the half-wild guinea fowl were also

[4] Stamp, D. S., 1953, pp. 270–278.   [5] Murdock, G. P., 1959, p. 67.
[6] Jones, W. O., 1960.   [7] Johnston, B. F., 1958.

D

tended. Pigs had a limited distribution, and were not eaten in many areas, including those where Islam had not penetrated. Horses were limited to the northern part of the savanna region because of their high susceptibility to the tsetse fly. Here they were used as prestige animals, and in warfare. Donkeys had a wider distribution, not only because of a higher toleration for the trypanosomes, but also because of their utility as beasts of burden.

Hunting and fishing were part-time activities. Elephants provided the ivory so valued in some African societies and in the Mediterranean lands. The numerous other animals in this region were often hunted for their meat as well as for their skins. Specialization in fishing was limited to some riverine, coastal, and lacustrine populations, who traded dried and smoked fish into distant inland areas.

Agricultural production was basic to the development of the economies in West Africa, as it was for other areas. There were no cases of chronic land shortage. "Farm tenure" gave most persons the right to some land, and social pressures in many societies often dictated that they cultivate it. Every Dahomean was a farmer; no matter what his occupation, whether craftsman or not, he cultivated a plot of ground.[8] Symbolically, not even the Dahomean king himself was able to hold himself "exempt from the command to participate in the cooperative labor of farming."[9] Farming was said by all Tiv to be their "great work," and provided most of the imagery and metaphor of labor.[10] Even the trade-minded populations of Djenne, Bamako, and Sansanding believed that "working the soil is the only noble profession."[11] The Mossi of the Upper Volta declare, "The hoe is the work of mankind." Similar attitudes towards food production can be found reported in the monographs dealing with most of the populations of West Africa.

The basic unit of agricultural production was the extended family. True, in most societies individuals were allowed, even encouraged, to produce commodities for their own use, but usually only after they had fulfilled their obligations to their kinsmen.[12] Nevertheless it appeared to be true for the Nupe, among others, that the extended family afforded "the only means of cultivating a large variety of both useful and profitable crops."[13] The actual amount of food produced by these units differed from society to society, and often depended upon the crops grown and whether or not there was crop specialization. Regardless of

[8] Herskovits, M. J., 1938, Vol. I, p. 49.   [9] *Ibid.*, p. 30.
[10] Bohannan, L. and P., 1953, p. 51.   [11] Pacques, V., 1954, p. 63.
[12] Skinner, Elliott P., 1960, p. 383; cf. also Nadel, S. F., 1942, p. 241; Bradbury, R. E., 1957, p. 23.
[13] Nadel, S. F., 1942, p. 246; cf. Herskovits, M. J., 1938, I, p. 31; Bohannan, L. and P., 1953, p. 51.

the society, however, the extended family apparently produced enough food to allow some of it to be disposed of in the market place.

The extended family which found that it could not produce enough foodstuff for itself or for sale often made use of larger cooperative units. A Dahomean had recourse to a cooperative working group known as the *dopkwe* when his fields were "too extensive to permit them to be hoed by his own labor and the labor of those whose services he has at his disposal."[14] The Nupe used a larger cooperative unit called the *egbe* for agricultural production when, for various reasons, the extended family was insufficient, or "simply because its ambitious program demands larger cooperation than is at its disposal."[15] The Jukun employed a cooperative unit similar to the *egbe* for the production of surplus food, part of which they sold "in exchange for clothes."[16] The informal cooperative work group among the Mossi, the *sosose*, also served the same function, that is, the production of agricultural commodities, some of which were often sold in the markets.

3

In many of the more highly developed societies, surplus agricultural products were produced by serfs and slaves. Much of what was grown by them was used to feed the personnel of royal or nobles' houses, and to entertain guests, but a large portion was sold locally or traded to passing merchants or caravans. In Dahomey, there was a class of men known as the *gletanu* (great cultivators) who even produced crops especially for sale to middlewomen. The farms of these men, cultivated by their relatives and slaves, comprised areas of from 15 to 25 kilometers in length and several kilometers in breadth, and specialized in the raising of some single food staple such as millet, maize, or yams. In some exceptional cases, all three crops were grown by the same planter.[17] The Yoruba also used slaves for the specialized production of foodstuffs for resale in the markets. Talbot reports that a large number of Yoruba slaves "remained out in the suburbs, where they farmed huge plantations, in consequence of which food supplies were remarkably cheap and plentiful."[18]

Whether or not this economic specialization among the Yoruba and the Dahomeans was a response to European contact on the coast is unknown, but the fact that it also developed indigenously is seen by its appearance in Djenne, in the Sudan. Here the large merchants kept

[14] Herskovits, M. J., 1938, I, p. 72. [15] Nadel, S. F., 1942, p. 248.
[16] Meek, C. K., 1931, pp. 409–410. [17] Herskovits, M. J., 1938, I, p. 55.
[18] Talbot, P. A., 1926, III, p. 699.

slaves in the rural districts to produce the foodstuffs so necessary for the survival of desert-surrounded Timbuktu. Thus we have in West Africa several levels of food production: subsistence crops, from which surplus food was taken to be sold in the markets; production for the nobility, some of which was also drawn off for sale: and specialized production for the markets.

Few West African societies were without craftsmen, who manufactured goods for local consumption and for external sale. Craftsmanship in the smaller groupings, such as the Ewe, Tiv, Katab, Lobi, Gurunsi, Birom, Ga and Tallensi was ancillary to farming and, except for the fact that craftsmen often belonged to the same lineage, was unorganized. For example, Manoukian tells us that

> The main handicrafts practiced by the Ewe are spinning, weaving, pottery-making, and black-smithing. With very few exceptions these are all part-time occupations, being combined with farming or trading. There does not seem to have been at any time any considerable development of economic specialization, comparable with that which obtained in Ashanti and Dahomey.[19]

Nevertheless, it was as true for the Ewe as for the other societies that part of the manufactured goods of even these smaller societies was eventually diffused into the larger market centers.[20]

Specialized production of manufactured goods for sale was more characteristic of the large state societies of the Guinea Coast and of the Sudan. The craftsmen and artisans here produced all manner of goods, and had highly developed social and economic organizations which facilitated production and dissemination. The Ashanti wove cotton cloth and dyed it; they also made barkcloth, pottery, numerous types of carved wooden objects and utensils, and produced many metal objects and articles, some of them by the cire-perdue process. Significantly, the *adwumfo*, or goldsmiths who played an important role in the economy of Ashanti, "were in the olden days an honoured class; they formed a sort of brotherhood and were privileged to wear gold ornaments, otherwise restricted to kings and their wives, and greater chiefs." The art was retained in certain families.[21]

The craftsmen and artisans of Dahomey and Benin produced a greater variety of manufactured goods, and were more highly organized, than in Ashanti. This fits in with other evidence that they were more highly developed than Ashanti as concerns trade and commerce. Most

[19] Manoukian, M., 1952, p. 17.   [20] *Ibid.*, p. 19.
[21] Manoukian, M., 1950, pp. 20–21.

of the more important craft groups in Dahomey lived in special quarters. The jewellers had their own quarters; the ironworkers who made agricultural implements and weapons were organized into "forges," each of which had its houses and workshops in a separate part of a town, or in a separate village. The weavers had special quarters where their looms were located; and the potters had their centers in those areas where the best clay were found.[22] Similarly, most of the "important crafts of the Benin kingdom were in the hands of special ward-guilds in Benin City. There were guilds of blacksmiths and brass-smiths, wood and ivory carvers (one group), leather workers, weavers of special embroidered cloth, drum-makers, locksmiths, etc."[23] Both in Dahomey and Benin the craft guildsmen were also members of specific families. In contrast to the smaller societies, however, guild heads, and therefore family heads, were able to control the production of goods, fix prices and also punish guildsmen who violated guild rules. The Benin ruler went even further. He granted some of the guilds virtual monopolies over certain products, but retained the products of such guilds as the brass-smiths and ivory carvers for himself.[24]

Craft guild production and guild organization reached their greatest development among the Nupe of Central Nigeria, and possibly also among the Hausa. There were iron ore miners and blacksmiths, brass and silver smiths, glassmakers, weavers, potters, bead workers, masons, wood workers and carpenters.[25] In contrast to Dahomey and Benin, however, not all who produced certain craft goods were members of guilds or had to join them. The guilds themselves, like most African craft guilds, were composed of members of the same families, but they were open to anyone who formally applied for admission and went through an apprenticeship. Some of these guilds, like that of the blacksmith, were found all over Nupe, and were controlled by chiefs who were often agents of the ruler. On the local level, they were fairly autonomous, setting their own standards of production. The other types of guilds in Nupe appear to have functioned on a slightly different basis. For example, the head of the bead workers treated his guildsmen as though they were journeymen. He procured work for them, supervised their work, and paid them out of the money he received. Most of the guildsmen of Nupe, however, were bound to their guilds and were controlled by a leader who was often admitted to the King's council. Nadel felt that the craftsmen of Nupe were "the king's craftsmen" and

[22] Herskovits, M. J., 1938, I, pp. 44–50; II, p. 354.
[23] Bradbury, R. E., 1952, p. 26; cf. Talbot, *op. cit.*, II, p. 308.
[24] Bradbury, R. E., *ibid.*, pp. 26, 34–35.
[25] Nadel, S. F., 1942, p. 257.

that their organization presented a picture "closely resembling the organization of craft guilds of Imperial Rome and the Middle Ages."[26]

The Kano Chronicle suggests that in Hausa country there were guilds of blacksmiths, brewers, miners, salt workers, and even medicine makers, archers, minstrels and dancers, long before the arrival of the Hausa invaders.[27] By the time Clapperton and Barth arrived in Kano several centuries later, there were crafts and more guilds in existence. It appears that these, like those in Nupe, Benin and Dahomey, also occupied separate sections of the city.[28] Kano was especially well-known for its leather work and cloth production; in addition, the people of this important trading center also worked iron, silver and brass, and there were potters, glass workers, bead makers and wood carvers.[29] But the industry that impressed Barth most of all was the production of cotton cloth. He enumerated and described about twenty different types of cloth made in Kano and other towns. In terms of the amount of cloth produced Barth had this to say:

> In taking a general view of the subject, I think myself justified in estimating the whole produce of this manufacture, as far as it is sold abroad, at the very least at about 3,000,000,000 [cowries]; and how great this national wealth is will be understood by my readers when they know that, with from fifty to sixty thousand kurdi,[30] or from four to five pounds sterling a year, a whole family may live in that country with ease . . . [moreover] this industry is not carried on here, as in Europe, in immense establishments, degrading man to the meanest condition of life, but . . . it gives employment and support to families without compelling them to sacrifice their domestic habits.[31]

The societies north and west of Hausa did not produce as much manufactured goods as those in Nigeria; nor were their craft guilds as complex. An interesting aspect of most of these craft guilds was that their members were often not respected, and occupied subordinate social positions. Rouch called Songhoi specialists in iron working, carpentering and canoe building, in weaving, leather working and pottery making "artisan castes."[32] The slipper makers, smiths, masons, tailors, and leather workers of nearby Timbuktu were said to have

[26] *Ibid.*, pp. 257–294, *passim.*
[27] Palmer, H. R., 1908, pp. 62–65.
[28] Denham, D. and Clapperton, H., 1826, Section II, p. 53.
[29] *Ibid.*, pp. 54–56; Barth, H., 1859, I, p. 512.
[30] Barth used the term kurdi for cowries. The exchange value of this currency was 2,500 cowries for one Spanish or Austrian dollar.
[31] Barth, H., 1839, I, pp. 511–512.
[32] Rouch, J., 1954, pp. 23–25.

belonged to a "sort of guild system of hereditary crafts." Nevertheless, this guild system did not prevent the elaboration of the crafts, since some guildsmen employed slaves and serfs to work for them. Some of the smiths here even specialized in working only one metal, such as silver or gold; other smiths worked all types of metals.[33]

The people of Djenne showed "vestiges of a division into corporations" when visited by Dubois in the 1890s. The crafts found here were not too different from those in the other areas of the Sudan. These were also honored professions, however, and the craft guild leaders were "among those personages of the town who deliberate and control public affairs."[34] In contrast, similar craftsmen along the river Niger at Bougouni and Bamako were held in low esteem and known by an "injurious sobriquet, Nyamamkala."[35] The nearby Senufo of the Ivory Coast apparently came from the Niger area, bringing with them similar notions about the inferior social position of craftsmen. Their most important crafts were carpentry, weaving, smithing, and jewel making. The production of all of these "caste guilds" was controlled by the elder of each family involved.[36] In Senegal, craft guilds whose members were considered as belonging to a low social stratum were well organized. Their work was supervised by their leading men, "with whom the bur [king] dealt when he had any matter concerning their groups."[37] Similar guilds were found in neighbouring Sierra Leone, Guinea, and Liberia. Among some of the groups in Liberia, however, the guilds extended far beyond the local communities, including "those practicing the same handicraft, regardless of clan or tribal affiliations."[38]

4

Markets were ubiquitous in West Africa. There were a few regions where aboriginal markets were absent—in parts of Liberia, southwestern Ivory Coast, and in certain portions of the plateau regions of Nigeria. Nevertheless, even here people engaged in trade, and benefited from the markets of contiguous areas. The markets served as local exchange points or nodes, and trade was the vascular system unifying all of West Africa, moving products to and from local markets, larger market centers, and still larger centers.

Important features of all the markets in the smaller West African societies and in the rural areas of the larger entities were their cyclical periodicities. These markets were held every three, four, five, eight, or

[33] Miner, H., 1953, pp. 52–54.   [34] Dubois, F., 1897, p. 196.
[35] Pacques, V., 1954, p. 63.   [36] Holas, B., 1957, p. 70.
[37] Gamble, D. P., 1957, pp. 57ff.   [38] Schwab, G., 1947, p. 121.

even sixteen days. Within a circumscribed area covered by a cycle, not more than one market was held on any one day, so that the people within the area had the opportunity to visit every market in turn. Small local markets, held daily, made it possible to buy food and other staples in small amounts on the days when the larger ones were "closed." Another feature of markets was the segregation of vendors or merchants according to the product sold.

The first Europeans to arrive at the lower Niger River in the eastern coast of West Africa reported that they saw Ibo traders from inland bringing yams, cows, goats and sheep for trading with such coastal peoples as the Ijaw in exchange for salt.[39] Nothing much is known, however, about the early markets in this region until they appeared full-blown with the manilla currencies during the height of the slave trade.[40] We know, however, that the Nupe traders brought goods from Kano and points north to Onitsha in exchange for such forest products as palm oil.[41] Yoruba markets had periodicities of four, eight, and even sixteen days. Those in the larger urban areas were held every day and even during the evening. Large numbers of women traders sold specific types of goods, leaving other types for sale by men. There was barter in these markets, but cowries, manillas, and iron bars were also used as currencies to buy such goods as live animals, cooked foods, cereals, salt, fish, palm oil and palm wine, cotton cloth clothes, pottery, soap, slaves, jewelry made of iron, brass and copper, weapons and implements made of iron.[42]

The rural trading centers of the neighboring Edo had a periodicity of four days, and formed a cycle of feeder markets which supplied the capital, Benin, and large towns outside the kingdom. There were two large markets at Benin, alternating daily. The types of goods sold here were probably no different from those among the Yoruba. A visitor to the Benin market in 1589 reported,

Pepper and elephant teeth, oyle of palme, cloth made of cotton woll very curiously woven, and cloth made of the barke of palme trees were procured in exchange for cloth both linen and wollen, iron works of sundry sorts, Manillos or bracelets of copper, glass beades and Corrall. . . . They have good store of soap and it smelleth like beaten vilets—Also many pretie fine mats and baskets that they make, and spoones of elephants' teeth very curiously wrought with divers proportions of foules and beasts made upon them.[43]

[39] Talbot, P. A. 1926, I, p. 184.   [40] Diké, K. O., 1956, pp. 42–43.
[41] Nadel, S. F., 1942, p. 319.
[42] Talbot, P. A., *op. cit.*, III, pp. 920–946.
[43] Quoted in Talbot, P. A., 1926, III, pp. 159–160.

These Edo people traded goods with Ibo and the Yoruba, and also with some unidentified "Dry Land" peoples from the hills behind Addamugu or Abela who "brought horses to them."[44] Yoruba trade to Nupe, Hausa and Dahomey was highly organized by "trade chiefs" who "furthered the commercial interests of their towns, settled disputes at the markets and made rules and regulations to ensure just prices and safeguard the standards of workmanship in crafts."[45]

The markets of Dahomey reached their height during the period of the slave trade, but like the markets of neighboring countries they maintained their African characteristics despite European influences. Herskovits reported three types in this country—small roadside stands which opened daily, large wholesale markets for the sale of agricultural products, and retail markets which served as the major instruments for the circulation of all types of goods. The larger markets met every four days, and constituted market cycles. The wholesale markets were run by the *gletanu*, the specialized farmers, who might send agents to neighboring retail markets to determine the resale price of their products before setting the proper discount for the middlewomen who brought their goods. There was little barter in Dahomean markets; the people here used cowry shells as currency. In some markets, prices were set by the first arrivals, and as the late comers followed suit there was no haggling. Some of the associations of market women established prices for the products they sold, and punished vendors who violated the set price. Many of the craft guilds, such as the iron workers, wood carvers and jewellers, permitted their members to haggle over the prices of their products.[46] Dahomey traded a great deal with the early Europeans; it also had fairly extensive indigenous foreign trade. Herskovits reports that Dahomeans traded agricultural products and salt both east and west. Some of their goods did go north to Kumasi, Sansanne Mango and Kandi, important caravan terminals for both Timbuktu and Kano. They imported large quantities of leather products from Kano along the same route.[47]

The Ewe people of what is now Ghana and Togo had small daily markets. These were held in most villages, whose women and children exchanged or bought foodstuffs and such products as soap, pottery, yarn and firewood for domestic use. Large markets were held every four days in the larger towns, which formed part of a market cycle. Such larger markets were patronized by Ewe from neighboring towns and villages, and by professional traders from Dahomey and Hausa country.

[44] *Ibid.*, p. 172.   [45] Biobaku, S. B., 1952, p. 38.
[46] Herskovits, M. J., 1938, I, pp. 51–62, *passim*; cf. *ibid.*, 1952a, pp. 217–220, 347.
[47] Herskovits, M. J., 1938, I, p. 108; *ibid.*, 1936, pp. 16–22.

The Ewe used both barter and cowrie shell currency in their small and larger markets. Foodstuffs were sold at fixed prices; in contrast, buyers and sellers of livestock and articles of craftmanship, such as pottery, mats, and cloth always haggled, especially foreign traders.[48]

The markets of the societies in the middle zone between the eastern coast of West Africa and the Hausa states in the north were important centers of exchange and trade in the period prior to European incursion. The Tiv of central Nigeria had "five-day" cycle markets. The smaller units in the cycle dealt mainly in local produce, but there was always one large one which served as a hub. Tiv conducted most of their small-scale commercial transactions by means of barter, occasionally using both rods and *tugudu* cloth as currency and as a standard for value. Their producers and middlemen brought their goods to the larger hub markets for resale to other Tiv, Hausa, Ibo, Jukun and Nupe merchants.[49]

Nupe country, which lay northeast of Tiv, was likened to "one big market." Nadel tells us that "the complexity of Nupe economics and . . . the far-reaching specialization of Nupe production . . . expresses itself most forcibly in the wide scope of trade and marketing."[50] The smaller markets were held every five days and also formed cycles. In the very small villages, markets were deserted on off days, but in the larger villages restricted trade in foodstuffs was carried on. Bida, the market center of Nupe, had six centers, three main day markets close to the three royal houses, two small day markets (one near the west gate of the town, and one in the "stranger's quarters"), and one night market which, according to Nadel, usually had ten times the attendance of even the largest of the village markets, and possessed all manner of goods. There were also many small shops throughout the town.

Nupe men and women traders usually sold different types of goods. Some vendors specialized in one product, or in several products which were usually sold together; others sold a little of all types of goods. Cowries were a universal currency, and little or no barter took place. Fixed prices were charged for most merchandise. Nevertheless, the Nupe saw to it that the prices of goods corresponded "closely to variations in supply and demand, above all, to seasonal fluctuations." They also made sure "that distance between area of production and market, and the additional labour and loss of time involved in transport, enter into the calculation of price and profit."[51] Many of the Nupe merchants were members of market guilds. Market guildsmen had booths where

[48] Manoukian, M., 1952, pp. 19–20.
[49] Bohannan, L. and P., 1953, p. 53; Bohannan, P. J., 1959, pp. 491ff.
[50] Nadel, S. F., 1942, p. 319.
[51] *Ibid., loc. cit.*

they acted as brokers, selling goods for client-traders on a commission basis. Their elected headman, who was confirmed by the king, was paid a fee. He inspected the goods in the caravans when they arrived at the market. He reported to the ruler in order to ascertain his wishes before placing the goods on sale in the market place. Once the guild-master received this permission, he then guaranteed to all guild members equal access to the goods, and sought to avoid unsound competition among them. He also tried to insure business integrity on the part of trader and broker alike.[52]

5

The list of the traditional trade routes which passed through Nupe country, and moved in all directions, reveals the complexity of the trade of these people. Nupe traders, travelling along these routes, tapped the "small circle of inter-village exchange which form no less part of the comprehensive marketing scheme of the country" than did the larger markets. They also visited the "relay stations" where, according to Nadel, people brought specific types of goods for trade. The palm oil, kola nuts, other forest products and goods they collected from Nupe were taken to Hausa country to be exchanged for trans-Saharan products, cloth from Kano, and potash from Bornu. These they brought back south, sending them to the Yoruba, Ibo and Tiv. Such traders, unlike craftsmen and market brokers, belonged to the larger fraternity of Nupe traders who formed colonies, especially in the larger towns in northern Nigeria and surrounding regions.[53]

Hausa markets were the most important in all of the eastern edge of the western Sudan. In the rural communities they were held in accordance with cycles of four days.[54] Clapperton found them filled with beef, mutton, fowls, gussub, beans, Indian corn and other products.[55] Markets in the larger towns met every day. Each was divided into sections where goods of various sorts, and occasionally slaves, were sold. Clapperton tells us that merchants came to these markets from "all parts of Africa, from the Mediterranean and the Mountains of the Moon, and from Sennar and Ashanti."[56] These merchants were reportedly quite fair in their dealings. If a purchase was later found to be defective, the broker or the seller was obliged by the laws of the market to refund the price paid for it. On the other hand, the merchants were very aware

[52] Nadel, S. F., 1942, p. 330.
[53] *Ibid.*, p. 320.
[54] Smith, M. F., 1959, p. 20.
[55] Denham, D. and Clapperton, H., 1826, Section II, p. 18.
[56] *Ibid.*, p. 50.

TABLE 4.1. *Volume, Value, Type, Source and Destination of Goods in Kano Market, 1851*

Product	Volume	Value	Source and Destination
Cloth	300 camel-loads per year	60 million cowries	Kano area to Timbuktu. *Comment:* According to Barth, this cloth was shipped as far North as Myrzuk, Ghat, and Tripoli; to the East as far as Bornu; and to the South and South-east to the Igbara, Igbo and Adamawa.
Nuts, Kola	500 ass-loads per year	200,000 cowries per ass-load; total: 80–100 million cowries	From Forest zone for shipment North to Sudan Zone. *Comment:* One-half value was profit.
Natron	20,000 loads per year	(?)	From Bornu to Nupe and Nyffi. *Comment:* Transit tax of 500 cowries per load, giving 10 million cowries carried by horses, asses and oxen.
Salt	1,000 camel-loads per year	50–80 million cowries	Salt merchants from Desert bought Kano merchandise with their money.
Ivory	100 "kantars" per year	75–100,000 cowries per kantar	Not an important trade item. *Comment:* Lowest price per kantar was "thirty dollars, or 75,000 cowries."
Silk, Coarse	3–400 camel-loads per year	200,000 cowries each, or 70 million cowries	From Tripoli by way of Ghadames.
Cloth, Woolen	(?)	15 million cowries	
Calicoes and Prints, Bleached and Unbleached (from Manchester)	(?)	Over 40 million cowries	Cloth comes through Ghadames, but some of it often dyed and re-imported.
Sugar	100 camel-loads per year	12 million cowries	

TABLE 4.1 (continued)

Product	Volume	Value	Source and Destination
Paper, Wrapping	(?)	5 million cowries	Probably from France, "Trés lune" trade-mark.
Needles and Looking Glasses	(?)	8 million cowries	Needles with emblem of a pig. Formerly came from Nuremberg, but lately from Leghorn. *Comment:* Needles sold for one cowrie each. Barth sold 1,000 for 600 cowries.
Blades, Sword	50,000 per year	50 million	Most blades sold out of the country to neighboring groups.
Silks, French (called "hattaya")	(?)	20 million cowries	Imported and re-imported to Yoruba country and Gonja.
Clothes, Arab	(?)	60 million cowries	From Tunis and Egypt, but some of it from Leghorn.
Beads	(?)	50 million cowries	
Frankincense, rose oil, spices, cloves	(?)	55 million cowries	Many of these luxury items for princes.
Copper and Zinc	70 loads per year	15–20 million cowries	From Tripoli and Darfur
Leather Products, such as sandals		15 million cowries	
Slaves	5,000 per year	150–200 million cowries	Sold mainly to American slave dealers. American produce found in Nupe markets.

of the principles of supply and demand, and held goods out of the market when prices fell, in order to obtain later higher prices. Currency in these markets was the *cowry*, but silver and other media were convertible.

An outstanding aspect of the Hausa country markets was the great volume of trade that passed through them. Barth described the Kano market in the following terms. "Here a caravan from Gonja arriving with the desired kolanut . . . or a caravan laden with natron, starting for Nupe, or a troop of Asbenawa going off with their salt for the neighboring towns, or some Arabs leading their camels, heavily laden with the luxuries of the North and East."[57] Due mainly to Barth's reportorial

[57] Barth, H., I, 1839, p. 498.

skill we have some data on the value, volume, type, source and destination of goods which passed through the Kano market in 1851.[58]

Barth estimated that over £80,000 worth of bulk merchandise passed through Kano market alone in any one year; and this without taking into account the petty trade.[59] Not all of this trade was in the hands of the Hausa, but so famous were Hausa traders in this part of West Africa that the name Hausa became synonymous with trader. Hausa traders visited Tiv, Nupe, Ibo, and probably Yoruba and Edo. In addition, they went to such Nigerian societies as the Katab, Jaba, Kagaro, Pyem, Jukun, the Kanuri, Bornu and even Bargirimi. They moved westward to Dendi in northern Dahomey; Tilho has given us a précis of their activities:

> The Dendi have a little of everything, the Zaberma [Songhoi] have only livestock and potash. The Bengou people have only salt, the inhabitants of Ilo foodstuffs which they produce, and the Hausa the cotton cloth which they weave. As it is, the Zaberma go to Bengou to sell their livestock in exchange for salt which they carry to Ilo. At Ilo they meet the Hausa who bring cotton cloth there to exchange and thereby procure merchandise, part of which they sell afterwards to the Dendi. Then the Zaberma and the Dendi go to Kani where they meet people from Togoland with whom they exchange their merchandise for kola nuts, which are then sent off to Sokoto.[60]

Hausa traders also went to Gao, Zinder and Dori in the country of the Songhoi, to Ouagadougou, Kaya and Tenkodogo in Mossi country, and to the markets of Salaga in the country which is now Ghana. Here they competed with traders who were involved in another trading complex—that between the western coastal and forest zones of West Africa, and the Sudanese emporiums along the Niger River to the north.

Few data exist about the traditional markets in the western coastal region, except those in the former Gold Coast. A report of 1602 tells us that in this area,

> Everie towne hath market daies specially appointed, upon the which you find more to bee bought than upon other daies, and everie towne hath his market upon such a day, as the others have it not, and so everie one differeth upon their daies, and when their market daies come, they have two daies market one after the other, wherein the principall boores or countrie people come from divers places to traffique with the ships. They have their Sunday also, but on that they doe nothing. The inhabitants of the seaside, come also to the market with their wares, which they buy of the Netherlands, as linen cloth, knives, ground corals, looking glasses, pinnes,

[58] *Ibid.*, pp. 507–525.   [59] Barth, H., 1859, vol. I, pp. 498–512.
[60] Noll, Ned, 1960, pp. 402–403.

arme rings, and fish, which their husbands have gotton in the sea, whereof the women buy much, and carrie them to other townes within the land, to get some profit by them, so that the fish which is taken in the sea, is carried at least an hundred or two miles up into the land.

The principal traders in these markets were women described as "very nimble about their businesse." Apparently linen cloth and gold were used as currency, since, according to most reports, the people in the coastal regions of the Gold Coast refused to accept or to use cowries.[61] Information on the markets in the forest zone of the western part of West Africa is very sparse. This area was famous for its trade, because it was a primary source of kola nuts. Binger, in 1892, stated that in parts of the Ivory Coast a secret society had control over the trade in this commodity, and tried to prevent the Dioula and other Sudanese merchants from gaining access to the areas of production.[62] However, when Ollone traveled in northern Liberia about two decades later, he found the trade well organized and, in meeting places near each village, he found "bales of kola nuts, well packed as though for a long journey, with marks painted on them, perhaps those of their owners or of the consignee."[63] Chevalier found in one Guerze village of the Ivory Coast a Monday market where, "1,500 buyers and sellers gathered . . . and about 100 charges of kolas and 20 charges of rubber were exchanged there for salt, cloth, iron, copper." At Nzo, two thousand individuals, men and women, came there each week from a radius of more than 70 kilometers to exchange about 100 charges of kolas.[64] Kola nuts and other forest products found their way to Niger river towns such as Bamako, Djenne, Timbuktu, and finally across the desert.[65] Goods which came to these markets in return were traded down to the coast and even in Liberia.[66] The Kwahu people of the forest region of eastern Akim, in what is now Ghana, took their kola nuts to Kumasi, Kintampo and especially to Salaga.[67]

Salaga had a unique role in the economic structure of West Africa. In contrast to Bida in Nupe, which acted as a staging center for goods going to Kano, and Djenne, which played a similar role for Timbuktu, Salaga traded with both areas. It was strictly a traders' town. Its life depended upon trade, and in contrast to Kumasi, cowries, gold and cloth were accepted here as currency, while those persons without currency could barter. It had a daily market where one encountered

[61] Marees, Pieter de [1602] from Wolfson, F., 1958, pp. 55–56.
[62] Binger, L. G., 1892, I, pp. 142–143.
[63] Ollone, L. G., 1901, p. 309.   [64] Chevalier, A., 1909, pp. 26–27.
[65] Bovill, E. W., 1958, pp. 240–241.   [66] Schwab, G., 1947, p. 121.
[67] Lonsdale, R. L. T. (1882), from Wolfson, F., 1958, p. 185.

the Mosi with his cattle, sheep and slaves . . . the natives of Dagomba, Sansanne Mango, and the many small countries on the interior with cattle, sheep, ivory, skins of wild animals, the various products of their countries, principally clothes, basketwork, mats, &c.; traders from Lagos with coast produce; the leather workers, basket and mat makers, saddle and pannier makers, water sellers, women selling various kinds of food; the whole presents a very animated though exceedingly hot scene.[68]

Salaga's real trade, however, was conducted outside of the market: "One may stroll for two hours in and out of the various streets before having seen the whole of the business which is carried on."[69] In its hey-day, 10,000 persons entered Salaga every day, and in season many caravans of from 200 to 500 and 600 persons arrived and left for such places as Sokoto, Kano, Sansanne Mango, Salfara, Hombori and Timbuktu. These caravans were themselves "moving markets, buying and selling everywhere along the road."[70]

The caravans which went north through Mossi country often traded in the rural markets, which had periodicities of three days and were members of market cycles. The caravaneers either bought or sold goods here for cowries, or bartered them against other products. The larger Mossi market centers were open every day and afforded the merchants a wider variety of goods, since they were the collecting points for products from many of the rural markets. From Mossi country, many of these caravans went northward to Dori, at whose markets they met Hausa caravans going north to Gao, then turning east to Timbuktu. Other caravans of Dioula came north from Kong and the kola markets, heading for the Niger river towns of Bamako, Segou, Djenne and Timbuktu.[71]

Djenne, the staging area for goods from the southern and western parts of West Africa to Timbuktu, was as much a trading center as it was a market. Dubois declared that,

Instead of confining her trade to the market-place, as in the case of other towns, Jenne cries "Commerce! Commerce!" at every step. . . . She sends her merchandise to the sea-coast; and when the first Europeans trading between Benin and Cape Palamas asked where the gold and produce offered for sale came from, the natives answered "from Jenne." Her name was thus given to the Gulf of Guinea, and indirectly, to an English coin, the guinea, so called because the first pieces were struck from gold coming from there.[72]

[68] *Ibid., loc. cit.*
[69] Gouldsbury, V. S., 1897, from Wolfson, F., 1958, p. 169.
[70] Lonsdale, R. L. T. (1882), from Wolfson, F., 1958, p. 184.
[71] Monteil, P. L., 1894, p. 91.   [72] Dubois, F., 1897, pp. 89, 182.

Whether Dubois is correct about the origin of the word Guinea or whether this is simply folk etymology, he did report that he saw virgin gold in the warehouses of Djenne as well as such exotic products as packets of ostrich feathers, civet musk, lead, marble, antimony. In addition, there were the local commodities, especially kola nuts and foodstuffs.

The merchants at Djenne appear to have organized their trade quite efficiently. Her inhabitants,

> organized "business firms" in the European sense of the word, which were provided with a routine and staff similar to our own. They established representatives in important centers and opened branches at Timbuktu. They sent out travelling agents who received percentages of the business they accomplished, and were, in fact, none other than "commercial travellers." The staff was composed of relatives and slaves, or free men who were obliged to earn their living.[73]

One merchant, when queried by Dubois as to how this commission-agents' system worked, replied: "We trust our merchandise to people who have no goods; they sell it for us throughout the country, and part of the profit is theirs. If they have the will they can become merchants in their turn."[74] These merchants shipped their goods up and down the river in boats measuring between fifty-eight and sixty-five feet long by ten feet wide. They were capable of carrying as much as twenty to thirty tons. According to Dubois, to convey the same load by land would have necessitated a caravan of a thousand porters, or two hundred camels, or three hundred bullocks.[75] Rene Caillie reported that he "frequently" saw flotillas of sixty to eighty such boats laden with various kinds of produce, making the passage between Djenne and Timbuktu.[76]

The two daily markets of Timbuktu, the Big Market and the Little Market, dealt mainly in provisions, household and personal articles for its inhabitants. Much of the trading there was in the hands of craftsmen and lower class persons. Serfs and slaves bought goods for their noble masters, who neither went to the market, nor allowed their women folk to go there.[77] There was little or no barter, cowries and gold being the media of exchange used. These two currencies fluctuated one against the other, especially during famines. At such times cowries were more important than gold because of the

> greater practicality of cowries for small market transactions and hence the greater demand for them under conditions of famine inflated prices. On the

[73] Dubois, F., 1897, p. 174.   [74] *Ibid.*, p. 195.   [75] *Ibid.*, p. 177.
[76] Caillie, R., 1830, II, p. 9.   [77] Miner, H., 1953, p. 66.

one known occasion when the cowrie value of gold did not decline during a famine—that of 1738—the evidence is positive that it was the shortage of gold which kept its value up.[78]

Haggling was common, and commerce was conducted on a basis of mutual suspicion. In contrast to Kano, the motto here might well have been *caveat emptor*. Perhaps this mutual suspicion reflects the fact that Timbuktu was a place where the economic practices and attitudes characteristic of West Africa came into contact with those of the Mediterranean world. For to paraphrase an old Sudanese saying: "Timbuktu was the place where the camels from across the desert met the canoes, donkeys and porters from Black Africa."

Almost the whole life of the city of Timbuktu was based upon foreign commerce. Caillie found the ten to twelve thousand people there nearly all "involved in trade."[79] The goods which came from innumerable West African producers to Timbuktu were sent to two areas. One portion, destined for the

> towns and nomadic tribes of the Sahara, consisted principally of matters of alimentation, such as millet, rice, karite butter, manioc, peanuts, honey, kola nuts, neta, baobab flour, monkey bread, tamarinds, onions and tobacco (cheaper and inferior to that of Tuat), dried fish, and in addition, soap, iron, antimony, cotton, straw hats, potteries, and calabashes. The other portion was specially allotted to Morocco, Tuat, and Ghadames, and comprised gold, ivory, ostrich plumes, raw leather, wax, incense, civet musk, indigo, gum, etc., and a few slaves.[80]

The goods which came across the desert from the salt mines and the Mediterranean area destined for diffusion throughout West Africa came along two main roads from the north, one from Morocco, and the other from Ghadames, which was linked to Egypt. Apparently two large salt caravans a year arrived in Timbuktu from the mines of Taodeni. The number of camel loads of salt varied from year to year, but according to Dubois, about 50,000 to 60,000 loads entered the city annually. The other caravans brought such Mediterranean products as red cloth, looking-glasses, cutlery, tobacco, bleached and unbleached calico, firearms, scissors, needles, silk, seed pearls for embroidery, large pearls for necklaces, amber, coral, spices (mainly cloves), sugar, coffee, tea, perfumes, teapots, cups, snuff-boxes, dates, carpets, fezzes, burnouses, caftans, in addition to other commodities.[81]

---

[78] Miner, H., 1953, pp. 48–49.   [79] Caillie, R., 1830, II, p. 56.
[80] Dubois, F., 1827, pp. 283–284.
[81] Dubois, F., 1897, pp. 270–301 *passim*; Barth, H., 1853, I, p. 366.

6

The coming of the Europeans had an important effect on West African economies. Some of the coastal states developed large commercial centers, but often did so at the expense of the smaller societies, whose populations were sold into chattel slavery. The abolition of slavery coincided with the desire of the Europeans to explore the interior of Africa, and capture the Saharan trade for themselves. What surprised many of the travellers who went there was the scale of the economies of societies relatively untouched by the slave trade. Mungo Park's reaction to Segou is an example: "The view of this extensive city; the numerous canoes upon the river; the crowded population, and the cultivated state of the surrounding country, formed altogether a prospect of civilization and magnificence, which I little expected to find in the bosom of Africa."[82] Wherever he and the other travellers went inland, they encountered "Commerce! Commerce!" Barth, Caillie, Clapperton and Monteil all compared the interior of Africa with contemporary Europe, and advocated trade with this region. Unfortunately for the advocates of liberal trading policies, who saw in the establishment of commercial relations between Africa and Europe excellent profits for all the groups concerned, the industrial system of Europe, which had now made the slave trade obsolete, demanded "controlled markets."[83] The scramble for markets in Africa took place in the latter half of the nineteenth century, and soon most of West Africa was under European rule. Its economies became subservient to those of the metropolitan countries.

European controls left in their wake economies geared to those of the metropolitan countries. Yet, in the hinterland, the markets continue their periodicities, traders roam as if frontiers did not exist, or try to escape them, and money changers, often using traditional currencies that no longer exist as units, convert francs of various vintages into different types of pounds, and even dollars. A few West African states have moved to recreate an economic unity of West Africa, but they cannot revive the caravan trails which directed goods across the Sahara. Salt and manufactured goods now come more easily by sea. Nevertheless, should the oil in the Sahara pass into African hands, it may stimulate the economies of many of the interior countries of West Africa which, though once brilliant, have since been by-passed by roads and railroads whose only goal is the sea.

[82] Park, M., 1799, I, p. 196.
[83] Diké, K. O., 1956, chapters ix and xi.

Land Holding and Social Organization

by Daniel Biebuyck

University of Delaware

As many writers have pointed out, the field of investigations covered by the analysis of African systems of land holding is very wide. Again and again it has been stressed that, in order to obtain a clear picture of these complex patterns, it is necessary to take into account various aspects of social organization, population density, agricultural methods and the broader economic field. Various other factors, such as religion und value systems, particular ways of thinking about geography and history of the groups involved, are also highly relevant. Many years ago, B. Malinowski in his writings on the Trobriand Islanders and M. Mauss in his *Manuel d'Ethnographie*[1] indicated the variety and complexity of factors involved.

The interplay of these factors has had widely different effects, since in many societies one or more of them are stressed. Thus in some West African and Congo societies the religious aspect is emphasized, whereas in the southern and eastern parts of the continent the political aspect seems often to predominate. And again among some Ghanaian peoples the economic aspect of land holding is clearly discernible, whereas among the Kongo principles of land holding have to be discussed with continual reference to the history of fluctuations in the segregation of lineage groupings and the expansion of Kongo on Teke lands. It is therefore no wonder that the subject of land holding has been treated in studies of African peoples under such diverse chapters as social and political organization, economic systems, agriculture, law, or as a separate category, and that the discussion of land rights tended to be inadequate where it has not been confused.

In this paper we will be essentially concerned with "analysing the cluster of rights of social personalities and groups in types of land used

[1] Mauss, M., 1947, pp. 144–147; Malinowski, B., 1938, I, pp. 328–330.

99

for specific purposes."[2] To show why the content and nature of these rights take particular forms, we have to relate them to other factors in the total cultural setting. We should also make clear that the concept "land holding" is somewhat misleading when applied to African practice. This is because rights do not necessarily relate to land as such, but more often to the use of it for specific purposes, to its products and resources, and to various other of its attributes, such as those that are religious or political. The rights to be discussed, then, are not always rights to land *per se*, but also rights of access to land, rights of ritual or political control over land, rights of allocating or distributing land, and rights of settling disputes over land.

It is quite clear from the studies which have been made that many of our current conceptions of the nature of land holding, and our ways of thinking about such matters as land resources and the incorporation of labor into the land, or about land ownership, transfer and alienability of land, or its meaning and value in the economic sphere, cannot be applied to the analysis of African land holding systems without considerable reinterpretation. It is too simple to reduce the variety and complexity of African systems of land tenure by approaching them in terms of Euro-american legal codes, or to translate the many shades of meaning contained in African conceptual categories which relate to the land and to the peculiar types of relationships between individuals and groups with regard to the land, into restrictive statements such as ownership, possession, usufruct, ultimate title, residuary right, sale, mortgage, loan, *chef de terre*, and the like. This is why the kinds of title held by individuals and groups with regard to the land, and the types of control they exercise over its resources, are extremely difficult to describe in precise terms.

The many reasons for this deserve our full attention, and will provide the basis for our discussion. Some of the rights ascribed to groups or individuals are essentially theoretical. Thus the Nsaw of the Cameroons Highlands hold, in theory, that parcels of land should be regularly re-allocated by the heads of patrilineal kin-groupings, but in practice the land remains in the hands of families and their descendants.[3] Furthermore, some of these heads assume political functions at the local level, either as local chiefs or village headmen, and control larger areas of land than the ordinary heads of kin-groupings. Finally, the paramount chief has the right to resume rights in land already held by these heads, but in practice he rarely does it.[4] This situation leads to various apparently contradictory statements on rights in land existing within the same

[2] Gluckman, M., 1944, p. 18.   [3] Kaberry, P., 1952, pp. 46–48.
[4] *Ibid.*, 1950, pp. 313–316.

society that can be given by students concerned with this problem, so that "ownership" of the land may be simultaneously attributed to ancestors and chiefs, to local chiefs and village headmen, to heads of larger kin-groupings and families. It becomes apparent that to hold a particular title in land is often merely a question of prestige or of ritual privilege, and has little or nothing to do with its allocation or actual usage.

The exercise of rights in land always implies various duties and liabilities. We rarely find rights having an absolute or exclusive character. The king of the Rotse of Northern Rhodesia is *mung'a*, "owner" of all the land, but he must give every subject land for his house and to cultivate. He protects the rights of all his subjects, allows them freely to hunt, fish and gather food on unoccupied land. Moreover, when he allocates land to a particular individual, the right of the latter is conditioned by his position and presence in a village. Thus despite the theory of Rotse land holding, and its phrasing, the Rotse king makes no use of his acknowledged right to all land.[5]

2

African concepts referring to various types of control and rights over land, as symbolized in their linguistic expressions, have been found to be extremely complex. This is the more so, since a single term may be used for describing apparently widely different relationships. It can be assumed that many writers have been misled by the tendency to translate these words by reference to well-established Euroamerican legal categories, without paying enough attention not only to the particular social, but also the linguistic contexts in which these concepts occur. Although we encounter occasional references to this problem, and occasionally the native terms are given, one can point to no study of African land systems that has fully analysed modes of land holding, by taking them adequately into account. The Nyanga of the central eastern Congo describe the different categories of persons that may lay claim to land or farms, or crops, by the use of the single concept *mine*.[6] Its primary meaning, as the people understand it, is "being with"; its full significance in a given instance becomes apparent only when it is combined with other words. Moreover, these various combinations can be applied only to well-defined categories of persons.

Thus, a woman, whether living in her father's or her husband's

[5] Gluckman, M., 1959, pp. 743–745.
[6] These notes are based upon field work among the Nyanga, carried out from 1954 to 1956 under the auspices of I.R.S.A.C.

village, is always *mine mereme* ("being with crops"); men who are descended from the local multilineal descent group are *mine ishwa* ("being with field," particularly with banana groves); men who simply come to join such a group, such as men who come to live with girls "married to spirits," or men who come to live with a mother's or wife's or sister's husband's group, can only claim the title of *mine mereme* ("being with crops"). The head of an extended family (*mutambo* of a *nkhumo*) is called *mine mutundu* ("being with hill such and so," or better, in Nyanga terms "being with children such and so of a mountain"). The senior of a local descent group (*mutambo* of a *rushu*) has claim to the title *mine butaka* or *mine ntata*, "being with unit of land" or "being with mountain." These usages obviate confusion, and underscore the fact that the content of the rights referred to is completely different.

The use of the plural, *bise*, is also possible. It refers, in the first instance, to husband and wife; in the second to a man and his brothers and sons; in the last two, to the effective members of the social groups involved. In some cases the content of *mine* is different according to whether it is used by oneself or in reference to someone else. No one in Nyanga country, not even the divine petty chiefs, can call themselves *mine cuo* ("being with the petty state"), but their subjects may refer to them in that way. There is no *mine oto* (soil as such), although it is often said that the ancestors are *bise oto*. Living individuals among the Nyanga can only establish *mine* relationships, firstly, with parcels or areas of land that "were subdivided by those who lived in ancient times," and in this case *bakare* ("those of old"), and not the word *bashumbu* ("ancestors"), is used. Secondly, they can establish *mine* relationships with land where labor has been or is being incorporated.

In African societies, groups of individuals do not always hold the same type of right with regard to a particular piece of land, nor is a particular parcel always controlled by the same group. This fact is linked to the incidence of migration and expansion, and to various forms of shifting cultivation and transfer of lands. It is also related to different economic activities. Among the Yumbe, who live in western Republic of the Congo, minor kinship groupings hold fairly exclusive rights in particular savannas and forests with respect to residence and agriculture, but rights in hunting, fishing and food gathering, as well as those in such sacred places as burial or initiation grounds, are vested in a larger local community, which will include several such kinship units. That is, in a particular society, several systems of land-holding may co-exist and overlap. Different sets of rules governing land-holding that are found in the same society can be the result of distinctions made between categories of economic activities or of mere ecological situations, such as distinctions between very fertile and very arid lands, as among the Toucouleur of West Africa or the Tonga of Rhodesia, or between the ethnically heterogeneous elements in a society as among the West African Tallensi or the Mandari of the Sudan Republic, or in regions where hunting groups live in social symbiosis with agriculturalists, as among the Lese, Bira and Pygmies in the Congo.

3

No simple correlation can be established between types of social and political organization and particular systems of land-holding. Let us borrow a few examples from societies with centralized political systems. In some societies of southeast Africa, land rights can be conveniently viewed in terms of what Gluckman has called "an hierarchy of estates of holding."[7] That is, chiefs assign their land and delegate their powers more or less permanently to territorial chiefs, who in turn confer them upon village headmen and family heads. Elsewhere, as among the Ashanti of Ghana, the role of descent groups in matters concerning the use and holding of land is predominant, though there an elaborate theory has developed as to the rights of ancestors, and the ritual powers of the chief.[8] Still elsewhere, as among the Lunda of the Congo, neither the paramount chief nor the many categories of territorial chiefs deal with matters of allocation and distribution of land, nor with land disputes. They are said to "look after the people" and to influence the well-being of the group as well as the fertility of the land. They do not, however, hold title to any particular piece of land, but live with their people on land attached to specific village titles.[9] Among the Ruanda or Shi of the Congo almost all land is "owned" and distributed by the king; various kinds of persons hold it under an elaborate system of tenancy. In still other African societies the land is held by villages which got it by way of first settlement; there is no theory whatever that the king or chief would have distributed it.[10]

Few generalizations would be valid about the nature and content of rights exercised by such social categories as women or village headmen. Consider, for example, two groups in Northern Rhodesia, the Bemba and Tonga. Among the Bemba, village headmen organize collective hunting and fishing, initiate the new agricultural cycle and settle disputes over land; but they do not allocate it.[11] Among the Tonga, on the other hand, a village headman has practically no other rights than

[7] Gluckman, M., 1945, p. 5. [8] Busia, K., 1951, pp. 44–45, 56.
[9] Personal information received from Fernand Crine, Anthropologist of I.R.S.A.C.
[10] White, C. M., 1958, pp. 124–130. [11] Richards, A., 1948, pp. 103–104.

those to the few fields he has personally acquired; he cannot allocate land, since he holds no more than the other members of his community.[12] Elsewhere, as among the Tswana of South Africa or the Mambwe of Northern Rhodesia, headmen and chiefs in general exercise a more thorough control on the allocation and distribution of the land and its resources, although they are not allowed to sell the land of their people or to give it away.[13] In some societies, as among the Nsaw of the Cameroons or the Tonga of Rhodesia or the Tswana of South Africa, women have clearly defined land rights in their kinship groups; in others, as among the Afikpo-Ibo or Tiv of Nigeria, women acquire rights to land essentially by virtue of marriage.[14] Most commonly women work land, rights in which are held by men.

How people work the land is part of their system of social relations. Lineages or other kinship groupings, villages or wards, chiefs or headmen, seniors of local kinship groups or ritual leaders exercise a good deal of control over land. Individuals have access to land essentially by virtue of their membership in lineages or villages. Kinship and residence rules determine the kind of people that live together and work the land together; kinship links determine where individuals cultivate.

However, land-holding is not merely a dimension of social organization. African peoples have developed theories about the land itself and its resources, and about the ways in which land can be acquired and should be preserved. They have concepts which enable them to refer to geographical and legal subdivisions of the land, and these concepts may be quite different from those relating to distinctions in their social structure. They have ideas about the particular geography of their country, about boundaries and limits, parts of land and types of land, savannas and forests, hills and valleys. They attach a series of values to it, both as resource and as patrimony; they have surrounded it with religious thinking.

It is in these terms that we may differentiate some of the general characteristics of African landholding that have been distinguished. In the first place, the general abundance of land allowed for various forms of extensive exploitation of the natural environment, and for the ready acquisition by all members of a given community of the right of access to land. Initial settlement and clearing of virgin land were held to be an important, if not the most essential, means for establishing secure title. A great many groups in Africa still hold land today by virtue of initial

[12] White, C. M., 1958, pp. 124–130.
[13] Schapera, I., 1955, p. 196; Watson, W., 1958, pp. 94–106.
[14] Kaberry, P., 1952, p. 48; Schapera, I., 1955, p. 206; Ottenberg, P., 1959, p. 208. For Tonga and Tiv, cf. communications presented by Colson, E. and Bohannan, P., at Second International African Seminar (Leopoldville 1960).

occupancy; individuals and families hold specific rights in parcels of land within a larger area, controlled by their lineage or village, because they or their forebears were the first to clear the land. These were by no means, however, the only ways in which land could be acquired. Gradual expansion on land previously occupied, or conquest, or pacific infiltration, or transhumance, conferred rights, though in many instances this led to ritual and political arrangements which counter-balanced the exclusiveness of the rights.

Generally the first settlers continued to have at least some claims under supernatural sanction, because of their mystical association with the soil. Partition of land between segmenting groups and various, often conditional, transfers of land between related or unrelated groups, through ritual exchange, symbolic sale, loan or mortgage were also current; but outright sale was exceptional.[15] In a great many instances, rights in land, either in well-defined areas or in vaguely separate tracts, were vested in villages, lineages or other descent groups, represented by their headmen, seniors or counsels. In some societies with centralized political institutions, such as among the Ganda of Uganda or the Shi of the Congo, the rights of these groups had been entirely or partially suppressed in favor of chiefs, princes, officials or courtesans.

Individuals had access to the use—even the permanent and hereditary use—of land through various channels. In all societies they could obtain this right in various ways, one of which seemed to be the most important and to offer the greatest security.[16] Usually, the essential mode was through membership in lineages, villages or other types of descent groups; in a few societies, through clientship and tenantry. But in the same societies, marriage, affinity, friendship, co-residence, ritual ties and various forms of "contract" could also lead to the acquisition of rights in land, which were conferred upon individuals and families in a more or less formal way, ranging from allocation to self-aid, and in a more or less permanent manner, that was valid as long as the land was actually under cultivation or even while it lay fallow. Where final say concerning allocation was vested in lineages or villages, various degrees of control were maintained by these groups over the parcels of land provided. Thus a lineage could retain "residual" rights over individual tenures, in the sense that it set limitations to the free transfer of such tenures to strangers. Its control could be greater where there were annual allocations of land, or where the seniors of the groups had a claim to some part of the harvest or of the game killed there. At the

---

[15] Cf. for example, Fortes, M., 1948, p. 249; Wagner, G., 1956, p. 98; Köbben, A. 1954, pp. 314–316.

[16] Cf. for example, Nadel, S., 1951, p. 181; Wagner, G., *op. cit.*, p. 77.

other extreme, the rights of the larger groups could be merely theoretical and in actuality individuals and immediate families had full control over the use of the land held by them.

Land was thus a most important part of the patrimony of the various social and political groups in African societies, not only because it provided subsistence, but also because in most instances it set the essential condition for the maintenance of sovereignty and their continuation as autonomous units. This was reinforced by the fact that, in the view of many African peoples, land was a sacred heritage that had come from the ancestors; it was where ancestors had lived and its integrity had therefore to be preserved.

4

In general, at least theoretically, all members of a given community had the right of access to land used for hunting, fishing, food gathering, cultivation and residence. Except perhaps in the case of a few states, organized along lines comparable to feudalism, there were no landless people, in the sense that all individuals could without difficulty acquire the right to live on the land and work it, although the sources and nature of their possession might take on various forms in different societies. That is, while it was not difficult for individuals to obtain use of the land, they could rarely obtain definite and full title to it or, in some cases, to enjoy full security. Generally, continued residence, continued use, incorporation of labor and acceptance of the local code made for sufficient individual security. Even if the rights were temporary, or were withdrawn as regards a particular piece of land, a person still had economic security, since he could always obtain other land.

Rights of women, though well recognized, were in general determined by those of their husbands, lovers, fathers, brothers or sons. This arose from the fact that the task of clearing land was most commonly done by men; and under the systems of shifting cultivation that were prevalent, this had to be done every few years. In many societies, women had either partial or total rights to a garden and its produce, acquiring these rights through kinship, marriage and residence. Husbands had to give their wives gardens; if they did not, there was ground for divorce.[17] In some societies, however, such as Nsaw, Tonga or some Ghanaian cocoa-farming peoples, women's rights were more extensive. Within their own kinship groupings, they had the same rights as men. They could have exclusive ownership of the produce of their gardens. Thus among the

[17] Gluckman, M., 1959, p. 746.

Kuba, women have their gardens in the savanna country and men in the forest; women are exclusive owners of whatever their gardens produce; men have to share the produce of their gardens with their wives.[18] Among the Lozi, man and wife are a kind of "joint owners" of the produce cultivated by the wife in the garden given her by the husband; if, however, the husband resides in his wife's village he has no right to her produce.[19]

The amount of land actually used for residence or cultivation was generally small; various magical, technological and economic reasons may account for this. Differences in rank were not necessarily expressed in size of holdings, but might as well be expressed in the acquisition of less remote gardens or more fertile areas.[20] The question of the ownership of vacant lands—or even of the very existence of such kind of lands —was generally not raised. Lineages or villages did not have to make full or continual use of all their lands in order to maintain full claims to them. In some regions, however, no-man's-lands existed. These vacant regions functioned as a zone of protection between hostile societies; they were also thought of as possible areas for expansion, as among the Logoli of Kenya.[21]

Alienation of land was by no means common, though several forms of transfer of rights were known, and there was great flexibility in the rights of use. Among the Tallensi of Northern Ghana, even the "rights of tillage" in lands situated in the neighborhood of settlements could only be alienated, under circumstances of extreme necessity, to kinsmen, or members of the local community, or members of the clan. The same regulations applied to a less extent to bush farms.[22] Generally speaking, in Africa, transfers of land and of rights in land could only be achieved under certain circumstances and with certain restrictions, and the categories of people, the kinds of valuables used and the procedures involved in the process were strictly circumscribed. Moreover it is often extremely difficult to assess what is the exact implication of such a transfer; whether it can be considered as loan, or mortgage, or sale, or gift, or whether it is transfer of land as such or simply of the rights to use the land.

In general, those who leave the land, or abandon it (even when forced to do so), or transfer it, retain some kind of right or claim to it. This may be expressed in various ways. Those who grant land may continue to live on it, or they may retain certain ritual rights, or they may be permitted to carry on certain economic activities on it, or they may be

---

[18] Personal information received from J. Vansina.
[19] Gluckman, M., 1945, pp. 8–11. [20] Kaberry, P., 1952, p. 48.
[21] Wagner, G., 1940, pp. 227–228. [22] Fortes, Meyer, 1948, p. 249.

entitled to tribute, or they may be enabled to take it back. Outright sales of land were, and still are, rare; the very idea of alienation of land was, and still is, very often absent.[23] Among the Kgatla of South Africa, land could never be sold, although transfer of land for cultivation from one man to another—say between relatives or friends—was common.[24] Among the Nupe of Nigeria strangers had to be adopted into the household, when they made a request for land on which to settle.[25] Among the Tallensi of Ghana alienation of land was possible only in favor of clansfolk, kinsfolk, or co-members of the same local community.[26] Among the Lega of the Congo, all property except land could be used as stakes in gambling.

The distinction between "owner of the farm" and "owner of the soil,"[27] between first settler and newcomer, between first "owner" and grantee is widely found. It would seem that, even in those societies where the principle of alienation of land was accepted, transfers occurred only when there was great need, as, for example, in paying debts, collecting initiation fees, or discharging urgent ritual and political obligations.[28] Moreover, some lands were always non-transferable; among the Nyakyusa of Tanganyika and Nyasaland the very scarce and valuable ground in the bottom of old volcanic craters could not be alienated;[29] among the Kongo and Yumbe of the Congo, burial and initiation grounds could not be transferred. When land was transferred, the agreement of all the members of the local "owning" group was necessary; as among the Kgatla of South Africa, they had to agree, not only upon the transfer itself, but also upon the acceptability of the particular grantee.[30] Among the matrilineal Yumbe of the Congo the transfer of land to sons or grandsons was accompanied by an elaborate ceremonial in which fetishes linked to the earth were handed over by their fathers; the transfer of land to non-kinsfolk implied the payment of a few slaves.[31] Many factors—the wide importance attached to first occupancy, often involving mythical relationships with the soil, or assigned to the preservation of the integrity of the patrimony of the group, or the desire to attract many people on one's own land, or the

[23] The very concept of alienation of land would have to be redefined, since it can hardly be applied to situations where adoption and integration in the local kinship group, or political allegiance and residence, or friendship, or various ritual arrangements, are prerequisite to the use of land by "strangers."

[24] Schapera, I., 1955, p. 203.   [25] Nadel, S., 1951, p. 182.

[26] Fortes, M., 1948, p. 249, n. 2.   [27] Fortes, M., 1945, p. 177.

[28] When, among the Nyanga of the Congo, a divine petty chief is consecrated, he has to give tracts of land held by his kinship grouping to various ritual leaders in the community and to his ritual wife.

[29] Wilson, M., 1951, p. 46.   [30] Schapera, I., 1955, p. 203.

[31] Personal inquiries among the Yumbe.

economic advantages derived from possessing land that is plentiful, or the prestige values attached to holding land—all seemed to enter.

The religious background was also relevant. One of the reasons commonly given for the inalienability of the land by the rural people, but also by African writers and by anthropologists, refers to its sacred character, which is particularly important where land is considered to be closely tied up with the ancestors.[32] Among the Bemba of northern Rhodesia the spirits of dead chiefs become tutelary deities of the land.[33] Among the Tallensi of Ghana, inherited farm-land belongs to the ancestors, it is their sacred trust; they represent the ritual sanction against its sale or pledging.[34] Among the Ashanti of Ghana, the chief cannot sell the land without the agreement of the lineage elders concerned, and without obtaining the ancestors' sanction through sacrifice.[35] This does not mean that African peoples are unable to distinguish between economic or utilitarian aspects of land and ritual relationships with it; neither does it mean that the mystical bonds with the land are everywhere recognized. Even in the same society, some groups or individuals may feel the sanction of a mystical relationship much more strongly than others. Among the Tallensi of Ghana the Tendaanditib clans are much more mystically linked to the soil than Namoo clans.[36] Among the Lunda of the Congo, heads of local descent groups are ritually much closer to the soil than local chiefs.

5

With the end of the colonial period, various new factors have increasingly entered to change African systems of land holding. Among the more important of them have been the application under the colonial regime of new legal systems and regulations relating to land holding, the introduction of new crops and the development of cash and export crops, the general demand for increased food production, the growing scarcity of land which in some parts of Africa has resulted from a greater demand for land, growing populations and persistence of rudimentary agricultural techniques, overstocking, impoverishment of the soils, and erosion, a higher degree of social mobility resulting in the presence on tribal lands of strangers, and the temporary or permanent absence of a good many members of the local land-controlling units, and the initiation of numerous schemes and programs of rural development. New situations have also arisen out of the policies of independent

[32] Little, K., 1951, pp. 86–87.   [33] Richards, A., 1948, p. 97.
[34] Fortes, M., 1945, p. 178.   [35] Busia, K., 1951, p. 44–45; p. 56.
[36] Fortes, M., 1945, p. 189.

African states having to do with land holding. Indeed, it would seem that land tenure poses an extremely difficult problem to be dealt with by the new states, the more so since they must reconcile traditional practices concerning land with the many precedents set by colonial land laws, and yet think about original and typically African solutions which they stand for.

The effects which several combinations of these new factors can be expected to have on fundamental principles of land holding are extremely varied. Only a few trends can be noted here, some of which set a challenge to current ideas about eventual changes or orientations in African social and economic life and legal theory.

Greater scarcity of land has not generally led to more extensive individual holdings or individual ownership of land, nor to the position that land is a marketable or saleable entity. The psychological attitude toward land has often remained what it was when land was still plentiful, so that the feeling that all persons should have the right of access to land has continued to be prominent in African thinking and practice. This has led, as among some societies of southern and eastern Africa, to continual fragmentation and subdivision of the parcels of land,[37] and elsewhere to the restructuring of lineage controls on land where rights, at one time, seemed to have become largely individualized.[38] Absentees have not lost their claims; some have even had these completely maintained by leaving their wives and children on the land.

The scarcity of land has very much stressed the desire to maintain the land and caused feelings of frustration to arise as soon as part of it is lost. Africans in the new setting have often been found to be less interested in increasing productivity or developing plantations than in protecting and reaffirming their existing rights, and this has led to a demand for some form of registration of customary title, and to greater stress on the notion of set boundaries. In regions where strangers are numerous, as among the Agni of the Ivory Coast or the Lulua of the Congo, growing hostility has been noted toward land holding by outsiders. The Lulua ousted most Luba strangers after the Congo gained its independence; as early as 1948, Agni chiefs decided to grant no more land to strangers; those who were already present at that time were allowed to stay on, but could not increase their area; new land could only be given them for cultivating food crops.[39] Scarcity has led elsewhere, as among the Yumbe of the Congo, to the consideration that

[37] These points were clearly stressed by Prof. Monica Wilson for Xhosa and Mr. Homan for Meru at the Second International Africa Seminar, Leopoldville 1960.

[38] Studies made on the Ghanaian cocoa-farmers by Dr. Polly Hill (1961) reveal this feature.

[39] Köbben, A., 1954, p. 316.

traditional rights to property in land have to be preserved by all means; the outright sale of it has simply become impossible.

Moreover, many rights of lineages and individuals who acquired parcels of land in the past through ritual arrangements or patrilateral ties have been questioned by the descendants of the first settlers and given rise to insoluble problems.[40] Among the Bete-Dida of the Ivory Coast and the Yumbe of the Congo, the combined effect of the growing importance of cash crops and the increasing population has been to bring about a considerable increase of litigation over land, not only between different kinship groupings, but even within these groupings between families and individuals.

Societies where descent is counted in the maternal line, in particular, have been faced by the complex problem of inheritance of rights in land and in plantations. Men who wish to see their plantations pass to their sons face the adverse reaction of their matrilineal kinship groups. This had led to much conflict between brothers, or between men and their nephews or cross-cousins, as customary law does not make provisions for this kind of situation, and sets limits as to the period during which kinsmen on the paternal side can stay on in the group. This is enhanced by the fact that in case of serious litigation, the courts have tended to favor the heirs who would succeed under customary law. New and intermediate solutions have had to be sought. Wills have been made, or fathers have given their farms to their sons during their lifetime, though even in such cases people did not accept a will as valid and the sons, on their part, could not obtain adequate protection from their father's maternal kinsfolk. In other cases, men gave their farms to their sons, but permitted houses, money and other valuables to pass to their brothers and nephews.

Most large-scale resettlement and consolidation schemes have either failed or have proved to be inefficient. Even though they had an adequate technical base, many of the schemes completely ignored the social organization of the people who were involved in them, or they misrepresented the relationships between the people and their land. Psychological attitudes were also powerful; people did not want to leave the ancestral land and to work new, though more fertile, land on which they had no customary claim; or, having left their land, they found it was better than that on which they had been settled. They felt that they had lost their security, or they did not like the districts where they had to live or their new neighborhoods.

Among the Mossi of Upper Volta who have been resettled at the *Office du Niger*, there seems to have been no major difficulty in adapting

[40] Personal information collected among the Yumbe in 1959–1960.

E

to the new natural environment, which was fairly similar to their original habitat in the Yatenga. Adjustment to some supernatural aspects of the new setting was somewhat more difficult; but through Bambara influence, they became somewhat superficial Moslems. Most difficult was to adjust to the social situation in which they found themselves. This they did not understand, since it derived from the reconstruction and maintenance by the French administration of a system of social organization that was incapable of being integrated with the economic and technological requirement of the Niger Scheme.[41]

In some regions the new factors at work led to the curtailment of women's rights; in others, to a considerable increase in the rights of chiefs and to a general confusion between political and ritual rights, on the one hand, and land rights, on the other hand; in still others, to the emergence of new categories of rich and poor in land, of tenants or hired laborers; still elsewhere, to landless individuals and even landless lineages or villages.

Generally speaking, the picture became more complex as the number of types and varieties of landholding increased. But there are almost no instances where spontaneous developments towards a Euroamerican type of land holding, or acceptance of Euroamerican legal theory, seem to have taken place.

[41] Hammond, P. B., 1959, pp. 252–256.

6

Social Stratification and Economic Processes

by Lloyd A. Fallers
University of Chicago

Social stratification is a relatively complex phenomenon. Studying it involves more than simply plotting the distribution of power and wealth in a society, and more than securing ratings by a society's members of one another's prestige. Such simplifications may for some purposes be quite appropriate, but they are unsatisfactory if we aim to reach an understanding of the various ways in which economic processes may be involved in social inequality. For this purpose, a broader conception of social stratification and its place in human societies is required.

In its essential character, social stratification is not an economic phenomenon at all. This is not to say that economic phenomena are not involved or are unimportant in stratification, but simply that the economic aspect of stratification is secondary to another, and more basic, aspect: the moral or cultural one. The heart of stratification—what makes it universal in human societies—is man's tendency to evaluate his fellows, and himself, as "better" or "worse" in terms of some cultural notion of "the good."[1] To be sure, the content of such notions varies over a wide spectrum, but the universality of moral ideas forms one of the common roots of stratification. At this most basic level, economic phenomena may be involved in varying degrees and ways; goods and services of different kinds, and goods and services as such, may be differently evaluated in different cultures.

Here we encounter the notion that "the economic" is founded upon a set of basic biological imperatives—a set of irreducible needs for food, clothing and shelter. It is true, of course, that there are some kinds of goods and services which no culture is in a position utterly to disregard,

[1] The general approach to stratification adopted here owes a great deal to Parsons, T., 1954.

but there are relatively few areas in Africa where considerations of this sort take us very far. The admirable reports and films on the Bushmen of the Kalahari produced by the Marshalls[2] impress upon us the precariousness of life in the desert and the marvelous ingenuity of the Bushmen in solving its problems through a single-minded adjustment of all aspects of life to the food quest, but for Africa as a whole, this is an extremely unusual situation.

The vast majority of Africans have in recent centuries been reasonably prosperous agriculturalists or pastoralists, or often both, employing relatively efficient technologies. As Jones has put it: "Diets are those of poor people, but they are not necessarily poor diets. The total supply of calories appears to be adequate, and Africans rarely know hunger in the sense of persisting shortage of food energy."[3] As a matter of fact, in many areas, such as the highlands of eastern Africa, sheer subsistence requires of the ordinary man a good deal less attention than it did, let us say, of the medieval European peasant. Subsistence production can be left mainly in the hands of the female part of the labor force so that men may be largely available to work and fight for the king or chief. Consequently, "biological imperatives" do not take us very far in explaining the ways in which goods and services are evaluated in traditional Africa. Africans are relatively well off, and hence their cultures are free to give varying kinds and degrees of attention to goods and services.

On the other hand, traditional African cultures do not use the freedom which a relatively efficient technology gives them to actively *devalue* goods and services as, we are told, some traditional Asian cultures do. One must be cautious here; the stereotype of the "spiritual, non-materialistic East" can be very misleading if taken to mean a simple lack of avarice among Asian peoples. As Geertz has shown in his study of religion and economics in a Javanese town, the matter is more complex.[4] The people of Modjokuto see things—persons, modes of behavior, psychic states and material objects—as ranging along a continuum of relative excellence bounded by the polar concepts *alus* and *kasar*—that is, roughly speaking, subtlety, control, inner serenity, as contrasted with crudity, awkwardness and uncontrolled animal passion. High rank, power and wealth should be held by persons who are *alus*. This does not mean that persons in Modjokuto lack the desire for goods and services, but it does mean that concern for such things receives no sanction from the cultural definitions of excellence which are associated with the élite and hence remains unregulated by them. Economic activities of a sort which involve attention to the rationalization of production and exchange

---

[2] Marshall, L., 1957, 1959, 1960; Thomas, E. M., 1959.
[3] Jones, W. O., 1961, p. 5.   [4] Geertz, C., 1956, *passim*.

tend to be devalued or ignored, even while the products themselves may be greatly desired. Such activities are the concern of the *santri*, a more fully Islamicized sub-group standing somewhat aside from the mainstream of Javanese life. No people—certainly not the people of overpopulated Java—are in a position totally to ignore the wants and needs of the biological man. But many Asian peoples do seem to have committed themselves to religious conceptions which regard the body as an unfortunate impediment to the perfection of the soul.

While recognizing that such generalizations, in the present very imperfect state of our understanding of such matters, inevitably oversimplify the cultural dynamics involved, it seems clear that this sort of cultural turning-away from things economic has not been prominent in Africa. Whatever features of traditional African life may stand in the way of more rapid economic development, an absorbing interest in achieving states of inner spiritual perfection is not among them. On the contrary, Africans seem to have, on the whole, a very utilitarian, matter-of-fact view of goods and services.

This is not to say that African cultures have made the organization of production and exchange a central concern. Except perhaps in those areas of Western Africa where trade has become a highly developed calling, this is clearly not the case. It will be argued below that, much more typically, production and exchange have been undertaken as an adjunct—a means—to the organization of power, the field in which, it appears, the African genius has really concentrated its efforts. But there is no evidence that in traditional Africa, economic concerns were rejected as spiritually unworthy. Far from viewing the biological man and his wants as base and unworthy of concern, there is a certain tendency for traditional African religions to make the health, fertility and prosperity of the living individual and the living community matters of central importance. A great deal of the ritual communication which takes place between living persons and the spirit world has as its object the maintenance or re-establishment of individual or group well-being in a quite material, biological sense.

With all the variation that may be found in traditional African religion, this seems to be one of the more persistent themes, appearing, for example, in the intricate cosmological religion of the Dogon of the western Sudan as well as in the ancestral cults of so many Bantu peoples.[5] In the context of this sort of cultural orientation, the production and exchange of goods and services, while not the primary objects of human endeavor, are good and useful insofar as they contribute to individual and group comfort and well-being. In their recent economic

[5] Griaule, M., 1954; Colson, E., 1954.

contacts with the outside world Africans have on the whole responded in this essentially utilitarian way.

2

Thus far we have been discussing culture as one of the bases of social stratification. We have concluded that traditional African cultures, while not regarding economic processes as ends in themselves, have nevertheless given them definite positive value. We may now turn to the other universal root of stratificatory phenomena, the differentiation of roles in the social structure. No human community is a completely undifferentiated aggregation of like beings. The mutual expectations on the basis of which persons are enabled to interact with one another are always to some extent arranged into bundles or clusters on the basis of age, sex and kinship—and usually, of course, upon other bases as well. Again economic phenomena may be involved—perhaps they always are, since the differentiation of roles always tends to involve some differential allocation of economic tasks and thus to be, in one of its aspects, a "division of labor." In general, the more complex the technological apparatus, the more complex the division of labor may become, though the relationship is by no means a simple and direct one. The division of labor between men and women, for example, seems to be largely independent of technological complexity.

The cultural and social structural roots of stratification are not, of course, discrete "things"; instead they come together in the tendency of the differentiated roles themselves, including their economic aspects, to be culturally evaluated. Since tasks are differentially allocated, the culture evaluates persons differentially; that is to say, not just pottery-making and praying are evaluated, but also potters and priests. Obviously, varying degrees of excellence in the performance of priests' and potters' tasks are also recognized.

In traditional African societies, the complexity of the differentiation of roles varies over a wide range, but it varies within definite limits. On the one hand, some degree of economic specialization beyond that represented by the sexual division of labor is present almost everywhere. Again the Bushmen, and perhaps some Pygmy groups, provide exceptions; but these, though they may be of great scientific interest for certain purposes, actually represent only an insignificant fragment of the population of Subsaharan Africa. In most African villages, an array of traditional crafts tends to be reflected in a corresponding array of semi-specialized craft roles: potter, smith, woodworker, musician, bark-cloth-maker or weaver, and often others as well. In recent decades the bicycle mechanic and the tailor with his treadle "Singer" have often joined the ranks of "traditional" village specialists.

On the other hand, in village Africa, as in the rest of the non-industrialized world, there is little differentiation of occupational from domestic organization. By far the greater part of the production of goods and services takes place in a domestic setting, that is, in some kind of local homestead unit. Workplace and homestead are the same and have the same inhabitants. Most homesteads in traditional Africa produce most of what they consume, and consume most of what they produce, and this probably remains true for a majority of African people today, despite the great changes of recent decades.

This relative lack of differentiation between homestead and work group has important conseqences for social stratification. It means that what is stratified is not a series of autonomous occupational categories and organizations, but rather a series of domestic and other kinship units whose economic functions are but one among a number of characteristics on the basis of which their relative worth, in terms of cultural values, is judged. One of the great differentiating characteristics of industrial societies, from the point of view of social stratification, is their tendency to develop such autonomous organizations in which occupational roles may be played outside the domestic context. The modern business firm and the governmental bureaucracy, in their ecological aspect, are places spatially and socially segregated from domestic and other kinship units.

It was one of Karl Marx's great contributions to social science to point out some of the consequences of this separation. The point is not, of course, that occupational and domestic roles cease in such cases to influence each other, but rather that the autonomous occupationa organizations tend to become the main foci of cultural evaluation, and hence of stratification. The domestic unit of the job-holder comes to depend for its status, and even for its basic existence, upon the occupational system to which it is linked by a more or less "purely economic" tie. It is for this reason that students of stratification in industrial societies tend to focus their attention upon occupational ranking. Where occupational roles remain embedded in multifunctional domestic units, it is these latter which tend to be the units of stratification. Such units may remain economically more self-sufficient; a wider range of their characteristics and performances may remain relevant to evaluation and stratification.

Thus we have in traditional Subsaharan Africa the following range of variation: Almost anywhere there is craft specialization, but everywhere we also find that the production of goods and services is household production. Within this range, there is room for a good deal of variation in the degree to which households specialize economically. In most of Africa, craft specialization is predominantly part-time. That is to say, almost every household engages in a basic subsistence activity—usually some combination of agriculture and animal husbandry, but in some cases fishing or transhumant pastoralism—and in addition some households also engage in a part-time specialty like smithing or pottery-making.

In eastern, central and southern Africa, crafts were almost always carried out in this part-time way. Even during late colonial times, in the villages of Buganda and Busoga, for example, one would be hard put to find a really full-time specialist of any kind. Potters, smiths, bark-cloth makers and tailors, as well as modern school teachers, shop keepers and clergymen, maintained gardens, flocks and herds to supply their staple diet. Even a large part of the employed population of the modern town of Kampala found it possible to grow much of their own food.

One gains the impression that this is common throughout the continent wherever urban dwellers are not crowded into "labor lines" or housing estates whose layout makes gardening impossible. In traditional eastern, central and southern Africa really full-time craft specialists only exist at the courts of the more powerful and affluent kings, where they form part of the royal household. In Buganda, only the king's, and perhaps a few of the more eminent chiefs', barkcloths, pots and music are produced by persons who work more or less full-time; those consumed by villagers are made by fellow-agriculturalists for whom the craft is a sideline.

In traditional western Africa, as Skinner points out in his discussion of the indigenous economies of this part of the continent, full-time craft specialists are more common and the crafts themselves more highly developed. The old Yoruba towns contain many—perhaps a majority of persons who maintain farms in the surrounding countryside, but they also contain weavers, smiths, carvers and traders who are full-time professionals, dependent upon the sale of their products for basic subsistence.[6] Here, too, one finds the closest approach to the development of autonomous occupational organizations in the guilds of craftsmen and traders, which control entrance into these occupations and whose leaders represent their members' interests in the governments of the towns. It is not clear, however, how far these guilds as corporate bodies engage in production and exchange and how far they are structurally distant from the lineage organization which is prominent in Yoruba society.[7] The craft guilds of Bida, the capital of the Moslem

[6] Bascom, W., 1959.   [7] Forde, D., 1951, pp. 10–16.

Nupe, which tend to be hereditary and hence to be made up of a series of related kinship groups, are highly organized bodies exercising a substantial measure of control over their members.[8]

Throughout traditional Africa, however, full-time occupational specialization, in the sense of freedom from participation in subsistence production, is more commonly related to political than to economic tasks. Whereas full-time specialization in craft production or trade is relatively rare, the specialist in government is quite common. Indeed, there is in Africa a certain political efflorescence which is perhaps a corollary of the lack of the particular kind of other-worldly religious orientation found in parts of Asia. Authority is sought for and admired, both as a goal of individual ambition and as a means toward, and symbol of, group prosperity and well-being. This is reflected in the African passion for litigation, as well as in the tendency toward formalized political hierarchy. This characterization does not apply only to the great traditional kingdoms, which included much less than half the continent, and were limited to relatively restricted areas of the Guinea coast, the western Sudan, the Great Lakes area and parts of southern Africa and the Congo basin. Political specialists, such as kings and chiefs, are by definition found only in policies with a degree of political centralization, but the absorbing interest in things political of which these states are but a particularly explicit expression is common also, for example, to the decentralized, descent-organized polity of the Tiv, with its elaborate system of moots. It is perhaps not going too far to assert that the *emphasis* in African systems of stratification is primarily political. The roles which are most highly regarded are usually authority roles, whether these involve the part-time political activity and adjudication of disputes which absorb the energies of the elders of a descent group, or the full-time exercise of authority engaged in by the rulers and chiefs of the great kingdoms.

One aspect of this peculiar prominence of the political in African systems of stratification, and perhaps the most important for the purposes of this discussion, is a tendency for economic structures and processes to be overshadowed by—or, perhaps better, *contained within—*political structures and processes. It would not be unreasonable to hazard the guess that in Subsaharan Africa the greater part of the exchanges of goods and services which take place outside domestic units occur as incidents to the exercise or acknowledgement of authority. Wherever there are kings or chiefs, or even petty headmen, goods and services pass upward in the form of taxes or tribute and back down

[8] Nadel, S. F., 1942, pp. 257–297.
[9] Bohannan, P. J., 1957, *passim.*

again in the form of hospitality and gifts. In societies organized on the basis of descent, exchanges serve to mark the political alignment of corporate groups. Land-holding, too, is commonly, in traditional society, a political matter. "*Omwami tafuga ttaka; afuga bantu,*" runs a proverb of the Baganda: "A chief does not rule land; he rules people."

Again the matter is fundamentally the same in both centralized and decentralized societies; landholding tends to be merely the territorial aspect of political relations and groupings, not a distinct and predominantly economic relationship in itself. "Landlords" and "tenants" are exceedingly rare in traditional Africa, perhaps in part because on the whole land is not scarce. Of course we must be careful not to overstate the case. Throughout Subsaharan Africa there is also trade for its own sake, particularly, as we have noted, in western Africa. And a few peoples, perhaps most notably the Kikuyu of Kenya, seem always to have regarded land as a commodity.[10] But throughout the region, at any rate prior to the extension of the money economy in recent times, the predominant tendency has been for political structures to dominate and enclose economic ones and hence for authority to be the principal basis for stratification.

3

Thus far we have considered the two basic sources of stratificatory phenomena—the system of values and the pattern according to which roles are differentiated. There is clearly, however, much more to stratification than this. If the allocation and performance of differentially evaluated roles were a simple mechanical process, a catalog of values and roles would suffice. But societies are not machines, and the persons and groups who make up societies are not cogs and levers. Culture is not a set of engineer's drawings. Persons and groups interpret, feel and strive, and in the process they react to, manipulate and even create both the structure of social relations and the ideas which go to make up culture. All this results in certain additional complexities in stratification and in the economic processes related to it.

By differentially evaluating roles, societies secure a commitment of energy and intelligence on the part of their members to tasks embodied in the roles which are more highly regarded, but in accomplishing this they assume the burden of assuring, explaining and justifying the ways in which particular persons are selected to fill these roles. The range of possibilities here is of course very wide. Access to the more honorific roles is never entirely free and, to the degree to which it is not, culture

[10] Sluiter, G., 1960; Middleton, J., 1953, pp. 52–56; Kenyatta, J., 1938, pp. 20–40.

may undertake to legitimatize inequality of access by means of an ideology of inborn differences in capacity or sanctity. Or it may attribute differential success to luck or the whim of the gods. Where a degree of openness is recognized, it may glorify competitive striving; and the qualities singled out for recognition may in varying degrees relate to actual superiority in the performance of the roles in question. The variations seem endless, but the problem is universal; as a result there develop what might be called "secondary cultures of stratification"— values and beliefs *about* stratification, in contrast with the basic values which give rise to stratification in the first instance.

These secondary cultures include both general public views of how stratification should or does work and also, commonly, a verdant growth of more or less "private," but typically standardized, ideas and beliefs through which persons and groups express their own aspirations, gratifications and frustrations with respect to the results. Thus in Buganda, as in contemporary United States, a public glorification of achievement is combined with an absorbing interest on the part of individuals and kinship groups in genealogy and the symbols of ascribed status, as well as in securing for their own children advantages in competition which are, from the point of view of the publicly expressed ideal, "unfair."[11]

The various elements which make up such a complex of ideas may in one sense, be "contradictory," but they relate to each other in perfectly understandable ways in the context of the problem of linking and reconciling individual and group motivation with the overall system of stratification. The example just given pertains to systems in which achievement is publicly endorsed; but systems of hereditary status also have their public and private secondary cultures of stratification which, as materials from India demonstrate, allow lower-caste persons both to "accept" the fact of low hereditary status and, at the same time, to protest and work against it.[12] One would no doubt discover similar phenomena in the few real caste societies which are found in Africa, such as those of Rwanda and Burundi.[13]

Where different groups within a society become sufficiently separate from each other, the secondary culture of stratification may develop into distinct sub-cultures, based upon class, of the sort which interested Robert Redfield.[14] That is to say, relatively distinct "folk" and "élite" versions of the common culture may develop, expressing the respective interests, values and beliefs of the élite and village levels of society. It

[11] Fallers, L., 1959.
[12] Berreman, G. D., 1960; Marriott, M., 1960, pp. 14ff.
[13] Albert, E., 1960.
[14] Redfield, R., 1956.

has been argued elsewhere that such cultural differentiation, which is one of the marks of the true "peasant society," has not been prominent in Africa, in part because of the lack of a written religious literature of the kind which has formed the basis for élite sub-cultures in Europe and Asia.[15]

In this cultural sense, Africa tends to be rather strikingly egalitarian. This does not mean that Africans reject inequality of any kind; on the contrary, there is among them, as we have noted, a strong tendency toward political hierarchy. But, lacking the degree of cultural differentiation between strata which was common in medieval Europe, Africans do tend to be egalitarian about a man's class origins. The person who manages to acquire a position of authority and wealth is accepted as such; since the élite culture is not greatly differentiated from that of the villages, he can easily learn it and hence does not carry about with him linguistic and behavioral stigmata of the sort which have tended to mark the socially mobile European as a *parvenu*.

Along with this secondary culture of stratification there also develops what we may call a secondary structural aspect of stratification, an aspect commonly symbolized in the literature on the subject by the figure of a pyramid. Such figures are meant to illustrate, beyond the basic differentiation and differential evaluation of roles, the relative numbers of roles of various kinds that are actually available for allocation. The "shape" of the pyramid is clearly related in an important way to degrees of technological complexity. Thus the systems of stratification in those relatively complex, but non-industrialized, societies which are commonly called "peasant" or "feudal" tend to be broad-based, with a small political and religious élite supported by a large mass of subsistence producers.

The traditional African kingdoms may be considered "peasant societies" in this structural sense, though they lacked the cultural differentiation characteristic of their Asian, Near Eastern and European counterparts. Economic modernization of such societies tends to increase the number of "middle class" roles, and thus to "push outward" the sides of the pyramid. Insofar as this image is an accurate one, it has important implications for the working of stratification. Peasant societies may to varying degrees emphasize achievement or hereditary status in their values, but if the élite is very small and the "common man" very numerous, the opportunity for mobility will be extremely slight, no matter how much the culture may glorify it, and no matter to what degree the small élite may actually be recruited from below.

There are other secondary structural aspects of stratification which

[15] Fallers, L., 1961.

are not so easily considered in terms of the pyramid image. Perhaps among the most important are family and descent systems, which greatly influence the allocation of roles and the nature of the units which are stratified. For example, systems of corporate unilineal descent groups, though of course by no means universal in Africa, are very common there. Given the sharply "peaked" shape of traditional stratification pyramids, that is, given the tendency for the powerful and rich to be relatively few and the weak and poor to be relatively numerous, with comparatively small numbers of persons in between, then it follows that extended kinship solidarities will tend to cut across stratification hierarchies in ways which are rather startling to Europeans and Americans. Solidary extended kinship groupings will tend to contain persons of widely varying degrees of power and wealth. This is particularly so where, as is common in Africa, persons of high status have higher rates of polygyny and fertility, with the result that in each generation there are many more élite children than can possibly inherit their parents' status.

In traditional European societies, although the phenomenon of the gradually declining "cadet" lines within a noble or gentry family is a familiar one, solidary kinship groups have tended to be narrower in range and more homogeneous as regards status. The kinship groups involved have been less ramified and marriage has tended to be endogamous with respect to class—or better, for the period of European history concerned, with respect to "estate." In Africa, however, solidary kinship groups tend to contain persons of widely varying power and wealth, both because they ramify widely and because marriage is seldom class-endogamous in any important sense. And this is particularly true of the kinship groups of élite persons, which status-differential polygyny and fertility tend to cause to expand more rapidly than others. Overall status distinctions, therefore, tend to be blurred and it is difficult to find clearly defined strata, even in the larger kingdoms.

African societies have worked out numerous ways of handling the apparent contradictions that result from the juxtaposition of sharp stratification of power and wealth and ramified kinship solidarity. Descent groups may be ranked, both internally and externally, by genealogical seniority, as in the southern Bantu states; or descent groups may be ranked *vis-à-vis* one another, while internal differentiation is determined by some form of election, as among the Akan peoples of the Guinea coast. Still another pattern is found in some of the interlacustrine Bantu states, where the political hierarchy, which here as elsewhere dominates stratification, is simply segregated structurally from the solidarities of descent groups. Except for the kingship, political office in these states is usually not hereditary. Chiefs are recruited by royal appointment, and thus a man's place in the state is one matter, his role in the internal domestic affairs of his lineage quite another.

Understandably, none of these ways of handling the problem entirely resolves the ultimate tension between stratification and the leveling influence of corporate descent groups, because every person remains influenced by both. This is another reason why relatively enduring, culturally defined, "horizontal" strata of the sort familiar in traditional Europe and Asia have not been prominent in Africa. Extended kinship solidarities work against their crystallization. Of course in the un-centralized societies organized on the basis of descent, where formal stratification and differentiation of authority are in any case relatively slight, these issues tend not to arise.

In the processes by means of which persons are distributed through the system of stratification of their society, economic phenomena may be involved in various ways and at different points. We have already, in discussing the cultural and structural roots of stratification, noted how the production of goods and services may be involved at the level of the primary evaluation of differentiated roles. Roles involving production and trade may to varying degrees be differentiated out and may in varying degrees be evaluated as élite roles. In traditional Africa, as we have seen, full-time specialization in non-agricultural production or trade is relatively uncommon, though it certainly exists, and in general authority roles tend to outrank those primarily associated with economic processes.

Apart from this primary evaluation of economic processes and roles, however, goods and services are also involved in other ways in the dynamics of stratification. For stratification, and indeed any element of social structure, always tends to have an economic aspect, even though this aspect may not predominate. Interaction between persons always involves the allocation of scarce goods and services—at a minimum those of space and time, and usually other things as well. Because they are scarce, their allocation is problematical, and this limits the ways in which interaction can proceed.[16] In the case of systems of stratification, it is useful to think of such goods and services as symbols and as facilities.[17] On the one hand, all systems of stratification tend to select some scarce goods and services as symbols of status. The differential allocation of such goods and services is in itself an expression of stratification

[16] Levy, M. J., 1952, pp. 95-98, 390-467.
[17] The distinction is related to that made by Herskovits, M. J., 1955, pp. 155-156, following DuBois, between "prestige" and "subsistence" economies, although facilities are of course not limited to subsistence goods.

and a reward to persons thereby favored. On the other hand, there are also goods and services, possession of which is not in itself particularly honorific, whose utilization is nevertheless essential to the achievement or maintenance of high position.

It is rarely possible to classify actual goods and services as falling wholly into one or the other of these categories, for the distinction is an analytic, not a concrete descriptive one. Thus the corvée labor which so many African kings and chiefs could demand from their people was simultaneously an expression of their superiority and a means of maintaining and strengthening it through the performance of useful work. But particular goods and services may vary considerably in the degree to which they function as symbols or as facilities and it is in the purer cases that the distinction becomes most clear.

Thus in eastern Africa cattle are particularly highly valued goods; indeed, they are valued to such a degree that Herskovits has given the name "East African cattle area" to the whole region.[18] But in many of these societies, cattle are very much in the nature of status symbols, while in others they are regarded as utilitarian goods. A good illustration of the contrast may be seen in the neighboring and closely related kingdoms of Rwanda and Buganda. In Rwanda, cattle are the élite symbols *par excellence*. Possession of large herds and consumption of a diet consisting as far as possible of dairy products are perhaps the most important expressions of Tutsi aristocracy.[19] Cattle are favorite subjects for poetry and exchanges of beasts validate the relationship of lord and vassal. The Baganda, also, value cattle—they are, for example, among the main objects sought in raids against neighboring peoples, just as they are in Rwanda.

But to Baganda, cattle are simply meat—the means by which king and chiefs may provide feasts for their followers. Mere possession of herds means nothing and cattle have no ritual significance in any context. Perhaps most striking of all, the tall, thin cattle people, whose Tutsi and Hima cousins in cattle kingdoms like Rwanda and Ankole form the ruling aristocracy, are in Buganda regarded simply as rustic and rather smelly herdsmen, who hire themselves out to look after the cattle of wealthy Baganda. However, the cattle of Baganda chiefs are not in any real sense more "economic" than are the more symbolic beasts of the Tutsi, though the uses to which they are put may be more mundane. Both facilities and symbols are "economic" in the sense that they are valuable and scarce and hence their allocation presents a problem in economizing for both persons and groups. The Tutsi chief in Rwanda,

[18] Herskovits, M. J., 1926, *passim*.
[19] Maquet, J., 1961, pp. 18–19, 129–142.

it is clear, allocates his cattle quite as carefully as he does his less symbolic possessions.

Here again we return to the point that in traditional Africa goods and services, both as symbols and as facilities, circulate primarily in terms of political relations, for it is the polity that dominates stratification. Persons and groups strive to control the symbols and facilities that are the expressions of authority and the means of strengthening and extending it. A good case could be made that, at least in eastern, central and southern Africa, the most important facilities are people. This does not mean that people are regarded by their rulers as mere "things", though of course various forms of slavery have sometimes been involved, but rather simply that in the production of goods and services in this part of Africa, the most problematic factor is usually human labor.

As we have seen, land is on the whole not scarce and agricultural and military technology are relatively simple. The means of production are therefore controlled by groups of village cultivators. For the chief who wishes to strengthen and extend his rule, the main problem consists in securing an adequate supply of labor. The solution of this problem lies in attracting and holding the maximum number of subjects who, as cultivators and warriors, can then produce the maximum amount of tribute and booty in craft and agricultural products. These in turn can be redistributed as largess to the maximum number of loyal supporters. The principal danger to the authority of the chief lies in the ultimate ability of his disaffected subjects simply to pick up and move away, leaving him to be "chief of the pumpkins." Thinking, as we tend to do, of land and capital goods as the problematic factors, this tribute-largess-labor-starved economy may seem a tenuous base upon which to erect a highly centralized and stratified society, but the examples of the eighteenth- and nineteenth-century kingdoms of the Zulu and Baganda show that this can be done by rulers able to manipulate shrewdly the symbols and facilities of authority.[20]

Trade has also tended to be dominated by the polity, that is, to be directed to the political ends of rulers. In eastern Africa, where trade with the coast came late, rulers strove to monopolize the trade in such new facilities as firearms, which greatly reinforced the ruler's authority if he was in fact successful in controlling it, and, through sumptuary laws, such new symbols as tailored clothing. The Reverend Batulumayo

---

[20] M. Gluckman (1960) says that the crucial factor in the creation of the Zulu "empire" of Shaka was land shortage, but he does not explain how this effect was produced and one does not find his argument convincing. On the contrary, the Zulu polity, as he himself so well describes it, seems an excellent example of state built upon military and political intelligence and charisma. Land shortage, if such existed, did not prevent the empire from disintegrating when Shaka's leadership ceased to be effective.

Musoke Zimbe, who as a boy served as a page at the court of King
Mutesa of Buganda, describes in his memoirs how Mutesa assigned
different types of clothing to various ranks.[21] Even in western Africa,
where trade is more extensive, more diversified, more professionalized
and of longer standing, it tends to be heavily influenced by political
considerations. Rosemary Arnold's account of the domination of the
port town of Whydah by the kingdom of Dahomey provides an excellent
example of the tendency toward "administered trade."[22] The independent trading town of the sort described in the diary of Antera Duke of
Calabar, where a kind of "lodge" or "guild" of trader-chiefs themselves
ruled the town in the interest of trade, is a much rarer phenomenon in
Africa.[23] Trade has most commonly been controlled in the interest of the
polity.

4

Traditional African societies, then, have characteristically exhibited
patterns of role differentiation in which political specialization has been
more prominent than economic. The ambitions of their members have
been directed primarily toward attaining authority, and economic processes have commonly been dominated by the political needs of individuals and groups. While sharply "peaked" systems of stratification
have been created in the great traditional kingdoms, even in these cases
there has been relatively little cultural differentiation between élite and
common folk and little concentration of the non-human means of production in élite hands. Extended kinship solidarities have worked against
rigid status stratification. Keeping these indigenous patterns in mind,
we may in conclusion draw attention to some of the consequences that
contemporary processes of economic modernization seem to be having
or, equally important in some respects, not having, for these traditional
patterns.

First of all, there has been taking place all over Africa, particularly
during the past half-century, an ever-increasing commercialization of
land and labor. This process was often initiated in the first instance by
the demand for money created by the imposition of taxation by colonial
governments, but it has also, and increasingly, been stimulated by the
desire for the vast array of new goods and services, both imported and
locally produced, which have become available. In some areas Africans
numbering in the hundreds of thousands have gone to work for wages
in mines and factories and on plantations; somewhat fewer have become
white-collar workers—the ubiquitous "clerks" who tend the machinery

[21] Zimbe, B. M., 1938, pp. 19–20.   [22] Arnold, R., 1957.
[23] Forde, D., 1956.

of bureaucracy in both government and business firms. Others, in still larger numbers, have become cash-crop cultivators, producing cocoa, coffee, tobacco, cotton and other crops for the export market.

Frequently cash-crop agriculture and wage work have competed for African labor, and in a great many areas vast numbers of men move back and forth between the two forms of money-making in cycles varying from daily commuting to periods of many years, combining agriculture and employment in ways that best suit their various situations and tastes.[24] Underlying all the variations in pattern, however, has been a pervasive and constantly deepening commitment to a money economy, in which both labor and land have increasingly become marketable commodities. If in very many areas traditional subsistence patterns have remained intact enough to make the money economy a rather superficial overlay, a source of "luxury" goods and services, the number for whom this is true has constantly diminished as the relationship of population to land has changed and as what were formerly merely "wants," have become "needs."

At the same time, ever-expanding educational systems have been busily producing practitioners of the learned professions—physicians, lawyers, clergymen, engineers and teachers. Expanding literacy and the nationalist movements have encouraged the rise of politicians and publicists. Africanization of governmental and business bureaucracies has produced civil servants and junior executives. New opportunities for trade have stimulated a few real African entrepreneurs.

All this has meant a great proliferation of differentiated roles and, in particular, of occupational roles. In fact, over much of Africa, true occupational roles, in the sense of full-time roles played outside the domestic context in exchange for basic income, have essentially come into existence for the first time during this period. As a result we may confidently expect the emergence of new patterns of stratification. However, we may also expect that in these new patterns there will remain important elements of continuity with the past.

Almost without exception, direct continuity with traditional systems of stratification has been rendered nearly impossible by the lack of congruence between traditional and modern societal and cultural boundaries. Most African countries, having acquired their boundaries through the maneuvers of European diplomats, are extremely heterogeneous, and those lying south of the Moslem Sudan and Christian Ethiopia lack over-arching literate élite cultures of the sort that, for example, give some unity to the otherwise quite diverse peoples of India. Thus, traditional élites, deriving their positions from societal and cultural units that

[24] Elkan, W., and Fallers, L., 1960, *passim*.

have been absorbed and superseded by the new states or proto-states, tend to have little legitimacy on a national level.

In Asia and the Near East, traditional élites can to a greater extent absorb and give birth to the new. Gandhi and Mohammed Abdu, for example, could in some measure reinterpret in modern terms traditional élite cultures that represented the common pasts of the peoples of their countries, thus contributing an essential element of continuity to the culture of new nations. In the African countries, however, there is inevitably a greater discontinuity between old and new cultures and between old and new élites. The only culture self-consciously shared by the new élites has tended to be that imported from France, Belgium or Britain—or that formed in reaction to French, Belgian or British domination. This is not to say that there are no underlying regional cultural unities in Subsaharan Africa, but these tend to be of a sort discovered by anthropological research. Not having been made explicit by being embodied in literary traditions, they are difficult for élites to utilize in the creation of new national cultures. Such concepts as "African personality" and "*négritude*" represent attempts by contemporary African leaders to solve this problem.

There are, however, other kinds of continuity between traditional and modern systems of stratification which may be even more important. Although direct cultural continuity may be difficult to achieve, some characteristic features of the traditional systems may perhaps persist and give a distinctly African character to the new independent nations. For example, in the new African nations, as in the old, political structures seem likely to continue to dominate economic ones, and political élites to retain their pre-eminence. To be sure, the place of economic processes in society has changed greatly. Whereas in traditional societies an essentially static economy was manipulated for political ends, the new independent states make rapid economic development the principal aim of public policy.

But this is precisely the point: Whereas in Europe and America economic modernization was in great measure carried out by private entrepreneurs under régimes of *laisser faire*, Africa is attempting to modernize at a speed, and under conditions, which require a more prominent role for state entrepreneurship. This means a greater prominence, both in numbers and in status, for civil servants, as compared with private business men. As a result, the élite of a country like Nigeria, recently studied by the Smythes, is perhaps as heavily political as was, say, that of the old Yoruba state of Oyo.[25] The traditional cultural emphasis upon authority coincides with, and perhaps helps to

[25] Smythe, H. and M., 1960.

produce, modern conceptions of planning for economic development.

It may be anticipated, also, that the new African states will continue to be relatively "classless" in the same sense in which the old ones were. To be sure, occupational differentiation has greatly increased and the new educational systems hold the potentiality for creating cultural stratifications of a kind unknown in traditional societies. In the colonial period, during the early phases of educational development, many African societies seemed to be producing new solidary élites of European-educated persons, and many writers have dwelt upon the gap between such persons and the uneducated masses, often, one suspects, reading into the African situation European attitudes toward status which were not really there. We certainly should not expect egalitarianism in the sense of a lack of differentiation according to power, wealth and prestige; such differentiation was prominent in the past and is likely to remain so.

At least in the short run, however, extended kinship solidarities will tend to check the development of clearly defined strata. Welfare-state policies in education and other fields, policies which modern populist politics make almost inevitable, also will militate against the solidification of the new élites into hereditary estates or castes. Furthermore, the modernization of economies tends to increase the number of intermediate, or middle class roles, thus increasing the structural opportunities for mobility. Thus, while the new African societies may be highly stratified economically and politically, they will probably remain relatively open to talent.

PART THREE

Induced
Economic
Phenomena

7

Land Use, Land Tenure and Land Reform

by Paul Bohannan
Northwestern University

Even a brief examination of the relevant literature shows that a discussion of land in any cross-cultural context is an undertaking ringed by pitfalls. The difficulty, although not easy to counteract, can be met if ethnocentric considerations of geography, agricultural technology, property, and legality are suspended, and images of historical societies such as feudal systems set aside. A careful view of the facts themselves, and the contrasting ways that they have been examined by Africans and non-Africans, provides a corrective.

The difficulty lies essentially in the fact that the word "land" immediately calls up the word "tenure," and hence prejudices the next step in any consideration of the position of land in non-European societies. "Tenure" refers to a limited type of relationship between people and land or, as lawyers would have it, between persons in terms of land; it further assumes a given type of institutional association between the means of production and the allocation of property.

Moreover, the word "land" itself has two meanings of immediate relevance, besides its many others. In the first place, land is a factor of production—a resource; no commodities can be produced without in some way using the resources associated with land. In the second place, space is a dimension of human society, and most of the space occupied by societies is in fact the land that is concomitantly exploited as a factor of production. Thus there is a necessary relationship between production and local grouping because both depend on land.

The problem, then, is clear. As Fallers has shown, it is not possible to discuss land as a factor of production, in the context of an economy, without reference to the political aspects of the problem. As a short-cut, one can thus say that "land use" presents jural and political problems, but that the two are only analytically separable from a common fund of data, and that either economic or legal facts put stringent limitations on the other.

There is an additional difficulty. In a capitalistic culture, land as a dimension of society is considered divisible into marketable parcels called "sites." The resources and products of the land are brought into the same market as is the site. Thus, there is a simplistic integration of these two items, in capitalist society, under the principle of the market. Such societies have not only a market economy, but in a sense and to a limited degree, also have a market polity. In even those few African societies which recognized sale of land, land entered into a market limited strictly as to who could buy and what could be used as exchange.

The constituency of any local community in capitalist society is, to a greater or lesser extent, the result of the working of the same market which creates the integration of the economy: that is, people buy and rent homesites just as firms buy and rent factory and shop sites, or as farmers buy and rent farms. The result of this situation is that the economic aspects of land, both as factor and as site, are predominant. Concomitantly, we may regard the local community as a mere epiphenomenon of market, to overstate the matter somewhat but not seriously to warp it. In a society integrated fundamentally by the principle of market, territorial groups are little more than concatenations of contract. Kinship is of minimal significance, and there is no contradiction between sale of sites and the ecological and chronological results of such sales on the one hand, and the distribution of factors of production on the other.

As is so often the case, however, Euroamerican culture simplifies the situation out of recognition. We are accustomed to thinking of our society and our culture as complex, when in fact complexity requires simplifying ideas in order to be accommodated. These simplifying ideas, once learned, are difficult to hold in abeyance. Yet they are not, for any reason, necessarily attributable to a less complex situation that can be organized, and hence analyzed, the better without them. "Market" and "money," as concepts, have simplified our lives. They have, however, vastly complicated the process of analyzing the economics of technologically less developed societies that are organized and operated without them as integrating principles.

In most cultures that are both non-capitalistic and technologically simple, the situation is the reverse of what it is in capitalistic societies. In the former, the political aspect of land—land as a territorial dimension of society—is dominant. The local group is ordered not by contractual practices concomitant on sale or rental on a market principle, but by kinship or by religious or some other principle. In such places, exploitation of land follows political and social organization rather than the opposite.

It is neither possible nor desirable to discuss two "types" of land custom. Rather, the discussion must center on principles, and the number of possible principles is not germane to our discussion. Because of the limitation to African society, our emphasis will be on the principles of kinship, which are those that most Africans use to view land custom, and on the principles of market and contract, which are those that most Europeans and Americans use to view land custom. That there are other principles needed to analyze other systems, such as that of hierarchy in India or in feudal Europe, is beside the point.

An obvious difficulty arises when changes are made in the principles which govern land custom. There is not merely a revolution in the distribution and use of land as a resource, but also a concomitant revolution in land tenure, which means a change in the composition, nature and social significance of the local group. The difficulty facing a people who adopt new methods of exploiting their environment must not be thought of as primarily economic. Members of any society are able to understand and appreciate methods which make production easier, products better and themselves richer. They are not, however, always or even often willing to pay the social price that the process of incorporating new methods into their productive and distributive activities actually demands.

We will here examine three African societies in terms of the correlation between prevailing systems of land use and land tenure as they are seen by the people themselves, and then examine the same practices either as they must necessarily be interpreted in order to accord with the statutes and codes of the country concerned, or as they are being administered by the relevant colonial power. This will in some measure provide a key to the basic social as well as cultural changes that are being required by "land reform" in African society. The examples will be the Tiv and the Yoruba of Nigeria and the Kikuyu of Kenya.

2

The Tiv, who number about 800,000 and live on both sides of the Benue River in central Nigeria, claim descent from a single male ancestor, Tiv.[1] The entire people form a single segmented lineage, seen in terms of a genealogy some 14 to 18 generations in depth. Every descent group is comprised of the living descendants of a single ancestor in the paternal line; each ancestor is a point of differentiation between his own

[1] Bohannan, P. J., 1954a and 1954b, *passim*.

descendants and those descended from his sibling. The two descent groups so formed comprise, in terms of the father of the two ancestors, a single descent group. Therefore, this people represents a concatenation of descent groups bound together in terms of a "master" genealogy. The groups, like the genealogy, run from small lineages of living people to the whole tribe, itself a lineage, the (children of) Tiv.

The smallest lineage called a "segment" (*ipaven*) is a descent group some three to six generations in depth which is associated with a discrete

CHART 7.I. *Relationship of Genealogy to Territory. Tiv. Tribe.*

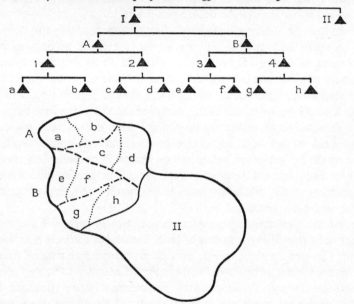

territory (*tar*). "Segments within the hut" are smaller kinship groupings and do not form the basis of recognized local entities. Larger ones, called merely "segment," always do so. In the few cases in which the two lineages of a larger, more inclusive grouping do not bound one another, they have a special set of historical myths to account for their separation. The population of a territory associated with the smallest "segment" is from 200 to 1200 people. The territory itself varies from about two square miles to over twenty.

A model of the system can be seen in Chart 7.1. The founder of segment *a* was a brother of the founder of segment *b*. Each is a minimal segment today, and each has its own territory. The two segments taken together all count descent from "1" and are known by his name—the children of "1." In the same way, the territory of lineage "1," made up as it is of the combined minimal territories *a* and *b*, combines with the territory of lineage "2," made up of the combined minimal territories of *c* and *d*, to form territory *A*, occupied by lineage segment *A*, all descended from a single ancestor *A*. This process is extended indefinitely to the apex of the genealogy, back in time to the founder who begot the entire people, and outwards in space to the edges of Tiv country. Most Tiv live in the territories of their own lineages. In five communities from three parts of the area, 83 per cent of the men resident in a lineage area were members of the patrilineal descent unit associated with it.

Every Tiv, as a condition of his membership through descent in his lineages, has a right to land within the territory or *tar* of his smallest territorial lineage. This principle does not apply to any specific piece of land, but recognizes the right of a man to enough land to support him and his family. Since the Tiv practice a slow and regular migration, lineages moving as units, a specific piece of land changes hands from year to year. The relevant question to Tiv is not position on the earth, but rather juxtaposition in space, as determined by genealogy. A man "hoes farms" for each of his wives; in the normal course of events, these farms bound one another, with a path only a little wider than ordinary between them. The sons of each wife "inherit her farm," not in the sense of possessing an actual piece of land, but in that of their juxtaposition among the various sets of half-brothers. The farms a man works are beside these of his full brother, and the combined farms of his groups of full siblings are beside those of his various sets of half-brothers. All together, the farms of the sons of one father are beside the farms of the sons of the father's various brothers. The important point is whom one bounds.

Actually, of course, brothers sometimes quarrel, and one finds fairly frequent examples of brothers whose farms do not bound one another. Always, however, there is said to be a reason in contrast to farms which are beside the farms of a brother, a situation that is regarded as being in the natural course of events.

The social unit is thus the important group, and is a "given"; land, as a resource, is dependent upon the dimensional aspects of Tiv social organization. However, two other practices must be considered here: land usage and the slow, constant migration which is characteristic of Tiv. Tiv break new land every year, mound it and plant yams and subsidiary crops on the mounds. The next year this field becomes a "second-year field," and is used to grow millet and sorghum. It may be used a third year to grow sesame or soy beans as a cash crop. It then reverts to fallow for as many as 6 to 20 years; as many as are required for it to regain full fertility. Thus every Tiv brings a new farm into cultivation each year, but also uses each of his farms for two or three years. When the land reverts to fallow, his rights to it lapse. In the southern sector of Tiv country, where land is scarce, individual Tiv may claim fallow they have once farmed, but often have difficulty in maintaining their claims in the traditional courts. Where there is no land shortage, there is no noticeable tendency to lay claim to fallow.

Land may be used by quite different people the second time it is brought into cultivation. Rights to individual parcels of land are not, by and large, carried over the period of fallow. Indeed it would be impossible to carry them over and maintain the migrations which are an important part of Tiv land custom.

Tiv see every lineage, at every level, as growing in numbers and therefore necessarily expanding in territory. They have a maxim, "Would I take land from my full brother when I can take it from my half brother?" which is a way of saying that when they must expand the area required for farms, they nudge the "brother" who bounds them, but who is most distantly related to them, demanding that he take his sufficiency further over. Insofar as the lineages are actually expanding—and population is in fact rising at the same time that cash cropping of food as well as of sesame and soy beans, which require more land, is on the increase— each is pressing outwards in all directions. In Chart 7.1, lineage *a* will, as part of lineage "1," expand against lineage "2" rather than against lineage *b*. If, however, lineage "2" does not have sufficient space for its farms, it will cooperate with "1", and therefore activate lineage *A* in expanding against lineage *B*. Thus, the outward pressure from every lineage, at every level, is maintained.

In the center of Tiv country, the pressure is fairly slight, and the readjustment is minimal. However, the pressure builds up as the periphery is approached so that every lineage away from the central portion has a direction of migration. In the south, before there was effective colonial administration and the maintenance of a boundary, each lineage moved four or five miles a generation. In the north, where the land before them was almost empty, the rate was and has continued to be much faster. Except in the center of the country, it was thus unlikely that a group would be found living on a piece of ground ready for farming which was there when it was previously farmed. This fact has continued to be the case in many parts of the north, and would be true throughout were it not for governmental maintenance of boundaries and the prohibition of warfare. "Title" to any specific piece of land was unthinkable in such a situation. Position was determined by social organization and was based on genealogy. One farmed wherever one happened to be.

This resembles the territoriality of birds far more than it does traditional views of "land tenure." Some birds, such as the English robin, whose territoriality has been well studied, allow no other members of their own species within a certain distance of their nests, and moreover exploit a rather wider area, which they also protect from too great competition. To say that Tiv have long-term "land tenure" is much like claiming it for robins.

There is another set of rights, however, which Tiv hold for brief periods of time, and which do resemble European notions of land tenure. During the time that a man and his wives are actually working a piece of land, they have specific rights in that piece of land which amount more or less to "ownership." These rights include those usually referred to loosely as "usufructory"; they also include rights to exclude others, or to erect shelters, and the like. A man can be said to "own" his farm—but not the land it is on. Tiv can be said to have "farm tenure" but not "land tenure." The rights which resemble those that we regard as land tenure are held in specific pieces of land only for periods of no more than three years. They are, however, held in some piece of land or other all the time.

One of the primary differences, in other words, between the legalistic "land tenure" of Europe and America, and Tiv land custom, is to be found in the time dimension, and ultimately in the way in which local groups are associated with the earth. With Euroamericans, land and its divisions are permanent; the people come and go by virtue of contractual activities. With Tiv, it is the social organization and its divisions that are permanent. The land, so to speak, comes and goes with fertility and with migrations.

The land laws of the Federation of Nigeria are, like most Nigerian law, based on an English model, with due deference usually given to what was called "native law and custom." The basic concept in this law is the so-called "right of occupancy," defined as "a title to the use and occupation of land." Statute Chapter 96 provides that such rights of occupancy shall be recognized in accordance with the native law and custom in the area. What it does not consider is the fact that, for the Tiv at any rate, this law assumes that a "title" exists, and moreover that that title is to a specific piece of land for an extended period of time.[2]

Thus, subtly and without intent, the law changed the whole basis of land practice. Instead of focusing on the body social, it focuses on the title to land. The Tiv, as we have seen, recognize something that can be called a title to a farm during its use—at most, three years. However, for them the greater and overriding right is to have sufficient land

[2] Cf. Nigeria, Federation of, 1959, *passim*.

wherever the lineage may in fact be. The result of the law, from the Tiv point of view, is thus two-fold. It deprives them of their social birthright, and at the same time it transfixes and ossifies the social structure into the narrow range considered suitable only for a single year. For periods of a single year, the land-dominated view of the economy and society is correct; but in the Tiv system, this situation changes annually.

Tiv have therefore resisted any attempt to "apply" the law—and indeed, the attempts have been few. However, the fact is that they are no longer able to migrate as freely as in earlier times, and thus either a new form of migration is changing the social organization, or else the land is becoming eroded from overuse, or both. Such are some of the factors behind the Tiv unrest that marred the independence celebrations of Nigeria.[3]

Another important factor in northern Nigerian land law is that it forbids sale or even sublease of land without permission of the Governor. It also provides that no single piece of land can be divided into more than two parts on inheritance without the consent of the Governor. These two provisions have serious potential effects. In the first place, Tiv did not sell land in their traditional system—as we have seen, they did not "own" it except for very short periods of time, and everybody had a right to land in his own lineage; it was also common practice to give a "daughter's child" or other kinsman farming rights for the time the farm was in production. Tiv did not sell "farms"—they gave them to their kinsmen. They could not sell land, for to do so would be tantamount to selling a place in the genealogy.

However, when new conditions came to be demanded by the shift from society to geography that the law assumed, to withhold the right to sell land had the same effect as it would have in any other developing country. The British administration, whose provisions had the purpose of protecting the rights of Nigerians, in fact subsidized and created a particular type of peasantry rather than merely "maintaining" native law and custom. But the result has, in sum, been that the Tiv have been asked to redirect their attention from social considerations of landed space, with concomitant economic security, to economic considerations of land as a factor of production, without what they consider to be concomitant social security.

It should be noted that nothing has been said about the "ownership" of land by the lineage as a corporate group. A kinship grouping has spatial dimension; lineage members have rights to sufficient land within

[3] Tiv rioting took place during late September and early October, 1960. The riots, which are periodic occurrences among Tiv, concerned problems of authority in local government and had nothing to do with independence.

its area and specific farms within it. But the lineage as a corporation has no right to anything. This point is important because it is at variance with the situation among the Kikuyu and the Yoruba.

3

The Yoruba, the dominant people of the Western region of Nigeria, number about six million. They are divided into kingdoms, each with its capital city and with the hinterland composed of large villages called "towns." The affairs of each of these towns, including the capital, are regulated by a group of chiefs, and each kingdom has at its head a ruler called an *oba*. As with the Tiv, the primary local group is made up of the descendents of a single ancestor. However, there the resemblance ends. In some areas, notably Ekiti, Oyo, and Egba, the descent group is called in Yoruba *idile*, and is made up of kinsmen related in the male line, who live together in a town compound and hold a large block of farmland. In other areas, notably in Ijebu and Ondo, the lineage is not patrilineal, but rather is an unlimited descent group called an *ebi*, membership in which is determined by the actual assumption of land rights.

Lloyd[4] has described in detail how each of these lineages, of either type, is associated with a chieftancy title in the town in which it lives, and also with a given block or blocks of land in the environs of the town. Each lineage also has a myth which justifies its presence in the town, usually a tale accounting for the relationship between its first chief or founding ancestor and the *oba* of the kingdom concerned.

Every lineage occupies and uses the block of land which is said to have been assigned to it by the *oba* and chiefs. In a few areas, notably in Ado Ekiti, some land is still controlled by the *oba* and chiefs which can be, and continues to be, assigned. In most parts of Yoruba country, however, all land has been taken up, so it is no longer possible for the chiefs and *obas* to assign further land holdings.

Once a block of land has been assigned to a lineage, the *oba* loses all rights in it, save those which we might compare to rights of eminent domain. Every member of the lineage, in virtue of his membership in it, has a right to sufficient land in the block which has been assigned to his lineage. He also has a right to a voice in the management of the property, and can speak up in family meetings, as they are called, at which decisions about the property and about farming policy are taken by the lineage members as a group. The man also has rights to a certain number of living rooms in the family or lineage compound in the town.

[4] Lloyd, P. C., 1954, 1955, *passim*.

Grievances among family members are almost always taken care of in these family meetings, and seldom reach the courts.

It is important to remember that although rights pass within this group, they are not inherited within it. Since being a member of the lineage entitles one to the use of sufficient land within it, one does not inherit land at all. Rather, one is born to it. A man cannot, of course, alienate these rights, even to other members of the kin group. He can merely forego them, and let the specific land which he has been using revert to other members of his kinship group. As with Tiv, for him to be able to sell such rights would be tantamount to selling positions in the kinship system.

The kinship group itself, however, may buy and sell all those rights which it in fact holds, which are all those not specifically reserved by written law, or by the customary rights of the *obas* and chiefs. So-called "family land" is indeed sold in most of those areas in which there is no further land to be allocated by the chiefs. The kinship group, as a group, under the presidency of the oldest man, can sell its rights to either an individual or to another kinship group.

Two processes can thus be seen at work. The first of these Lloyd has called "allocation."[5] Allocation is the act of deciding which member of the lineage shall have rights to farm in which specific parts of the land block and to live in which specific rooms of the compound. The second, which is more formal, he has called "partition," in which two groups of descendants of a single man agree on the part of the family property to which each will have rights. Under the process of partition, each quits his claim to the rest of the property. Partition, however, involves the entire community, with its chiefs and *obas*, and is carried out according to rigid rules.

A man's son has preferential rights in his specific fields and in his specific house rooms. However, he must use them within a given time, or they revert to the group. He may be given rights some place else if he returns home and asks to take them up.

There are thus two types of owner of rights in land. On the one hand there is the individual owner, on the other there is the community owner, called "family" by Yoruba. If a man buys land individually it remains individual land only until his death. After that all of his sons have rights in it; it therefore again becomes community property, belonging to a small lineage. In such a situation no individual child can alienate his rights; only the group can do so. It is important to make it clear that the rights of these offspring are in no wise rights of joint tenancy, devolving on the last survivor. Rather, descendants of each

[5] Lloyd, P. C., 1959a, *passim*.

male owner in the paternal line become a part of the owning group. Thus lineage rights are created in all individual property, no matter how acquired, at or before the time of inheritance.

There are thus two aspects to the idea of what the Yoruba call "family property." There is first the corporate holding of the property by the kinship group, and in this case the individual has no alienable share, for all that he has specific rights in the property because of his kinship membership. Secondly, there is the constant re-entailment, so to speak, of all self-acquired individual interests in real property on the death of their creator.

For these reasons, most Yoruba property is "owned" by kinship groups. At least it is so most of the time. It may be partitioned and come into the ownership of individuals. It may be sold to an individual by a kinship group. But barring resale or a single heir, the individual ownership is of a temporary nature. However, the important factor here is not whether the owner or holder of the rights in land is a group or an individual. It is, rather, that the rights each may hold are of exactly the same sort.

In this situation, unlike the Tiv, a concept is patently present that resembles what jurists call the "corporation aggregate," which holds rights in specific blocks of land. Within this corporation, the type of rights is very like those held by the Tiv. However, the organization of the groups, and of their rights, into greater unities is done by the political method of chiefship and kingship rather than by the Tiv method described above.

Lloyd[6] makes a specific point of the fact that the executive head of the family is not its trustee. Rather, he says, all policy must be decided at family meetings, and the head merely implements their decisions. However, with the Communal Land Rights (Vesting in Trustees) Law of 1958 of the Western Region of Nigeria, the executive head of the family was in law recognized as the trustee for the group. This law was the final step in making it irrelevant whether an individual, or a group with a trustee, is the "owner." Yoruba land tenure, both customary and modern, was thereby brought under the control of the courts administering an English-inspired type of law. What had once been a type of territoriality combined with a political organization based on a form of the state now had become an easily recognized form of "land tenure." The change was accomplished by declaring the kinship group to be a legal corporate aggregate, capable of holding a specific title, and having a trustee to act as its representative.

This particular transition to European models was without doubt the

[6] Lloyd, P. C., 1959b, p. 110.

F

easiest of the three that we shall consider here, but it is to be noted that
the transition is in all cases of the same order. Land among the Yoruba
entered the market. However, a modicum of traditional social organization was maintained by the device of turning the kinship group into the
corporate aggregate before the law.

The Yoruba were more fortunately situated to make the specific
change required of them than were the Tiv, specifically because, among
Yoruba, lineages were traced back only a few generations, and were
associated with one another by means of a "state"-like organization,
rather than by means of a comprehensive genealogy. Thus when the
nature of the Yoruba state and its accompanying law was changed, the
Yoruba lineage could, as a unit, survive in the new system.

4

It has been known for some time that Kikuyu land use and land tenure
was complicated by the fact that it embodied two principles and two sets
of local groupings which did not coincide.[7] The first of these principles
was that which gave rise to what has been called the estate system of the
Kikuyu, and which the Kikuyu themselves refer to as *githaka*. The
second principle is that which leads to demarcation of ridges, called
rugongo, which are the political units. Kikuyu country is crossed by
fast-flowing streams that have cut canyons out of the hillsides, so the
word "ridge" is to be taken more or less literally. Ridges were "gov-
erned" by a committee called "the council of nine," chosen by the
various councils of nine of its subordinate, territorially bounded units,
called "fire-units" or *mwaki*. These fire-unit councils were appointed by
the councils of nine of the village-group or *itura*. Matters concerning
law and warfare were handled by the smallest possible council of nine.
The British, on their arrival, put a chieftainship system on top of this
indigenous committee system. The ridge with its subdivisions was a
specifically compact and demarcated territorial unit, but it had nothing
to do with exploitation of the environment. That was rather a feature of
the estate system.

Thus, whereas the Tiv and early Yoruba emphasize the social system,
leaving the economic system as an epiphenomenon thereof, and whereas
Europeans emphasize the economic system, leaving the system of local
groups more or less as an epiphenomenon, the Kikuyu have quite completely separated the two aspects of land, and have in fact two maps or
two sets of relationships between men and soil to take care of these two
different characteristics.

[7] Cf. Sluiter, G., 1960; Leakey, L. S. B., 1952; and Middleton, J. F. M., 1953.

Kikuyu divide themselves into nine non-localized, patrilineal clans. These clans are composed of a series of sub-clans called *mbari*, each group having a common ancestor. The sub-clan is a localized group; each has one or more "estates." Estates have recognized boundaries, and employ trees, ridges, stones, streams and the like as markers. Inalienable right to land in the estate is a condition of membership in the associated sub-clan.

A single "estate" might be laid out in such a way that it crossed several ridges. Land disputes were apparently settled by the councils of nine, not by the sub-clan heads.

The Kikuyu image for viewing the relationship between man and social groups on the one hand, and land on the other, is a complex one for foreigners because it is put into a kinship idiom which, in English at any rate, would seem to be highly fanciful. The analogy, if such it be, hinges on the complexity of the concept *mbari*. An *mbari* results when a lineage (*nyumba*) is in possession of an estate (*githaka*). The lineage plus the estate (*nyumba* plus *githaka*), taken as a unit, is the *mbari*. Both the people, organized as a patrilineal lineage, and the land area are "members" of the *mbari*. Kikuyu describe the *mbari* as "one person" comprising the kinship groups and the land. They say that the two parts of the *mbari* are the male lineage, and the female land. The image which the Kikuyu use to explain the *mbari* is the image of the married couple.

There are two sorts of *mbari*. The first is that which is formed by all Kikuyu, who are descendants of Gikuyu and Muumbi, the mythical first parents, with all of Kikuyu land as its *githaka*. The second is that which is formed by the descendants in the male line of more recent ancestors—usually no more than five or six generations removed from the living, and specific estates or *githaka* which have been purchased or inherited by the smaller lineage. This distinction becomes vital, as will become apparent, in matters pertaining to the sale and purchase of estates.

To the image of marriage is added that of descent, for there may be sub-lineages which hive off to form what might be called colonies, which are regarded as "sons" of the *mbari*. Pieces of the land may, furthermore, be sold outright to other lineages, which is regarded as analogous to marrying off a virgin daughter. Sluiter[8] has used the diagrams of Charts 7.2a and b to represent the Kikuyu ideas. Any piece of land sold is regarded as a virgin daughter for whom bridewealth has been received. Sale of the total *githaka* of any *mbari* is, however, the equivalent of divorce. Thus transfer of rights in land is considered a precise equivalent of transfer of rights in women. Rights in land and rights in women

[8] Sluiter, G., 1960, *passim.*

are, in some contexts at least, equated as a single type of "commodity."

There is a complicating factor, however. Those who are buried in the soil of the *githaka* must, by definition, be members of the *nyumba* if a true *mbari* is to result. The *nyumba* may be the whole Kikuyu tribe, seen in this context as the *nyumba* of Gikuyu and Muumbi, the two founding ancestors of all Kikuyu. Thus, land can be sold outright to any Kikuyu

CHART 7.2a. *The Kikuyu* mbari. *In the Kikuyu view, the* mbari *is a combination or marriage of the male lineage (P) and the female land (L).*

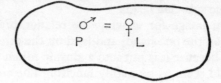

CHART 7.2b. *Expansion of the* mbari. *The lineage (nyumba) of the* mbari *becomes, with time, a collection of subordinate lineages, descended from different sons of the original founder. Each small lineage may leave the estate (githaka) of the parent* mbari, *taking up land elsewhere, thereupon becoming a full-fledged* mbari *of male lineage and female land. The Kikuyu analogy is to the marriage of sons.*

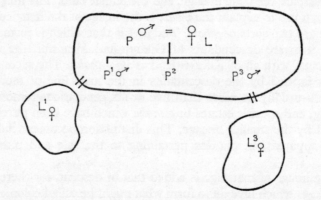

individual or groups; as with Yoruba, this makes little difference after a generation has passed, for the same rights can be held by a *nyumba* as by an individual. Obviously, the minimal necessity, that the persons buried in the ground are of the *nyumba* of the purchasers, has been achieved.

However, to sell land to non-Kikuyu is tantamount to deserting the ancestors, and can produce serious results. It is this aspect of the man-land relationship which was foremost in the Mau Mau uprising, since in Kikuyu terms any Kikuyu would have more right to the land than would any non-Kikuyu, unless the latter had undergone the adoption ceremony into the *mbari* of the tribe. Moreover, land that was formerly not "owned" by Kikuyu in this sense, that is, land which formed the *githaka* aspect of a Kikuyu *mbari*, could not be bought without first turning the land into Kikuyu land by a method of "adopting" the ancestors buried in it. Leakey[9] has described in detail the "adoption" ceremony.

Most non-Kikuyu land purchased by Kikuyu, and all that of which we have any record, was bought from the Ndorobo people. It would seem to be about the middle of the 18th century that Kikuyu began to cross to the southern bank of the Chania River into what is now Kiambu, an area controlled by the Ndorobo. The Kikuyu "bought" land from them by means of the adoption or birth ceremony of land, whereby the Ndorobo became Kikuyu while remaining Ndorobo. All the male members of the Kikuyu *nyumba* buying the land attended the ceremony; the individual Ndorobo who had rights in the land, accompanied by his wives and at least one son, also attended. By the exchange of seven oaths on either side, the Ndorobo was adopted into Kikuyu society, and because of this his ancestors buried there became Kikuyu—that is, they became adopted members of the *nyumba* of Gikuyu and Muumbi. It was then, and only then, that it became possible for the incoming Kikuyu small *nyumba* to buy land. The purchase was made in goats, which the Ndorobo used as bridewealth.

The Ndorobo, then, became a member of the *mbari* of all Kikuyu, and sold his land to an individual *nyumba* as its *githaka*. He did not, however, become a member of the smaller *nyumba*. Rather, he became its *muhoi*. A *muhoi* (plural *ahoi*) is a sort of client who is given specific, limited rights of tillage and pasturage within the *githaka* by the members of the *nyumba* associated with it.

One of the many difficulties which led to the Mau Mau uprising of the early 1950s was the problem of land, and the fact that the British and Kikuyu looked at the matter in very different terms. The British claim either to have taken up empty land, or to have bought land from the Kikuyu. To the Kikuyu, much of the "vacant" land was considered to be unused *githaka* belonging to some lineage; moreover Kikuyu land can be "bought" only by other Kikuyu, and the British had not been through the adoption or birth ceremonies. Therefore, the ancestors buried in the land taken over by the British were thought to be giving trouble to the whole Kikuyu nation.

The relocation of Kikuyu after the end of the "Emergency" ran into similar difficulties. Kikuyu land was, indeed, fragmented through sale and inheritance. But the fragmentation was tied intimately to the lineage

[9] Leakey, L. S. B., 1952, *passim*.

system and ultimately to the kinship system. The new "rationalization" in which every group received the same amount of land, of the same quality, as it had before, overlooks the tie of space to the social structure —even though it made a fetish of taking cognizance of it.[10] Ideas among Kikuyu may be changing, but even in the late 1950s, Kikuyu told incredulous land-law inquirers, "You are taking away my wife." And one old Kikuyu woman, looking at her new farmland which she admitted vastly superior to her old, cried out, "It is not my grandfather!"[11]

The "relocation" of the Kikuyu, by putting fundamental emphasis on the economic, so called "rational" aspect of land tenure, dealt a serious blow to social organization. Apologists may say that the old social organization is doomed in any case, and they may be right. Be that as it may, when "land tenure" of people who have traditionally seen land and kinship in a single set of images is "reformed," the kinship system and ultimately the whole social fabric also undergoes "reformation." New images must replace the old. It is a notoriously difficult situation; no matter how easily people accept new cultural items for carrying out old processes and old relationships, they resist the suppression or shattering of the old relationships when the form of the new ones is not clear.

5

Thus, even among Kikuyu, the African society in which buying and selling of bounded parcels of land seemed most nearly like that of Europeans, the problem is present in a virulent form. "Land reform" for the rationalization of the economy, whereby land is treated as a factor of production, means concomitant "reform" of the social structure, and in the imagery in which the spatial dimension of social organization is seen and valued.

It is clear that the generalization of Sir Henry Maine was right. In the trend from a society which holds social and political organization to be central, which Maine called "status," to one which holds organization of production to be central, which is one aspect of Maine's "contract," a fundamental, basic change is occuring. There is probably no single force greater than rapid change in "land tenure" for creating *anomie* by establishing new factual situations of neighborhood and local groups, while not affecting greatly the values of kinship and neighborhood.

Industrial society demands that the factor aspect of land be uppermost, and the only way Europeans and Americans have found to achieve this situation is through a social organization based on the principle of

[10] Kenya, Colony and Protectorate of, 1958, *passim.*
[11] B. E. Thomas, personal communication.

contract. Non-industrial African societies, for all their variety, have in common the fact that the spatial aspect of land is uppermost, and it is integrated by non-economic, certainly non-contractual, mechanisms. Industrialization apparently means the end of such forms of social integration. It will be interesting to see the extent to which the emergent nations develop in accordance with the hypothesis that industrialization means enlarging the sphere of contract as the principle of social organization, with concomitant shrinking of the spheres of other principles such as kinship or hierarchy.

Changes in the land custom of African countries have been induced by colonial powers, by economic development, and by the people of African nations in their drive toward industrialization and modernization. These changes usually stem from economic considerations, and draw political and social consequences in their wake. Probably there is no area of change to which less conscious attention has been given. And probably there is no area of change that has been more far-reaching.

8

Changes in Agricultural Productivity*

by Bruce F. Johnston
Stanford University

The best indication of the extent to which overall agricultural productivity in tropical Africa may have increased is provided by data concerning the growth of agricultural exports. During the past half century, production of export crops has emerged as an important element in the economies of virtually all countries of tropical Africa; with the exception of Northern Rhodesia, the Republic of the Congo and Sierra Leone, agricultural exports constitute the principal source of foreign exchange. Although there is no really satisfactory way to compare the importance of production of export crops and crops for domestic food consumption, some notion of the order of magnitudes of the two categories is suggested by the fact that the foreign exchange proceeds from agricultural exports, a little over 1.5 billion dollars for the years 1953–1955, represent about one-third of the landed cost of the 33 million tons of wheat flour that would be required to provide 2,000 calories daily per person for the population of tropical Africa.

Knowledge of the rate of increase of a country's agricultural exports is obviously not a sufficient basis for measuring the change in agricultural productivity. Under the conditions that have prevailed in tropical Africa since 1910, however, an increase in farm productivity can usually be inferred from an appreciable increase in agricultural exports. This inference rests on two propositions: first, that the expansion of export production in tropical Africa has typically represented a net addition to farm output, not a substitute for traditional cultivation of

* I am indebted to William O. Jones, R. J. Hammond, A. M. M. McFarquhar, and James Maina for valuable criticisms and suggestions. Miss Rosamond H. Peirce, Associate Statistician at the Food Research Institute, Mrs. Catherine Whittemore, and George Beckford have done most of the work of assembling the statistical material that I have used; and Mrs. Patricia Cedarleaf prepared the chart summarizing Africa's agricultural exports, 1909–1959.

food crops; secondly, that the expansion of export production has been achieved with only a relatively small increase in farm inputs.

Although it is impossible to test the first proposition directly against statistics showing the changes in food production that have been associated with the expansion of exports, indirect evidence suggests that the production of food has probably increased at about the same rate as the growth of population. The present dependence on cereals, roots or tubers, or plantains—cheap starchy staple foods of the sort that invariably bulk large in the diets of low-income communities—is so great that it is hard to believe that African diets 50 or 100 years ago were any more dependent on these starchy staple foods. We may infer, therefore, that there has probably been little qualitative improvement in the average diet; and it also seems unlikely that per capita calorie intake has increased appreciably. But neither is there any evidence that suggests a general reduction in per capita food supplies. On balance, the fragments of information available point to a modest improvement in the food position of most of the countries of tropical Africa. Improvements in transportation and the introduction and spread of new crops have almost certainly alleviated the scourge of famine and the pinch of pre-harvest hunger.[1]

Fears have often been expressed concerning the food shortages that would emerge as a result of the neglect of food crops owing to preoccupation with export production. In general, however, such fears have not been justified by experience. The sharp rise in the prices of staple foods in West Africa during 1948/49 and 1950/51 provoked considerable anxiety at the time, and gave currency to the view that the supply of food was particularly inelastic in tropical Africa. In retrospect it seems clear that these were largely due to special factors—a sharp increase in cocoa prices that led to an abrupt rise in consumer purchasing power and a substantial reduction in maize supplies, that resulted from a serious outbreak of maize rust that was introduced into West Africa from the Americas for the first time in 1949.[2]

The expansion of food supplies to keep pace with demand must be attributed almost entirely to enlarged domestic production. The percentage increase in food imports in recent decades has been substantial, but the absolute quantities involved are small. Even today food imports probably account for less than 3 per cent of total supplies in tropical Africa in terms of food calories, although enlarged imports have made a significant contribution to the growing requirements of certain cities such as Dakar and Douala.

[1] Johnston, B. F., 1958, pp. 193–203 and 209–210; Jones, W. O., 1959, pp. 224–226; 232–234; 241–243.
[2] Johnston, B. F., *op. cit.,* pp. 5–6 and 259–264; Poleman, T. T., 1961, pp. 122–124.

Because of an almost complete lack of quantitative evidence, it is difficult to document the proposition that the expansion of export production has been achieved with a relatively small increase in farm inputs. A good deal of qualitative evidence, however, including intensive studies of particular localities, seems to indicate that it has usually been possible to superimpose production of an export crop or crops on to the traditional agriculture without affecting food crop production adversely.

A particularly interesting example of a district in which the production of export crops has been grafted on to the traditional cultivation of food crops is provided by the Bongouanou District of the Ivory Coast, the object of an intensive sample survey in 1955/56. As is true of much of tropical Africa, this is a region where land has been abundant; even though the population of the district increased from some 15–20 thousand in 1910 to close to 65 thousand in 1955, shortage of land has not yet emerged as a significant problem. Bongouanou lies in the forest zone north of Abidjan, and the traditional food crops—yams and plantains—give high yields per unit of land and of labor. Much of the area is now planted to coffee and cocoa; in fact, these crops now require more labor than food crops, and account for more than half of the average farm income, including in this the imputed value of subsistence food production. The description in the survey reporting changes in local agriculture that have resulted from the introduction of cocoa and coffee cultivation emphasizes that this represented a "remarkable adaptation of the traditional cultivation practices which was accomplished without causing the farmers to neglect their food crops."[3] In attempting to explain why food crop production did not suffer even though the new coffee and cocoa crops became the principal economic activity, a number of factors are mentioned.[4]

> The tree crops are cultivated on the same land as the food crops which provide needed shade during the first three or four years after the cash crops are planted. On the other hand, in the traditional agricultural system certain periods of the year were fairly slack, being marked by the seasonal unemployment that still characterizes many African economies; and in the present system the heaviest labor requirements for cocoa and coffee— notably the harvest periods of August and December—occur precisely at these slack periods. In fact, it is probably the secondary activities, hunting and fishing, which have declined somewhat to the advantage of the new crops, a decline which in the case of hunting has probably been largely offset by the present widespread use of firearms.

[3] Cote d'Ivoire, Service de la Statistique, 1958c, p. 17.
[4] *Ibid.*, p. 18.

This explanation seems plausible, and the evidence makes it clear that the farm families in Bongouanou have continued to produce virtually all of their food requirements—89 per cent in terms of value and a still higher proportion of the food calories consumed.[5] Moreover, the factors mentioned probably apply to many of the areas in which agricultural export crops have been introduced.

An additional factor of considerable importance in a large part of tropical Africa, though it is apparently not applicable to the Agni population of the Bongouanou district, is related to the traditional division of labor by sex.[6] The agricultural activity of men in many African societies was traditionally limited to the heavy work of felling trees and clearing bush plots for food crops, the remaining work of producing and preparing food crops falling to women and children. The role of the man was that of a warrior and hunter. Even in an era when tribal warfare was frequent and game relatively abundant, this pattern of division of labor by sex probably left men a good deal of leisure time. As domestic peace came generally to prevail and game tended to become less abundant, the leisure of the male "labor force" undoubtedly increased substantially. In most instances in which export production has been introduced, however, traditional restrictions have been put aside, and the new cash crop has been a "man's crop." It would thus appear that the large quota of leisure that so often prevailed reflected in considerable measure a lack of sufficiently remunerative ways for a man to employ his labor. Hence, it is not clear to what extent this increase in the effective labor force resulting from male participation in the production of an export crop is truly an additional cost.

Expansion of export production has involved other costs that are difficult to evaluate but nonetheless need to be recognized. Sometimes the introduction of an export crop led to a change in the local food crops. In Ubangi-Shari, now the Central African Republic, the newly introduced cotton crop conflicted with the seasonal peaks in labor requirements for the traditional millet and sorghum crops. This was the chief factor underlying the expansion of manioc production at the expense of those cereal crops, a shift which represented deterioration in the quality of the diet from a nutritional and economic point of view.[7] The spread of plantain cultivation in Uganda has been attributed in part to the low labor requirements for that crop, which gave it an important advantage when cotton was being introduced.[8]

[5] *Ibid.*, p. 129.
[6] See Murdock, G. P., 1959, p. 255; Baumann, H., 1928, p. 303.
[7] Guillemin, R., 1956, pp. 281 and 299.
[8] Personal communication from Dr. David MacMaster, Kampala, May 6, 1961.

A still more intangible but probably more important cost associated with the expansion of export or other cash crops in some areas has been the exhaustion of soil fertility as a result of keeping land in cultivation for too long a period, or not allowing sufficient time for natural regeneration under a forest or bush fallow. In his discussion of the productivity of African labor, de Briey cites articles by Guilloteau, Malengreau, Humphrey, Dumont and others which, he claims, "have shown that the exhaustion of the soil and resulting drop in the incomes of African farmers are tending to become general."[9] There is scant evidence to support such a statement, and available evidence for limited areas is difficult to evaluate.[10] But continued population growth and further expansion of production for export will in time necessitate the development of more intensive farming systems that will maintain soil fertility by the use of cover crops, fertilizers, or other methods.

It seems likely, however, that for much of rural Africa this sort of intensification of agricultural production is still not economically justified. Many of the critical appraisals of African farming methods represent the viewpoint of technicians and conservationists, who give insufficient weight to the economic aspects of the problem. Such critics have also failed to appreciate the extent to which traditional practices are adapted to the physical environment of tropical Africa, and the economic conditions that have existed and still exist throughout much of the continent.[11] In the economist's view it may well be advisable to "mine the soil" for a period of time in order to increase incomes and foreign exchange earnings during the early stages of development, whereas in the eyes of the conservationist "mining the soil" is *ipso facto* a heinous crime. In any event, it seems questionable whether serious erosion resulting from expansion of export production is a problem of wide importance in tropical Africa; and experience in Kenya suggests that it may be possible to make good erosion damage more rapidly than had been anticipated.[12]

Even when allowance is made for the direct and indirect costs involved, it seems clear that the expansion of export production has largely

[9] De Briey, P., 1955, p. 123.
[10] Guilloteau, J., 1950, pp. 91–100, stresses particularly the deterioration of soils in Senegal as a result of persistent cropping to peanuts followed by millets or sorghum and the "sterilization of the soil" and development of lateritic crusts in the Fouta Djallon of Guinea. B. Floyd (1960) and others have stressed the seriousness of problems of erosion in Southern Rhodesia. For a brief review of some of the facts and views that have been expressed concerning the extent and seriousness of soil deterioration and erosion in western tropical Africa, see B. F. Johnston, 1958, pp. 9–11, 64–65, 238–239, and 268–272.
[11] Jones, W. O., 1961, pp. 9–10.
[12] Kenya, Colony and Protectorate of, Ministry of Agriculture, 1956, p. 7.

been a net addition to farm output. It is impossible to measure the rate
of change, but the considerable expansion of exports since 1910 does
undoubtedly reflect an appreciable increase in agricultural productivity.
Furthermore, these agricultural exports have made a highly strategic
contribution to furthering economic development in tropical Africa—
in providing foreign exchange, in generating increased incomes, in
furthering the spread of a money economy, and in stimulating the
development of transportation and communications. The significance
of enlarged export production varies considerably from country to
country; and there have been large fluctuations in the incomes derived
from these crops as a result of variations in their prices on world markets.
A summary picture of the expansion of agricultural exports is given in
Chart 8.1 A-I, which shows annual exports of nine major commodities
for the period 1909–1959 for the countries in which these exports were
significant.[13]

It is important to consider why expanded production of export crops
has provided the principal opportunity for increasing the productivity
of African agriculture. Measured agricultural productivity is a ratio of
agricultural output, aggregated by money value, to some measure of
inputs. Since there is only limited scope for increasing this ratio by
reducing inputs, the availability of market outlets which can absorb
enlarged production of agricultural commodities is a necessary condition
for achieving an increase in productivity. Otherwise, the increase in the
value of agricultural output will be small relative to the physical expansion of production; indeed, enlarged production may even reduce the
value of agricultural output if the expanded supplies lead to sharp
declines in the prices of important commodities. Production of export
crops, however, has been expanded to cater to an existing world market,
and expanded shipments of commodities such as coffee and rubber by
an individual African country have been easily absorbed with only
limited impact on the world price.

In contrast to the market for export crops, enlarged demand to
absorb increased production of food crops for domestic consumption
depends upon population growth, increased per capita consumption, in
value terms, by food producers and by a growing non-farm population,
or displacement of food imports. In most countries that have achieved
substantial economic progress, a huge increase in the absolute and relative size of the non-farm population has been the really important way

[13] The cocoa series is extended through 1960 to show the important expansion of
exports in that year. The sources on which Chart 8.1 is based were described in an
Appendix Note to the mimeographed version of this paper presented at the
Conference.

CHART 8.1(A-I). *Agricultural Exports of Selected African Countries, 1909-59.* (*Thousand metric tons*).

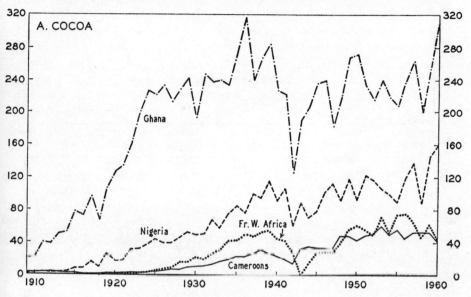

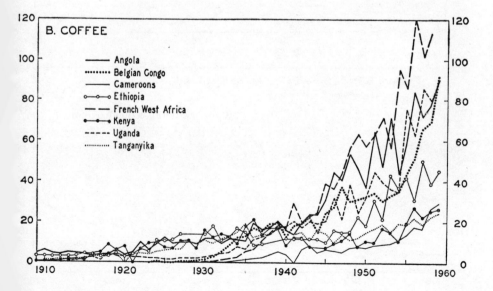

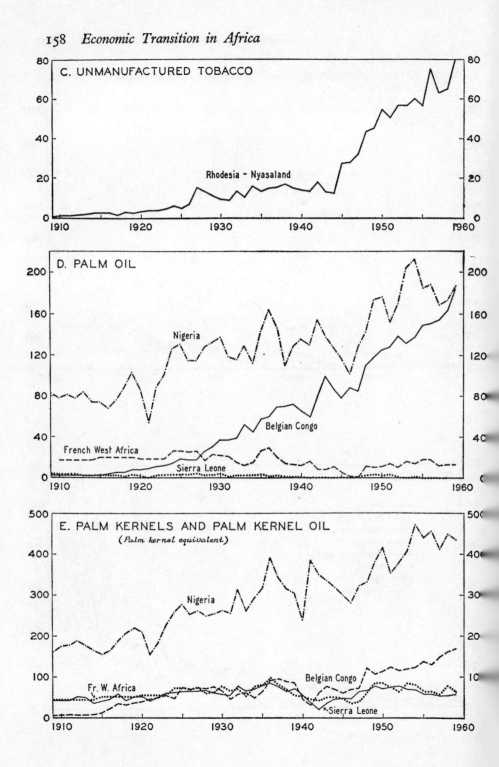

C. UNMANUFACTURED TOBACCO

Rhodesia – Nyasaland

D. PALM OIL

Nigeria

Belgian Congo

French West Africa

Sierra Leone

E. PALM KERNELS AND PALM KERNEL OIL
(Palm kernel equivalent)

Nigeria

Fr. W. Africa

Belgian Congo

Sierra Leone

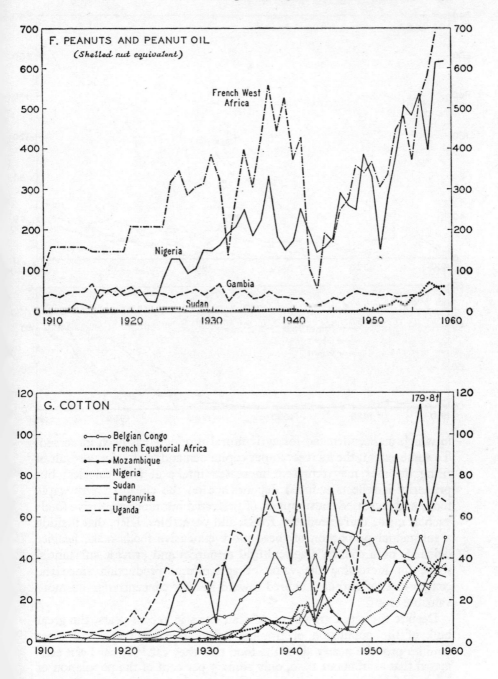

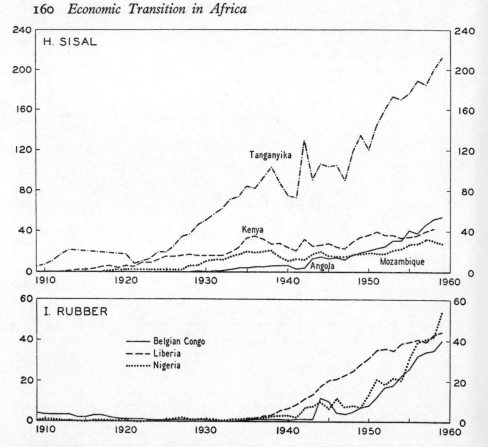

in which market demand for agricultural products has been increased. To some extent, the increase in per capita demand for food as a result of rising incomes may represent increased intake of food calories; but primarily it reflects reduced dependence on the cheap starchy staple foods and increased consumption of preferred but more expensive foods such as meat, dairy products, fruits, and vegetables. Diets that include a substantial proportion of these more expensive foods make heavier demands on a country's agricultural resources and provide substantial scope for increasing the value of agricultural production since the composition of output is altered toward heavier concentration on more valuable crops.

Despite the rapid growth of African cities in recent years, the great bulk of the population of tropical Africa remains rural, and most families produce nearly all of the food that they eat.[14] It has been estimated that as of about 1950, only some 5 per cent of the population of

[14] See Table 11.5., p. 258, *infra*.

TABLE 8.1. *Prewar and Postwar Population of Selected Cities of Tropical Africa* (*Thousand persons*)

City	Country or Territory	Pre- war (a)	Post- war (a)	Per- centage increase
Abidjan	Ivory Coast	10 (1931)	128 (1955)	1180
Accra	Ghana	70 (1931)	165 (1954)	136
			388 (1960)	454
Addis Ababa	Ethiopia	150 (1959)	400 (1952)	167
Bamako	Mali	20 (1931)	100 (1951)	400
Bangui	Ubangi-Shari	14 (1937)	85 (1957)	507
Brazzaville	Republic of the Congo	40 (1937)	99 (1957)	148
Conakry	Guinea	7 (1931)	53 (1951)	657
Dakar	Senegal	93 (1936)	231 (1955)	148
Dar-es-Salaam	Tanganyika	34 (1937)	99 (1952)	191
Douala	Cameroun	28 (1931)	118 (1951)	321
Freetown	Sierra Leone	55 (1931)	77 (1956)	40
Ibadan	Nigeria	387 (1931)	459 (1952)	19
Kano	Nigeria	89 (1931)	130 (1952)	46
Khartoum	Sudan	45 (1938)	93 (1956)	107
Lagos	Nigeria	126 (1931)	312 (1956)	148
Leopoldville	Republic of the Congo	36 (1938)	300 (1955)	733
Luanda	Angola	40 (1934)	190 (1955)	375
Monrovia	Liberia	10 (1938)	41 (1956)	310
Nairobi	Kenya	65 (1939)	210 (1956)(b)	223
Salisbury	Southern Rhodesia	33 (1936)	168 (1956)(b)	409

General Note: Data for postwar years from United Nations, Statistical Office, 1957, *Demographic Yearbook 1957*, pp. 150–151, with the following exceptions: Bangui from French Equatorial Africa, Haut Commisariat, 1959, *Afrique Equatoriale Française Economique et Sociale, 1947–1958*, p. 8; Accra from Ghana, Office of the Government Statistician, 1960, *Quarterly Digest of Statistics*, June 1960, p. 1 (this is the provisional estimate from the 1960 census; the mid-1959 estimate of Accra's population given in Ghana, Ministry of Finance, 1960, *Economic Survey 1959*, p. 47, was 208,000); and Bamako, Conakry, and Douala from France, Ministère de la France d'Outre-Mer, 1957, p. 27. Prewar data from Yust, Walter, ed., 1942, *Encyclopedia Britannica World Atlas*, pp. 182–211, except for Abidjan, Bamako, Conakry, and Douala, which are from France, Ministère d'Outre-Mer, 1957, p. 27, and Accra, which is from Gold Coast (Ghana), Office of the Government Statistician, 1950, *Census of Population, 1948, Report and Tables*.

Notes to Table:
(a) Figures in parentheses are the year of census or estimate.
(b) These figures apply to the urban agglomeration.

Middle Africa was to be found in cities of 20,000 population or larger.[15] The data in Table 8.2 showing the proportion of able-bodied males engaged in wage employment outside of agriculture indicates that,

[15] Poleman, T. T., 1961, p. 121.

TABLE 8.2. *Percentage of Able-bodied Males Engaged in Wage Employment, Prewar and Postwar*

Country or Territory	Prewar		Postwar Percentage		
	Year	Percentage	Year	All Wage Earners	Excluding Agriculture and Forestry
Belgian Congo	1938	19.9	1954	38.1	29.3
French Equatorial Africa	—	—	1954	13.1	9.7
French W. Africa	1936	4.8	1954	7.5	5.8
Ghana	1938	7.1	1952	16.5	14.6
Kenya	1938	21.0	1954	27.3	12.0
Uganda	1938	7.8	1954	16.2	12.0
Mozambique	1938	17.5	1953	32.5	24.1
Nigeria	1938	4.4	1953	3.8	3.2
Northern Rhodesia	1938	44.5	1953	61.0	52.0
Southern Rhodesia	1936	38.6	1951	55.5	6.6
Nyasaland	1938	41.7	1953	33.6	23.2
Sierra Leone	1938	4.9	1952	8.4	7.9
Tanganyika	1938	15.8	1954	15.8	5.0

General Note: Computed from population and employment data in International Labour Office, "The Development of Wage-Earning Employment in Tropical Africa," *International Labour Review*, Vol. LXXIV, September 1956, pp. 242, 248. The source emphasizes that many of the labor force estimates are only rough approximations and that in a number of instances the number of able-bodied males was approximated by simply taking 25 per cent of the estimated population in the appropriate year. The indicated decline between 1938 and 1953 in Nigeria is probably due to substantial under-estimation in the population figure for 1938 (20.6 million). See source for details concerning migrants and other categories included or excluded in the estimated number of wage earners in various territories. Particularly important in that regard is the fact that the figure for wage earners in Southern Rhodesia excludes migrants from other territories (246,772 in 1951, a slightly higher figure than for the indigenous wage labor force). It should also be noted that the figures for the wage labor force in Nyasaland and Mozambique included more migrants working in other territories than at home (152,000 out of 216,000 in the case of Nyasaland and 321,000 out of 458,000 for Mozambique to the 1953 estimates).

apart from Northern Rhodesia and the former Belgian Congo, only a small fraction of the population is dependent upon purchased food.[16] Among the regions of specialized agricultural production, the cocoa region of Western Nigeria appears to be the only one where a sizeable fraction of family food requirements are purchased.[17]

[16] P. 162, *supra*.
[17] Johnston, B. F., 1958, pp. 16–18.

Although urban areas and mining and industrial centers have provided a growing market for an increasing number of African farmers, this outlet is still small relative to the value of agricultural exports. Accra is an important example of a city in which food requirements have increased enormously; the city's population increased more than five-fold between 1931 and 1958. Nevertheless, the farm value of indigenous foods supplied to the Accra market in 1958, which can be estimated very roughly at between $25 and $40 million, was still fairly small compared to the export market for Ghanaian cocoa—$175 million in 1958.[18]

In economically advanced countries, a rise in labor productivity and per capita incomes in the agricultural sector has also been accompanied by a reduction in the farm labor force. Expansion of manufacturing and other non-agricultural sectors has not proceeded far enough in tropical Africa to provide substantial opportunities for employment outside of agriculture. Thus, although it is theoretically possible for a rise in the productivity of labor in agriculture to be associated with little or no change in the level of output but rather with a reduction in labor inputs, this factor has not been of much importance. Among the countries of tropical Africa, it is only in Northern Rhodesia and the former Belgian Congo that a sizeable fraction of the labor force has found employment outside of agriculture.[19] Further gains in agricultural productivity and economic progress generally will, of course, depend upon expansion of output and employment in the non-agricultural sectors as part of the "structural transformation" that characterizes the process of economic development, a point to which we will later return.

2

Although measurement of changes in farm productivity in tropical Africa is not yet possible, a good deal can be said about the ways in which farming techniques and the organization of agricultural production have changed. Broadly speaking, it is possible to identify four ways in which such changes have occurred. First, we can identify *spontaneous changes*, such as the introduction of a new crop, that have involved little alteration in traditional agricultural technique. Second, we can identify instances of *substantial modification of traditional agriculture* as a result of the application of modern technology and the introduction of new

[18] Alternative approximations were derived from T. T. Poleman's estimates of staple food consumption by Accra residents (1961, p. 167), based upon a produce movement census carried out by the Office of the Government Statistician, and by assuming that Accra residents spent 50 per cent of their income on indigenous foods, using an arbitrary figure of $225 for average per capita income.

[19] See Table 8.2, p. 162, and Table 11.4, p. 257.

inputs. Traditional agriculture has also been changed drastically by the launching of *large-scale projects,* such as the Gezira Scheme and the Office du Niger in the former French Sudan. The fourth type of change in patterns of agricultural production is represented by the introduction of *European-operated farms or plantations.*

Although they have accounted for the bulk of the increase in farm output in tropical Africa during the past half century, there is not a great deal to be said concerning the *spontaneous changes in traditional agriculture.* Their one common denominator is that they all represent a response to disequilibrating factors that have led to modification of the traditional agricultural system. The most important of these factors appear to have been knowledge of a new crop, population growth and increased food requirements, access to a market—domestic or export— as a result of improved transportation and reduction of the male labor force in agriculture in certain areas, owing to the absence of adult males employed as migratory workers in mines, on European farms, or in industry.

The nature and extent of the spontaneous changes in response to these various disequilibrating factors has varied greatly; and our understanding of these changes is extremely limited. The adoption of new crops such as manioc or maize that give a higher yield, require less labor, especially at seasonal peaks of activity, or that are less exacting in their soil requirements has clearly been of great importance. The area under cultivation has been increased, making possible a more or less proportionate expansion of agricultural output. Frequently, this has been done by lengthening the period of cultivation of a plot that has been cleared and by shortening the period of bush fallow. Such changes, particularly when combined with a change in the combination of crops grown, have often made possible an increase in productivity, since output could be expanded more than proportionately to the increase in labor inputs.

This type of spontaneous change in African agriculture has, of course, been in progress for centuries, as is evidenced by the early adoption of the Southeast Asian complex of food plants and by the subsequent introduction and spread of manioc, maize, and other New World crops. But the extent and rate of these spontaneous changes increased greatly during the colonial period, if only because two of the major disequilibrating factors—the expansion of opportunities to participate in the money economy through sale of crops or labor and the acceleration of population growth—have become really important. These changes, individually so unimportant but in aggregate such a dominant factor, have been so numerous and so diverse that they tend to be ignored. To give an adequate treatment even of those areas that have been studied and described would be a huge task.

Two examples must suffice. In the Ghanaian town of Ejura, located some 50 miles north of Kumasi on the highway to the Northern Territories, within a relatively short period after the opening of the highway, the local farmers had expanded their output substantially and were taking advantage of the low freight charges on southbound traffic. By 1930, some 75 per cent of the yam crop and half of the maize output were being commercialized.[20] The response of the African farmers in the vicinity of Jinja, in Uganda, to increased opportunity has been recorded by E. H. Jones in connection with the failure of an ambitious scheme for mechanized cultivation of food crops.[21]

> In the first half of 1949 the then Governor of Uganda directed that preliminary investigations be carried out into a scheme for the bulk production of African foodstuffs by mechanization on an area of land in the vicinity of Jinja. It was considered desirable to plan for the feeding of 5,000 employed labourers and on this basis it was estimated that 5,000 acres farmed on a 6 year rotation of three years cropping and three years rest would produce enough starch and vegetable protein to feed this number....
>
> At this time the main consideration behind the urgency to start this scheme was the assumed need to provide food for the large labour force which would be employed in the development projects being undertaken at Jinja. *It was assumed that peasant farmers in the vicinity would not be able to meet the increased demand for foodstuffs which would arise.*

Fortunately, the farmers in the vicinity were able to meet the increased demand for foodstuffs, because only 750 acres had been cleared when the scheme was wound up in 1954 after four years of heavy losses.[22]

Substantial modification of traditional agriculture resulting from the introduction of new technology and new inputs covers a wide range of innovations, including (1) compulsory introduction of new cash crops, (2) changes in agricultural techniques as a result of the impact of agricultural research and extension-education activities, (3) systematization and improvement of existing practices by settlement or re-settlement schemes such as the *paysannats indigènes* in the former Belgian Congo, (4) introduction of plowing with animal draft power, (5) irrigation projects and (6) mechanization schemes.

Changes resulting from compulsory introduction of new crops or from the impact of extension-education activities obviously cannot be

[20] Hunter, T., and Danso, T. V., n.d., pp. 218 and 223.
[21] Jones, E. H., 1960, p. 75. Italics in original.
[22] *Ibid.*, pp. 78–81.

differentiated sharply from the "spontaneous changes in traditional agriculture" discussed above. The initial introduction and spread of cocoa in the Gold Coast at the end of the 19th century was an important example of spontaneous change relating to an export crop. Almost from the beginning, however, the introduction of cocoa in the Gold Coast was facilitated to some extent by a limited amount of research and dissemination of information by government and by mission stations. In the years since World War II government agricultural programs have had much greater impact on cocoa production in Ghana. The large-scale campaign against swollen shoot disease was a major factor in controlling a grave threat to the country's cocoa industry. Government programs for spraying and for encouragement of spraying and related control measures by individual farmers appear to have had considerable success in reducing the adverse effect on cocoa yields of capsid bugs and black pod disease. These measures have apparently been major factors accounting for the upsurge in cocoa production in Ghana during 1959 and 1960.

The introduction of cotton in Uganda early in the present century provides another example of how a profitable export crop can be grafted on to the traditional food economy. This seems clearly to have been an example of a "substantial change." A new "input"—compulsion by government and the local chiefs—was involved, and organized research, seed distribution, extension, and planting regulations had a fairly important impact on the Uganda cotton industry, especially following the 1907 crisis when serious problems arose in marketing Uganda cotton on world markets owing to the bad reputation it had acquired.

The Uganda cotton industry illustrates some of the salient features of the superimposition of an agricultural export crop on a traditional system. After a period of testing various crops, it was found that American Upland varieties of cotton could be grown successfully in Buganda and other areas and thus provide the promising cash crop that had been eagerly sought as a source of foreign exchange and as a base for tax revenues. Seed farms were established to supply seed to the local farmers, and as early as 1908 the government issued instructions on the approved methods of planting and cultivating the new crop. The country's first cotton experiment station was established in 1911, and research activities relating to the selection, breeding, hybridization, and cultivation of cotton were intensified over the years.[23] This basic pattern of introducing an export crop, which is then incorporated with its associated technology into the traditional farming system, is one that is common to a number of export crops in various countries and terri-

[23] See Nye, G. W. and Hosking, H. R., 1940, pp. 183–185; Nye, G. W., 1940, pp. 207–208.

tories. It has been substantially repeated in Uganda itself with the introduction of coffee, which has come to rival cotton as the country's leading crop.

Three major programs have been launched to systematize and increase the efficiency of African agriculture by settlement or resettlement schemes. The first of these was the program in the former Belgian Congo for establishing *paysannats indigènes*, which began to be promoted actively from about 1948.[24] The *paysannats indigènes* organized in various regions of the Congo have varied considerably, but the basic idea has been to evolve an improved and more stable version of "Bantu agriculture." The technical arrangements incorporated in the *paysannats* were based on a recognition of the special problems that arise when tropical forests are cleared for cropping and the soils are exposed to direct sunlight and rain, with a resulting rise in soil temperatures and rapid loss of humus. The customary long fallow of natural regeneration is employed to restore the fertility and structure of the soil following a period of cultivation, but the prescribed agricultural pattern modifies the traditional shifting cultivation in a number of respects. Frequently the rotation of fields is systematized according to a "corridor system", with the land divided into strips about 100 meters wide. Forest strips are left on each side of the cultivated strips to facilitate natural regeneration when the cropped area is returned to fallow. Under this systematic pattern of assigning fields with a prescribed rotation of crops, shifting cultivation becomes stabilized farming. It thus facilitates the establishment of marketing and processing facilities as well as community services such as schools and dispensaries.

The plans devised by INÉAC (*l'Institut National pour l'Étude Agronomique du Congo Belge*) for a technically sound and economical solution of the special problems of tropical agriculture also followed the example of "Bantu agriculture" in avoiding unnecessary tillage and using mixed and succession crops to keep the soil shaded most of the time and to extract nutrients from different soil levels. In addition, the INÉAC research program has stressed (1) plant breeding and selection of improved varieties, (2) study of improved agricultural techniques with respect to such practices as time of planting, spacing of plants, and the use of composts, (3) determination of the most suitable combination or sequence of crops and the positioning of crops in a field in relation to their requirements for sunlight and (4) measures for the control of insects and plant disease. The systematic layout of the fields in the *paysannats indigènes* and the technical supervision which was part of the paysannat program provided an environment that was particularly

[24] For references to more detailed discussions, see Johnston, B. F., 1958, p. 274.

favorable to the introduction of improved agricultural practices developed by the INÉAC research stations. By 1956 approximately 150,000 families had been settled in *paysannats indigènes*, and the number was to be tripled within a decade. It is reported, however, that in the period since independence most of the families have left their *paysannat* holdings because of uncertainty with respect to their tenure rights.[25]

The Native Land Husbandry Act, which was enacted in Southern Rhodesia in 1951, defined "in terse legal terms a nation-wide program of those changes considered necessary if a harmonious and viable relationship between man and land was to be achieved in the reserves."[26] An accelerated program to implement the Native Land Husbandry Act was launched in 1956 as "a five year plan that will revolutionize African agriculture"; however, owing to technical and financial difficulties, the plan period was subsequently extended to seven years, to be fully implemented in 1962.

Several distinct considerations motivated the Native Land Husbandry Act. On the one hand there was keen concern in Southern Rhodesia over the deterioration of agricultural land in the native reserves. Overstocking and shortening of the fallow period under the pressure of population growth had caused serious problems of erosion. It was estimated that between 1902 and 1953 the population in the native reserves increased threefold and that the cattle population in the reserves rose from 55 thousand to 1.8 million.[27] In addition, fragmentation of the available land into uneconomical units had aggravated the problem of agricultural inefficiency.

The territorial government was convinced that prompt and drastic measures were needed to halt the process and to introduce improved agricultural practices that would insure the conservation of agricultural resources. Moreover, it had reached the conclusion that a gradual program to introduce improved agricultural methods in the reserves by education and persuasion would not be sufficient.[28] Finally, it was considered important to raise agricultural output and incomes in the native reserves not only to improve the economic welfare of the African population, but also as an attack on the social problems that had arisen as a result of the system of migrant labor that had evolved in Southern Rhodesia. Typically, some 50 per cent of the able-bodied males were absent from their homes at any one time under the arrangement commonly described as keeping one foot in the reserve and one foot in the modern, money economy. The framers of the act envisaged a transi-

[25] Personal communication from Daniel Biebuyck, November 17, 1961.
[26] Floyd, B. N., 1960, p. 1.
[27] Southern Rhodesia, 1955, p. 29.
[28] *Ibid.*, p. 1.

tion to a situation in which farm families would operate economic units as a full-time, stable, and remunerative activity while those engaged in wage-employment would become a settled labor force. It was further anticipated that the increased productivity attainable with continuity of employment would make it possible for employers to pay a wage sufficient for the worker to maintain himself and his family in the community where he worked and thereby lessen the social and moral problems that arose when families were divided and single men led a rootless existence in the city while leaving their families in the rural village.

The Native Husbandry Act was expected to achieve its multiple goals, essentially through the conversion of "what is predominantly a 'squatter' system at bare subsistence level to a peasant farming structure operating in a market economy."[29] This was to be accomplished by the registration of individual rights in the land, subject to regulation and supervision designed to prevent further fragmentation of land holdings, and by measures to improve farming practices and prevent overstocking. During a transitional phase, such practices as communal grazing were to be maintained because of the prohibitive costs of the necessary demarcation, fencing, and provision of water. However, regulation of the total number of livestock in a given area was to be enforced, and pro rata reduction of herds carried out where necessary. The regulation of farming practices extended to such details as contour terracing, crop rotations, manuring, and general farm practices.

Implementation of the act begins with a survey of the physical and human resources of the area to be improved, thereby providing a foundation for detailed allocations of land suitable for cropping or only for grazing to individual cultivators. Prior to allocation, facilities such as roads and water supplies are provided, and villages are relocated on new sites considered to be suitable. After implementation, provision is made for inspection and for appropriate means of ensuring compliance with the requirements imposed by the government.

Such a fundamental transformation of the traditional agricultural system was bound to provoke strong criticism. In Southern Rhodesia, the problem of implementation was doubtless further aggravated by the suddenness of the transition, by the heavy reliance placed on regulation by a European administrative staff, and by the political issues surrounding the Land Apportionment Act, which allotted to 200,000 Europeans some 50 per cent of the total land area, while reserving 35–40 per cent for the African majority. A balanced evaluation of successes and failures under the act, even if it was possible, would involve the examination of issues far beyond the scope of our topic.

[29] *Ibid.*, p. 4.

The third of these major programs to systematize and increase the efficiency of African agriculture by a settlement or resettlement scheme was the so-called "Swynnerton Plan" launched in Kenya in 1954. This "plan to intensify the development of African agriculture" was similar to the program introduced in Southern Rhodesia by the Native Land Husbandry Act, in that it provided for the creation of consolidated farm units which gave individual farmers security of tenure and incentive to improve their holdings. There are also similarities in that the farm planning or farm layouts emphasized the introduction of an agricultural system that would maintain soil fertility and avoid soil deterioration or erosion.

The Swynnerton Plan appears to differ from the program in Southern Rhodesia, however, in two important respects. To a much greater extent than in Southern Rhodesia the program in Kenya depended upon voluntary acceptance of land consolidation and related measures by the African community concerned. Secondly, greater emphasis seems to have been given in the Swynnerton Plan to introducing farm plans or layouts that would result in really substantial increases in agricultural income.[30] The Department of Native Affairs in Southern Rhodesia estimated that with complete implementation of the program of land consolidation and the associated extension work, crop production would be increased by 50 per cent in five years and livestock output by the same amount in eight years. Cash income from the sale of produce was expected to increase threefold, reaching a level of about £40 per family at the end of eight years.[31]

The Swynnerton Plan set its sights considerably higher, aiming at raising income from cash sales of produce to at least £100 per family; and some of the outstanding consolidated holdings attained a net income of £400 to £600 a year.[32] It was recognized that the average cultivator would not be easily convinced of the value of "sound farming practice" merely because of its effect on soil structure and control of erosion, especially since the improved farm practices increase substantially the physical effort required of the farmer. The problem and its solution have been tersely summarized by Clayton:

[30] In the terminology used in Kenya, "farm planning" refers to the preparation of a detailed plan designed to fit the resources and requirements of a particular farm, whereas a farm layout is a standard pattern for crop rotations and related farm management arrangements to be applied to all farms in a locality. Owing to shortage of field staff, major reliance was placed on the introdution of simple farm layouts rather than the more time-consuming operation of devising individual farm plans.

[31] Southern Rhodesia, 1955, p. 11.

[32] Brown, L. H., 1957, p. 71; Kenya, Colony and Protectorate of, Ministry of Agriculture, 1958(?), App. Table II.

[33] Clayton, E. S., 1959, p. 147.

The problem was to persuade the cultivator to adopt sound farm practices on his consolidated holding despite his ignorance of basic principles and his natural disinclination for more work. It was resolved by including in the farm plan a high-value cash crop, for example, coffee, tea, pyrethrum, pineapples, etc. The advantages of a more secure tenure and of increased cash incomes following from consolidation and farm planning were quickly recognized and in certain areas demands to effect these reforms were soon stretching the administration's limited resources.

Similarly, the plan provided for the introduction of improved, highly productive livestock so that the planted grass fallow or ley, which is a central element in the farming system applied on the consolidated holdings, would not only play its key role in maintaining fertility and preventing soil erosion but would yield a substantial cash return as well.[34]

One of the most basic features of the plan was that it went beyond general policies such as the changes in land tenure referred to above, and outlined specific crops and farming systems for each of the major ecological zones of Kenya. The program for consolidation and enclosure of holdings was only to be applied in areas of "high potential," with measures of an entirely different character being specified for the semiarid pastoral areas. Specific targets were set for the "phased development of cash crops" in the zones in which research and experience had demonstrated that these crops could be successfully grown. Planting material has been distributed by nurseries, the extension service has provided technical assistance on production methods and quality control, and marketing has been facilitated by establishing cooperative societies, marketing boards, and processing plants.[35]

In a relatively short period, the Swynnerton Plan provided impressive evidence of its success. Progress was most rapid in the Central Province, where 227 thousand farms, comprising 1.1 million acres, had been established on consolidated holdings by 1960. This means that land consolidation in this province had been virtually completed in about five years, whereas it had been expected to take fifteen to twenty years.[36] Elsewhere, progress was much slower, but interest in land consolidation was seen to spread.

An impressive feature of the program was the performance of the African farmers in producing high-quality Arabica coffee and other demanding export crops, and in managing high-quality livestock.

[34] Personal communication from R. J. M. Swynnerton, Nairobi, May 9, 1961.
[35] Kenya, Colony and Protectorate of, Department of Agriculture, 1954, pp. 13–14; *ibid.*, Ministry of Agriculture, 1958, p. 2.
[36] *Ibid.*, p. 46; Clayton, E. S., 1959, p. 148.

Because of fear that the high reputation of Kenya coffee would be spoiled, reinforced no doubt by the conservatism of a vested interest, it was not possible for an African farmer to obtain a license for production of Arabica coffee until about 1950. Since that time, coffee production in African areas increased dramatically, and by 1960 there were 105 thousand African growers producing Arabica, their production increasing as follows:[37]

Item	51/52	52/53	53/54	54/55	55/56	56/57	57/58	58/59	59/60
Quantity (ton)	83	180	338	750	781	1,522	2,047	3,642	4,607
Value (£M)	34	78	172	280	323	788	891	1,432	1,793

Another indicator of the success of the Swynnerton plan was the fact that attacks leveled against the plan seemed to be largely confined to criticism of certain aspects of its implementation, particularly charges of irregularities and favoritism in the allocation of land in carrying out consolidation. The basic ideas of the program appeared to be widely accepted, with a fairly general recognition of its impact on farm incomes.

It is important to recognize that a number of special conditions contributed to the success of the plan. The Mau Mau Emergency was responsible for a program of "villagisation" and for increasing the available field staff, both significant factors. Moreover, most of those who stirred up local opposition to land consolidation in the past were interned during the Emergency. Probably the most important elements were, however, that the plan itself was an intensification and acceleration of policies already tested, and that the increased activity was adequately financed by a grant of £5 million and further resources of £3½ million. This support made it possible to strengthen the agricultural field staff, expand nurseries, make loans and grants to support production and processing, and help develop marketing organizations. A fund of knowledge had been accumulated by Kenya's research stations and in the experience of European farmers that could be drawn upon to provide a basis for a technically sound plan for accelerated agricultural development. Finally, there was undoubtedly a pent-up desire on the part of the African population to undertake production of coffee and other cash crops that had long been restricted to European farmers.

Examples of substantial modification of traditional agriculture by the other types of change in farming methods referred to above—introduction of plowing with animal draft power, irrigation projects, and mechanization schemes—are too numerous to review in detail. It appears that the most widespread adoption of plowing with animal draft power has

[37] Kenya, Colony and Protectorate of, Department of Agriculture, 1961, and unpublished report, May 6, 1961.

taken place in Southern Rhodesia, where the use of plows by African farmers seems to have become common by the 1920's. Efforts to promote mixed farming and use of animal draft power were initiated in the Northern Region of Nigeria in the 1920's, but progress here was slow. Similar efforts were made to introduce the use of animal draft power in the Northern Territories of Ghana, in Guinea, and in the former French Sudan, where most of the rice area has come to be cultivated with animal draft power.[38]

The introduction of irrigation and mechanization has often taken the form of *large-scale agricultural projects*, usually involving some sort of partnership between the local people, the government, and a private or governmental corporation responsible for the operation of the scheme. By far the most important of the schemes of this nature is the Gezira Project, which led to a notable expansion of cotton production and exports in the Sudan in the years following 1925, when the Sennar Dam was completed.[39] The project, described in detail in Gaitskell's admirable study, has been an outstanding success as a highly productive investment that yielded large returns in raising incomes and export earnings in the Sudan, and in improving the level of living of those who participated in the scheme as tenants or laborers. It is also important to emphasize that the plan had the benefit of flat land admirably suited to irrigation and soil and climatic conditions favorable to the production of long-staple cotton, a high-value export crop that has generally been in strong demand in world markets.

The Office du Niger was created in 1932 as a public corporation to launch a large-scale irrigation project in the former French Sudan.[40] The original plans envisaged the cultivation of 500,000 hectares of cotton and 450,000 hectares of rice, but to 1960 only about 38,000 hectares have been placed under cultivation, most of the land being devoted to rice. The project has been continuously dependent upon annual subsidies from the French government. Despite the lack of information concerning costs and returns from the project, it seems clear that it has not been a profitable investment, and that the large financial and personnel resources devoted to the scheme have been completely out of proportion to its contribution to the economy of Mali and to the magnitude of the project which embraces only some four thousand families and 8,500 laborers. Soil conditions and other factors proved to be better suited to rice than cotton; but owing to the high cost of rail

[38] Barber, W. J., 1961; Johnston, B. F., 1958, p. 233.
[39] Gaitskell, Arthur, 1959; Hance, W. A., 1958, pp. 18–45.
[40] See Coyand, Yves, 1956, and other references cited in Johnston, B. F., 1958, pp. 231–232; also Food and Agricultural Organization of the United Nations, 1961.

transport in exporting rice to Dakar, Abidjan, or other potential markets, it is doubtful whether rice from the Office du Niger can compete on an economic basis with rice from Burma or other major exporting countries.[41]

Many other agricultural projects involving irrigation or mechanization, or both, were launched in tropical Africa after World War II. The failure of the Tanganyika Groundnut Scheme launched by Britain's Overseas Food Corporation in 1947 attracted much attention. In fact, there has come to be general recognition of the more obvious lessons of that experience—the need for adequate information concerning such basic elements as soils and rainfall and its variability, and the necessity of starting with a pilot-scale project because of the many unknowns that characterize African agriculture.[42]

The Niger Agricultural Project for mechanized production of sorghum and other food crops at Mokwa in Nigeria, another example of an unsuccessful project, has been examined in a valuable study by Baldwin.[43] Many factors contributed to the failure of this scheme, but one of the fundamental difficulties was the simple fact that investment of scarce resources in mechanized production of local food crops was bound to be uneconomic under the conditions that prevailed. The Damongo, or Gonja, Scheme for mechanized production of food crops in the Northern Territories of Ghana seems to have been a failure for much the same reasons.

A project for mechanized rice production in the Bonthe-Pujehun District of Sierra Leone stands out as one of the few examples of a successful mechanization project. This is an area of level grassland with rich and fertile soil replenished by annual flooding. The flooding is deep, but the land is dry enough during the dry season to support crawler tractors. Owing to the heavy grass cover and the short dry season, rice cultivation would be impossible without the heavy tractors used for clearing and preparing the seed beds. The mechanical cultivation is done on a contract basis with payment in kind at harvest time. There has been steady expansion of the area under rice, and the district is well on its way to becoming one of the main rice producing centres of Sierra Leone.[44]

[41] Special efforts have been made in recent years to develop improved techniques for cultivating cotton; the 1960–64 program for the Office envisaged a doubling of the cotton area (to 12,000 hectares) and a reduction in the area devoted to rice. Likewise, costs have been reduced by increased reliance on animal draft power rather than mechanical equipment. Cf. Food and Agricultural Organization of the United Nations, 1961, country report for the Mali Republic, pp. 178–183.

[42] Wood, A., 1950, pp. 231–240.

[43] Baldwin, K. D. S., 1957.

[44] See Johnston, B. F., 1958, pp. 227–236, for a discussion of these and other large-scale agricultural projects in western tropical Africa, and for more complete citations.

No attempt is made here to consider the agricultural changes in tropical Africa that have resulted from the introduction of *European-operated farms or plantations*. Production of export crops by European-operated farms or plantations has been of considerable importance in a number of countries. This has been conspicuously the case in Kenya, where European farms have accounted for nearly 75 per cent of the value of the country's agricultural exports. It was also true to a considerable extent of Tanganyika and the Congo and to a very great extent in Southern Rhodesia and Angola. European plantations or farms have accounted for most African exports of Arabica coffee, tea, pyrethrum, tobacco, sisal, and rubber. In Southern and Northern Rhodesia, Tanganyika, Kenya, and Angola, European farmers have also accounted for a substantial part of the commercial production of local food crops.

3

Most of the increase in total agricultural output during the past half century seems to have resulted from spontaneous changes in traditional agriculture and from the superimposition of an export crop and its associated technology on to the pre-existing food economy. Relative to their contribution to total agricultural output and its increase, a disproportionate amount of space has been devoted here, and in the literature generally, to settlement or resettlement schemes such as the Swynnerton Plan or the *paysannats indigènes* of the Congo and to irrigation and mechanization projects. There are, however, cogent reasons for giving close attention to these various approaches that have been adopted for substantially modifying the traditional farming systems in tropical Africa.

It is clear that it will become increasingly difficult to rely on the more or less spontaneous, "horizontal" expansion of output that has largely sufficed in the past. As a result of the accelerated growth of population and enlarged demand for cash crops, land is becoming increasingly a scarce resource; and the traditional techniques of shifting cultivation, which depend on a great abundance of land, are in the process of becoming untenable; indeed, those techniques have become untenable in certain areas, either because population density is exceptionally high or because the land is especially vulnerable to erosion. Technical difficulties arise because of the shortening of the fallow period which leads to a decline in soil fertility, reduced crop yields, and often to serious soil erosion.

Economic considerations emphasize the fact that the traditional shifting cultivation is not well suited to a commercially oriented economy.

G

Arrangements for bulking produce, for processing, and for transportation are difficult to rationalize because production takes place on scattered plots in forest or bush clearings which are cultivated for perhaps one to three years before the cultivator moves on to a new plot. Moreover, the strictly temporary occupation of the land under shifting cultivation, and the traditional tenure arrangements that can be roughly described as "communal," constitute an environment that is not conducive to agricultural improvement. There is little incentive for investing labor or other resources in improving land that is held only in temporary usufruct, and long-term planning and rational management of a well-defined farm unit is impossible. These factors have impaired the effectiveness of agricultural extension programs, and have limited the responsiveness of African farmers to technical innovations that would increase output and productivity.

There is no doubt that in the long run the pressure to modify existing farming systems will become increasingly strong and widespread. The real questions concern the rate of change and the nature of the modifications of these systems that is economical in different countries and in different farming districts. We do not know enough about the technical and economic results attainable by various approaches to agricultural development in tropical Africa to reach firm conclusions as to the most promising approach. And of course the great diversity of physical, cultural, and economic conditions means that no single approach would be optimal for all of tropical Africa. Nevertheless, past experience throws some light on the type of approach that is most appropriate, even though our understanding of the agricultural changes that have occurred is woefully inadequate.[45]

One important conclusion is that the ability of traditional agriculture to adjust to changed conditions and to expand output should not be under-estimated. Many of the large-scale agricultural projects that were launched since the second World War were based on the notion that efforts to enhance the efficiency of the existing agriculture would be too slow and uncertain and that a fundamentally different line of attack was needed. In the immediate postwar period this attitude was heavily influenced by the world shortage of food and other primary commodities; and resort to mechanical equipment was expected to make possible a large increase in agricultural output in a short period of time.

Experience in Africa and elsewhere suggests that the "required"

[45] The *Africa Survey* (1961) of the Food and Agricultural Organization is an interesting treatise on African agriculture and its relation to economic development. The project was carried through with great speed, however, and the survey report contains very little comparative analysis and evaluation of various approaches to agricultural development. See pp. 92–94.

expansion of agricultural output and productivity can be achieved mainly by introducing technological innovations within the framework of the existing labor-intensive methods of production, and with only modest requirements for capital and other resources that are particularly scarce in a developing economy. A number of general considerations indicate that the most promising and economical approach to increasing farm output and productivity lies in enhancing the efficiency of the existing agricultural economy by methods that emphasize achieving more effective use of existing resources of labor and land in the agricultural sector, and minimize requirements for the scarce resources, such as investible funds, foreign exchange, and certain types of entrepreneurial talent, that are indispensable for expansion of the non-agricultural sectors.[46]

Historical experience and certain theoretical considerations point to the conclusion that transformation of a country's economic structure, involving a secular decline in the agricultural sector and relatively rapid expansion of manufacturing and other non-agricultural sectors, is a necessary condition for cumulative and self-sustaining economic growth. This structural transformation that characterizes the dynamics of growth underscores the great importance and difficulty of capital accumulation in a developing economy. Requirements for capital to be invested in transportation, utilities, and communications, for the expansion of education and technical training, and for the creation and expansion of manufacturing enterprises are almost certain to strain the supply of funds available. Because of the sheer size of the agricultural sector and the lack of alternative sources of capital, it is usually impossible to achieve a "satisfactory" rate of economic growth unless the agricultural sector makes a net contribution to the capital required for investment in social overhead and for the expansion of secondary industry. This consideration also reinforces the proposition that agricultural output and productivity should be increased mainly through more effective use of the resources already in the agricultural sector and with only modest demands upon the scarce resources that are indispensable for industrial development.

This view of agricultural development points up the importance of "developmental services," such as agricultural research and extension-education programs, and the need to modify land tenure and other institutional arrangements that seriously impede the adoption of agricultural innovations. For a variety of reasons, relatively little effort has been made in the past to enhance the efficiency of the existing agricultural economy in tropical Africa by this type of emphasis on the intro-

[46] Johnston, B. F. and Mellor, J. W., 1961, *passim*.

duction of technological innovations. Agricultural research, especially in relation to food crops, has been so limited that frequently, "neither the teachers nor the specialists who advised them had sufficiently valuable technical improvements to propose." It has already been noted that certain characteristics of shifting cultivation and the traditional systems of land tenure make it difficult to carry out agricultural extension programs and weaken the incentive for land improvement and adoption of better practices. In addition, lack of funds, heavy reliance on expensive European agricultural officers, and language problems have restricted the intensity and effectiveness of agricultural extension activities. Moreover, the small degree of commercialization that characterizes a large part of African agriculture has limited the return to be anticipated from extension activities and has also limited the responsiveness of Africans to output-increasing innovations.

A number of these unfavorable factors, which have been important in the past, are in the process of changing, and there is reason to believe that significant gains in farm output and productivity can be achieved at modest cost. To do so will require intelligent and vigorous efforts to strengthen agricultural research and extension programs and to identify the most strategic opportunities for increasing productivity and output. The Swynnerton Plan in Kenya is of particular interest as an example of essentially this type of approach to agricultural development.

9

The Role of the Small Entrepreneur

by Margaret Katzin
Northwestern University

The indigenous economies of British and former British territories of Subsaharan Africa are, to varying degrees, in transition from subsistence to exchange economies. The functions of the commercial middle class have largely been carried out by Europeans, Levantines and East Indians. However, particularly in Ghana and Nigeria, where a complex trading system with markets and middlemen existed in pre-British times, Africans conduct almost all internal trade and are responsible for most of the collection of export products and the distribution of imported goods. African-owned businesses and workshops include building contractors, laundries, bakeries, brick and tile manufacturers, printing, confectionaries, light engineering shops, oil expressing plants, woodworking and weaving shops, transport by trucking and taxis, and auto repair shops, to name but some. Apart from government officials, members of the learned professions and employees of government and foreign-owned enterprises, Africans are employed as farmers, traders, processors of foodstuffs and produce, truck and taxi drivers, barbers, hairdressers, dressmakers, and rural and urban laborers. Except in the cities and towns, complete specialization is rare. Most adults engage in more than one occupation during the year, and almost everybody occasionally trades.

In West Africa, trade is conducted by individuals and trading firms. Some individuals keep shops,[1] but the great majority of them conduct their businesses in public markets, on the street, or from their homes. Firms, but with few exceptions, are owned by non-Africans, Europeans,

---

[1] Any place, other than a market stall, where goods are kept for sale, whether wholesale or retail, is called a "shop" in British Africa. The term "store," which is used in the United States to designate such establishments, almost always refers to a storage place for goods. This usage will be followed here.

Indians or Levantines. Those having substantial capitalization are engaged in foreign trade, the great bulk of which is done by European organizations which carry on two-way trade in imports and exports. Some African firms also both import and buy produce for export, but African, Levantine and Indian firms are small as compared to the great European trading concerns.

African trading organizations are typically one-man or one-woman enterprises, in the sense that they seldom reach a scale of organization involving the delegation of executive responsibility to employees who can conduct the business in the owner-operator's absence. The typical organization of the established trader in Onitsha in 1961 included the trader and a number of "boys," ranging in age from twelve years to the early twenties, who were both domestic servants to the master and apprentices in the trade. Most of them were unpaid, although this is changing; but the master obligates himself, usually orally but occasionally in writing, to assist the "boys" who complete the apprenticeship to establish themselves independently, either by a lump cash payment or extension of credit on goods, or both. In the past, most "boys" were from the master's family or village, but with time those from elsewhere came to be engaged on the recommendation of a trusted friend or fellow trader. Considerable traveling is involved in large-scale trade. Either the master leaves "boys" in charge of the shop or market stall and travels to distant markets himself, or trained "boys" may be sent on such errands or stationed for a time in a distant trade center, from which they communicate market information to the master, buy and send goods to him, sell goods sent by him, or both. In Onitsha, only one Nigerian trading organization could be found in which executive responsibility was delegated; in this case, the owner's principal subordinates were Europeans.

The scale of activity of these essentially individual traders ranges from that of itinerant peddlers and street vendors, who sell to final consumers in small quantities, to that of merchant wholesalers, or more usually wholesaler-retailers, with substantial amounts of capital, some of whom import at least part of their stock. Between the extremes are market traders and shopkeepers, whose transactions vary greatly in scale. Traders tend to specialize in import, export or internal trade, and within the various types, in certain lines of goods, although shifts to other lines offering greater possibilities of profit are common.

The primary object of most traders is not to change the system of trade but to advance their own position within the existing system, by building up trading capital, expanding the range of their trading contacts and thereby increasing their volume of trade. The biographies of typical successful women traders, most of whom do not read or write, indicate that they began as petty traders, gradually gained experience, accumulated capital and a sound credit rating, shifted to more profitable lines and finally became wholesaler-retailers, specializing in lines that were expected to yield the highest returns.[2] The successful male trader, as depicted in the literature, is usually literate, has had some previous experience in business or related occupations, conducts his business from a specialized establishment, such as a shop, and has accumulated a relatively substantial amount of capital before he sets up as an independent trader.[3]

In Onitsha, the careers of successful women traders follow the general pattern of women traders elsewhere in West Africa, but successful men traders differ in some respects. Though they are nearly all literate and conduct their businesses from shops, they entered trade in a small way with no previous business experience other than as "boys" serving a master, and built up their capital from such small beginnings as £5 or £10. In 1960–1961, of 34 Onitsha traders, each with capital of more than £1,000, 11 entered trade with less than £10; 6 with between £25 and £50, 5 with between £50 and £100; 3 with between £200 and £300; 3 with £300; and 1 with £475. Of two men engaged in truck transport, one entered business with £6 and the other with £50. Similarly, of five small manufacturing concerns, the beginning capital of one was £30, of another £50, of another, £70, of another £265; still another, the owner of which was helped by a wealthy brother, began with £2,000.

The indigenous populations of British territories of East and Central Africa have not moved nearly so far toward an exchange economy as have those of West Africa,[4] due to ecological, cultural and ethnic differences in the two areas. In pre-British times, household self-sufficiency was the rule in East Africa.[5] Trade was local, for the most part, and achieved by barter without the intervention of middlemen. The culturally dictated level of wants was met by subsistence production; the idea of profit was almost unknown, and there was no need for costs, in the economic sense, to be considered, or for habits of thrift or shrewdness in trade. Imported commodities were introduced by non-African traders, mostly East Indians who were equipped to handle foreign trade. As the volume of

[2] Leith-Ross, S., 1938, pp. 338ff; Comhaire-Sylvain, S., 1951, p. 177; Addae, G., 1956, p. 25.

[3] Garlick, P. C., 1959, *passim*; McCall, D. F., 1956, p. 40. Successful men traders in East Africa are similarly described by Wright, F. D., 1953, p. 24; Watson, Wm., 1958, pp. 207–208; and Leubuscher, C., 1944, p. 23.

[4] United Nations, 1954, p. 34.

[5] Cf. Herskovits, M. J., 1962, chapters 3 and 4, *passim*, esp. pp. 80–82.

trade grew, the numbers of non-Africans were augmented, and those who had come earlier and had accumulated capital expanded the range of their activities so as to secure and maintain a virtual monopoly in foreign trade. Possible African competition was reduced by the use of the licensing power by government to grant licenses to only a comparatively few Africans and to set fees above the ability of most Africans to pay.

By the time Africans had become familiar with the money economy and the new types of trade, non-Africans were entrenched and able to discourage African competitors. European settlers not only interfered with the growing of export crops by African farmers but competed with them in supplying foodstuffs to urban centers. As a result, Africans came to derive cash incomes mainly from labor for government or non-ndigenous enterprise, and the sale of export products. They thus participated in foreign trade chiefly as small shopkeepers and peddlers, who dealt in imported merchandise, and as small middlemen, buyers of export produce which they sold to larger-scale middlemen or exporters.[6] Regular internal trade through African markets and middlemen developed late, with the growth of urban centers, and was largely limited to supplying urban populations with African-produced foodstuffs.[7] Few traditional craft products were traded beyond the local community, but Africans came to do such work as bicycle and automobile repairing, building, truck and taxi driving and the like. As would be expected, indigenous entrepreneurs were fewer, and operated on a smaller scale than in West Africa.

2

Analysis of indigenous African entrepreneurship requires a broad definition of the term entrepreneur, since those devised for analysis of developed economies would exclude all but a few African business men.[8; 9] We propose an operational definition of the entrepreneur as "an independent self-employed manager, who carries the risk and claims the gains of an enterprise conducted with the object of obtaining money profits." "Manager," as used here, does not necessarily entail a high degree of administrative or organizational skill, but rather connotes the responsibility for all decisions in the conduct of a business in which subordinates are responsible only for carrying out orders and

[6] Hearn, H., 1956, *passim.*
[7] Cf. Nyirenda, A. A., 1957, *passim.*
[8] Cole, A. H., 1959, p. 6; Hoselitz, B. M., 1952, p. 98; Redlich, F., p. 223.
[9] Tax, S. (1953, p. 12), at the opposite extreme, uses the term "entrepreneur" to designate anyone who exerts efforts to earn cash income.

performing routine tasks. African entrepreneurs, other than farmers producing crops for sale, are nearly all engaged in trade or transport, but a few operate enterprises producing goods which require investment of capital and administrative skill above that of the independent craftsman and his "boys." Of African-owned enterprises of this sort in Onitsha, there are three bakeries with power-driven machinery and fleets of trucks, two small umbrella factories assembling imported parts, one phonograph record factory, one shoemaker and repairer using power-driven machinery, and several printing establishments.

As will be seen below, it is useful to distinguish between types of African entrepreneurs. We shall use the term "innovating entrepreneur"[10] to designate the person who conceives an idea and introduces a new element into the economy. This may be a totally new product, or one known elsewhere but previously unknown in the area, or a new use for a known product, or new markets for known products, or a new procedure, or a new type of economic organization.[11] The term "imitating entrepreneur" designates one who adopts a new economic practice after a local innovator has demonstrated it to be practical and profitable. The term "traditional entrepreneur" designates one who follows established practices.

There are three reasons why all African enterprises treated in this paper may be considered small. First, most African enterprises are anything but large by any definition, even smaller than the category "infinitesimal," used by Samuelson in his classification of American businesses.[12] Second, insufficient information exists on which a classification according to size of business can be based, such as amount of invested capital or volume of business. Third, though there are some African enterprises of substantial size, no details of their organization or operations are available other than the fact that they employ Europeans in executive positions.[13]

[10] The terms "innovating" and "imitating entrepreneur" are taken from Schumpeter and used in much the same sense. Cf. Clemence, R. V., and Doody, F. S., 1950, p. 9.
[11] The argument that the adoption of an element originating outside the indigenous economy is not an innovation has only limited validity, since the innovator in this case must envision the possibility of integrating the new element into the ongoing culture and must be willing and able to meet the obstacles that are likely to confront him. This is as true of the element borrowed from an outsider practicing new ways in the local area, as of an element introduced by a person native to the area who has learned it abroad, for the outsider is seldom a total participant in the local culture and is not so judged by the local community. For example, European men traded at Onitsha and Sierra Leonian men imitated them, setting up small shops; but it was nevertheless an innovation for indigenous men to take up trading as an occupation, since traditionally this had been done by women.
[12] Samuelson, P. A., 1951, pp. 110–112.
[13] International Bank for Reconstruction and Development, 1955, p. 346.

3

The introduction of the fundamental innovations that stimulated the change from primarily subsistence production to production for exchange, and the correlated expansion of trade, has usually been attributed to sources external to the indigenous economies, that is, to governments or non-indigenous firms and individuals.[14] But an examination of the means by which these innovations were accepted and integrated into the existing indigenous economic systems has been largely neglected. The explanation undoubtedly lies in the fact that this was accomplished through the accumulation of a great variety of individually small acts of numerous innovators, operating on a minuscule scale, in diverse ways in different regions. African craftsmen adopted imported tools; a few small manufacturers operate imported power-driven machinery; bicycles and motorized transport have come to be widely used commercially; farmers began to cultivate cash crops on an increasing scale; and indigenous traders fostered cultivation of cash crops by bringing imported merchandise, both from overseas and from a distance within Africa, to distant areas and linking remote producers to markets.[15]

Documented instances of innovations due almost entirely to African initiative are the trading institution of the "House" in Eastern Nigeria,[16] the introduction of cocoa and its development as a cash crop in the then Gold Coast,[17] and the development of the Kamba woodcarving industry of Kenya.[18] Still another innovation is the "company," a type of business organization found among the Bantu of Kavirondo, the Kikuyu and the Baganda.[19] A "company" may be organized to carry on any type of business. Several persons contribute capital, and profits are shared according to the proportion of original capital contributed. In some "companies," all contributors participate in the operation of the business; in others, one or a few direct the business and the remaining investors only share in the profits. In 1955 Leakey wrote:

"The Kikuyu have over the past ten years developed an absolute craze for 'company' formation. There are hundreds, possibly thousands, of unregistered 'Companies,' as they call them, comprising anything from three to ten shareholders, who invest their money with the hope, often a forlorn

[14] Bauer, P. T., 1954, p. 167; Hancock, W. K., 1942, Chapter II; United Nations, 1954, p. 1.
[15] Bauer, *op. cit.*, p. 30, describes the career of one Hausa trader whose commercial activities played a valuable part in the spread of the groundnut industry in Northern Nigeria.
[16] Dike, K. O., 1956, pp. 34–37.   [17] Hill, P., 1956, pp. 102–103.
[18] Elkan, W., 1959, pp. 314–323.   [19] Hoyt, E., 1952, p. 170.

one, that it will multiply much more quickly than it would in the Post Office Savings Bank or in any other recognized concern."

"Companies" were organized to conduct truck transport, to carry on internal and external commerce, to build and operate shops of various kinds, and to run almost any kind of commercial enterprise.[20]

An innovation of the Chagga of Tanganyika was the formation of the Kilimanjaro Native Planters Association to combat the opposition of Europeans to the growing of coffee by the Chagga. In 1932 the Association became the Kilimanjaro Native Cooperative Union, one of the most successful African organizations of its kind. It survived many difficulties and became an agent of the Native Coffee Board, supervising the cultivation and marketing of coffee. In 1952 there were 30 societies affiliated to the Union, with a total of 31,000 members; it held deposits of over £18,000, and played a considerable part in promoting education among the Chagga.[21]

Elsewhere, cooperatives were introduced on the initiative of government, with control and operation retained in the hands of the members. They are of various types: thrift and credit societies, consumers' societies and marketing organizations, the latter being the most important in most areas. Cocoa marketing cooperatives have been successful in Nigeria and Ghana, particularly the latter. A development of the cooperative movement, that may prove to be a means of achieving some of the benefits of larger scale production without changing the existing system of land tenure, is the organization in Ghana, Nigeria and Uganda of a few farmers' cooperatives which collectively own or hire farm animals and equipment and market the products. In Uganda, the government has also fostered operation of cotton ginneries by African cooperatives as a means of freeing growers from dependence on Asian middlemen.

Other innovations are the diverse types of savings, credit and community "improvement" associations common in southern Nigeria, such as the *esusu* and the "meeting."[22] Some of these associations are open to anyone, others are restricted to members of a given occupational group, lineage, or community. The *esusu* are primarily economic, but the others serve social and educational functions as well. As far as is known, Ibo Progressive Unions originated not in the home districts but in distant urban centers where migrants from the same area, chiefly traders and

[20] Leakey, L. S. B., 1956, pp. 177–179.
[21] Hailey, Lord M., 1957, p. 1468.
[22] Bascom, W. R., 1952, pp. 63–69; Amogu, O. O., 1951, pp. 202–209; Green, M. M., 1947, pp. 44–48; Ezeabasili, A. N., 1960, p. 10.

wage and salaried workers, banded together for mutual aid in an unfamiliar situation, and to maintain close ties with the home district. Almost every community in Iboland has come to have such an association, comprised of a central body in the home district and branches in all the distant centers to which its people have migrated, united under one administration, often with a written constitution. General meetings are held when most migrants visit the home district at the same time— Easter and Christmas. Traditional village loyalty has stimulated the unions to become channels of development of rural areas. Migrants resident in urban areas communicate to the home community ideas for developmental projects, schools, maternity homes, post offices, roads, piped water and the like, and tax themselves to provide necessary funds.

It is generally held that one of the most important, if not the most important, factors bringing Africans into the exchange economy is the development of new wants for imported merchandise that can be purchased only with cash. Until recently these goods were imported into Africa by non-Africans, who also provided Africans with cash to purchase imported goods by buying goods produced in Africa for export. To a limited extent in Ghana and Nigeria, non-indigenous trading firms were in direct contact with African producers and consumers through small trading stations established in remote districts. Only a fraction of the total volume of their transactions was ever done in this way, and in recent years they have largely abandoned this aspect of their business. The trader who has been most in direct contact with producers and consumers is the African middleman, who plays an important part in effecting the transitions from subsistence production to production for exchange.[23] Moreover, the great expansion in Ghana and Nigeria of cultivation of crops for sale in internal markets, and long-distance trade in African-produced goods, must be attributed to African entrepreneurs.

Several instances of innovating and imitating entrepreneurship in trade may be cited from Onitsha. As elsewhere in non-Moslem West Africa, men were traditionally farmers and craftsmen, and most trading in the markets was done by women. When European firms established stations at Onitsha, some women began buying palm produce to exchange with these firms for imported goods, which they sold in markets. Some men also became produce buyers, and a few of them took up trading as a full-time occupation, taking space in the market to sell imported goods, even though the community disapproved. Women resented their invasion in an activity that had always been reserved to

[23] Bauer, P. T., 1957, p. 70; Uganda Government Report, 1955, p. 10.

them, while men taunted them for doing women's work, and their families tried to dissuade them. One of these men stated that he was unable to marry for a number of years because women and their families refused to accept a trader as a husband, though they would have consented if he had abandoned trading for farming, or for his previous occupation of teaching. However, after the pioneers had demonstrated that trading could be a lucrative occupation for men, more and more of them entered the market and community disapproval was overcome. Some of the original innovators were the first Nigerians to open shops outside the market, and to import goods direct from overseas. They have become among the most successful merchants in Onitsha.

Before the expansion of trade following the Second World War, women distributed the great bulk of imported goods. During the wartime period of scarcity, foreign firms channeled the bulk of their imports through their established customers, most of whom were women. Men who had previously been importing in a small way, and other men who had returned from military service with some savings and had entered trade, had great difficulty obtaining stock. As soon as the wartime restrictions on importing were lifted, however, Nigerian men in such numbers began direct importing that non-African firms stopped trading in some items, and the smaller firms were anticipating a time when their business would be largely confined to goods which Nigerian traders could not yet handle because of the capital, service facilities, and the like required. A considerable part of the business of the small non-African firms at Onitsha came to consist of placing orders overseas for Nigerian importers; some Nigerians, with the necessary capital and knowledge, began ordering goods for other Nigerian traders.

In domestic trade, Nigerian men have found and exploited new markets for existing products, and have changed traditional channels of trade to take advantage of improved transportation facilities. One example among many is the trade at Onitsha in *mangala*, a type of dried fish produced in the Northern Region. Traditionally this trade was carried on between Northern fishermen and women traders established at Onitsha. The fisherman caught and dried fish until he had enough to fill a large canoe, which he floated down the rivers to Onitsha, where he turned over his goods to his "customer," who sold the cargo for him, retaining a commission for herself. Typically the relationship was established and maintained by the trader advancing money to the fisherman, often as much as £100 or more, to cover his expenses in obtaining the cargo, and also to feed and house him while at Onitsha. After the development of motor transport, Ibo men began going to the Northern fishing centers, buying from the fishermen and trucking the fish to Onitsha, where it was sold to women traders. The formerly successful women wholesalers in fish complained bitterly that their "customers" no longer brought cargoes by water, but preferred to sell to the male traders in their home territory.

Similarly, after the railway was completed and Southerners settled in some numbers in the urban centers of the north, they began a two-way trade in agricultural produce between stations on the railway. At the outset, a Southerner living in the North saw trade possibilities in products of the South, such as palm wine, palm oil and gari, and commissioned a relative in a Southern station to buy these commodities and send them to him. In return he sent Northern products, such as beans and peanut oil, to the Southern agent, who sold them and purchased Southern produce to send North.

An example of trading ingenuity is the widespread practice, known in Lagos and Western Nigeria as "gold-coasting," which is a means of overcoming a lack of capital. A trader who is able to obtain merchandise on credit for which payment is not required for a period of time, usually one month, sells the goods for cash at cost, or below if necessary. He employs the funds to finance other trading ventures, or in money-lending ventures in which he earns more than enough to repay the advance when it is due.[24] Nadel states that between 1920 and 1940 the Nupe had learned to use this device to the full.[25]

Other innovations are exemplified by small factories established in Onitsha by Nigerians. In one case, two brothers who were traders dealing in general merchandise specialized in imported umbrellas. When they learned that Indian firms in Lagos were importing parts and assembling umbrellas locally to obtain the advantage of the lower duty on umbrella parts, one of the brothers went to Lagos to observe the assembly operations, and learned the source of supply of parts. They subsequently developed a flourishing small business at Onitsha, importing and assembling parts and selling the umbrellas. Another small firm has made a success of the same type of business.

In another case, a man who had been a successful trader in general merchandise began importing records in the late 1930s. He found he could do well in that line even against the competition of non-African firms because, while he was not a musician, he could tell by listening to a record whether Nigerians would buy it. On the basis of his belief that Nigerians would prefer records of Nigerian music with Nigerian performers to those made abroad, he organized an orchestra to play at local functions and cut records which he sent to Europe for processing.

[24] Bauer, P. T., 1954, p. 17.
[25] Nadel, S. F., 1942, p. 328.

When the sale of these records proved him right, he hired a European sound engineer and other non-Africans, obtained a £30,000 government loan, and built a sound-studio and factory with modern equipment for cutting and producing records. Technological innovations have not been beyond Nigerians. In one instance, a Nigerian bakery owner, who had been using imported power-driven machinery, invented a machine, equally efficient at one of the operations, that could be produced at a fraction of the cost of its imported counterpart.

Despite the important part women have had and continued to have in trade, they were, by and large, traditional entrepreneurs holding to established trade practices. All twelve outstandingly successful women traders at Onitsha were established customers of one or another of the great European trading firms, from whom they bought goods on credit to resell to the large clientele of smaller traders, which each of them had built up over many years of trading. Innovating and imitating entrepreneurs seem all to have been men. As far as could be ascertained, not a single women trader has done any direct importing, though occasionally they place special orders with the European firms; and among hundreds of Nigerians using current accounts with one Onitsha bank for business purposes, only two were women.

Whatever the final judgment may be of Africans as innovating entrepreneurs, there can be no doubt of their proficiency as imitating entrepreneurs. This holds true especially of the Ibo. At Onitsha, a common complaint of traders who formerly carried on a profitable business in a particular line is that so many others have taken it up that the margin of profit has been reduced. The search for new ways of earning a profit is unremitting. Non-African firms and Nigerian traders exert efforts to preserve trade secrets, but they are seldom successful for long. Competitors ferret out sources of supply, or have a duplicate made of any item that can be sold at a profit. One European firm manager never reorders a shoe pattern that sells well, because before a new shipment could arrive, Nigerian traders would have sent a sample abroad to have a cheaper version made. Agents buying or selling for Onitsha traders in distant markets communicate favorable price changes to their principals by coded telegrams in an attempt to keep the information from competitors. Ibo men import produce from the North and control the butcher trade, both formerly carried on by Hausa. They import directly about one quarter of the overseas merchandise sold at Onitsha, and appear to be displacing Ibo women as regular customers of non-African firms. After a comparatively late start, they have come to dominate nearly all aspects of the trade at Onitsha that was formerly carried on by other groups.

4

Capital formation involves two related processes, saving and investment. For capital formation to occur, the population of a given country must consume less than its total annual output, and the margin between total output and total consumption must be directed into productive investment which will increase its future capacity to produce. Both saving and productive investment are generally expected to be relatively slight in underdeveloped countries; the first, because incomes are so low that little saving is possible, and the second, because the savings that are accumulated are likely to be hoarded in the form of currency or trinkets because of the lack of, or unfamiliarity with, institutions for mobilizing the savings of numerous small savers.[26]

The indigenous populations of East and Central Africa conform to the general pattern; but in Ghana, where income per capita is relatively high, and even in Nigeria, where it is much lower, the indigenous population contributes substantially to savings. The major sources of net saving are the forced saving of farmers, obtained through accumulation of Marketing Board profits and export taxes, and the voluntary saving of depositors in cooperative accounts, commercial banks, and the Post Office Savings accounts. The proportion of the population that saves in banks or post offices is small, but steadily increasing. In Nigeria, savings bank deposits have increased every year since 1943, and the number of accounts in the Post Office Savings Bank has increased every year since 1938. But, though the accumulated deposits grew annually from 1938 to 1957, they show an annual decline in subsequent years.[27] This may be due to the fact that savers became familiar with banks, and preferred them to the Post Office Savings Banks, because withdrawals could be more easily made from the former than the latter, where a depositor had to be identified each time he wished to make a withdrawal and, to take an amount in excess of £5, he had to wait, often for several weeks, for authorization from the comptroller's office in Lagos.

At Onitsha, it would seem that the banks and the attitude of Nigerians toward them have changed markedly since Bauer described them in 1954.[28] At that time there was only the British Bank of West Africa, and its business was largely confined to transactions for government and non-African firms. Subsequently, both Barclays and the African Continental Bank established branches and the BWA, which had moved into a new, larger building, found it necessary to build a new extension and

[26] Samuelson, P. A., 1951, p. 49.
[27] Nigeria, Federation of, 1961, pp. 14, 17.
[28] Bauer, P. T., 1954, p. 187.

also to establish a branch office near the market. All of these banks are thronged with Nigerians during business hours; credit is extended to qualified Nigerians in the form of overdrafts; and many Nigerian business men consider the European bank managers as valued friends and advisors. In the opinion of one bank manager, the number of savings accounts would compare very favorably with any bank in England. In 1960, one bank was opening five or more new accounts every business day, whereas only a few years earlier no more than that many were opened in a month; another bank had as many as 200 new accounts each month. Formerly, savings depositors were nearly all teachers or clerks, but knowledge of the use of banks has spread throughout the population. In the list of occupations of depositors who opened accounts in one bank during the first few months of 1961, traders were the largest occupational group, numbering more than the next two occupations, teachers and clerks, combined. More than one hundred other occupations were represented, including farmers, who ranked tenth on the list. Savers varied from the lad selling cigarettes by the "stick," to the wealthy trader who owned real estate and deposited the rents in a savings account. One bank held more than £500,000 in "petty-petty" savings accounts.

Undoubtedly, the true volume of savings of Nigerians is greater than the total deposited in formal institutions. A part of these savings is kept in idle hoards; it is common for currency notes damaged by moisture or insects to be brought into the banks for redemption. Nigerians avoid formal savings institutions because of unfamiliarity with them, to conceal resources from tax authorities and relatives and because many rural savers live far from any bank, so that the cost and trouble of transporting money is not compensated by low net yields on bank deposits. Another reason is the availability of other opportunities for short-term investment that bring a higher return. Almost anyone can employ small savings in trade, and money-lenders use private borrowings in their business. Individuals place their savings with money-lenders because money-lenders pay a rate much higher than the banks.[29]

Moreover, additional savings and investments are channeled through the numerous informal savings, credit and "improvement" associations in southern Nigeria, such as the *esusu*, among the Yoruba, and the "meeting" of the Ibo, in which each member contributes a specified amount at regular intervals and the total contributed on each round is drawn by each member in turn.[30] In some *esusu*, the participants make

[29] Amogu, O. O., 1956, p. 203.
[30] Bascom, W. R., 1952, pp. 63–69; Green, M. M., 1947, pp. 44–48.

regular specified contributions, but receive in return only the right to borrow, at a relatively low rate of interest, from the fund thus contributed. The interest charge serves as an inducement for the borrower to employ the money productively, which he can do either by himself engaging in petty trade or by lending the money. The period of the loan is usually one month, at the end of which time full repayment of the principal and of any interest due is expected.[31]

"Improvement" unions, as mentioned above, are more elaborate, also serving social, political and community developmental functions. Membership and payment of dues is compulsory or morally obligatory for all adults, as well as special assessments for community projects. In Ibo country, which is agriculturally poor, traders contribute to community unions more than their proportionate numbers would indicate, because a man with cash is expected to pay the dues and assessments of his poorer relatives. Many of the various branches also make loans to members for business purposes for periods of three months or more.[32]

The voluntary contribution of funds for community development is not confined to West Africa. The Kikuyu of Kenya have for a long time taxed themselves fairly heavily through local native councils, mainly for educational purposes. In certain districts they pay as much as 10 shillings as Local Native Council tax in addition to the government tax, as a contribution to local development.[33]

In Onitsha there is another type of informal savings institution, known locally as "the poor man's savings bank." Many persons, particularly petty traders, prefer these to the savings banks because such institutions enable them to save small amounts regularly, without wasting time in the long lines at the banks. A collector calls daily at the place of business of each customer and records his contribution in a book retained by the saver. At the end of each month, the total contributed during the month is returned, less one day's contribution, retained by the "bank" in payment for its service. It is probable that the money is put out on short-term loans by the "bank" during the month it has these funds.

Savings and productive investment also occur in other forms, often overlooked by economists, such as the establishment, extension and improvement of agricultural properties, livestock, and various types of equipment inventories.[34] Investments in agriculture may be individually small and unimpressive, consisting of such items as simple structures,

[31] Amogu, O. O., *op. cit.*, p. 204.
[32] *Ibid.*, pp. 204–205; Ezeabasili, A. N., p. 10; Ottenberg, S., 1956, *passim*.
[33] Leakey, L. S. B., 1956, p. 180.
[34] Bauer, P. T., 1957, pp. 60–63.

fertilizer, or improved seeds and tools, but they are nevertheless important in the overall picture for their role in increasing productivity. Although the evidence is not available to substantiate it, the opinion is widely held that much of Ghanaian small enterprise in trade and transport was originally financed from the savings of cocoa farmers.[35]

Investment of savings in traders' inventories has probably been substantial in Ghana and Nigeria. All available information indicates that the primary drive of regular traders is to build up their capital position in order to increase their volume of trade. As a general rule, those with substantial assets have started with relatively small amounts of invested capital, and have gradually built up their position through reinvestment of earnings.[36] The rate of capital growth appears to be highest at the lowest levels, when the trader is struggling to become established.[37] The slower rate of growth at upper levels may be due to other factors than unwillingness to invest further in business. Smith has reported the successful Hausa merchant trader of Zaria as accumulating capital faster than he can find productive uses for it.[38] One inhibiting factor would seem to be the limit to the size of a business operation that can be controlled within the type of organization with which Africans are familiar, the one-man or one-woman enterprise. After a certain size is attained, an increasing proportion of earnings may be withdrawn from the business and invested elsewhere. This spreads the risk for the owner, and also contributes to capital formation in real estate—farms, houses or apartment buildings—in other businesses, such as transport, or in the education of children and relatives. In Onitsha, the successful trader may own a private car, a cement block house in his native village, a modern "upstairs" house in the township which he himself occupies, and other houses or apartment buildings which he rents. Such investments are not without benefit to him as a businessman, for they provide concrete evidence that he is a man of means, the car is used in his business, and property in the township can serve as security for loans.

5

Thus, no lack of the spirit of enterprise obtains among Africans, nor is there a shortage of entrepreneurs within the limits of our operational definition. The statement so frequently encountered, that one of the most important, if not the most important, barriers to growth and

[35] Herskovits, M. J., 1952, p. 103.
[36] Bauer, P. T., 1954, pp. 30–31; Addae, G., 1956, p. 53; Nypan, A., 1960a, p. 10; Garlick, P. C., 1959, pp. 29–30.
[37] Nypan, A., 1960b, p. 36.
[38] Smith, M. G., 1955, pp. 100–101, 168.

development of African economies is the lack of indigenous entrepreneurs, arises from the use of the term in a more restricted sense, to
mean business men with the type of administrative ability needed to
organize and conduct a medium or large-scale enterprise. It seems para-
doxical that in Ghana and Nigeria, where trading is almost a universal
occupation, there are comparatively few African trading firms; that,
though there are numerous craftsmen, there are still fewer African
manufacturing firms. Research among African traders has been done for
the purpose, among others, of ascertaining the factors that may be
responsible for the general failure to develop a strong, commercial
middle class with substantial capital resources.

The impediment to the growth of African trading enterprises most
frequently mentioned in the reports of this research is the failure of
African business to amass capital in sufficient amounts to finance larger
enterprises than the one-man type. This failure is attributed to the
relative poverty of Africans, to the scarcity of loan capital, to the inability
or unwillingness of Africans to form business associations, such as
partnerships or joint-stock companies, which could combine the capital
of small savers into significant amounts, or to the failure of Africans to
conserve such capital as they have. Let us examine the validity of these
propositions.

As we have seen, relatively low per capita incomes does not
prevent the accumulation of savings, while, for the most part, savings
are not hoarded but invested in ways offering the possibility of profits.
Onitsha traders, actually, have seemed to suffer not so much from lack
of capital as from over-commitment of the capital they had, leaving no
cash resources to meet exigencies of trade. With all their resources
invested in inventory, they are often caught short, and forced to sell at
a loss to obtain cash to meet pressing obligations. For example, overseas
orders are accompanied by a deposit of 25 per cent, and the balance
must be paid at the time of arrival to secure the release of the goods. If,
as often happens, the importer has insufficient cash when the goods
arrive, he is forced to sell the goods to other traders at cost or below to
avoid the loss of his deposit.

Short-term loans for trading purposes are available to qualified
Africans, through West African banks and other institutions, and the
organization of government development corporations may provide a
source of long-term investment capital. The situation may be less favorable in East Africa, where statutory limits on the amount of debt for
goods received that is collectible from an African by a non-African in
practice limits the credit extended to Africans by non-Africans to the
collectible amount.

The reluctance of Africans to form partnerships and joint-stock companies is usually attributed to extreme individualism in business, and to an atmosphere of mutual distrust. Generally speaking, Africans prefer direct control of their investments, and lack confidence in the competence and honesty of fellow Africans; but caution in entering into such associations is not surprising if one considers the fact that, in Onitsha at least, prominent traders have lost heavily by investing in overambitious undertakings that failed because of incompetent management, while probably more important, the protection of stockholders' interests has not reached a high level. Even so, a few such ventures have operated successfully and there are individuals with capital willing to invest in enterprises under competent, responsible management that offer reasonable security and the possibility of profit.[39] The availability of private investment capital for sound enterprises has also been reported in Lagos.[40]

Failure to conserve capital has been attributed to the practice of withdrawing money from business to meet family obligations, to expend on conspicuous consumption, to build houses and to invest in farms or other businesses. There can be no doubt that family obligations can be a drain on business capital, but the effect may have been exaggerated. Many Onitsha traders could not state the amount spent in this way, saying that they did not themselves know because no record was kept for fear that the total contribution for the year might discourage them. However, some Africans have been able to hold such expenditures within tolerable limits, because they have built up substantial capital through reinvestment of earnings, while meeting these obligations and remaining on the best of terms with their families. While the charge of wasteful expenditure on items of conspicuous consumption is frequently heard as concerns clerks, it is never made in regard to traders. On the contrary, traders are criticized for maintaining an unnecessarily low standard of living. As stated above, outside investments spread the risk for the trader and may benefit his business. Furthermore, Africans are well aware of the fluctuation of earnings in trade and place a high value on investments, such as rental property in towns, that yield a certain, regular income.

Widespread illiteracy with the resulting incapacity to keep proper accounts results in the inability of many traders to distinguish between gross and net profits, so that they never know their true profit position.

[39] Willingness to invest in joint-stock companies was demonstrated when shares in Nigerian companies under European management were made available to the public and purchased by many Onitsha traders.

[40] Fleming, R. I., 1961, p. 241.

This is true of the majority of small traders; but in their businesses, in which expenses are rigorously kept to an irreducible minimum, it is not essential that they know the precise cost of their operations. They have learned through experience the average mark-up that will enable them to meet their expenses and have something left over, and they conduct their business in accordance with this rule of thumb. Moreover, most successful traders of Onitsha, at least, are literate and capable of understanding simple accounts. Many of them have assistants, often those who have attended one of the local schools of commerce, who can keep their accounts. Onitsha has some qualified accountants, who either keep books for a number of traders, or supervise books kept by shop assistants, auditing them regularly. Some few traders regularly record all disbursements, distinguishing between business expenditures and personal or family expenditures, and have come to appreciate the necessity of keeping a reserve of cash. The Regional Ministry of Trade and Commerce encourages traders to keep books by providing a simple textbook and the advice of an officer stationed at Onitsha. Moreover, traders are motivated to keep accounts because the income tax department is authorized to set taxes arbitrarily in the absence of documentary proof of income.

Lack of familiarity with procedures of ordering, shipping and importing tends to limit many African traders to buying from local wholesalers, whose prices are higher than those which might be obtainable closer to the sources of supply. This does not apply where banks, non-African firms and Africans regularly perform these services for traders, but traders will buy from local wholesalers any item that can be sold at a profit, at least until they learn the source of supply.

Lack of administrative ability capable of conducting a relatively complex organization, and the correlated scarcity of reliable, trained subordinates, limits African business to the one-man enterprise. For this there is no simple or quick remedy. Entrepreneurship of this type cannot be taught in schools, and experience as managerial assistants or even departmental managers in foreign concerns does not train a man in all of the skills required to plan and operate a small business independently. Lewis has suggested that the Ghanaian government should provide managerial and technical assistance to small entrepreneurs,[41] and the Mission of the International Bank for Reconstruction and Development made the same recommendation for Nigeria.[42] Fleming, of the Rockefeller Brothers' Fund, stated that American firms might be helpful in establishing small enterprises that could train Africans for

[41] Lewis, W. A., 1953, p. 12.
[42] International Bank for Reconstruction and Development, 1955, p. 51.

total responsibility of management by working with them as friends and equals.[43]

The fact that even successful traders and merchants occupy positions in the prestige structure below traditional rulers, government officials and members of the learned professions[44] may partially explain the widespread attitude toward business as only a means of making money, to be dropped whenever something more profitable appears, something that Williams observed among Ghanaians. For them a business does not take on a personality of its own with which the owner identifies, deriving creative satisfaction from its prosperity and growth, as is typical of owners of small business in Europe and the United States.[45] Conditions in Onitsha, however, are not so unfavorable to this point of view. It is true that the position of trading on an occupational preference scale is well below the above-named occupations, but the most successful traders are among the first citizens of the community, highly respected by the general population and by local and regional government officials. Their pictures and accounts of their activities appear frequently in local newspapers, and the acknowledged leader of the business community is always invited to the most exclusive functions. Moreover, trade is not considered a denigrating occupation. One of the most successful business men of Onitsha is the traditional ruler of a nearby community, and a member of the Eastern Regional House of Chiefs. Furthermore, many traders hold offices in local governments, churches, and in their town "unions."

6

In addition to the above obstacles that have been observed in English-speaking Africa, scholars working in other underdeveloped areas have designated still other factors as critical to the development and growth of indigenous entrepreneurship, particularly in industry:

1. There must have been previous investment in social overhead capital.

2. There must be competent, honest administration, that recognizes the importance of small and medium-scale enterprise in economic development, and formulates and strenuously pursues policies that foster it.[46]

3. There must also be entrepreneurial security, which means relative

[43] Fleming, R. I., 1961, p. 242.
[44] McCall, D. F., 1956, p. 69; Smith, M. G., 1955, p. 101.
[45] Williams, J. W., 1956, p. 26.
[46] Singer, H. W., 1953, pp. 20, 22; Deyrup, F., 1957, p. 195; International Bank for Reconstruction and Development, 1955, p. 21.

freedom from government control, other than the prevention of restraints on competition, and a tax policy that allows entrepreneurs to
retain a large part of their earnings.[47]

4. The culture must allow individual advancement through initiative
and enterprise, and accord high status to entrepreneurs.[48]

5. The technology applied in economically less-developed areas must
be suited to local conditions, which often do not allow a simple transfer
of techniques from more industrialized countries.[49]

The development of entrepreneurs in small industry is inhibited by
the fact that a logical consideration of the choices available to prospective investors, in the light of their relative security and profitability under
prevailing conditions in underdeveloped countries, favors investment in
trade, money-lending, inventory speculation and real estate, over that
in industry. These make for an unbalanced economy, with consequent
marked price fluctuations, unfamiliarity with and distrust of one's
competence in industrial enterprise, lack of reliable information concerning the problems and possibilities of profit in industry, bank
policies that grant short-term credit but extend no long-term loans, and
lack of protection of interests of stockholders.[50]

Generally speaking, the present state of the factors listed above is
unfavorable to the development of individual entrepreneurship in
British and former British territories of Africa. A beginning has been
made in the provision of social overhead capital, but such facilities are
by no means ideal and are confined to some degree to the larger urban
centers. Many of the principal indigenous cultures find economic innovations congruent with earlier practices, however, and individual
advancement is possible. A final judgment as to the degree to which the
above factors inhibit the growth of entrepreneurship in African Territories is not possible as long as the necessary factual information is
lacking. African countries, particularly Ghana and Nigeria, present a
fertile field for research to test hypotheses regarding the nature of
entrepreneurship and the environmental conditions essential to its
development, because of the historical and geographical variations,
diverse cultures and differential rates of economic development that are
found both within and between these territories.

[47] Brozen, Y., 1954, p. 355; Easterbrook, W. T., 1949, p. 325.

[48] Levy, M. J., Jun., 1955, p. 472; Brozen, Y., 1954, p. 342; Easterbrook, W. T.,
1949, p. 326; Cole, A. H., 1959, p. 21.

[49] Aubrey, H. C., 1959, pp. 273–274; Fleming, R. I., 1961, pp. 203–204; Hoselitz,
B. F., 1952, p. 99.

[50] Aubrey, H. C., 1955, pp. 397–398.

10

Real Income Trends in West Africa
1939-1960

by Elliot J. Berg
Harvard University

During the decades 1939-1960, West Africa, like Africa generally, experienced unparalleled economic growth. This is registered in all available indicators—volume and value of trade with the rest of the world, size of the labor force in paid employment, rates of capital formation, volume of public expenditure, the stock of physical facilities in transport, communication, education, public health.[1] The extent to which this general expansion of economic activity increased African personal incomes in real terms has, however, been a matter of some controversy. Indeed, even the direction of change of African real incomes over these years has been called into question. Thus Bauer, in his study of West African trade, argued that the real incomes of many West African agricultural producers in the early 1950's were below what they had been in the 1930's.[2] Later, another writer tried to show that over most of the post-World War II period real wages in Ghana were lower than in 1939.[3]

In this paper we shall attempt to give a broad evaluation of changes in African real incomes during the decades we are considering, focusing on the major African groups in the money economy—export crop producers and wage earners—in four countries, Senegal, Ivory Coast, Ghana and Nigeria. Price and income data relevant for purposes of the measurement of income will be assembled and analyzed, income movements briefly compared, both within and between countries, and some explanations put forward to account for the differences in the behavior of real income that emerge from the data.

[1] See, for example, United Nations, Department of Economic Affairs, 1951, 1959a.
[2] Bauer, P. T., 1954b, pp. 304-308, and Appendix 2.
[3] Birmingham, W., 1960, pp. 2-6.

I

Tables 10.1 to 10.12 summarize money and real income movements between the late 1930's and 1960 for export crop growers and wage earners in Nigeria, Ghana and key territories in French West Africa. For each country two sets of tables are given, one on a base year of 1938 for French Africa or 1939 for Ghana and Nigeria, the other based on 1949 figures. There are several reasons for dividing the series in this way. The data before 1949 are much less reliable than post-World War II data; it is particularly difficult to find continuous series of consumer prices since 1939. The division is made more reasonable when the difficulties of interpreting consumer price indices calculated for an unchanging commodity basket in countries of rapidly changing economic structure are also taken into account. A number of indices are available for the post-1949 period which did not exist in earlier years. Finally, there is in fact a difference in the behaviour of real incomes in the two periods, so that treating them on separate base periods underlines the difference.[4]

Before turning to a detailed analysis of the data, it is important to set out two elementary distinctions that will make clear the significance of the various indices recorded in the tables: the distinction between the income of a given group of producers and income per producer, and the distinction between earnings and rates of remuneration.

The money income of any given producer of an export crop can increase in one or both of two ways. The price at which he sells his crop can increase; or he may sell a larger amount. Income of growers of this crop as a group can increase in either of these ways, and in yet another, since the group may become larger through the entry of new growers. In our discussion it is implicitly assumed that changes in income per producer are adequately measured by changes in the price of the crop. This assumption is valid only under two conditions; that output per man or per acre has not been significantly changed by technological improvements, and that average size of farming units has not significantly changed. If technological improvement brings about greater output with a given input, then a fall in the price of the output does not necessarily imply a decline in income. And if the size of farms has increased, then total income of the individual farmer may increase despite a fall in the price of his crop. In West Africa during the period under study there is no reason to believe either that the size of farming

---

[4] The underlying series of absolute prices and outputs are provided in the Appendix. In the Appendix can also be found a discussion of the sources of the data, and their degree of reliability.

units changed, or except in very recent years in the cocoa industry that there were significant changes in productivity.[5] It is therefore legitimate to take changes in price as indicative of changes in income per individual producer.

It should be clear that the income of growers of a given export crop as a group can increase, while incomes of individual producers decline or stay the same. This would be the case if output increases at a faster rate than prices decline, the increase in output resulting from entry of new producers—that is, from the transfer of resources out of subsistence into the production of export crops.

The second distinction is between earnings and rates of remuneration. The rate of remuneration is payment per constant unit of output—for example, wage rate per hour of unskilled labor. It takes no account of numbers of people at work for wages, or the amount of time each works. Earnings, being the total payment to a worker or group of workers, reflect numbers employed and time worked, as well as changes in the nature of the skills the work force possesses. Thus rates of wages may remain unchanged, or even decline, and earnings may rise, because more people are working or because they are working longer, or because their average level of skill is higher.

Tables 10.1 to 10.6 provide data on changes in money income per producer—that is, export-crop producer-price indices and wage-rate indices for unskilled labor in major urban centers—and on changes in incomes for export crop producers as a group, these being shown by indices of aggregate receipts. Lack of information prevents assessing the earnings of wage earners as a group. Indeed, since there are no usable series giving average earnings for these years, no information is presented in the tables about average individual earnings, as opposed to rates of remuneration.

The limitations of the indicators of changes in real income, whether of individual producers or groups of producers, should be obvious. To measure movements of real income, it is not only necessary to know changes in money incomes over time, but how the individuals in question spend their incomes, and what has happened to the prices of the commodities they buy. But these data are not available, except for urban wage earners. It is therefore necessary to use substitute measures of consumer price-changes—mainly prices of imported consumer goods. A comparison of import prices with producer prices and with wage rates tells us much about the "real gains from international trade" that

[5] In Ghana especially, but also in Nigeria and the Ivory Coast, the adoption of cocoa spraying aimed at capsid control has in recent years had the effect of increasing output from existing trees. Cf. Ghana, Office of the Government Statistician, 1960a.

accrued to African farmers and wage earners. The relationship between these prices is also highly indicative of changes in real incomes and living standards, since expenditure on imported goods is a significant portion of total expenditure of all Africans in the money economy.[6]

The various indicators of real income may now be defined. The "net barter" terms of trade of agricultural producers, the index of import purchasing power of wages, and the index of textile purchasing power per unit of agricultural output and of wages—all these are taken to measure changes in real income per producer. The net barter terms-of-trade measures the import purchasing power per unit of export crop. It is derived by dividing an index of producer prices by an import price-index, and is the agricultural counterpart of the index of import purchasing power of wages, derived by dividing an index of wage rates by an import price index. The textile purchasing-power index for wages and major crops in Tables 10.1 to 10.4 is a related concept, also designed to measure changes in real income per producer. It is derived by dividing export crop price-indices by the index of landed costs of cotton textiles constructed by Bauer in his *West African Trade*.[7]

The concept "income terms of trade" is useful in taking account of changing volumes of output. Indices of the income terms of trade relate changes in aggregate receipts of export crop farmers as a group to changes in prices of imported goods. These indices are constructed by dividing indices of aggregate producer payments for each crop by an import price-index and, in the 1939–1949 tables for Ghana and Nigeria, by Bauer's textile price index.

An increase in the income terms of trade represents an increase in group purchasing power regardless of what happens to net barter terms of trade. For while some growers of a crop may have constant or declining incomes, there are more growers, and higher incomes for the group as a whole. The gains in income accruing to the group as a whole outweigh any losses suffered by individuals within it. There may be a loss of "leisure," or possibly—though doubtfully, given West African conditions of production—a significant decline in food crop production. It can be inferred, on a basis of revealed preference, that the new entrants

[6] The relevant budget studies are to be found in Nigeria, Federation of, Department of Statistics, 1958, 1959; Ghana, 1955, 1956a and b, 1958; Côte d'Ivoire, Service de Statistique, 1958b and c.

[7] Cf. Appendix to this paper. Bauer (1954b) argues that the index of landed costs of cotton textiles is a closer approximation to actual retail price changes of imports than is the available general import price-index, for two main reasons: (a) it includes duties, as compared with the general import price index, which is of c.i.f. prices; (b) because of wage increases, increased distribution costs and scarcities during the period 1939–1947, the retail prices of import goods increased more during this period than did c.i.f. import prices.

into the production of cash crops preferred more production and higher money incomes to more "leisure" with production of food crops, and their gains are greater than losses suffered by existing producers. Economic "welfare" is therefore greater than before. The income terms of trade are, in this sense, a more general indicator of changes in living standards than are net barter terms of trade.

2

The most striking fact underscored by the data in Tables 10.1 to 10.6, covering World War II and the immediate post-war period, is the universality and severity of the decline in real incomes during these years. The terms of trade, both net barter and income, of agricultural producers, and real wages of urban laborers fell precipitously. A large margin of error must be allowed for the data concerning price on which these indices rest. The direction of error, however, almost certainly is in understating the decline in real incomes. In many instances goods were unavailable at any price, while some of the price indices apparently record officially fixed prices, not actual market prices.

Whatever series of prices to consumers is used, it is clear that during the second World War, African real incomes were far lower than those known in the prewar period. Only Nigerian wage earners seem to have maintained their incomes during these years, but the data regarding retail prices in Nigeria are particularly suspect.[8] For wage earners in the other West African countries, and all export crop producers, wartime incomes fell between 25 and 70 per cent. In 1949 a number of groups had not yet recaptured their prewar position as regards real income; this was the case for wage earners in Ghana, coffee growers in the Ivory Coast, and peanut growers in Nigeria.

Comparison of trends in real income, between countries and between different economic groups yields the following principal conclusions:

(a) The sharpest contractions in income of Africans took place in the Ivory Coast. Table 10.6 shows that net barter terms of trade, at least as measured by the very imperfect data available for this period, fell by two-thirds for cocoa and by half for coffee between 1938 and 1945. These terms of trade remained substantially below prewar levels until 1948 for cocoa, and until 1950 for coffee. Ivory Coast wage earners,

[8] For data cf. United Kingdom, Colonial Office, 1946. Certain costs of food quoted therein are scarcely creditable.

TABLE 10.1. *Changes in Money Incomes and Prices of Consumer Goods, Nigeria, 1939–1949 (1939=100)*

Year	Indicators of Changes in Money Incomes					Changes in Prices of Consumer Goods		
	Producer's Prices and Aggregate Receipts to Farmers				Wage Rate, Unskilled Laborer, Lagos	Index of Import Prices	Landed Costs of Imported Cotton Piece Goods	Lagos Cost of Living Index
	Cocoa		Peanuts					
	Price	Receipts	Price	Receipts				
	(1)	(2)	(3)	(4)	(5)	(6)	(7)	(8)
1939	100	100	100	100	100	100	100	100
1940	82	101	82	119	100	134	125	—
1941	88	107	82	94	106–125	146	158	—
1942	76	104	98	83	175–200	166	172	151
1943	76	66	136	156	200	222	245	167
1944	135	142	182	245	200	—	224	163
1945	162	204	182	321	214–238	223	255	176
1946	294	398	242	462	258	248	265	—
1947	368	333	242	471	258	290	342	—
1948	706	942	291	563	258	301	386	—
1949	588	719	321	357	258	328	377	—

Sources: Infra, pp. 230, 231, 234, 235.

TABLE 10.2. Indicators of Changes in Real Incomes, Nigeria, 1939–1949 (1939=100)

	Terms of Trade of Farmers								Wage Earners		
	Cocoa				Peanuts						
			Textile Purchasing Power				Textile Purchasing Power				
Year	Terms of Trade Net Barter	Income	Per Unit of Cocoa	Income	Terms of Trade Net Barter	Income	Per Unit of Peanuts	Of Peanut Income	Real Wage, Unskilled Laborer, Lagos	Import Purchasing Power of Wages	Textile Purchasing Power of Wages
	(1)	(2)	(3)	(4)	(5)	(6)	(7)	(8)	(9)	(10)	(11)
1939	100	100	100	100	100	100	100	100	100	100	100
1940	61	75	66	81	61	89	66	95	—	75	80
1941	60	73	56	68	56	64	52	59	—	73–87	67–79
1942	46	63	44	60	59	50	57	48	116–132	105–120	102–116
1943	34	30	31	27	61	70	56	64	120	90	82
1944	—	—	60	63	—	—	81	109	123	—	89
1945	73	91	64	80	42	144	71	126	122–135	96–107	84–93
1946	119	160	111	150	98	186	91	174	—	104	97
1947	127	115	108	97	83	162	71	138	—	89	75
1948	235	313	183	244	97	187	75	146	—	86	67
1949	179	219	156	191	98	109	85	95	—	79	68

Sources: Infra, pp. 230, 231, 234, 235.

TABLE 10.3. *Changes in Money Incomes and Prices of Consumer Goods, Ghana (Gold Coast), 1939–1949 (1939=100)*

| | Indicators of Changes in Money Incomes | | | Changes in Prices of Consumer Goods | | |
| | *Cocoa Farmers* | | *Wage Earners Wage Rate Unskilled Laborer, Accra* | *Index of Prices of African-Consumed Imports* | *Landed Costs of Imported Cotton Piece Goods* | *Accra Cost of Living Index* |
	Producer Price	Aggregate Receipts				
Year	(1)	(2)	(3)	(4)	(5)	(6)
1939	100	100	100	100	100	100
1940	80	104	112	—	126	—
1941	93	131	129	—	141	151
1942	81	92	129	153	160	159
1943	90	96	129	—	216	168
1944	156	196	129	—	228	168
1945	188	215	129	198	238	186
1946	356	377	143–194	—	264	198
1947	519	590	170–194	285	328	207
1948	842	1,296	194	—	372	—
1949	583	800	206	—	373	—

Sources: Infra, pp. 232, 235, 236.

TABLE 10.4. *Indicators of Changes in Real Incomes, Ghana (Gold Coast), 1939–1949 (1939=100)*

Year	Cocoa Farmers				Wage Earners		Relative Returns Cocoa-Unskilled Labor
	Terms of Trade		Textile Purchasing Power				
	Net Barter	Income	Per Unit of Cocoa	Of Cocoa Income	Real Wage, Accra	Textile Purchasing Power of Accra Wages	
	(1)	(2)	(3)	(4)	(5)	(6)	(7)
1939	100	100	100	100	100	100	100
1940	—	—	63	83	—	89	71
1941	—	—	66	93	85	91	72
1942	53	60	51	58	81	81	63
1943	—	—	42	44	77	60	70
1944	—	—	68	86	77	57	121
1945	95	95	79	90	69	54	146
1946	—	—	135	143	72–98	54–73	249–184
1947	182	207	158	180	82–94	52–59	305–268
1948	—	—	226	348	—	52	434
1949	—	—	156	214	—	55	283

Sources: Infra, pp. 232, 235, 236.

H

TABLE 10.5. *Changes in Money Incomes and Prices of Consumer Goods, French West Africa, 1938–1949*

	Indicators of Changes in Money Incomes								Changes in Prices of Consumer Goods		
	Export Crop Farmers						Wage Earners			Retail	
	Senegalese Peanuts		Ivory Coast Cocoa		Ivory Coast Coffee		Wage Rate, Unskilled Laborer		Prices of African-Consumed Imports (1938=100)	Prices of African-Consumed Goods, Dakar (1938=100)	Prices of Goods in Rural Budget (1938=100)
Year	Producer Price (1938=100)	Aggregate Receipts (1938=100)	f.o.b. Price (1938=100)	Sales (000 tons)	f.o.b. Price (1938=100)	Sales (000 tons)	Dakar (1938=100)	Abidjan (1938=100)			
	(1)	(2)	(3)	(4)	(5)	(6)	(7)	(8)	(9)	(10)	(11)
1938	100	100	100	—	100	—	100	100	100	100	100
1939	96	94	—	55.2	—	18	114	100	—	—	—
1940	101	75	—	45.4	—	15.6	123	—	—	—	—
1941	149	53	—	43.0	—	28.4	134	117	—	—	—
1942	197	40	—	28.6	—	19.8	153	200	—	—	—
1943	200	98	—	0.5	—	23.0	169	—	—	—	—
1944	323	133	—	14.7	—	24.1	171	300	—	—	—
1945	372	226	165	26.3	215	37.9	251	367	431	536	498
1946	638	415	256	28.4	251	36.3	629	467	491	703	618
1947	745	604	401	29.1	472	55.9	777	640	616	842	816
1948	1,542	1,189	1,140	63.0	845	54.9	1,269	773	1,247	905	928
1949	1,542	1,170	2,260	60.0	1,234	63.5	1,909	1,253	1,599	—	1,360

Sources: Infra, pp. 233, 236–238.

TABLE 10.6. *Indicators of Changes in Real Incomes, French West Africa, 1938–1949 (1938=100)*

Year	Terms of Trade of Farmers (Net Barter)			Wage Earners			Relative Returns Export Crops: Wage Earning Peanut Price: Cocoa Price:	
	Peanuts	Cocoa	Coffee	Index of Real Wage, Unskilled Laborer, Dakar	Import Purchasing Power of Wages		Unskilled Labor Rate, Dakar	Unskilled Labor Rate, Abidjan
					Dakar	Abidjan		
	(1)	(2)	(3)	(4)	(5)	(6)	(7)	(8)
1938	100	100	100	100	100	100	100	100
1945	86	38	50	47	58	85	148	45
1946	130	52	51	89	128	95	101	55
1947	121	65	77	92	126	104	96	63
1948	124	91	68	140	102	62	122	147
1949	96	141	77	—	119	78	81	180

Sources: Infra, pp. 233, 236–238.

similarly, suffered sharp reductions in real income during the war and particularly dramatic declines in the period 1945–1949.

(b) Wartime incomes of cocoa farmers everywhere tended to fall more than did incomes of growers of other crops. They recovered most quickly after the war, however, and reached new heights in the immediate postwar period. Peanut growers fared better than cocoa farmers during the war, but not so well in the years that followed; real incomes of Nigerian peanut farmers were below their 1939 level until the end of the period, though peanut growers as a group had rising incomes between 1945 and 1948, due to increases in marketed output. Senegalese peanut prices were markedly higher, relative to prewar return, than Nigerian, and were also relatively higher than prices paid for other export crops, though marketed Senegalese output fell sharply during the war and did not reach prewar levels until the mid-fifties. Hence aggregate incomes from peanut growing increased more slowly, until 1948, than in Nigeria.

(c) Wartime real wages in Accra, Abidjan and Dakar fell between 25 and 50 per cent from prewar figures. If the official Lagos cost-of-living index for the period 1939–1945 is taken at face value, then Lagos laborers enjoyed a real wage some 20 per cent higher than before the war. As we have seen, however, the reliability of this index of price is highly questionable. The import and textile price indices probably reflect more realistically the behavior of prices paid for consumer goods during these years. Nonetheless, the wartime rise in money wages was much more substantial in Lagos than in Accra. Since import prices and relative supplies of imports were not very different in the two cities, it is safe to conclude that the Lagos laborer suffered less during the war than his counterpart in Accra.

In 1945–1949, real wages seem to have remained roughly unchanged in Accra, to have fallen to a significant extent in Lagos and Abidjan, and to have risen sharply only in Senegal. The difference in the behavior of wage-rates in Dakar and Abidjan is especially striking. From 1942 to 1945 absolute wage rates appear to have been higher in Abidjan; this situation was spectacularly altered after 1945, when wage rates in Dakar were between 40 and 90 per cent higher.

(d) In general, wage earners suffered less wartime deterioration in their apparent position as regards real income than producers of export crops. It is, however, necessary to be cautious in making inferences from this fact as to welfare. Most growers of export crops could, and surely did grow more of their own food as its price rose relative to other prices. Farmers also avoided the burden of rising rents. Urban workers, on the other hand, by reason of proximity probably enjoyed easier access to scarce consumer imports. Except for Nigeria, where the urban wage earner's advantage was very large, it is hard to be sure whether the standard of living of the wage earners really increased significantly relative to that of producers of export crops. In the period 1945–1949, the incomes of farmers rose much more than wage rates, except for producers of peanuts and Ivory Coast cocoa and coffee farmers.

3

Three main factors explain the general decline in West African real incomes during the war and immediate postwar years. These were the disruption of trade relations with the rest of the world, inflationary tendencies in industrial countries, and marketing policies in the agricultural export sector of West African economies. Most fundamental was the disruption of foreign trade. Wartime shipping shortages and priorities meant that some West African exports could not be sent abroad at all. About 230,000 tons of cocoa were thus affected in Ghana and Nigeria, while in the Ivory Coast almost all of the 1942–1943 crop was left to rot. More important than this inability to market exports, however, was the drastic curtailment of import supplies. World-wide wartime cuts in the production of consumer goods, the closing down of important prewar sources of supply in the Far East, and the decrease in available shipping space combined to deprive West African markets of many of their customary supplies of consumer goods.[9]

There were few import-competing industries in West Africa that could expand output as imports were shut off after 1940. With respect to

[9] The following figures indicate the extent to which key consumer goods imports contracted during the war. It should be noted that imports of these commodities were greater in some earlier years during the 1930's, than in 1938–1939.

Volume of Selected Imports, Average 1940–1945 as a percentage of average in 1938–1939

	Country		
	Nigeria	Ghana	French W. Africa
Commodity	(percentage)	(percentage)	(percentage)
Wheat flour	31	63	70
Sugar	33	55	41
Cotton Textiles	123	99	30
Bicycles	75	87	28
Rice	—	16	29

Sources: United Kingdom, Colonial Office, 1946, pp. 126–127; Ghana, Office of the Government Statistician, 1960b; Afrique Occidentale Francaise, 1950, pp. 260–267. The Nigerian textile figure includes only the major groups of textile imports—white, prints and colored cottons; the Ghanaian includes only prints; the French West African, all cotton textiles.

foodstuffs, some substitution of local production for imports doubtless took place; bread-eaters, for example, had to shift to millet, maize or other grains in the absence of wheat flour imports. There is reason to believe, however, that increased supplies of local foodstuffs were slow in coming to market. The quantity of food most African farmers offer for sale depends on the size of harvests and on relative prices of consumer goods and food crops. Since imported consumer goods were scarce or unobtainable during many of the war and immediate postwar years, and were very high-priced, many farmers doubtless felt that it was not worthwhile to expand food output for sale, or even to continue to market customary proportions of their output. In those years when import goods were unobtainable at any price, an actual decline in locally-produced foodstuffs offered for sale could be anticipated. These hypotheses seem to be borne out by data on prices and quantities in French West Africa, though data from Ghana and Nigeria are less convincing.[10]

In any case, the smaller supply of goods available to consumers meant that some reduction of real consumption was inevitable. This being the case, the shrinkage in import supplies was thus the major factor in making for the general wartime decline in African real incomes. In the immediate postwar years, until about 1948, a second factor came into play—inflationary developments in the industrialized countries from which West Africa imported, whose rising prices were quickly reflected in higher West African price levels. This was an especially important element in the French areas, since the French inflation of these years was particularly severe. Prices of some export crops rose as fast or faster than those of imports, but in all areas wage rates tended to lag behind.

Finally, in both French and British colonies special marketing arrangements were created at the outset of the war, and in most cases these had the effect of reducing prices received by agricultural producers to figures well below what they would have been without controls. The rationale, procedures and some of the consequences of marketing schemes in British West Africa over this period have been extensively discussed elsewhere, notably by Bauer.[11] Much less is known about governmental marketing arrangements and price policies in French Africa during the war than in the territories controlled by Great Britain, though it appears that French marketing regulations there were such as to keep Ivory Coast cocoa and coffee prices below world market prices until the late 1940s.[12]

---

[10] See: Afrique Occidentale Francaise, 1951, pp. 185ff; France, Republic of, 1960, Table 18, p. 233; United Kingdom, Colonial Office, 1946 and 1948.

[11] Bauer, P. T., 1954a; Ady, P., 1953; Niculescu, B., 1954; Green, R. H., 1960.

[12] Bertrand, R., 1956, p. 289.

4

A great many factors account for the observed differences in the behavior of real incomes in various countries and between groups of producers during these years. Some are obvious. Prices on world markets, for example, are clearly of great importance. Thus producers of oilseeds maintained their income positions better than producers of cocoa during World War II because oilseeds, an essential item of basic food consumption whose supply was restricted during the war, fared better than cocoa on world markets. But because of differing conditions of supply and demand in world markets during the postwar period, cocoa producers tended to do better than oil seed sellers.

Other explanatory factors are not so easy to discern, nor does space allow all differences in the behavior of income to be discussed here. We shall therefore focus on three sets of comparisons—between general movements of income in French and British areas; between wage earners in different countries, and between agricultural producers and wage earners.

French Africa was harder hit during this period than was British Africa, in part because the disruption of trade relations was more severe there. As a result of its attachment to Vichy until November, 1942, French West Africa was cut off not only from North America, but almost as effectively from France as well. Imports of consumer goods during most of the war fell to slightly more than a third of their prewar averages,[13] and exports did only a little better. Isolation did, however, bring some beneficial effects. Senegal became a source of supply of oil fats for North Africa, and domestic refining of peanut oil expanded. But only peanut growers benefited.

Further difficulties arose from the inflation in France and the incorporation of French Africa into the French monetary system. After November 1942, when French West Africa rejoined the war on the side of the Allies, London and New York markets were re-opened to its exports, but inflation had been transmitted naturally to the French colonial areas, so that prices of African export crops on non-French markets at the official, fixed rate of exchange were much higher than world market prices. The remedy was to reduce the regulated prices of export crops to parity with world prices—a kind of selective devaluation of the franc. For cocoa, the crop most affected, this resulted in a cut in f. o. b. prices of some 50 per cent, part of which came from reduced export duties and reduction of buying fees of export firms, more from a reduction in prices to producers.[14]

[13] See above, page 211, footnote 9.   [14] Poquin, J. J., 1957, pp. 24ff.

In the postwar period, when inflation in France was greater than elsewhere in Europe, rises in prices were again transmitted to French Africa. At the same time French African consumers were denied access to markets outside the Franc zone because of quantitative restrictions on trade with non-franc zone suppliers. Of all areas of French West Africa, the Ivory Coast suffered most. During the war forced labor had been introduced on a wide scale in that territory, while African cocoa farmers particularly had been harassed by a battery of discriminatory measures imposed by the French administration at the insistence of European planters.

The differences in the behavior of wage rates in the countries being considered are less amenable to analysis than are movements of income within countries. Why did Nigerian real wages improve relative to those in Ghana during the war? And why did Ivory Coast and Nigerian wage rates lag so badly in the period 1945–1949, while in Senegal they increased?

Three factors seem most significant in this connection: conditions in the labor market, government policies regarding wages, and the effectiveness of trade union organization. During the war conditions of the labor market were not appreciably different in the four countries; in all of them the demand for labor in the non-agricultural sector was buoyant, while supply, because of the scarcity of imported incentive goods, was relatively unresponsive. In the postwar years, however, it appears likely that the growth of opportunities for wage employment was slower in Nigeria, and the supply of labor relatively more abundant, than in the other countries.

Governmental policies as concerns wages were important in Nigeria and the Ivory Coast. During the war it was explicit policy in Nigeria to prevent deterioration of real wages, and this was realized more successfully there than elsewhere. In the Ivory Coast, a policy of wage restraint was followed, at the behest of planters and timber operators, who pleaded inability to pay higher wages;[15] because the role of government in the labor market was dominant, this meant that increases in wages were more slowly realized than in other areas.

Before 1949 the trade union seems to have been a significant factor only in Senegal. African trade unions were given limited legal recognition in French Africa in 1937; in 1944 their legal existence became secure. They grew rapidly in Senegal, particularly among civil servants and clerks, but also among industrial workers. After 1945 they exerted steady pressure on the administration and private employers to force increases in wages that were in line with rising prices. Senegal was the

[15] Côte d'Ivoire, Inspection Territoriale de Travail, 1952.

scene of more well-organized strikes during this period than any other area in West Africa,[16] something relevant to the fact that the postwar rate of increase in Senegal was greater than in neighboring territories, where labor was much more weakly organized.

In Ghana and Nigeria, the birth of trade unionism coincided with the beginning of the war. The relative effectiveness of organized labor in the two countries does not seem, however, to be a significant factor in explaining movements of real wages. In both Lagos and Accra retail prices followed roughly the same path, but in Lagos the rate of money wages for workers doubled in 1942, while in Accra it rose by only some 30 per cent. In both countries no further major increase was granted between 1942 and 1945. A difference in the effectiveness of the trade unions in the two countries does not explain this lag of real wages in Accra behind those in Lagos, since the Lagos advantage was won in 1942, before trade unions attained significant proportions. Nor does it explain the behavior of wages in the period 1945–1959, when they rose almost twice as much in Ghana as in Nigeria, resulting in the reappearance in the early 1950's of prewar differentials in wages of unskilled labor between the two countries.

Explanation of differences in the movements of wages and agricultural income rests on many factors already mentioned. Wage earners tended to do better than agricultural producers during the war because of marketing difficulties for export crops and the behavior of prices paid for these crops on foreign markets. The price policies of marketing boards were particularly important during the war and postwar years. The boards in Ghana and Nigeria made unfavorable arrangements with the Ministry of Food in England in setting prices for bulk sales of West African crops in Britain.[17] During the early years of their existence the boards tended to be concerned with accumulation of reserves, and so were disposed to fix producer prices at a very low level relative to world prices. This was particularly the case for cocoa prices, since responsible individuals were inclined to be pessimistic.

In contrast, government policy in the wage-earning sector was concerned with the level of real wages, in the sense that cost-of-living changes in urban areas were the most influential guides for setting wages paid by official agencies. That real wage levels were not consistently maintained, however, is evident from the data in the tables. In the

[16] Berg, E., 1959, *passim*.

[17] The price paid by the Ministry of Food for Gold Coast cocoa was appreciably below New York prices between 1939 and 1947. Between 1941 and 1946 the controlled New York price was about £50 per ton, whereas the Ministry of Food price was between £31 and £36 per ton. In 1946–1947 the New York price rose to £155 a ton the Ministry price to £112. Cf. Green, R. H., 1960, Table I.

1945–1949 period, a more active concern with the effects of wage increases on prices, coupled with sharply rising agricultural prices on world markets, tended to reverse the wartime situation and caused wage incomes to lag behind agricultural incomes, most strikingly in Nigeria and the Ivory Coast.

5

In any attempt to assess the economic consequences of the movements of income sketched above, one question is especially important: Did the general decline in real incomes experienced by so many of West Africa's people affect the supply of effort in the exchange economy? More specifically, do rates of new planting of export crops appear to have been adversely affected, and did the fall in purchasing power of a day's labor lead to reductions in the supply of effort offered for hire?

With respect to the latter, it is clear that during the war years the supply of paid labor did contract in the Ivory Coast and in Nigeria. In the former country compulsion was necessary to maintain a work force, especially on the European plantations. The contraction was temporary, however. A year after the abandonment of forced labor in the Ivory Coast in 1946, men were migrating to seek work outside the villages, drawn by higher wages and the reappearance of consumer goods.[18] In Nigeria, similarly, the demands for tin mining labor could not be met by resort to the free labor market, and compulsory labor was introduced. Some 93,000 men were conscripted between 1942 and 1944, with an average period of employment of four months.[19] But in Nigeria, as in the Ivory Coast, the rising postwar demands for labor were met without serious difficulty, once consumer goods and hence incentives to work for wages reappeared.

One effect of differential movements of real incomes may have had more long-term significance. The supply of migrant labor from the Sudanese belt, and particularly from the Upper Volta, appears to have expanded in the immediate postwar years more substantially in Ghana than in the Ivory Coast. The two coastal territories have long been in competition for migrant northerners; in both countries they have provided the backbone of the agricultural labor supply. The relative disadvantage of Ivory Coast farmers compared with those of Ghana permitted the latter to offer better wages and working conditions, and hence attract a larger portion of the total migrant labor force from the north. Observers on both sides of the frontier believe that this occurred in the

[18] Côte d'Ivoire, Inspection Territoriale de Travail, 1947.
[19] Federation of Nigeria, Department of Labour, 1940–1945.

immediate postwar years, though there is no way to confirm the supposition by quantitative data.

As to the responses of rates of planting in agriculture to the total situation, the evidence is inconclusive, though it does suggest that the rate of new planting was adversely affected. Output of cocoa in Ghana remained below the levels attained in most of the 1930's until the latter part of the 1950's, which would indicate that little net new planting occurred during the low price periods of the '30's and '40's. On the other hand, swollen shoot disease ravaged wide areas, having a decisive impact on output. With over 112 million trees cut out in anti-swollen shoot efforts, and an estimated additional 50 million trees dying, a reduced output of some 75,000 tons resulted.[20] Replanting at an appreciable rate must have been going on to maintain aggregate production even at the levels it attained in the late '40's and early '50's, particularly in view of the major relocation of production during this period. In Nigeria, rates of increase of output are likewise unimpressive until the second half of the '50's.[21] In the Ivory Coast, the picture is similar. Until the early 1950's, new planting would seem to have been at a minimum.

The trends in real income during the war and immediate postwar years also had political consequences worth mentioning. In the light of what happened to African incomes, it is in fact difficult to avoid a crude economic determinism in interpreting the political history of this period. Except for cocoa farmers in Ghana and Nigeria after 1947, this was a period of sharply reduced living standards throughout the area. It was also marked by political protest and turbulence. These are the years of the Lagos general strike in 1945, the Accra riots in 1948, the "positive action" movement of 1949–1950 in Ghana, the Ivory Coast "incidents" of the same years. It is the time when West African political and labor movements attained peaks of radicalism unknown in the past, and which were in many instances not subsequently attained. During these years, for example, Nigerian labor conducted its only flirtation with political action. And in the Ivory Coast, whose African planters and wage earners suffered the hardest trials of any West African people, the radical nationalist Rassemblement Démocratique Africain came into power, based largely on support from African planters. In all of these, of course, powerful forces with many different origins were at work. But there is little doubt that these forces were focused and catalyzed by the deteriorating standards of living that characterized the period 1939–1949.

[20] Green, R. H., 1960, p. 32.
[21] See *Infra*, Table 10.13.

6

The last years of the 1940's represent a turning point in West African economic history. By 1948 or 1949 the immediate economic effects of the war had worn off. Exports from the industrial countries were easier to obtain. The world-wide postwar inflation was largely over. New plans for public investment were on the drafting boards or actually in operation, and there began thereafter the great surge of economic activity that characterized the early part of the 1950's.

The late 1940's also mark a turning point in the behavior of African real incomes. From 1948 or 1949 onward, the general trend turned upward, and African standards of life underwent marked improvement. And though, as we have seen,[22] the data for this period remain inadequate in many respects, they nonetheless permit a sharper picture of income movements than was possible for earlier years. Some of the principal trends that become apparent in scanning the data in Tables 10.7 to 10.12 and Appendix Tables 10.13 to 10.15 are as follows:

1. In comparison with the late 1940's, West African real incomes of almost all groups steadily rose throughout most of the decade of the 1950's.

2. Africans in the Ivory Coast made the most rapid gains.

3. In the decade of the 1950's, sellers of palm kernels in Nigeria did relatively less well than other farmers, and coffee growers in the Ivory Coast did relatively better.

4. After the mid-1950's, wage earners everywhere gained relative to agriculturalists.

Just as there were variations in levels of income during the period, there were differences between West African countries in the extent to which economic improvement occurred. In Ghana, average real income per cocoa producer, as measured by the movement of the net barter terms of trade, averaged about 45 per cent above the 1949 level during the eleven years between 1950 and 1960. In Nigeria the real incomes of cocoa farmers by this same measure averaged only about 30 per cent higher than in 1949. Differences in the absolute level of prices paid cocoa producers in our second base year of 1949 are, however, important in this comparison, since in 1949 prices paid producers for cocoa were almost 20 per cent higher in Nigeria than in Ghana.[23] Furthermore, after 1954 the income terms of trade in Nigeria, relative to 1949, were significantly higher than in Ghana; output in Nigeria, that is, showed a greater rate of increase than in Ghana, though heavy crops

[22] *Supra*, pp. 200–203.
[23] *Infra*, Tables 10.13 and 10.14.

TABLE 10.7. Changes in Money Incomes and Prices of Consumer Goods, Nigeria, 1946–1960 (1949=100)

	Indicators of Changes in Money Incomes							Price Changes			
	Producer Prices and Aggregate Receipts of Farmers						Wage Rate, Unskilled Laborer, Lagos	United Africa Company Index Wholesale Prices of Imported Goods			Retail Price Index, Lagos
	Cocoa		Peanuts		Palm Kernels			Lagos	Lagos	Kano	
Year	Producer Receipts Price	Producer Receipts	Producer Receipts Price	Producer Receipts	Producer Receipts Price	Producer Receipts		Cal. yr.	Crop yr.	Crop yr.	
	(1)	(2)	(3)	(4)	(5)	(6)	(7)	(8)	(9)	(10)	(11)
1946	50	56	75	129	—	—	100	—	—	—	—
1947	63	47	75	132	63	61	100	98	100	98	—
1948	120	130	91	158	81	83	100	99	103	104	—
1949	100	100	100	100	100	100	100	100	100	100	100
1950	120	132	100	76	123	127	103	101	118	124	133
1951	170	180	170	384	138	126	115	128	131	136	140
1952	170	184	170	388	129	147	129	124	120	116	131
1953	164	161	165	372	117	140	132	111	112	105	136
1954	196	174	165	327	117	149	144	108	109	98	143
1955	196	225	167	469	117	135	181	105	112	102	148
1956	146	197	153	289	115	148	181	114	120	105	162
1957	146	118	153	579	115	131	181	119	120	104	163
1958	146	206	136	385	115	147	181	118	125	106	163
1959	156	242	208	493	112	132	181	128	130	111	170
1960	144	252	—	—	112	130	226	130	136	116	179

Sources: Infra, pp. 230, 231, 234 235.

TABLE 10.8. *Indicators of Changes in Real Incomes, Nigeria, 1946–1960 (1949=100)*

Year	Cocoa		Terms of Trade of Farmers Peanuts		Palm Kernels		Wage Earners		Relative Returns Cocoa Price: Unskilled Labor Rate, Lagos
	Net Barter	Income	Net Barter	Income	Net Barter	Income	Real Wage, Unskilled Laborer, Lagos	Import Purchasing Power of Wages, Lagos	
	(1)	(2)	(3)	(4)	(5)	(6)	(7)	(8)	(9)
1946	—	—	—	—	—	—	—	—	50
1947	63	47	76	134	63	61	—	102	63
1948	117	126	88	152	79	81	—	101	120
1949	100	100	100	100	100	100	100	100	100
1950	102	112	81	61	104	108	77	102	117
1951	130	137	125	282	105	96	82	90	148
1952	142	154	147	334	108	123	98	104	132
1953	146	144	157	354	104	125	97	119	124
1954	175	160	168	334	107	137	101	133	136
1955	175	201	164	460	104	121	122	172	108
1956	122	164	146	275	96	123	112	159	81
1957	122	98	147	557	96	109	111	152	81
1958	117	165	128	363	92	118	111	153	81
1959	120	186	187	444	86	102	106	141	86
1960	106	185	—	—	82	96	126	174	64

Sources: Infra, pp. 230, 231, 234, 235.

TABLE 10.9. *Changes in Money Incomes and Prices of Consumer Goods, Ghana (Gold Coast),* 1946–1960 (1949=100)

	Indicators of Changes in Money Incomes		Wage Earners	Changes in Prices of Consumer Goods		
	Cocoa Farmers		Wage Rate, Unskilled	UAC Index of Wholesale Prices, Imports, Accra		Consumer Price Index,
	Producer Price	Aggregate Receipts	Laborer, Accra	Cal. yr.	Crop yr.	Accra
Year	(1)	(2)	(3)	(4)	(5)	(6)
1946	61	47	68–95	—	—	—
1947	89	75	82–95	103	100	—
1948	144	163	95	98	96	91
1949	100	100	100	100	100	100
1950	156	165	112	105	115	115
1951	178	151	112	125	123	134
1952	156	155	148	121	117	131
1953	160	136	154	117	114	133
1954	160	143	154	113	110	132
1955	178	164	154	110	107	137
1956	178	189	163	109	111	139
1957	160	134	183	114	111	143
1958	160	165	190	112	111	140
1959	133	171	190	113	112	150
1960	133	185	197	117	117	148

Sources: Infra, pp. 232, 235, 236.

TABLE 10.10. *Indicators of Changes in Real Incomes, Ghana (Gold Coast),*
1946–1960 (1949 = 100)

| | Cocoa Farmers | | Wage Earners | | Relative Returns |
| | Terms of Trade | | Real Wages, Labourer, Accra | Import Purchasing Power of Wages | Cocoa Price: Unskilled Labour Rate, Accra |
	Net Barter	Income			
Year	(1)	(2)	(3)	(4)	(5)
1946	—	—	—	—	90–64
1947	89	75	—	80–92	109–94
1948	151	170	104	98	152
1949	100	100	100	100	100
1950	136	143	97	107	139
1951	145	123	84	90	159
1952	133	132	113	122	105
1953	141	119	116	132	104
1954	145	130	117	136	104
1955	166	153	112	139	116
1956	160	170	117	150	109
1957	144	121	128	161	87
1958	144	149	136	170	84
1959	119	153	127	168	70
1960	114	158	133	168	68

Sources: Infra, pp. 232, 235, 236.

TABLE 10.11. *Changes in Money Incomes and Prices of Consumer Goods, French West Africa, 1946–1960 (1949 = 100)*

	Indicators of Changes in Money Incomes								Price Changes			
	Producer Prices and Estimated Receipts of Farmers						Wage Earners					
	Senegalese Peanuts		Ivory Coast Cocoa		Ivory Coast Coffee		Wage Rate Unskilled Laborer		Prices of African-Consumed Imports	Retail Prices African-Consumed Goods, Dakar	Cost of Living Index, European Families	
Year	Producer Price	Receipts	Producer Price	Receipts	Producer Price	Receipts	Dakar	Abidjan			Dakar	Abidjan
	(1)	(2)	(3)	(4)	(5)	(6)	(7)	(8)	(9)	(10)	(11)	(12)
1946	41	35	—	—	—	—	33	37	31	36	32	—
1947	48	52	—	—	—	—	41	51	39	47	40	57
1948	100	102	—	—	48	—	67	62	78	68	67	71
1949	100	100	100	100	100	100	100	100	100	100	100	100
1950	166	132	105	109	209	193	110	117	102	107	105	109
1951	128	132	165	121	311	317	124	133	111	112	120	118
1952	130	137	169	172	314	251	140	167	124	132	131	137
1953	138	177	354	349	463	600	151	194	106	135	137	138
1954	148	134	231	280	317	422	168	223	97	133	136	135
1955	138	174	147	170	291	477	168	232	96	132	138	141
1956	139	231	143	172	343	582	175	284	—	125	141	144
1957	147	285	343	261	409	616	190	318	—	146	150	163
1958	147	244	310	289	346	883	210	353	—	156	184	199
1959	152	255	300	219	300	632	240	394	—	168	191	211
1960	152	289	271	330	271	791	240	394	—	—	195	213

Sources: Infra, pp. 233, 236–238.

TABLE 10.12. *Indicators of Changes in Real Incomes, French West Africa, 1946-1960 (1949=100)*

| | Terms of Trade of Farmers (Net Barter) | | | Wage Earners | | | Relative Returns of Export Crops: Wage Earning | |
	Senegalese Peanuts	Ivory Coast Cocoa	Ivory Coast Coffee	Real Wage, Unskilled Laborer, Dakar	Import Purchasing Power of Wages Dakar	Abidjan	Coffee Price: Unskilled Labor Rate, Abidjan	Peanut Price: Unskilled Labor Rate, Dakar
Year	(1)	(2)	(3)	(4)	(5)	(6)	(7)	(8)
1946	132	—	—	92	106	119	—	124
1947	123	—	—	87	105	131	—	117
1948	128	—	62	99	86	79	77	149
1949	100	100	100	100	100	100	100	100
1950	163	103	205	103	108	115	179	151
1951	115	149	280	111	112	120	234	103
1952	105	136	253	106	113	135	188	93
1953	130	334	437	112	142	183	239	91
1954	153	238	327	126	173	213	142	88
1955	144	153	303	127	175	243	125	82
1956	—	—	—	140	—	—	120	79
1957	—	—	—	130	—	—	129	77
1958	—	—	—	135	—	—	98	70
1959	—	—	—	148	—	—	76	63
1960	—	—	—	—	—	—	69	63

Sources: See Appendix, *infra*, pp. 233, 236–238.

in Ghana narrowed this difference after 1959. For these reasons it can be argued that despite the generally more favorable evolution of the Ghanaian farmer's net barter terms of trade since 1949, real incomes have increased more in the Nigerian cocoa industry as a whole than in the Ghanaian. The Lagos laborer, on the other hand, saw his real income rise little over the decade of the 1950's. In no year was it more than 20 per cent higher than in 1949; the annual average real wage over the 11-year period was in fact lower than in 1949. Real wages of the Accra laborer showed a more distinct upward trend after 1951, which became especially marked after 1957; over the decade real wage rates averaged about 12 per cent higher than in 1949.

The most striking increase in African real incomes occurred in the Ivory Coast. Full data to measure the true extent of this increase are not available, as the unfilled spaces in Tables 10.11 and 10.12 and Appendix Table 10.15 suggest. But it does not require more information to confirm that the Ivory Coast has been the scene of extraordinary prosperity. While producers in neighboring territories were enjoying relatively slow increases through the decade, Ivory Coast cocoa farmers, as Table 10.11 shows, were receiving high, and in some years extremely high, prices; and coffee prices fluctuated between two and four times their 1949 level. Combined with the tremendous increases in coffee output over the period, these prices led to increases in income at a rate unequalled anywhere in the region.[24]

Ivory Coast wage earners, similarly, won money wage increases at a far faster rate than their counterparts in Dakar, Lagos or Accra. While money wage rates rose some two and a half times in Dakar between 1949 and 1960, they went up almost four times in Abidjan during the same period. However, Abidjan wage earners started at a much lower absolute level in 1949, while their absolute rate remained below that prevailing in Dakar until January 1961, when parity was temporarily achieved. It is also likely that consumer prices increased more rapidly in the Ivory Coast than in Senegal during this period. This is suggested by the increase in the cost of living index for European families in Abidjan; in the absence of usable data on African consumer prices, however, it is hard to be certain on this point. In any event, neither slightly greater price increases nor the fact of a lower absolute level of wages alters the significance of the rapid increase in money wages in Abidjan since 1949.

On comparing the relative returns to urban wage earners and producers of export crops, one observes different trends in the French- and English-speaking areas until the mid-fifties. In Ghana and Nigeria the

[24] The price of coffee in 1949 was relatively low. This tends to exaggerate somewhat the increase since 1949. Cf. Table 10.15, *infra*.

agriculturalists more than held their own relative to wage earners until 1955, except for Nigerian palm kernel producers. In Senegal and the Ivory Coast, however, wage rates increased more rapidly than producer prices of peanuts and cocoa after 1951, though this was not true in the case of coffee. After 1955, for all crop exporters in all areas, wage rates in the towns tended to increase relative to price per unit of export crop.

This suggests that the standards of living of wage earners tended to improve more than those of export crop farmers. But such a judgement must remain tentative, because of uncertainties as to changes in prices paid by members of the groups in question. Food is the largest element in the budgets of all groups, and since farmers raise much of their own food, it is not clear that the "prices" they paid for foodstuffs can be considered to have risen as much as the actual prices paid by urban workers. Furthermore, charges for rent, which are a significant part of the budgets of urban workers and a much less important element of the farmer's expenditure, have tended to rise faster than other prices everywhere in West Africa. In the absence of price series for goods consumed by farmers, one may only note two opposed tendencies. On the one hand, local foods have tended to be cheaper where they are grown than in cities, because of high transportation charges per unit of value; on the other, costs of transport and lack of competition among sellers have tended to make imported goods more expensive in rural than in urban areas. The changes in consumption patterns implied by all these changes in relative prices render welfare judgements impracticable. Further, improvements in the net barter terms of trade of cocoa farmers may, in this case, understate the improvement in each producer's real remuneration, because of increased productivity resulting from higher-yielding trees and widespread use of anti-capsid sprays.

A variety of elements enter into the explanation of the real income trends just outlined. Differences in the movement of net barter terms of trade realized by producers of various crops are explicable by differences in the behavior of the market prices of these crops. But large inter-country differences were caused by differences in the price and tax policies of the countries of West Africa. Because of Marketing Board levies and high export duties, producers in Ghana and Nigeria were paid a relatively small share of realized prices; between 1951 and 1959 Ghanaian cocoa farmers received an average of only 55 per cent of total proceeds from cocoa exports.[25] Furthermore, the export crops of Ghana and Nigeria had no protection in the markets of consuming countries.

In French Africa, by contrast, special protective arrangements with the franc zone led to substantially higher prices for some African exports

[25] Green, R. H., 1960, Table XIII.

than prevailed on world markets. Franc zone prices for peanuts, for example, were from 10 to 30 per cent above non-franc prices during the 1950's. And extraordinary support was given to coffee prices after the collapse of the world coffee market that began in 1958; franc zone coffee prices were actually two-thirds again as high as non-franc prices in 1960.[26]

In French Africa, moreover, there were no state marketing agencies at all until the mid-fifties, when "Stabilization Funds" for cocoa and coffee were established. Nor, after their establishment, did these organizations act (as in Ghana and Nigeria) as disguised taxing agencies by fixing producer prices at a relatively low level compared with selling prices abroad. Finally, duties on major exports were lower in French Africa than in Ghana and Nigeria; export taxes on cocoa and coffee averaged 14 per cent in the Ivory Coast in 1958,[27] for example, compared with cocoa duties of over 35 per cent in Ghana.[28]

With respect to the behavior of wages during these years, two sets of questions demand special attention: Why did wage incomes rise relative to farm incomes after the mid-fifties, and why did wages rise faster in the French-speaking areas than in Ghana and Nigeria?

Concerning the first question, three factors seem basic. First, wages in West Africa, as elsewhere in the world, are extremely sticky; a declining rate in money wages became an unusual event in postwar Africa. In the wage-earning sector of these economies, a decline in activity leads not to changes in wage rates but to reductions in the level of employment and earnings. In the agricultural sector worsening market conditions lead to a fall in the level of prices. After 1955, and especially after 1958, there was a tendency for prices of most of West Africa's export crops to weaken. Money wage showed no such tendency.

Related to this has been the fact that the principal criterion determining changes in money wages in West Africa over most of this decade has been changes in the cost of living, at least insofar as workers of unskilled and semi-skilled grades are concerned. In periods when domestic price levels are stable or declining, money wage rates remain unchanged, and sometimes even increase. In periods of rising domestic prices, wage rates catch up, though there may be in some instances a sizeable lag. Prices to producers of agricultural goods, on the other hand, are not set with an eye to cost of living changes.

[26] See, for example, Ady, P., 1960; Côte d'Ivoire, Gouverneur, pp. 127ff; Côte d'Ivoire, Service de la Statistique, 1959(?), pp. 243ff; Banque Centraledes Etats de l'Afrique de l'Ouest, 1960, pp. 11–12; and note 10, p. 212, above.

[27] Beyrard, N., 1960, Table XIX.

[28] Cf. note 11, p. 212, above.

Finally, the political factors that have been at work must be considered. One of the more tangible political gestures open to new African governments is the introduction of a general increase in wage rates. This was an important factor in the several wage increases that occurred in Ghana since independence in 1957. It was also a factor in Nigeria, where, partly because of political competition between the regions, Western Nigeria raised its wage level well above the level prevailing in other regions, ultimately forcing some of the others to match the increase.

In all of West Africa, government is a principal factor in the labor market, both because it is the largest non-agricultural employer and because it can establish statutory minimum wages, as it did in French West Africa during the entire period and as it did in Ghana in 1960. Determination of government wage scales or a minimum wage has, in all countries, involved close attention to the level of real wages, hence to some cost-of-living index. But government real wage adjustments were relatively infrequent in Ghana and Nigeria, since changes in wage rates required full-scale commissions of inquiry. In French West Africa, the committees charged with establishing the minimum wage met annually, so that adjustments occurred with a smaller lag. Whether or not this procedural difference actually operated in favor of the French West African wage earner over the whole period of the 1950s depends on the base years chosen for comparison, however.

Another factor at work in Senegal was the existence of an effective labor movement, capable of securing for its members a greater share in total output than could the labor movements in other countries in West Africa. With the coming of independence and concomitant responsibility for general economic policy, the Senegalese labor movement put less emphasis on this aggressive aspect of its behavior. This fact, together with a more rapid increase in productivity in the Ivory Coast during the late fifties, led to achievement of near-parity in real wages between these countries early in 1961.

The main explanatory factor, however, is the fact that increases in personal disposable incomes reflect the rise in national product more closely in French West Africa than they do in Ghana and Nigeria. The reason for this is that expenditure for development in French West Africa was mainly financed by the metropolitan government, while that of Ghana and Nigeria was largely self-financed.[29] Thus, disposable incomes rose less in the latter countries than in the former.

The general or "indiscriminate" benefits of development must not be forgotten. "Public goods" were, during the decade 1950–1960, spread

[29] United Nations, Department of Economic and Social Affairs, 1959a, chapter 4; Banque Centrale des États de l'Afrique de l'Ouest, 1959.

more lavishly and intensively among the people of West Africa than ever before. Medical services, education, access to positions of skill and responsibility, all became available for the first time to large numbers of Africans, and modern transport and communications systems brought the world closer to immeasurably more villages than in the past.[30] It is in this regard, rather than in increasing levels of personal income, that the improvement in African living standards has been most striking and significant.

[30] See United Nations, Department of Trusteeship and Non-self-Governing Territories, 1955, 1958, 1960a and b.

Notes to Tables 10.1 to 10.12
and Appendix Tables 10.13 to 10.15

The data from which the indices in Tables 1 to 12 are constructed are given in Tables 10.13 to 10.15 below. Unless otherwise noted, price and output figures refer to crop years.

NIGERIA

Cocoa

Prices are naked, ex-scale, Grade I, main crop, at port of shipment. Since 1953 a tax of £4 a ton has been levied on producers; this has been deducted from the gazetted price. The 1960–1961 price is a weighted average for the main crop; in January 1961 after 130,000 tons had been purchased at a price of £160, the price was cut to £112 for the remainder of the crop season. The tonnage for 1960 is a preliminary estimate. The aggregate payment series is derived by multiplying producer price for Grade I main crop cocoa by tonnage purchased. This involves an overstatement of aggregate payments on two counts: (a) mid-crop prices were £2–3 a ton lower than main crop in 1947–1948, and £5 lower from 1948–1953; (b) not all marketed cocoa is Grade I. With regard to the latter consideration, however, the method used here understates the increase in producer incomes over time, since the proportion of the total crop classified as Grade I has increased. Source of data up to 1947 is Bauer, 1954b, Appendix I; after 1947, *Statistical Digests*, Nigeria.

Peanuts

Standard Grade, Kano, Naked, ex-scale at railhead. Since 1953 a tax of £1 per ton has been levied on sales; this has been deducted from the gazetted price. Data for years before 1942 from Ady, *Economic Journal*, 1953; for years 1942–1947 from Bauer, Appendix I; from 1947–1957, *Statistical Digests*. For some of the earlier years substantially different prices are given by different sources, most of which seems due to different bases of calculation—i.e., crop year or calendar year. Postwar data are much more consistent. Terms of trade indexes use Kano prices of imported goods. (See discussion of the UAC price index below.) Income increases are understated since special grade peanuts form an increasing portion of total output.

Palm Kernels

Naked, ex-scale at port of shipment. Since 1953 a tax of £1 per ton has been levied in the North and West. Since roughly half of Nigeria's palm kernel out-

1939–1960

Year	Cocoa Producer Price (£ per ton)	Cocoa Sales (000)(tons)	Cocoa Receipts £ m.	Peanuts Producer Price (£ per ton)	Peanuts Sales (000)(tons)	Peanuts Receipts £ m.	Palm Kernels Producer Price (£ per ton)	Palm Kernels Sales (000)(tons)	Palm Kernels Receipts £ m.	Wage Rate, Unskilled Laborer, Lagos Sh. per day
1939	17	82	1.39	6.6	169	1.12	—	—	—	1/0
1940	14	101	1.41	5.4	247	1.33	—	—	—	1/0
1941	15	99	1.49	5.4	194	1.05	—	—	—	1/1–1/3
1942	13	111	1.44	6.5	143	.93	—	—	—	1/9–2/0
1943	13	71	.92	9.0	194	1.75	—	—	—	2/0
1944	23	86	1.98	12.0	228	2.74	—	—	—	2/0
1945	27.5	103	2.83	12.0	300	3.60	—	—	—	2/2–2/5
1946	50	111	5.55	16.0	323	5.17	—	—	—	2/7
1947	62.5	74	4.63	16.0	330	5.28	16.3	356	5.80	2/7
1948	120	109	13.1	19.2	328	6.30	21.0	374	7.85	2/7
1949	100	100	10.0	21.2	188	4.00	26.0	363	9.44	2/7
1950	120	110	13.2	21.2	143	3.03	32.0	376	12.03	2/8
1951	170	106	18.0	36.0	426	15.34	36.0	330	11.88	3/0
1952	170	108	18.4	36.0	431	15.52	33.5	413	13.84	3/4
1953	164	98	16.1	35.0	425	14.88	30.5	434	13.24	3/5
1954	196	89	17.4	35.0	373	13.06	30.5	462	14.09	3/9
1955	196	115	22.5	35.4	530	18.76	30.5	418	12.75	4/8
1956	146	135	19.7	32.4	357	11.57	30	466	13.98	4/8
1957	146	81	11.8	32.4	715	23.17	30	412	12.36	4/8
1958	146	141	20.6	28.9	533	15.40	30	461	13.83	4/8
1959	156	155	24.2	44.2	446	19.71	29	429	12.44	4/8
1960	144	175	25.2	—	619	—	29	422	12.24	5/10

TABLE 10.14. *GHANA (GOLD COAST). Producer Prices, Sales and Aggregate Receipts of Cocoa Farmers, and Wage Rates, 1939–1960*

Year	Cocoa Producer Price £ per ton	Sh. per load	Cocoa Purchases 000 tons	Receipts £ m.	Wage Rate, Unskilled Laborer, Accra Sh. per day
1939	14.4	8/4	181	2.6	1/5
1940	11.5	7	237	2.7	1/7
1941	13.4	7/10	251	3.4	1/10
1942	11.6	6/11	207	2.4	1/10
1943	13.0	7/3	196	2.5	1/10
1944	22.4	11/9	229	5.1	1/10
1945	27.0	14/6	209	5.6	1/10
1946	51.3	21/6	192	9.8	2/0–2/9
1947	74.7	40	208	15.5	2/5–2/9
1948	121.3	65	278	33.7	2/9
1949	84	45	248	20.8	2/11
1950	130.7	70	262	34.2	3/3
1951	149.3	80	211	31.5	3/3
1952	130.7	70	247	32.3	4/2
1953	134.4	72	211	28.4	4/6
1954	134.4	72	220	29.6	4/6
1955	149.3	80	229	34.2	4/6
1956	149.3	80	264	39.4	4/9
1957	134.4	72	207	27.8	5/4
1958	134.4	72	256	34.4	5/6
1959	112	60	317	35.5	5/6
1960	112	60	343	38.4	5/9

TABLE 10.15. FRENCH WEST AFRICA. Prices, Sales and Estimated Aggregate Receipts of Export Crop Growers, and Wage Rates, 1938-1960

Year	Peanuts (Senegal) Producer Price (000 Fr. per Ton)	Peanuts Sales (000) (tons)	Peanuts Receipts (Billions of Francs)	Coffee (Ivory Coast) 'Official' Price (000 Francs per Ton)	Coffee Producer Price (000 Francs per Ton)	Coffee Sales (000) (Tons)	Coffee Estimated Receipts (Bill. of Francs)	Cocoa (Ivory Coast) 'Official' Price (000 Francs per Ton)	Cocoa Producer Price (000 Francs per Ton)	Cocoa Sales (000) (Tons)	Cocoa Estimated Receipts (Bill. of Francs)	Unskilled Labor, Wage Rates, Francs per Hour — Dakar	Abidjan
1938	.94	569	.53	8	—	18		3.9	—	55.2		.875	.75
1939	.90	560	.50	8.7	—	15.6		3.7	—	45.4		1.0	.75
1940	.95	419	.40	10.4	—	28.4		5.1	—	43.0		1.075	—
1941	1.40	199	.28	16.1	—	19.8		8.5	—	28.6		1.175	.875
1942	1.85	114	.21	18.9	—	23		4.4	—	.5		1.34	1.5
1943	1.88	274	.52	13.5	—	24.1		5.2	—	14.7		1.48	—
1944	3.04	234	.71	20.0	—	37.9		8.8	—	26.3		1.50	2.25
1945	3.5	354	1.2	28.0	—	36.3		25.7	—	28.4		2.2	2.75
1946	6.0	365	2.2	50.4	—	55.9		50.4	—	29.1		5.5	3.5
1947	7.0	452	3.2	72.0	—	54.9		74.0	—	63.0		6.8	4.8
1948	14.5	434	6.3	—	35	63.5	2.2	—	45.5	60	2.7	11.1	5.8
1949	14.5	429	6.2	—	73	58.8	4.3	—	48	62	3.0	16.7	9.4
1950	24.0	342	8.2	—	109	63.7	6.9	—	75	44	3.3	18.4	11.0
1951	18.6	443	8.2	—	110	50.7	5.6	—	77	61	4.7	20.7	12.5
1952	18.9	449	8.5	—	162	82.3	13.3	—	161	59	9.5	23.4	15.7
1953	20.0	550	11.0	—	111	84.3	9.4	—	105	73	7.6	25.3	18.2
1954	21.4	390	8.3	—	102	103.8	10.6	—	67	69	4.6	28.1	21.0
1955	20.0	539	10.8	—	120	107.6	12.9	—	65	72	4.7	28.1	21.8
1956	20.1	712	14.3	—	143	95.7	13.7	—	156	45.5	7.1	29.3	26.7
1957	21.3	830	17.7	—	121	162	19.6	—	141	56	7.9	31.7	29.9
1958	21.3	709	15.1	—	(105)	134	14.1	—	(95)	62	5.9	35	33.2
1959	22.0	720	15.8	—	(95)	185	17.4	—	(95)	94	8.9	40	37.0
1960	22.0	812	17.9									40	37.0

put is produced in the East, 10 shillings per ton has been deducted from the gazetted price to account for the tax. There are particularly great divergencies in pre-1947 prices of palm kernels given in different sources; between Bauer and Ady, for example, differences of as much as 50 per cent appear in some years. I have, therefore, not included palm kernel data for years before 1947; from 1949 on, prices and tonnages are from *Statistical Digests*.

Wages

The wage rate refers to the entering rate for unskilled labor ("general labor") in government employment in Lagos. While this wage rate does not give an accurate picture of general movements in wage rates because of large regional and skill differentials, it is the closest approach to a key rate. The rates given in the table are annual averages. Dual rates in 1941, 1942 and 1945 are due to the granting of retroactive wage awards in 1942 and 1945. The lower figure excludes the retroactive payment, the higher includes it. Sources of data are: United Kingdom, Colonial Office, 1946; Nigeria, Federation of, Department of Labour, 1940–1960; and Nigeria, Federation of, 1955. Real wage indices refer to calendar years.

Prices

For the war and immediate postwar years there exist three indices of import goods prices, one computed by the Colonial Office, a second computed by the Nigerian Government, and a third constructed by Peter Ady. The first two are reproduced in Bauer, 1956b, Appendix II; Ady's index is given in Ady, 1949. The Ady index is in a c.i.f. value index weighted according to purported rural expenditure patterns; the others are composed of twenty items, including several (motor vehicles, fuel oil, whiskey, cement) not consumed by Africans, and weighted by import values. The Nigerian Government and Colonial Office index move together for years in which they overlap; I have therefore linked them together to form the index given in Table 1. Bauer argues that these indices substantially understate the true rise in import prices, and that the index of landed costs of cotton piece goods is a closer approximation to the true rise. Ady's index tends to bear this out; in the postwar years it follows Bauer's textile price index much more closely than the Nigerian Government and Colonial Office indices. Both the Ady index and Bauer's textile index show prices some 15 per cent greater than the index used in Tables 1 and 2.

The Lagos Cost of Living Index was constructed by the Labour Department. It appears in the annual reports of the Labour Department, and in the Tudor-Davies Report. The index was discontinued after April 1945, though food prices were collected on an informal basis until 1947. The collection was hardly rigorous; the *Annual Report* of the Labour Department for 1947 notes that "volunteer ladies" did the price collecting. From 1949–1953, the Lagos retail price index is interpolated from a graph given in the appendix to Nigeria, Federation of, 1955. The possible margin of error is substantial. After 1953 the official Lagos Cost of Living Index is used, as found in the *Statistical Digests*.

The United Africa Company Index of Wholesale Prices of Imported Goods is computed on a crop year basis to make it comparable to price and tonnage data. For years 1947–1957 the index is weighted by the value of sales of certain main groups of goods in the year 1947–1958. The major components and their weight is as follows: Textiles 47 per cent, drinks and tobacco 22 per cent, food, 14 per cent, hardware 8 per cent. The description of its construction is in United Africa Company, 1949, pp. 40–43. From 1958 on, a new current weight index was published by the United Africa Company (see United Africa Company, 1959, pp. 56–58). It has been linked to the old index. All terms of trade indices use crop year wholesale import prices: the "import purchasing power of wages" indexes use calendar year prices.

The UAC publishes a "producer's terms of trade" index, computed by dividing indices of gazetted prices of main crops by their wholesale price index (since 1957, by a retail price index). The UAC producer terms of trade indices are in some instances markedly lower than the net barter terms of trade indices used in the text—sometimes as much as 30 per cent. There is no apparent explanation for these differences.

GHANA

Cocoa

Cocoa price and tonnage data for years up to 1947 are from Bauer, 1954b, Appendix I. His prices are adjusted statutory producer prices at railheads; they are consistently lower than those given by other students—for example, by Ady, 1953. Bauer's tonnage figures are also significantly lower for 1939— 188,000 tons as compared with Ady's figure of 242,000 tons. From 1947 Cocoa Marketing Board statistics are used. Prices are for Grade I main crop cocoa. Mid-crop prices were lower in several years.

Wages

The wage rate for unskilled labor is the starting rate for government laborers in Accra. All rates are averages for the calendar year, taking account of the time of the year changes were introduced. The dual figures for 1946 and 1947 are due to the Korsah award which granted an increase retroactive to January 1946. The lower figure for each year is the rate for the year exclusive of the retroactive payment; the higher rate includes it.

Prices

The import price index is from Ady (1949). The textile price index is from Bauer, Appendix II. The Accra Cost of Living Index for the years 1939–1947 is from Ghana, Department of Labour, 1939–1948; from 1948–1960 it is from Ghana, Office of the Government Statistician, 1948–1961. The UAC Wholesale Price Index is similar to the Nigerian index discussed above. In Table 9 (column 4) the index is presented both on a crop year (Fall–Summer) and calendar year basis. The UAC "producer's terms of trade" index for Ghanaian cocoa shows differences from the net barter terms of trade index, as in the Nigerian case.

FRENCH WEST AFRICA

Senegal Peanuts

Peanut prices are average producer prices for unshelled nuts at Kaolack: until 1956–1957 average prices actually paid over the crop year; after 1957, minimum guaranteed price at Kaolack. There is a small discrepancy—of the order of 5 per cent—in prices cited in different official sources. Sources of data are France, Ministère de l'Outre-Mer, Services de Statistiques Outre-Mer, 1960; Banque Centrale des États de l'Afrique de l'Ouest, 1961; and Senegal, Service de la Statistique, 1953–1960.

Ivory Coast Cocoa

No data are available for producer prices up to 1949. From 1939–1949 there is a series of undefined "official prices", given in Afrique Occidentale Francaise, 1951, p. 394. These are used in the tables. From 1949–1958 prices are for "courant" grade cocoa, naked ex-scale Abidjan, c.f.a. francs per ton, average price to producer, crop year. Prices for 1959 and 1960 crop years are guaranteed minimum producer prices, Abidjan. There are large differences in producer prices cited in different official sources. (See Afrique Occidentale Française, 1956, p. 333, and France, Ministère de l'Outre-Mer, Service des Statistiques Outre-Mer, 1960, p. 257, where prices differing by nearly 40 per cent appear for some years.) Prices used in the tables are from Afrique Occidentale Française, 1956, p. 333 (for the years 1949–1953), and from Côte d'Ivoire, Service de la Statistique, 1959 (?), p. 177 (for the years 1953–1958).

Tonnage figures refer, for year 1939–1946, to calendar year exports. From 1947–1957 crop year "exported production" figures are used, as cited in Côte d'Ivoire, Service de la Statistique, 1958a, p. 34. From 1957–1960 output refers to crop year "marketed production," as given in reports of the Banque Centrale des États de l'Ouest, and in Côte d'Ivoire, Service de la Statistique, 1957–1962, January 1962. The use of differently defined output figures introduces some error into the data, but there is no acceptable alternative.

No deduction is made in output figures for European production. The European share of output is in any case small and declining; it fell from an estimated 4 tons in 1948 to about 1 ton in 1958. (Côte d'Ivoire, Service de la Statistique, 1958a.) The extraordinary increase in sales in 1960–1961 is probably due in part to a massive increase in smuggling of cocoa from Ghana.

Ivory Coast Coffee

Prices for years after 1948 are for Robusta, *"courant"* quality, naked ex-scale, Abidjan, average for crop year. As with cocoa prices, widely different quotations are given in different sources. For the years 1939–1949, "official prices" are found in Afrique Occidentale Française, 1951. For 1949–1952 prices, the source is Afrique Occidentale Française, 1956, p. 333; for 1952–1953, Côte d'Ivoire, Gouverneur, 1958, p. 89; for 1953–1959 (10 months), Côte d'Ivoire, Service de la Statistique, 1958a, p. 177, and 1959 (?), p. 135. From 1949–1959 prices are actual producer prices, Abidjan. For 1959 and 1960 guaranteed minimum producer price, Abidjan, is used.

Output figures for the period 1939–1946 refer to tonnages exported, calendar year; "exported production," crop year, as reported in Côte d'Ivoire, Service de la Statistique, 1958a is used for the period 1947–1956 and "marketed production," crop year, for years 1957–1960, as reported in Côte d'Ivoire, Service de la Statistique, 1957–1962. No deduction is made for output from European plantations; Europeans occupy less than 3,000 hectares of coffee plantations as against 500,000 by Africans. (Côte d'Ivoire, Service de la Statistique, 1961, p. 3.)

Prices

Import price indices have been constructed by three French students: M. Lengellé, in Lengellé, M., 1954, pp. 3ff; Poquin, J.-J., 1957; Bertrand, R., 1956. Lengellé's study is the basic one; the others build on it. But there are significant differences in each of these series, as the following comparison shows.

Import Prices, French West Africa
(1949=100)

	Bertrand	Poquin
1946	31	30
1947	39	50
1948	80	98
1949	100	100
1950	102	133
1951	111	144
1952	124	152
1953	106	136
1954	97	127
1955	—	123

Differences of such magnitude obviously demand caution in interpreting terms of trade movements in this country. Bertrand's series is used in the Tables because it apparently incorporates some revisions made by Lengellé in his original enquiries. Poquin's index is used for 1955. Both indices are c.i.f. value indices, composed of items in common African consumption and weighted according to the 1950–1951 import pattern, as follows: rice 12 per cent, wheat flour 10 per cent, sugar 18 per cent, wine 4 per cent, tobacco 4 per cent, salt 1 per cent, cotton yarn 4 per cent, cotton textiles 42 per cent, clothing 3 per cent. After 1955 there are no import price data.

There are two sources of retail price data for goods consumed by Africans. One is an unpublished index computed by the Inspection du Travail in Dakar, given in column (1D) Table V. The other appears in an unpublished Service des Statistiques memorandum entitled *Le Pouvoir d'Achat du Franc du Territoire à diverses époques en A. O. F.* (n.d., mimeographed); it is from this latter source that the "rural budget" index of Table 5 comes. For the years 1946–1958 the index in column 10, Table 11, is constructed from price data collected by the Services des Statistiques and published in various statistical bulletins. The raw data are weakened by imprecise definition of items and uncertain methods of price collection. But I have used them, with a weighting based on the findings of the Abidjan budget study adapted in line with some of the findings of the general urban budget survey by Y. Mersadier (1957) published by I.F.A.N. That the resulting index is indicative of general price trends is suggested by its rough correspondence with such unpublished partial indices as exist in the studies of the Service des Statistiques.

On the basis of this weighting and using the sources noted above it is possible to construct an index of retail prices of African consumed foods for the war years. The index, not set down in the tables in the text, is as follows: (1938=100): 1939, 136; 1940, 209; 1941, 267; 1942, 410; 1943, 614; 1944, 897; 1945, 653.

PART FOUR

The
Changing Economic
Scene

Demographic Factors in Subsaharan Economic Development*

by H. W. Singer
United Nations

Africa south of the Sahara presents a degree of variation in its demographic patterns that makes generalization difficult. There are islands of very high population density: Zanzibar and Ruanda-Urundi are examples that come readily to mind. There are areas of very low density of population: South-West Africa, Somalia, or parts of what was French West Africa, such as the Central African Republic, the Chad, the Republic of the Congo, and Gabon. In many cases, such as Somalia, Mauritania or South-West Africa, the low density of population clearly corresponds to the low capacity of the country to carry a numerous population, that is, to a basic ecological condition, such as might be exhibited by a desert country without natural resources. The example of Libya should show us, however, that we ought not to assume that such a picture will remain without change. Libya was at one time cited as a country where a poor endowment of resources would make economic development very difficult. Recent discoveries of oil, however, have changed the interpretation of the Libyan ecology quite dramatically. Obviously the population-carrying capacity of Libya is greater than it was assumed to be before the existence of oil was known.

Taken as a whole, Africa is clearly not over-populated in the same sense as is China or India. It is more like Latin America, where we also find islands of over-population in a continent which, as a whole, is clearly not over-populated.

The mobility of the African population is great, in that both intra-

---

* In preparing this paper I have had the benefit of being able to revise earlier notes in the light of the discussions at the Conference of the International Economic Association on Economic Development in Africa south of the Sahara which took place in July 1961 at Addis Ababa. In particular, I refer to the paper prepared for this Conference by Professor J. J. Spengler on "Population and Population Trends."

territorial and inter-territorial migrations are important. However, statistical information is scanty, especially on internal migration; and the direction of the major inter-territorial flows is better known than their volume. By and large, just as in the process of urbanization that will be considered later in this paper, the groups involved in these movements, whether internal or inter-territorial, originate in areas that are remote from markets, where the economy is predominantly of the subsistence type, and where opportunities to earn cash are rare. In some territories, such as Nyasaland, population pressures on land resources and employment opportunities have for some time been feeding migratory flows toward territories in which primary-exporting industries have developed rapidly during the last decades. In 1956, half of Nyasaland wage-earners were employed outside of that territory, mainly in Southern and Northern Rhodesia. As Table 11.2 shows, in Southern Rhodesia half of the wage-earners were non-local, while in South Africa two thirds of the Africans employed in the mining industry came from other territories. The mining industries of Ghana, of Katanga, and of Senegal attract migrants from considerable distances. Commercial farming areas of Ghana and of Senegal also receive large numbers of migrants, mainly seasonal, during harvesting of cocoa and groundnuts. These movements afford relief to areas such as Ruanda-Urundi, Nyasaland, Upper Volta, or Northern Guinea that are over-populated in relation to their present opportunities for employment.

The distribution of demographic pressures in Subsaharan Africa, therefore, presents one aspect if one can assume free migration and opportunities for the redistribution of the population, but quite a different one if this assumption cannot be made. If the independence of African countries should result in the interference with migration across the national frontiers, demographic pressure in certain less-developed countries could become quite acute, while the shortage of labor could reduce the rate of industrial growth in more rapidly developing areas.

The potential economic importance of migration has been reduced to some extent by the fact that much of this migration has been only temporary. Temporary migration makes labor productivity lower than it would be if the same labor force were permanent, prevents the establishment of a permanent industrial labor force, prevents the acquisition of skill and labor organization, and leads to grave social problems in towns or mining areas where male migrants from different ethnic groups are often thrown together in an unfamiliar environment without the benefit of family situations. However, temporary migration can sometimes be well adjusted to social and economic conditions and requirements. It has frequently been pointed out that where women do most of the agricultural labor, the men may return just often enough to take care of the periodic need for work that is usually done by men, such as building or fencing, and may improve their farms by using the money accumulated during their wage-earning periods.

The structure of manpower in African countries reflects the coexistence of heterogeneous economies and diverse cultural and ethnic groups. It should be borne in mind that estimates of the economically active population in African countries are on the whole subject to wide margins of error. Not only are census and survey questions regarding the labor force not always understood by the population and the enumerators, but the base population by which proportions of the labor force are computed is not well established. International comparisons which, in this field, are difficult enough to draw as between industrialized countries, become quite impracticable between African countries, because the official definition of "economically active population" varies greatly from one country to another. For instance, in the Republic of the Congo recorded rates for female activity are higher than the rates for males, and, in several other countries, rates in excess of 50 per cent have been recorded, so that one can hardly believe that in fact only five per cent of females are economically active in Mozambique.

2

Great care must be taken in the interpretation of the rather frequent statements that designate tropical Africa as under-populated or over-populated. Such terms as "under-population," "over-population" or "optimum population" make sense only in relation to a given or assumed economic structure, a given state of available resources, whether potential or actual, and a given state of market opportunities. It was the condition of world markets in the years during and after World War II that gave Africa the chance to take a larger share of these markets for primary commodities. In some cases, like Kenya and Uganda, population pressure on agricultural land resources is clearly acute; but since Africa remains largely unexplored as to these resources, it is not possible to undertake a comprehensive appraisal of its economic possibilities, even without regard to the consequences of possible future variation in market potential. Although the soil and mineral potentials of tropical Africa are generally listed as poor, this assessment must be considered as premature or at best not proved. A great effort to intensify research and survey projects directed toward revealing the nature and extent of African resources is essential for drawing valid judgements.

The problem of making such judgements is further complicated by the complex interconnections between present prospects for economic development, current levels of population, and future rates of growth of both output and population. In those areas where the rate of industrialization is very low—areas comprising most of tropical Africa—the population-carrying capacity of the region would be greatly increased if productivity in food-producing industries could be increased sufficiently to free labor resources for the development of export-producing industries. But the obstacles to this increase in food-raising productivity, and to the subsequent development of successful export industries, are formidable. What, then, should be assumed? The safest assumption, for purposes of the present analysis, is a projection of trends which indicate that while some parts of Africa will continue to develop quite rapidly, others will more or less stagnate. However, there are unpredictable elements that might well arise from the intensification of the resource surveys, which may quite easily result in the discovery of entirely new ranges of resources.

In the absence of surveys of resources and population, it is difficult to say whether or not a given country in tropical Africa is underpopulated or not, even when assumptions as to future economic developments are made. In certain countries, the actual population is not really known. For instance, although a population figure of 20 million people is often suggested for Ethiopia, the correct figure may be as high as 25 millions or as low as 12 millions. Even in some areas where the size of the population was generally supposed to be well known, recent censuses and sample surveys have indicated that actual population may be significantly higher than earlier supposedly accurate estimates had predicted. A case in point is Uganda, where estimates based on figures believed to be reliable,[1] put the population of that country in 1959 at a level 12 per cent above that for the same year based on earlier information. Ghana, on the other side of the continent, is an even more extreme example of the same phenomenon. Clearly, population estimates for the countries of Africa should only be accepted subject to a wide margin of uncertainty.

Furthermore, underpopulation and overpopulation are not uniform characteristics of a country as a whole, even though the overall density of population per acre or per acre of arable land may seem low or high. This is another result of the interaction between levels of economic development and population-carrying capacity. At a given moment in its history, a country may present a picture of over-all low density, while in detail the structure is one of islands of urban development, with a sparsely-populated hinterland linked to the urban centers by a transportation system of very limited capacity. In such a situation, the current

[1] Cf. Table 11.1.

demand for transportation services would clearly be low, and it would appear unprofitable to expand the transportation system. But it should be noted that the structure indicated is generally associated with low per capita income in the hinterland, and this low per capita income is itself associated with the fact that a limited transportation system imposes high costs of movement and therefore limits per capita incomes in the hinterland. The crucial point is that sparse population should not be thought of as the cause of the unprofitability of building new rail lines or improved roads or waterways. The real obstacle, insofar as there is one, is the low productivity—the low income, in other words—of the hinterland, and the connected concentration in these regions on production for local consumption, usually using traditional methods for traditional products. A good index of the importance of this "localization" of activity[2] is the generally low proportion of wage-earners in the populations of the regions being examined, which shows a low degree of monetization of the economy, and indicates that much of the real output of the area is not destined for markets where money is in general use.

The argument is not complete, however. Why is production so localized? One reason is precisely that high transportation costs make it impossible for goods produced in the hinterland to compete, either in urban markets or in ports, with goods produced in regions where transportation to the markets is cheaper. It follows that an improvement in the transportation system may well provide the impetus for major increases in productivity and income in outlying districts, as monetization proceeds and local products enter wider markets.

The growth of urban areas also expands the monetization of the economy. Since the second World War, owing to the increased demand for cash crops and minerals for exports, there has been a rapid growth in the populations of African cities, the main economic function of which has been to provide a link between the local economy and the developed countries. Moreover, postwar efforts of governments to support development have been mainly concentrated in capital cities and administrative centers. The result of these two main factors, and others as well, has been a rapid growth of the urban areas, though the relative size of the non-urban population in African countries is still higher than in other parts of the world, including Asia and Latin America. The number of cities in tropical Africa with 100,000 inhabitants or more by 1960 had increased from five in the pre-war period to 28. Among these are 17 capital cities and 12 port cities, of which 11 are both capital and port cities. Although African governments have had to cope with formidable economic and social problems that have become more threatening than

[2] Cf. Table 11.4.

were similar ones in developed countries in earlier decades, and even though unemployment is apparently widespread and income per capita low, rapid urbanization provides an abundant labor supply and a ready and relatively extended market for large-scale and rural-cottage industries. Also, in the immediate hinterland of these urban areas, traditional agriculture gradually changed from the subsistence type to the cash-earning type, thus extending more and more the areas connected to the monetized "islands" of Africa.

Many observers of the African rural scene have concluded that, in the given state of agricultural knowledge and tribal or village organization, with its strong elements of subsistence production, African populations have achieved an ecological equilibrium between population and resources at a low level of output. Such a situation may be taken as representing a sort of Malthusian equilibrium, at a comparatively low density of population. This judgement, however, seems to neglect the possibility that the population-carrying capacity can be sharply increased, even within the existing production structure, by comparatively minor, inexpensive improvements. Particularly important among these are health measures, especially the control of malaria, controls on pest populations, such as the tsetse fly and the desert locust, better rotation of crops, which would reduce the need for shifting cultivation and burning soil cover, and the regrouping of villages. Thus it has been observed that where villagers live close together, perhaps for reasons of mutual protection and lack of security, the total amount of land they can cultivate is sharply limited by the requirement that all fields must be within daily walking distance of the village. If the agricultural population could be placed on individual holdings, or in smaller settlements, the amount of land cultivated even with existing methods could be greatly increased, without any new investment or change in methods of cultivation. In many parts of Subsaharan Africa there is a good deal of soil erosion caused by wind, rain, an excessive cattle population, or poor agricultural methods. Populations have often been decimated, primarily by epidemics, and secondarily by slave trading, tribal wars, and other causes. In these circumstances, it seems difficult to attach any precise meaning to the term "ecological equilibrium." Indeed, it would appear to be a somewhat romantic concept which at best is not very helpful.

The sparsity of population in large parts of tropical Africa, and the lack of transport which is both cause and effect, have a number of other important economic consequences. There is often no general market and price system in African countries, but only localized markets, with local prices that may differ very sharply from one region to another. Conditions of food shortages and high prices may exist in one part of a country, while there are surpluses and low prices in another. The small markets make the development of large-scale industries very difficult; in many cases, the development of efficient small-scale industries, including rural industries, would seem to be one of the most urgent requirements.[3] High costs of transport place a premium on subsistence production and afford powerful protection against external competition to such local activities as already exist, thus removing an incentive to economic efficiency. The lack of transport and the lack of power, which are also connected with the sparsity of population, make it uneconomic to exploit many local deposits of mineral and other resources. Improvements of transport and power, in spite of the sparsity of population, could clearly have multiple economic effects, especially in connection with the application of new techniques.

3

Two statements that were made above concerning the size or density of population are also true of the rate of increase of population, since our knowledge of the facts is deficient, and tropical Subsaharan Africa presents a patchwork that makes generalization difficult.

As regards the first point, it has already been mentioned that recent censuses and enumerations have often resulted in higher figures than had been previously estimated or assumed. From this the conclusion is sometimes drawn that the rate of population increase must be higher than was previously believed, or that it must have been speeded considerably. However, we do not know to what extent the higher figures are due to better statistical coverage or to what extent they reflect an actual acceleration in the rate of population growth. One might hazard a guess that while most of the apparent discrepancy is due to improved statistical coverage, there also has been some acceleration in the rate of increase, resulting from lower death rates, which reflect more effective control of disease, higher standards of living, better education and also the progress of urbanization.

It is often contended that unsanitary living conditions, bad housing, and widespread unemployment found in many Subsaharan towns may offset improved health services. However, this widespread idea is not verified by research conducted by the United Nations on the structure of mortality. At a high level of mortality, the greater part of deaths can be attributed to infectious, parasitic and respiratory diseases. These causes

[3] Cf. Singer, H. W., "Problems of Small Scale Industries in Tropical Africa," a paper presented to the Conference of the International Economic Association on Development in Africa South of the Sahara, July 1961, at Addis Ababa.

of death have been reduced drastically at low costs by modern medical techniques, which in Africa are mostly available in urban areas. Therefore it seems unlikely, except in extreme cases, themselves unlikely, that death-rates of the urban population could be higher than those of the rural population.

With regard to urban fertility trends, it is often argued that the abandonment of tribal and rural customs and taboos that reduce the number of births may act to prevent birth-rates from falling. But this attractive and folkloric explanation of fertility trends should also be approached with extreme caution. Should an increase be observed in the fertility of urban women, other causes, certainly less intellectually seductive, like the improvement of health conditions, should also be studied closely. Otherwise, African demography may, as did demographic theories for more developed continents at an earlier period, lag behind the facts during some decades, at a time when the growth of African populations must be predicted with fair accuracy as part of any solution of African economic problems.

It is thus difficult, where Subsaharan Africa is concerned, to distinguish between speculation and demographic fact. Because the statistics are inconclusive, we cannot ascertain on the one hand to what extent recorded births and deaths in the towns relate to people from the countryside who utilize hospitals in urban areas or, on the other hand, to what extent townspeople go back to their villages to die.

Coming to the second point, concerning the patchwork impression from the available figures, we find that some of these show very rapid recent population growth, as in the Ivory Coast, in the Upper Volta, in Uganda and in Ruanda-Urundi, while other areas show a practically stationary population or even a declining one, as is the case in Gabon, Somalia and the Gambia. These statistical differences may be assumed to correspond only very broadly to real differences. Qualified observers estimate the current rate of population increase as around 2 per cent per annum, a figure that agrees fairly well with United Nations estimates. If this is true, it must mean an acceleration in the rate of population growth compared with the period between European colonization and the second World War, during which the population cannot have increased by more than perhaps .5 per cent per annum.

In view of the fairly well-established differences between different countries of Subsaharan Africa, an over-all rate of 2 per cent would also mean that there must be some territories in which population growth is very rapid even in comparison with fast-growing areas in other parts of the world, although much of this growth may be due to migration, while in other countries the increase in population must be quite slow. However, it should be borne in mind that the figures in Table 11.7 are estimates derived from census, survey and vital-statistics data, the validity of which cannot be assessed as yet. It seems likely that the wide variations of birth and death rates might be due more to errors than to real differences, so that explanation of well-established inter-territorial differences in gross rates of change must await better knowledge of the components of change.

In a country like Ethiopia, conclusions drawn from existing historical sources, village structure, the absence of major conurbations, and general observation, as well as such sample data as exist, seem to suggest that the rate of population increase during the period 1935–1960 must have been quite modest, most probably 1 per cent per annum. On somewhat similar grounds, it would seem a reasonable guess that the current over-all rate of population increase in Subsaharan Africa is more likely to be below than above 2 per cent per annum. The naïve picture sometimes encountered outside Africa that virtually all African women bear the physiological maximum of children is certainly far from the truth. It must not be forgotten that, over wide parts of the Continent, effective methods of regulating the number of births are found in the form of long nursing periods for infants and taboos of many kinds against sexual intercourse during such nursing and other periods; and that customary ages at marriage are high in some parts of the Continent. Moreover, if the incidence of mortality is relatively low during child-bearing ages, diseases that reduce fertility through these ages are widespread, and many women complete their maternal life long before reaching the menopause. The prevalence of migratory labor means that men and women of reproductive ages are often separated for considerable periods of time.

Yet, by the same token, all this implies that a potential acceleration in the rate of increase of population is also present. Nursing periods for infants may be reduced under the impact of the European "demonstration effect," taboos may be given over with urbanization, the dissolution of tribal society, the spread of schooling and literacy, and diseases that reduce fertility may be controlled. Hence, even if the guess should be correct that the rate of 2 per cent usually given may be too high, it is quite possible that it may be exceeded in the near future, if it has not been surpassed already in some countries.[4]

In any case, it is not so much the rate of increase in population that matters economically as the way it is brought about. The gross rate represents a combination of birth and death rates, and, in an analysis of economic effects, it is the components rather than the aggregate that

[4] Cf. Table 11.7.

must be considered. A growth rate of 2 per cent per annum can be brought about either by a birth rate of 30 per thousand and a death rate of 10 per thousand, or by birth rate of 50 per thousand and the death rate of 30 per thousand.[5] While the net result is numerically the same, the economic implications are quite different in the two cases. A combination of high birth rates and high death rates is economically highly unfavorable.

In the first place, it results in an unfavorable age composition of the population with a very high rate of dependency, that is, with a preponderance of children below the productive age. In that respect, African countries reproduce the pattern found in the countries of Asia and of Latin America. In some countries of Africa, recorded dependency rates are rather low, but they are inconsistent with the trends in mortality and fertility that apparently prevail, so that it is likely that the observations are by-products of under-enumeration of young children during census and survey operations. With high dependency rates, resources that might otherwise go into capital formation have to be diverted to the feeding and clothing of a high proportion of dependents. The resulting low proportion of producers in the total population may be sufficient by itself to account for a considerable reduction of the rate of capital formation and economic growth below its potential maximum, and over long periods could of itself explain the present disparity between rich and poor countries.[6]

Again, the vast expenditure on the feeding, clothing and care of children that should normally be considered as a productive investment of the community in raising the next generation of producers remains unproductive consumption expenditure because, in consequence of high death rates, a sizeable proportion of the children die before they complete, or even reach, the age when they can be producers. This is clearly implied in the average expectation of life in Subsaharan Africa, which is estimated at 40 years or even, in a number of African countries, as low as 30 years. It is clearly uneconomical to give children, to say nothing of producing workers, the same amount of education and training as would be worthwhile if death rates were lower, when such expenditures could be repaid over the full productive period of a given recipient's life. At the same time as the incentive for education and training is diminished, so are the resources available for this purpose, since the high rate of dependency pre-empts the existing scarce

[5] Cf. Singer, H. W., 1954.
[6] Cf. Singer, H. W., *op. cit.*; Coale, A. J. and Hoover, E. M., 1958. Spengler, in his paper to the Conference of the International Economic Association quoted in the introductory footnote, also provides quantitative data bearing upon this point.

resources in the sheer cost of feeding and caring for children to ensure survival.

Thus the combination of high birth rates and high death rates tends in two ways to result in a lower level of quality of "human capital." Thinking on problems of economic growth has tended increasingly to emphasize the importance of the human factor and of expenditures on education, training and research. This further highlights the import- ance of the obstacle presented by the demographic combination of high birth rates and high death rates. Deficiencies in education and training in Africa, and the high cost of the removal of these handicaps, are strikingly discussed in the Report of the Conference of African States on the Development of Education in Africa, held in Addis Ababa in May 1961.[7]

Whatever the uncertainties concerning the actual rate of increase in the population of Africa south of the Sahara, there can be little doubt that both birth and death rates are comparatively high. The statement in the preceding paragraph concerning the unfavorable effect of the combination of high birth rates and high death rates therefore applies with full force to the area.

It should be emphasized that a decline of mortality alone will not reduce the burden of dependency. One of the major contributions of demographic theory is to demonstrate clearly that a uniform decline of age-specific mortality, as observed in almost all economically under-developed areas, cannot be expected to bring any significant change in the age structure, which, in such a case, continues to be determined principally by the level of fertility with modifications due to migration. Thus, given a level of national income and the costs per child 'of up- bringing and education, the proportion of income that has to be invested in the maintenance and education of the dependents, in accord with fixed standards, is determined uniquely by the proportion of children in the population. As uniformly declining mortality will not significantly affect this proportion, no savings are freed for capital formation or other forms of consumption by an over-all decline in mortality. Of course, there is less waste, since the cost of up-bringing and education are paid back by a larger participation in the labor force; however, even in the long run, mortality decline will not make dependency ratios more favorable, unless fertility also declines.

At the meeting of economists held under the auspices of the Inter- national Economic Association in Addis Ababa in July 1961, when the general development problems of Africa south of the Sahara were

[7] United Nations Economic Commission for Africa and United Nations Educational, Scientific and Cultural Organization, 1961.

considered, the consensus of opinion seemed to be that while obviously the population-carrying capacity of the area could be much higher than the present population after economic growth had taken place and after a certain measure of industrialization had been realized, it would on the other hand be of economic advantage if the rate of population increase could be kept down to a level of from about 1 per cent to $1\frac{1}{2}$ per cent per annum, in such a way that while death rates should be lowered as rapidly as possible, birth rates should adjust themselves to the falling death rates with a minimum lag. This formulation would probably be supported by practically all those familiar with the area, even though it must be clear that it is more easily prescribed than realized. Obviously, a multitude of historical, social, and medical factors are at work that may make the realization of this ideal nearly impossible, since an accelerating rate of increase in the population above this economic ideal seems almost certain.

To some extent, the acceleration of population growth should finance itself. Control of disease should not only make for falling death rates, and hence more rapid growth of population, but also for better health and hence higher productivity. High birth rates and a low average age of the population favor economic mobility, increase the chances of modernization, and perhaps also expand receptiveness to new methods of production. On the other hand, greater longevity and improved health conditions may bring about, in the long run, greater concern for the future and greater emphasis upon up-bringing of children, which may bring a change in reproductive behavior conducive to a decline in fertility. But these effects are obviously not easy to measure, and the change of attitude in reproductive behavior belongs to long-run trends. Thus, we cannot rely on such hypothetical built-in compensations to solve the economic problems raised by increase in population. This must be done by the successful execution of programs that raise the productivity of agriculture, lead toward industrialization, and lay the necessary physical and, above all, human infrastructure for self-sustaining economic growth. This formidable task, it must be understood, has social, technical, and political components as well as economic ones.

TABLE II.I. *Estimated Population and Population Density by Total Land Area and Agricultural Land Area for African Countries, and Range of Densities for Administrative Divisions within Countries*

Country	Estimated Population 1959 (000s)	Density per Km²		Range of Density of Land Area within Administrative Divisions (a)
		of Land Area	of Agricultural Land	
West Africa				
Total	75,395	8	27	
Cameroun	3,225	7	22	1–94
Former French West Africa	21,502	5	14	
Dahomey	2,000	17	—	4–55
Guinea	2,727	11	—	5–24
Ivory Coast	3,103	10	—	2–14
Mali	4,300	4	—	0–16
Mauritania	730	1	—	0–06
Niger	2,555	2	—	0–11
Senegal	2,550	13	—	2–47
Upper Volta	3,537	13	—	4–37
Former French Equatorial Africa	5,000	2	6	—
Central African Republic	1,185	2	—	—
Chad	2,600	2	—	—
Congo Republic	795	2	—	—
Gabon	420	2	—	—
Gambia	301	29	151 (b)	—
Ghana (c)	6,612	28	125	2–84
Liberia	1,250	11	60	—
Nigeria (d)	33,663	38	151	7–157
Sierra Leone	2,400	33	41	—
Togo	1,442	25	63	7–71
Southern and Eastern Africa				
Total	117,929	8	21	—
Angola	4,550	4	15	—
Basutoland	674	22	169 (e)	—
Bechuanaland	337	1	1	—
Republic of Congo	13,821	6	27	3–9
Ethiopia	21,800	18	31	—

TABLE II.I. (*continued*)

Country	Estimated Population 1959 (000s)	Density per Km²		Range of Density of Land Area within Administrative Divisions (a)
		of Land Area	of Agricultural Land	
French Somaliland	70	3	35	—
Kenya	6,450	11	248	1–49
Mozambique	6,310	8	14	2–19
Rhodesia and Nyasaland	8,130	7	20	—
Ruanda-Urundi	4,780	88	120	32–177
Somalia	1,990	3	9	1–9
Sudan	11,459	5	37	2–24
South-West Africa (f)	554	1	1	—
Swaziland	250	14	16	—
Tanganyika	9,076	10	—	4–17
Uganda	6,517	27	225	15–41
Republic of South Africa (g)	14,673	12	15	—
Zanzibar and Pemba	304	115	152	—

General Note: The 1959 population estimate for Ghana is derived from preliminary result of census held in 1960. Data on population (total area) are for mid-year 1959, except for Liberia (1956).

Notes to Table:

(a) For each country the smaller administrative division for which census or survey data exists has been considered. Thus in some cases the districts are given by large tracts such as regions and governorates. In the figures presented for range of densities within countries, urban densities have been excluded wherever possible.

(b) Density of estimated area of shifting cultivation and of bush fallow.

(c) Includes Togoland under British Administration.

(d) Excludes Cameroons under British Administration.

(e) When calculating density data for area, permanent meadows and pasture are not considered.

(f) Includes Walvis Bay.

(g) Excludes Walvis Bay.

TABLE II.2. *Africans Employed in Selected Countries, by Country of Origin (Local and Non-local)*

Country of Employment	Date	"Local" Aggregate (000s)	Per Cent	Country of Origin "Non-local" Aggregate (000s)	Per Cent	Total Aggregate (000s)
Northern Rhodesia	1956	217.8	83	45.6	17	263.2
Southern Rhodesia	1956	300.2	49	309.8	51	610.0
Nyasaland	1956	155.6	94	8.9	6	164.3
Republic of South Africa (a)	1957	108.1	33	217.3	67	325.4
Republic of the Congo	1956	1,121.3	94	76.6	6	1,197.9
Tanganyika (b)	1957	290.6	88	40.6	12	331.2
Uganda	1957	162.3	72	64.6	28	226.9

Source: United Nations, Department of Economic and Social Affairs, 1959a, p. 49.

Notes to Table:

(a) Africans employed in gold mines and coal mines only.
(b) Males only.

TABLE 11.3. *Economically Active Population by Sex in Selected African Countries*

| Country | Date | Percentage Economically Active | | |
		Males	Females	Total
Western Africa				
Former French West Africa	1955–56	58.3	51.8	55.2
Former French Equatorial Africa	1956	76.7	53.3	65.0
Nigeria	1952–53	57.0	43.6	47.9
Southern and Eastern Africa				
Republic of the Congo	1957	47.2	51.7	49.4
Mozambique (*a*)	1950	55.1	5.1	28.9
Republic of South Africa (*b*)	1946	63.4	26.3	45.1
Zanzibar and Pemba	1948	74.7	39.8	58.1

Notes to Table:

(*a*) Indigenous population only.

(*b*) Obtained by weighing the activity rates of each of four population groups (Bantu, European, "Coloreds," and Asians).

TABLE 11.4. *Estimated Economically Active Population Classified as Engaged in Agriculture and in Non-agricultural Activities, and Proportions of Wage and Salary Earners in the Total Population for Selected African Countries*

| Country | Percentage of Economically Active Population | | Percentage of Wage and Salary Earners in Total Population |
	In Agriculture	In Non-agricultural activities	
Ethiopia	90	10	0
Guinea	87	13	4
Nigeria	78	22	2
Cameroun	91	9	4
Ghana	70	30	5
Ivory Coast	91	9	6
Republic of the Congo	85	15	8
Kenya	80	20	9
Federation of Rhodesia and Nyasaland	80	20	13

Source: Estimates by the United Nations Economic Commission for Africa.

TABLE 11.5. *Percentage of Population in Selected Countries of Africa Classified as Residing in Urban Areas, in Cities of 20,000 Population and Over, and in Largest Cities*

Country	Date	Urban Areas	Urban Areas 20,000 and Over	Largest City
Western Africa				
Dahomey	1955	7.1	5.5	3.5
Guinea	1955	6.5	5.1	1.1
Ivory Coast	1956	11.1	6.8	5.1
Mali	1956	5.1	1.8	1.8
Mauritania	1956	6.5	—	1.4
Niger	1956	2.7	—	0.8
Senegal	1956	22.9	19.0	9.9
Upper Volta	1956	4.0	2.3	1.3
Ghana	1948	16.3	5.0	3.3
Nigeria	1952–53	17.5	11.4	1.5
Togo	1958	9.6	4.5	4.5
Gambia	1957	71.8	—	71.8
Southern and Eastern Africa				
Angola	1955	7.6	6.0	4.6
Republic of the Congo	1957	9.8	7.1	2.2
Kenya	1948	15.0	3.8	2.2 (a)
Mozambique	1956	13.9	13.9	2.5
Federation of Rhodesia and Nyasaland	1950	13.6	—	1.7
Sudan	1955–56	8.3	4.5	2.4 (b)
Tanganyika	1957	3.3	1.9	1.5
Uganda	1948	0.8	—	0.4
Republic of South Africa	1957	42.6	30.7	5.0
Zanzibar and Pemba	1948	20.0	17.1	17.1

Source: United Nations, Economic Commission for Africa, Working Party on Economic and Social Development, 1961.

Notes to Table:
(a) Represents the population of Nairobi.
(b) Khartoum, Khartoum North and Omdurman are taken together.

TABLE 11.6. *Estimated Dependency Ratios in Selected African Countries*

Country	Census or Sample Survey Date	Dependency Ratio
Western Africa		
Cameroun (*a*)	1958	47
Guinea (*a*)	1955	89
Ivory Coast (*a*)	1958	96
Mali (*a*)	1958	80
Senegal (*a*)	1958	87
Central African Republic (*a*)	1958	59
Congo Republic (*a*)	1959	77
Chad (*a*)	1959	79
Ghana	1948	63
Gambia	1959	67
Nigeria	1952–53	86
Southern and Eastern and Central Africa		
Angola	1950	79
Basutoland	1946	89
Bechuanaland	1946	80
Republic of the Congo	1953	71
Mozambique	1956	83
Sudan	1956	101

Source: United Nations, Economic Commission for Africa, Working Party on Economic and Social Development, 1961.

Notes to Table:

(*a*) Based on the results of demographic surveys covering only parts of the national area.

TABLE 11.7. *Birth Rates, Death Rates and Natural Increase Rates, 1950–1959, and Rates of Population Growth, 1941–1960, for Selected African Countries*

Country	Official or Country Data (a)			Estimated Rate (b)		Rates of Natural Increase (per 1,000)		Rate of Population Increase During Decade (per cent) (c)	
	Date of Reference	Birth (a) Rate (per 1,000)	Death (d) Rate (per 1,000)	Birth Rate (per 1,000)	Death Rate (per 1,000)	Official (a)	Estimated (b)	1941–1950	1951–1960
(1)	(2)	(3)	(4)	(5)	(6)	(7)	(8)	(9)	(10)
Western Africa									
Cameroun	1954–55 1957	25	8	35	27	17	8	2.3	0.5
Guinea (e)	1954	62	40	60	40	22	20	—	2.9
Ivory Coast (f)	1956–58	59	28	58	26	31	32	—	4.0
Senegal (f,g)	1955	54	21	50	25	33	25	—	1.2 (m)
Central African Republic (f)	1959	39	26	40	30	13	10	1.6	4.7
Congo Republic (f)	—	—	—	45	24	—	21	—	1.9 (m)
Chad	—	—	—	45	23	—	22	—	1.9 (m)
Ghana (h)	1957–58	52	21	51	29	31	22	1.6	4.6
Nigeria (i)	1955–59	50	13	54	35	37	19	—	3.5
Togo	1955	35	13	35	23	22	12	1.9	3.7
Southern and Eastern and Central Africa									
Angola	1956–58	22	7	45	35	15	10	1.5	1.2
Republic of the Congo	1956–57	48	20	44	22	28	22	0.7	2.3
Ruanda-Urundi	1956–57	45 (l)	14	42	13	31	29	—	2.2
Sudan (k)	1956	52	19	51	23	33	28	—	—
Republic of South Africa (j)	1954–56	17	11	—	—	6	—	—	—

Notes to Table:

(a) Estimates based on official vital statistics, sample survey or census information.

(b) Estimates obtained by using stable population model with reference to the values for rates of population increase and size of population groups aged under 15 from census or survey data.

(c) Average of rates of increase, where available, within each decade.

(d) Average of rates for period signified; in case of wide fluctuation, average for recent period only given.

(e) Results obtained from a demographic sample survey covering the whole national area.

(f) Results obtained from a demographic sample survey of only part of the national area.

(g) Birth and death rates refer to Dakar only.

(h) Birth and death rates refer only to compulsory registration area of 36 towns comprising 12 per cent of the total population.

(i) Birth and death rates refer to Lagos only.

(j) For Bantu population.

(k) Estimates given by 1955–1956 sample census of population.

(l) Data on births available for 1955–1957 indicate birth rate in the range of 50 per 1000.

(m) Applies to increase over period 1951–1958.

12

The Development of the Economic Infrastructure

by A. M. Kamarck
International Bank for Reconstruction and Development

There is no easy, completely satisfactory measure of the development of the economic infrastructure in Subsaharan Africa. Economic infrastructure essentially refers to the basic services, or public utilities, which are necessary to the commodity-producing sectors of the economy. Provision of these basic services is essential but not sufficient for the growth of the commodity-producing sectors. Over the years, with the development of Africa, the needs for the basic services have not only grown but changed in character. The concept of "necessary economic infrastructure" has widened considerably over the last sixty years, as will be seen in somewhat greater detail in later pages.

Because the economic infrastructure is there to serve the rest of the economy, physical measures are not of great use as a standard of adequacy. If one compares the number of miles of railway per square mile of area in one country to another, the fact that country A has a smaller railway density than country B does not mean that its railway network is less adequate for the needs of its economy. In fact, if the railway is running at less than capacity, it may be that country A has actually over-built in railways. In other words, a proper appraisal of the adequacy of the development of an economic infrastructure can only be made country-by-country, in relation to the economic needs of a given country. We will not try to present here an evaluation of each country in Subsaharan Africa, but will rather be content to make a kind of *tour d'horizon* of the subject.

2

The beginning of any appreciable pace of economic development in Subsaharan Africa essentially depended on the discovery of mechanical

263

means of transport outside Africa, and on the willingness of outside sources to provide the capital to invest in introducing these mechanical means of transport into the continent. Until late in the colonial period, the main impediment to economic development there was lack of transport, which meant impossibly high transport costs. This held up not only the economic development of Africa, but her development in most lines of human interest.[1] For the African standard of living to rise above a bare subsistence it was necessary for the inhabitants to be able to produce a surplus of commodities which could be transported and sold abroad so that they could purchase, in exchange, the products of the industrial societies and the skilled services of foreign technicians and administrators. Transport had to be made available that was cheap enough so that African products could reach world markets and sell for a price that, after paying for the cost of transport, would leave an adequate return for the producer. And this could not be provided for most of Africa before railways had been built.

As long ago as the time of Adam Smith, it was recognized that economic development depended on the division of labor, and that this in turn depended on the size of the market. Access to world markets has been perhaps the most powerful engine of economic development for formerly backward countries such as the United States, Australia and Canada; and it continues to fulfill this role for the countries of Africa today.

The transport of goods and the economic development of Africa was impeded, first, by difficulty of access to the continent caused by the scarcity of good natural harbors and deep inlets of the sea, by the plateau which, ending near the coast in much of Africa, prevented the use of the rivers as roads into the interior, and by the presence of coastal swamps when no other obstacles were present. Once a landing was made, moreover, penetration into the interior in nearly every case depended initially on land transport. Internal trade routes, however, were difficult to establish because of the impossibility of using draft or pack animals in much of Africa due to trypanosomiasis, carried by the tsetse fly, and the other animal diseases, because of the presence of dense forests in part of the region and the deserts and steppes in other parts, and in many cases because of the resistance of the indigenous peoples. Reliance in most of Africa, in any event, had to be placed on the wholly inadequate transport capacity of human carriers. This limited trade effectively to commodities with much value in relation to weight, like ivory and gold, or to a commodity provided with its own legs, such as slaves.

"The bulk of the African resources lay inland and their development

[1] Wrigley, C., 1961, *passim.*

could not begin until the railroads made it possible."[2] Modern economic development of Africa had to await the coming of the "iron horse" which was immune to the tsetse fly and other animal enemies. But, the railway is almost *par excellence* a capital-intensive activity, requiring amounts of investment that no non-industrialized economy can hope to muster. It came into tropical Africa, therefore, only when the

TABLE 12.1. *Railways, Subsaharan Africa,* 1959

	Length (Track Miles)
Sudan	4,780
British East Africa	4,000
Republic of the Congo	3,730
Angola	2,290
Nigeria	2,230
Rhodesia and Nyasaland	2,160*
Mali and Senegal	1,260
Mozambique	1,890
Ivory Coast	820
Ghana	750
Madagascar	580
Ethiopia	520
Guinea	440
Dahomey	400
Sierra Leone	350
Nyasaland	340
Congo Republic	320*
Kamerun	310
Togo	300
Eritrea	220
Total	27,690

* Route length. Source: *World Railways,* 1960, pp. 104–110.

colonial countries were ready to turn from their own railway building in Europe and North America, and looked abroad to the Argentine, Australia and Africa. The railway building effort in Africa came initially from about 1885 to about 1914. Railways, accompanied by investment in ports and in some cases in steamers on the internal river and lake waterways, brought a substantial part of Africa within reasonably easy reach of the oceans and the world markets beyond them. This opened a new economic era, the era of economic development presenting new opportunities and new problems to the peoples of Africa.

[2] Van Dongen, I. S., 1954, p. 3.

Africa continues to be the only region in the world where there is still a justifiable reason for large-scale building of railways, though this does not of course imply that all the railways under construction or projected are really needed. These include considerable mileage: In Nigeria, to make the Bornu province accessible and stretch out towards the north east; in Sudan, to open up new areas towards the south and west; in East Africa, to replace a most costly and complicated land-water transport route to northwestern Uganda and to tie the Tanganyika and Kenya–Uganda lines together; in Swaziland, to give a new outlet to the sea and make possible exploitation of iron ore deposits; in Mauritania, Congo Republic and Liberia, for the exploitation of new ore deposits for export; and in Angola and Mozambique to open up new areas.

Tropical Africa in 1960 had about 28,000 miles of railway, plus over 2,000 miles under construction or projected; this for an area of over 6 million square miles. Such a figure can be contrasted with that for the Republic of South Africa and South-West Africa, an area one-twelfth this size where there are 18,000 miles of railway, traffic on which is considerably greater than on all the other African railways. Thus in 1948, the South African railways carried 11.3 billion ton-miles, while for all the African tropical railway systems the figure was 7.5 billion; in 1959, 19.3 billion ton miles and 11.6 billion ton miles, respectively. This means that by 1959 the traffic in the rest of Subsaharan Africa had caught up to the position of South Africa 11 years earlier.

The railways arrived in Africa just before the beginning of the road age. The main expansion in ground transport in Africa, as elsewhere, came to be in roads, since road-building as an important part of the investment plan in every country has become a world-wide phenomenon. The statistics on road mileage in Africa are unfortunately not very good; a reasonable estimate is that there are about 125,000 miles of road in Subsaharan Africa.[3]

Table 12.2, which gives the number of vehicles by country, provides some insight into the development of road transport. The total, 708,000, is about 300,000 less than the Republic of South Africa, and about equal to the number that the 10 million people of the Netherlands possess. However, there has been the beginning of an automotive industry in tropical Africa with the opening of truck assembly plants in Ghana and Nigeria, for example, and automobile assembly plants in the Rhodesias and Kenya.

The oil marketing companies have become some of the largest investors in Subsaharan Africa. Certainly in one respect, Africa is like

[3] The United Africa Company Limited, 1961.

the industrialized countries; the gasoline service stations that have been scattered across Africa are duplicates of the stations in the United States and Europe. The ultimate economic and cultural impact of this development is likely to be staggering.

TABLE 12.2. *Motor Vehicles in Circulation* (a), 1959
(*in thousands*)

	Passenger Cars	Commercial Vehicles	Total
Rhodesia and Nyasaland	110	45	155
Former French West Africa (a)	34	52	86
Kenya	57	11	68
Republic of the Congo (a)	35	23	58
Nigeria	30	23	53
Mozambique	30	9	39
Angola	27	11	38
Ghana	18	16	34
Tanganyika	23	9	32
Uganda	24	5	29
Kamerun	9	19	28
Sudan	11	14	25
Former French Equatorial Africa	10	16	26
Ethiopia	14	8	22
Somalia	2	4	6
Sierra Leone (b)	3	2	5
French Somaliland	2	(c)	2
Gambia	1	1	2
Total	440	268	708

Source: United Nations, 1960, pp. 332–334.

Notes to Table:

(a) 1958.
(b) 1956.
(c) Less than 500.

Most of the African countries have also had to make large investments in ports, a very large share of this going to make up for the deficiencies of nature in providing ships with shelter from weather and deep-enough anchorage. In Ghana, for example, both of the ocean ports, Takoradi and Tema, are artificial. The latter, Africa's largest artificial port, cost £17 million. Since 1939, an enormous effort has been made in building and expanding ports all around Africa. Conakry, Guinea; Port Harcourt and Lagos, Nigeria; Matadi, Republic of the Congo; Lourenço Marques and Beira, Mozambique; Dar-es-Salaam, Tanganyika; and Mombasa,

Kenya have been expanded. In addition to Tema, new ports of Abidjan, Ivory Coast; Cotonou, Dahomey; and Monrovia, Liberia, deserve special mention. In Liberia, also, another artificial port, Buchanan, will handle iron ore shipments from new mines.

In the provision and use of ports, tropical Africa has moved ahead more rapidly than in inland transport. In 1959, ports in this area handled over 40 million tons of shipments in international trade. This is

TABLE 12.3. *International Port Traffic*, 1959

	Millions of Tons
Mozambique	6.0
Nigeria	5.7
Former French West Africa	5.3
Ghana	3.4
Kenya	2.6
Liberia	2.5
Sierra Leone	2.3
Republic of the Congo	1.9
Former French Equatorial Africa (*a*)	1.8
Sudan	1.7
French Somaliland	1.2
Guinea	1.1
Tanganyika	1.1
Kamerun	0.8
Zanzibar	0.1
Togo	0.1
Gambia	0.1
Total	37.7

Source: United Nations, 1960, pp. 343–345.
Note to Table:
  (*a*) 1958.

about three times the volume of the trade handled in the Republic of South Africa. Table 12.3 shows how this traffic was distributed.

In air transport, Africa at least started on a par with the rest of the world. In fact, since the general practice is for government to subsidize air travel, Africa suffers a smaller absolute economic loss from the uneconomic over-rapid development of air travel than other countries, since she has a smaller investment in other forms of transport to lose in the process. The relative size of this loss is another matter, however, and cannot easily be estimated.

The African countries are likely to put a higher proportion of their total investment into transport than the industrialized countries, for a number of reasons. Whereas investment in roads, bridges and ports has gone on for 2,000 years in Europe, the Africans have a patrimony of infrastructure that goes back scarcely 60 years. In Cyprus, for example, expansion of the port of Kyrenia is changing the contour of a port, which was fixed by the Venetians, to one which takes advantage of a breakwater left by the Romans. The African populations are usually spread very thinly over enormous areas requiring relatively high investment per head for transport. As internal production gradually changes from subsistence to the market, more and more transport facilities are needed. Topography and climate are harder, and the investment in providing a given level of transport must consequently be greater; thus the Kenya–Uganda railway from Mombasa to Kampala has to climb from sea level to 7,600 feet, descend into the Rift Valley to 6,000 feet and rise again to 9,000 feet, finally reaching Kampala at an altitude of 4,000 feet. Commodities make up a much larger share of gross national product than in an industrialized country, where services are important. And, finally, the commodities to be transported are mostly primary products, which are bulkier in relation to value than fabricated industrial products.

Of the roughly £360 million capital investment carried out by this government and public agencies in Nigeria, 1955–1962, transport was allocated about 34 per cent. In the French-speaking territories, about half of the commitments undertaken by the French aid agencies, Fonds des Investissements pour le Développement Economique et Sociale (FIDES) and Caisse Centrale de la France d'Outre-Mer (CCFOM), in 1946–1954, were for transport and communications. In the second FIDES plan, 1954–1958, transport and communications were allocated 42 per cent of the total amount provided, even though a special attempt was made to allocate a greater proportion of funds to commodity-producing sectors.[4] Of World Bank loans of $860 million in Africa, 55 per cent went to develop transport facilities. It is, of course, partly accidental, but whereas in the rest of the world, the Bank loans for power and transport were about equal, in Africa, for every $1 loaned for power, $2.50 went for transport.

3

Though adequate transport infrastructure in railways, ports, roads and airways must remain an indispensable part of economic development, the word "infrastructure" has a broader meaning in the development of

[4] United Nations, Economic Commission for Africa, 1960b, pp. 79–80.

Africa than just transport. Earlier need was essentially for transport facilities—African farmers, or European concessionaires or miners required little else than a way of getting their products out to markets. In this stage, Lugard's comment was essentially right: "The material development of Africa may be summed up in one word—transport." But as the economy of Africa broadened and the first stages of industrialization and urbanization began, the necessary "infrastructure" also broadened. That is to say, the basic services that the government has to provide for the commodity-producing sector of the economy could no longer be limited to transport. As mines and agriculture developed and the first beginning of industrialization took hold, electric power became essential if products were to be processed and transformed in Africa itself. Assuring electric power for industry has thus come to be generally accepted as an integral part of the basic services that governments hold to be their responsibility.

Electric power output has been growing rapidly; between 1951 and 1960, it more than doubled. The rate of increase has been higher than the world average, even though the absolute level reached is still very small. It has been estimated that Africa produced 1.3 per cent of the world output of electricity in 1950; in 1960, the proportion was 1.6[5] per cent. Table 12.4 shows the distribution of output among the African countries for the latest years for which comparable data are available. The very great unevenness in the production of power shown by different countries is an indication of the degree of industrialization or mining development reached by them; production in the Republic of South Africa was almost triple that of the total of the other countries combined.

The spread of modern government administration into Africa carried with it the need to provide the communications—the post office, telephones and telegraphs—to make administration possible, and for use by the developing economies. Private arrangements by no means disappeared in this field. In Uganda, for example, the volume of mail transported privately may well exceed the volume that the post office handles. The growth of urbanization has made water supply and sewerage essential public utilities, although over most of Africa individuals and companies still make their own provision for these, so that they have still to become fully a part of the economic infrastructure.

Education was not always considered a part of the economic infrastructure, but was regarded more as an expensive consumer good than as a necessary prerequisite of economic growth. It is not possible to make a reasonable estimate of the part education plays in this regard; the part, that is, which merely increases satisfactions is difficult to dis-

[5] European Economic Community, Office Statistiques, 1961.

tinguish from that part which can reasonably be assessed as a cost of increased productive capacity. It was only in the 1920's that governments in Africa began to take an active role in the education of Africans,

TABLE 12.4. *Electric Power Output in African Countries*[1]

	Millions of kw.
Republic of the Congo (a)	2,750
Rhodesia and Nyasaland (a)	2,425
Uganda (c)	278
Nigeria (b)	273
Kenya (c)	214
Tanganyika (c)	141
Former French West Africa (b)	138
Ghana (b)	67
Sudan (b)	47
Angola (b)	43
Former French Equatorial Africa (b)	33
Ethiopia (b)	31
Kamerun (b)	29
Mozambique (d)	25
Sierra Leone (b)	14
Somalia (b)	6
Zanzibar (b)	6
Gambia (b)	3
Togo (b)	2
Total of foregoing	6,525

Notes to Table:
(a) 1957.
(b) 1956.
(c) 1958.
(d) 1955.

[1]*Sources:* World Power Conference, 1960, pp. 134–139, 160–162; Belgian Congo and Ruanda-Urundi Information and Public Relations Office, 1959, Vol. II, p. 113; East African High Commission Statistical Office, 1961.

this field having been left earlier almost exclusively to the missionaries; so that major development of education mostly came since 1950. It is practically only since 1960 that the high economic yield of expenditures on education has been widely recognized, and investment plans influenced by this fact.

In Africa, there has been a special reason for this. During most of the post-World War II period, the general approach to government policy in economic development in Africa was that the provision of economic

K

infrastructure, strictly defined, was the main essential. It was true that during a large part of this period, the capacity of the infrastructure in many African countries was the major bottleneck which held back economic development. The infrastructure, that is, had been neglected during the world depression and during World War II. With the larger world markets for African products after World War II, investment in the infrastructure was imperative to make it possible to get these products to market.

Investment in infrastructure, as narrowly conceived, has continued to be the decisive element in a number of countries where new ore bodies are being developed and railways and ports are needed to get the ore to world markets. But in many of the African countries once the infrastructure, in this sense, caught up with or even ran ahead of the needs of the rest of the economy, governments were faced with the central problem of stimulating the growth of the commodity-producing sectors directly. This is to say that they were faced with the need of increasing agricultural production by the voluntary action of millions of small farmers and of developing entrepreneurial, managerial and skilled worker groups where none had existed before. The problem was one of economic development through development of individual skills and attitudes. It is quite understandable that governments began to grope towards investment in education as a means of achieving this.

The development of the educational infrastructure in Africa, however, was no less uneven than in the other fields we have considered. W. Arthur Lewis made the rough judgement that, "If one considers only the investment aspects of education, the typical country in Subsaharan Africa might set as its first target 50 per cent of each age cohort of children in primary school, 5 per cent in secondary school, and 0.5 per cent in university."[6] By secondary education Lewis meant the grammar school level, while university education does not include other types of secondary education short of university. There are no comprehensive statistics on education in the African countries on this basis. The best available is in Table 12.5, on elementary and secondary education, where the definition of secondary education is considerably broader than that given by Lewis, probably including, in most cases, junior secondary schools, or the seventh and eighth years of schooling. The figures as given cast a dim light on the extent to which the educational infrastructure in the various African countries has developed and still requires development even to meet Lewis' first target.

The next stage in the evolution of the concept of economic infrastructure will probably be in agriculture, where such a change in

[6] Lewis, W. A., 1961, p. 77.

approach would be of immeasurable help in African economic growth. The first point to be made here is that rapid progress in agriculture in African countries depends on a revolution in the techniques of farming.

TABLE 12.5. *Percentage of Enrolment to School-Age Population*[1]

Country	Year	Primary School (Percentage)	Secondary School (Percentage)
Ghana	1959	67	29
Sudan	1959–60	13	6.5
Zanzibar	1958	25	5
Basutoland	1958	91	4.5
Swaziland	1958	56	4.5
Uganda	1959	52	4.4
Kenya	1958	52	3.9
Liberia	1959–60	22	3.3
Southern Rhodesia	1958	84	3.0
Kamerun	1959–60	78	3.0
Republic of the Congo	1959–60	72	3.0
Congo Republic	1957–58	70	3.0
Nigeria	1958	43	2.9
Sierra Leone	1959	21	2.8
Northern Rhodesia	1958–59	54	2.6
Gambia	1958	24	2.1
Tanganyika	1957–58	66	2.0
Senegal	1957–58	24	1.9
Nyasaland	1958	51	1.4
Bechuanaland	1958	46	1.4
Ivory Coast	1957–58	33	1.4
Dahomey	1959–60	31	1.4
Guinea	1959–60	20	1.1
Togo	1959	32	1.0
Ruanda-Urundi	1958	36	0.9
Central African Republic	1957–58	27	0.9
Cameroun (UK)	1958	20	0.8
Somalia	1958–59	10	0.8
Mali	1957–58	7	0.5
Ethiopia	1958–59	4	0.5
Chad	1959–60	14	0.4
Upper Volta	1959–60	7	0.4
Mauritania	1957–58	7	0.3
Niger	1957–58	3	0.1

[1]*Source:* United Nations, Economic Commission for Africa, and United Nations, Educational, Scientific and Cultural Organization, 1961, p. 7.

And this particularly depends on governmental expenditures on agricultural research and extension, as well as on education.[8] Expenditures on research and extension workers, however, have not been regarded as investment in needed infrastructure, but simply as recurrent expenditures. In consequence, countries have not included such expenditures in development plans for which a major national effort is justified, nor have such expenditures been regarded as clearly eligible for financing by external sources of finance. Actually, expenditure in creating and maintaining a network of extension agents is as much investment in building up the productive capacity of the economy as investment in a network of roads. Some realization of this fact has begun to be apparent. In 1960, the World Bank made a loan to the Republic of the Congo for agricultural development in which a portion of the loan was to pay the salaries of extension workers. The development plan of Uganda includes a large item under agriculture for the development of the extension service and agricultural research.

4

The foregoing paragraphs have considered some aspects of the evolution of the concept of economic infrastructure and the development in Subsaharan Africa. In general it has come to be regarded as almost axiomatic that African governments have the responsibility to provide this infrastructure. This has happened largely by default. In the early years of the twentieth century, the chartered companies, concessionaires, and other private interests generally undertook this responsibility. The private ownership of the B.C.K. railway and the power plants in the Katanga by Union Minière interests, the control of the Benguela railway by Tanganyika Concessions, Limited, and the important role that has continued to be played by missionaries in education in many countries, are relics of this previous point of view. In most cases, the fact that private investors received no dividends, frequently losing a part or all of their capital investment in addition, restricted the supply of private capital even before political uncertainties complicated the problem. Consequently, most governments, with a few exceptions, came to hold themselves responsible for the development of these sectors of the economy, and are held responsible for this by their citizens.

The introduction of modern transport into Africa was completely financed from abroad. Generally speaking, dependence on foreign sources of capital for financing a substantial part of the infrastructure remained throughout the twentieth century, even though indigenous

[8] Johnston, B. F., and Mellor, J. W., 1961, *passim.*

governments and not foreign interests came to provide these services.

The external financing provided Africa south of the Sahara was appreciable, when absolute amounts are taken into account. There is no comprehensive study available on this since Frankel's work,[9] but it is clear that in relation to total capital investment, external assistance in most African countries was vital. The Economic Commission for Africa estimated that, including the Republic of South Africa, external funds financed on the average about one-third of total capital formation, both public and private, in the period 1950–1957.[10] If South Africa were excluded, the proportion of external funds to total capital formation would rise to around 50 per cent.

After World War II, practically the whole of the infrastructure of the French-speaking countries of Africa was financed by external help. In the English-speaking countries, only part of their investment needs in this field were externally financed, but the proportion is growing. Ghana, Nigeria, Uganda were able to finance nearly all their needs from their own resources, but in their post-independence development plans, at least half of the public capital investment is to be financed from abroad. In Tanganyika's plan, about 90 per cent of the public investment is supposed to come from elsewhere; in the Sudan, 30 per cent. In Kenya most of the public investment after the Mau Mau troubles was financed externally.

The development of the economic infrastructure of Africa, consequently, has depended and has continued to depend especially heavily on outside sources of finance. This is a unique characteristic of Africa; no other region of the world is in a similar position.

[9] Frankel, S. H., 1938.
[10] United Nations, Department of Economic and Social Affairs, 1959a, p. 211.

13

The Adaptation of African Labor
Systems to Social Change

by Wilbert E. Moore*
Princeton University

The pre-modern forms of economic production in Subsaharan Africa range from extremely "primitive" hunting and food-gathering to settled agricultural systems of varying degrees of technical proficiency. Handicraft production, either utilitarian or esthetic, has been rather highly developed in some areas, minimal in others. The notion of a "subsistence" economy—that is, low levels of productive specialization and meager if any capital accumulation—does not necessarily imply the economic self-sufficiency of every family as the ultimate consuming unit. Considerable interdependence within and even between villages, mediated by various forms of trade, may modify the picture of an undifferentiated productive system.

It is characteristic of pre-modern social systems that most productive activities are carried out by units that are not specialized: in other words, by social units with "diffuse" functions. The primary family, and often other elements of the kinship system, have important economic functions. Larger units, such as villages, or tribes, may provide the boundaries and network for specialization and exchange.

It follows from the primarily non-economic basis of economic organization in such social systems that various productive and distributive activities are assigned less on grounds of efficiency than on the basis of other roles. The distinction is not precise, of course. For example, the division of productive tasks between men and women is to a large degree "arbitrary" from a technical point of view, but the recurrence of some patterns in widely scattered places suggests some quasi-rational basis for role assignments.

* The preparation of this study was supported in part by the National Academy of Sciences–National Research Council, under Contract No. DA–19–129–AM–1309 with the Quartermaster Research and Engineering Command, U.S. Army.

Women commonly perform the relatively light but routine and recurrent agricultural and household tasks.[1] Men do heavier work such as breaking up fields for new cultivation, cutting branches or trees for shifting forest cultivation and, commonly, hunting.[2] An interesting extension of the sexual division of labor is the greater probability that men will work in cooperative groups. This type of organization usually takes the form of mutual aid, with the farmer who benefits being responsible for food.[3] In Central and East Africa the beneficiary supplies beer, which is not regarded as payment to the working party, but as something to induce social conviviality,[4] since reciprocity of obligation still holds. One function of such work cooperative parties in the "transitional" situation of labor migration of men is the maintenance of family agriculture even in the absence of the male.

The age-grading of labor, which may simply provide for non-working infants and children, working youths and adults, and non-working aged persons, can on occasion be quite complex. Thus the Adioukrou of the Ivory Coast, of former French West Africa, have an elaborate seven-fold age-grading of adult tasks in the cultivation and preparation of palm oil.[5]

Since technical efficiency has not been the primary criterion for productive organization, it is not surprising that levels of efficiency in indigenous agriculture are generally low. The International Labour Office has concluded that,

> ... the present basis of subsistence production represents one of the lowest levels of utilization of human resources in the world and is at the root of the low standards of living in Africa. Until a greater quantity of food can be produced by a much smaller number of persons and a considerable portion of those engaged in subsistence production can be released for more productive activity, this situation is likely to remain unchanged. ... Work ... is dictated by the rhythm of the seasons ... and all activities developed into a tradition sanctified by usage and surrounded by ritual. ... Work in the tribal setting requires neither foresight nor planning; it includes no notion of time, there is no specialization and no order other than that ordained by the seasons.[6]

While it may be noted that the migratory system discussed in the first of the preceding excerpts provides at least the opportunity for greater

[1] International Labour Office, 1958, pp. 13, 68, 88.
[2] De Schlippe, P., 1956, pp. 140–148; Gulliver, P. H., 1955, pp. 33–41; Richards, A. I., 1958; Southall, A. W., 1953, pp. 271–279; Watson, W., 1958, pp. 2–22, 33.
[3] International Labour Office, *op. cit.*, p. 66; Little, K. L., 1948.
[4] For example, Watson, *op. cit.*, pp. 106–110.
[5] Dupire, M., 1956, *passim*.
[6] International Labour Office, 1958, pp. 32, 140.

efficiency of labor on the part of those remaining behind but continuing traditional production, the second part of the quotation indulges in gross, though poetic, exaggeration, since even in one of the most "primitive" modes of agricultural technology—that of the clearing, burning, shifting cultivation in forest lands—a cycle of several years is both planned and implemented.

Although there is a fairly standard doctrine that a "rational" organization of work is dependent on a monetary economy—a view maintained in the International Labour Office Survey[7]—Udy has made out a considerable case for the appearance of such organizations in many nonindustrial societies, including some African ones.[8] As previously noted, there are some "technical" elements in the sexual division of labor—particularly the assignment of physically arduous tasks to males. The role of the male as hunter, warrior, and construction worker is common. But to this sexual division of labor must be added the difference in organization of work by sexes. The common appearance of the workgroup, despite the obvious note of conviviality introduced by beer drinking, can be assumed to rest upon a technical distinction between individual and group tasks. A major finding of Udy's comparative study, which includes some twenty-six African tribal societies, is that "rational" work groups in nonindustrial societies are likely to be organized on a temporary basis, being employed for tasks that are not daily and routine.[9] Although this contrasts with the organization of work in commercialized economies, the evidence does suggest that transition to such economies may be somewhat less radical than is commonly supposed.

2

It is not ordinarily realized that Africa has been subjected to a great variety of external influences over a period of several centuries. The rapidity of contemporary change in political and economic structures, and the resulting heightened tensions, should not lead to the casual assumption that the continent remained in a stable *status quo ante* until the colonial period. The slave trade to North Africa, the New World and Asia Minor, the introduction of "trade goods" by Europeans and Arab traders, the later political and religious imperialism that started more than a century ago, and the educational and economic transformations instituted by colonial governments—all have had their major and subtle effects on labor systems.

[7] *Op. cit.*, pp. 66–68.
[8] Udy, S. H., Jr., 1959.
[9] *Ibid.*, pp. 41–43, 49, 127, 128.

In the most general terms, the experience in Africa is a repetition of that in other technologically underdeveloped areas, although the details differ greatly. Workers have been induced to enter into new forms of activity by measures ranging from direct coercion to the indirect appeal of goods that only money will secure. They have been given training in varying degrees appropriate to new tasks and opportunities. They have been "pushed" out of traditional economic pursuits by contraction of the land available to them, and by population growth as a by-product of increased sanitation.[10]

The details, however, are not inconsequential. The meeting of civilizations in Africa seems to have produced a richer variety of adjustments than in any other area of the world. Some of the adjustments considered here as "transitional" have proved remarkably stable and persistent, whether because of the underlying strength of the indigenous cultures, or because the policies of alien rulers have prevented more rapid and radical transformation.

Enterprisers in Africa seeking local labor commonly encountered a situation that was an extreme illustration of a type, namely, an indigenous population insensitive to financial inducements. In the absence of a monetary market in the traditions of many African societies, and with relatively inelastic demand schedules for products in any case, this behavior was inconvenient. Slavery in various forms as well as many types of obligatory service at the instance of political rulers existed in many African areas prior to contact with Europe and America. Although in a sense providing a prior cultural base for new systems of forced labor, there were also negative consequences for new labor systems, even of a non-coercive type. The International Labour Office *Survey* observed that "for many tribes any form of organized manual work for others has associations with slavery and is therefore despised. ..."[11]

There are at least three rather different situations in which forced labor has been sanctioned by governing authorities. First, there are personal services for recognized native chiefs, including agricultural work on the chief's land and the upkeep of his buildings. Second, there are various forms of the *corvée*, that is, obligatory work for public purposes such as porterage, road construction, and military service. Third, there have been types of essentially compulsory public recruiting for private economic activities, particularly in the earlier days of colonial rule, when local supplies of labor were inadequate and additional workers had to be sought at considerable distances.

The first form of compulsory labor, various services to native chiefs, has of course the superficial justification of preserving elements of the

[10] Moore, W. E., 1951. [11] *Op. cit.*, p. 140.

traditional social order. However, the combination of increasing legal restrictions and the evolution of the socio-economic structure has operated to modify and transform such services. Thus, commuting of forced labor by cash payments is reported to have been possible in the Congo and Ruanda-Urundi.[12] Among the Alur of Uganda the service is viewed as a tax payment in cash, and actual performance is regarded as a penalty for default of payment rather than the normal method of fulfilling the obligation.[13]

The distinctions to be made among the three types of forced labor are not entirely clear-cut. For example, services to native chiefs in Portuguese Guinea are in part for the purpose of supporting orphans, the sick and infirm, and the destitute,[14] which in the light of concepts of public welfare has a distinctly public flavor. On the other hand, forced labor "for the purpose of agricultural instruction" in the Congo, and compulsory agricultural work for the purpose of protecting against famine, recognized in Gambia and Tanganyika,[15] has a distinct flavor of public intervention for private economic interests.

Direct coercion of workers, even for public works, was scarcely consistent with the legal standards that prevailed in the metropolitan powers. This was particularly true if labor was uncompensated. A widely used form was the head or hut tax, payable only in cash, and thus in most areas payable only by the acceptance of employment for wages. "This coercion by indirection, which is more in keeping with European canons of law and ethics and conceptions of productive relationships, has been accomplished mainly by the power of taxation as a prerogative of constituted governmental authority."[16] Under German administration in Tanganyika, a variant of the cash tax was imposed. In one section of the colony every adult native male had to work 30 days within every four-month period for a private employer. If he failed to comply with this regulation he was conscripted for an equal amount of time on public roads.[17] Taxation, however, has lost its importance as a factor in labor recruitment. A considerable expansion of wage earning in the absence of indirect compulsion would seem to indicate that "normal economic incentives have proved increasingly effective in inducing Africans to seek paid employment of their own accord."[18]

Certainly the outstanding feature of the contemporary system of employment in central and southern Africa is the pattern of relatively temporary employment of native workers who migrate to places of

[12] *Ibid.*, p. 298.　　　　　　　[13] Southall, A. W., 1953, pp. 304–305.
[14] Carriera, A., 1948.　　　　　[15] International Labour Office, *op. cit.*, pp. 297–299.
[16] Moore, W. E., 1946, p. 401.　　[17] Leubuscher, C., 1944, pp. 64–66.
[18] International Labour Office, *op. cit.*, p. 295.

employment and then return to their villages. Like many migratory movements, this transfer of workers is compounded of various elements of "push" and "pull". Contraction of farm and grazing lands, coupled with population "pressure," results in a deteriorating relation of the indigenous population to the traditional means of subsistence.[19] The "pull" factors include the usual ones associated with urbanization everywhere—ranging from economic opportunity, real or imagined, through various social amenities, to the mere excitement of urban life.

The variant in the African scene is the temporary character of much labor migration, and the rather specific character of the economic goals. This latter characteristic has led to the concept of the "target worker." The targets may themselves be compulsory, as in the case of getting money for taxes. They may be derivatives of traditional patterns, as in the commutation of bride-price from cattle to money, the substitution of migration for more traditional and sometimes violent forms of activities calculated to gain prestige for young men, or the investment of money in improved agriculture. They may be specific consumer products, from clothes to bicycles.[20] As long as economic "wants" remain highly specific and inelastic, higher wages are likely to mean that the worker stops sooner, and non-financial incentives such as conditions of work must then be used in competition for workers.[21]

The "targets" of workers differ in both space and time. Where indigenous agriculture has become substantially commercialized, as in parts of both western and eastern Africa, there is not only a greater probability that temporary migratory workers will work for native employers, but also some probability that the income from such employment will be used to pay for capital improvements on the worker's own farm. In other areas, the temporary employee is much more likely to be oriented to current consumption.

Through time, it is understandable that just as some migration that seems to be temporary is in fact relatively permanent, so the targets of workers become generalized through their increasing incorporation in the market system of pecuniary, industrialized economies. The target, in other words, becomes money, for whatever it will buy. For the "target worker," strictly speaking, the retention of village ties is unproblematical. It is his base of operations. Put in economic terms, his two sources of "income" are complementary. For the worker rather more fully incorporated into the labor and commodity markets, such

[19] Moore, W. E., 1951, pp. 48–55; Stephens, R. W., 1958. For a negative view: Burden, G. N., 1951.

[20] For example: cf. Southall, A. W., 1954.

[21] Berg, E. J., 1961.

ties may still be operative, and commentators have emphasized the economic security based on rights in land, and the social security based on kinship reciprocities and traditional political structures.[22]

The sheer volume of labor migration would appear to have some impact at the places of origin as well as at places of destination. Figures of migrants in the tens and even hundreds of thousands, from relatively restricted geographical areas, repeatedly appear in the reports.[23] Perhaps more significant are the proportions of men absent from their villages, which various studies indicate may range from 25 to as high as 70 per cent of the adult males.[24] The effects of migratory patterns on traditional structures are, surely, a function at least of the volume and duration of migration, as well as the extent to which the "traditional" structures were, in fact, relatively integrated.

In Africa, the migratory labor system has taken on a quasi-permanent character. In the Republic of South Africa it has a legal status which stems from the restrictions laid on African urban residence and the attempt to "retribalize" all Africans. The official policy of *apartheid* looks eventually to the near-cessation of the migratory system, however, by setting up separate geographical entities ("Bantustans") for Africans, and the substitution of European workers for the displaced Africans. Granting the sincerity of government in attempting to avoid for the Europeans the fate of becoming a minority in a multiracial state, it is extremely doubtful that the extremely tense political situation will become less so,[25] or that meanwhile *apartheid* will mean anything except the most rigorous system of racial domination in the contemporary world.

In all of Subsaharan Africa the numerical magnitude of migratory labor appears to be increasing. Apart from the somewhat special, or at least extreme, situation in South Africa, the reasons for this rather peculiar adaptation have been summarized by the East African Royal Commission:

> In the existing situation the migrant labour system appears to be the only one through which a considerable section of the African population can meet its needs, because the economic opportunities for more effective specialization have either been absent or have been seriously circumscribed by legal and customary restrictions. For many Africans it is not now possible to attain a higher income level for the support of their families without working both on the land and in urban employment. This means that,

[22] Delarozière, R., 1950; International Labour Office, *op. cit.*, pp. 82–83, 138–141.
[23] *Ibid.*, pp. 137–144.
[24] Gulliver, P. H., 1955, pp. 1–15; Richards, A. I., 1958.
[25] Northwestern University. Program of African Studies, 1959, pp. 59–61.

given the present productivity of Africans over large parts of the rural and urban sector of the economy, the migrant labour system appears as the most economic choice which the African can make, however socially deleterious or otherwise undesirable it may be. Notwithstanding these disadvantages the system brings about an improvement in the economic conditions of those who go out in search of paid employment. It follows that, if it is desired to curtail the system, it is necessary that the production opportunities in agriculture and in industry should be such that they can yield an income in cash and in kind that will be sufficient to enable the majority who work in either sphere to avoid working temporarily in the other. The replacement of the migrant labour system cannot be effectively accomplished merely by the introduction of special devices in the urban areas, but only as the result of a successfully long-term policy which includes both agricultural and non-agricultural improvement.[26]

A reasoned guess, however, is that the seeming stability of this structured compromise between divergent economic systems is spurious. "If this system provides a sort of statistical equilibrium it does not follow that it produces anything like a stable social equilibrium. Native labor migration serves as a bridge between rigid and otherwise incompatible types of social restraint. . . . The restraints . . . appear to be subject to pressure that may lead to their collapse."[27]

Another type of migratory movement of workers, seasonal labor, is less peculiar to the African situation than is the longer-term contractual worker. Although the two types of migration seem to merge in some instances, and to spring from some of the same sources, the seasonal migrant is almost exclusively an agricultural worker. The opportunity for seasonal wage employment stems in part from the relative underemployment of labor in the subsistence sector, making it possible for part of the labor force to aid in periods of peak demand for labor in commercialized agriculture. In part, the variations in climate, technology, and type of crop provide opportunities for farmers to work for other farmers during slack periods. The development of commercialized agriculture in West Africa has provided a considerable volume of employment for workers from neighboring regions.[28] An example of relatively long-distance seasonal migration is that of the migratory workers in the cotton fields of the Sudan. The bulk of the seasonal workers come from French Equatorial Africa and Nigeria, consisting of men who return annually to till their own crops.[29] The explanation of

[26] East African Royal Commission, 1955, p. 154.
[27] Moore, W. E., 1946, p. 419.
[28] Rouch, J., 1956.
[29] Fawzi, Saad El Din, 1957, pp. 4–7; Hassoun, Isam Ahmad, 1952.

the uncommitted worker has been put succinctly in the ILO *Survey.* If the worker

> . . . has ventured into the wage economy with the vague intention of remaining in it indefinitely, his native village or land unit remains in many areas an effective alternative to town life; no social or economic factors have yet arisen which link him and his fellows to industry and to town life. . . . That he should try to return such security as his rural background has to offer him is therefore normal. That his work in the wage economy should be conditioned by the complex of circumstances, largely unfavorable to him, which exist there is equally natural.[30]

In African multiracial territories, and to some extent throughout the Subsaharan area, some form or degree of the "color bar" has continued to exist. Official policy ranged from the denial of discrimination in French territories, through forms of "indirect rule" of predominantly African populations in some British territories, to open and legal racism in the Rhodesias and South Africa. African political ascendency in the newly independent states has not entirely ended the advantageous position held by the white merchant or employer.

Although much discontent incident upon racial discrimination arises from strictly social and political sources, its economic aspect cannot be set aside entirely. Two principal problems that affect the position of the African workers are the establishment of non-competing occupational categories for African and European workers, giving the latter immunity from African competition for skilled, prestigeful, and well-paid jobs, and discriminatory legislation or customary practices that not only bar any common European-African labor organization, but often prevent or sharply restrict the freedom of association of the African workers. The forms of the color bar have been modified in Rhodesia, with provisions for Africans to enter a wider range of "intermediate" occupations, and to present their views and grievance through union organization.[31] As one observer has noted, however, the ending of formal restrictions on access to occupations, whether imposed by law or by European workers, does not automatically produce Africans with the appropriate skills to claim the new opportunities.[32]

Secondary manufacturing industry has had little development. Where it has, the flexibility of occupational organization in view of changing physical or administrative technology has tended to give the employer a freer hand in opening positions to African workers, and thus

[30] International Labour Office, *op. cit.*, p. 142.
[31] Oppenheimer, H. F., 1956, *passim.*
[32] Prain, R. L., 1956, *passim.*

avoiding the exceptionally high wages exacted by European workers who are firmly protected from native competition. The International Labour Office *Survey* notes with reference to labor organization that,

> ... in some of the multi-racial societies ... the policies and legal provisions relating to freedom of association, the right to organize and bargain collectively, and the settlement of trade disputes, are different for the various racial groups in the community. Such anomalies are generally stated to be justified because of the different stages of social evolution of the various elements of the societies concerned.[33]

One may note, however, that the legislative imposition of racial inequality is itself a clear denial of the claimed justification, namely natural inequality, for if the latter prevented acquisition of higher skills, biology would need no help from politicians in keeping African workers "in their place."

3

The concept of a "stabilized sector" of African labor must be viewed in the special context of comparison with the clearly transitional adjustments between radically different soci-economic systems. The stabilized sector refers to those portions of the economy, and particularly that portion of the labor force, that are fully and irretrievably bound up with the commodity and labor market systems. In view of the inherent dynamics of modern commercial and industrial systems, these segments are clearly not stabilized in any static sense.

The assessment of the extent and significance of relatively complete departure from traditional economic usages presents in the first instance a merely factual problem: what is its quantitative importance? Some detailed field studies indicate that the truly transformed or committed workers, even among the urban-born and long-term employees, represent a fairly small minority.[34] However, as Mitchell has pointed out,[35] the mere factual question is complicated by the conceptual one, and he rejects as synonymous the concepts of urbanization, detribalization, and stabilization. Even if stabilization is defined as "permanence" of residence in towns and participation in the labor markets, as a predictive measure it must have an attitudinal component—that is, intent and identification. But it is precisely intention and identification that set the distinction between the "transitional" and "stabilized" forms of

[33] *Op. cit.,* p. 255.
[34] For example, Wilson, G., 1941–1942, *passim.*
[35] Mitchell, J. C., 1956, *passim.*

labor adopted in this paper. Moreover, the very high turnover of African workers represents a mixture, in unknown proportions, of migratory labor in the distinctly African pattern, and of workers simply changing employers. The latter may be somewhat whimsical or otherwise unreliable in their employment behavior, but they are acting within the modern labor-market system.

By implication, all or most forms of economic organization and labor systems not in conformity with the norms and patterns of the older industrial economies are "transitional." This is a view that some scholars concerned with Africa would reject. They argue that the viable strength of indigenous social systems is such that the future forms of African economies will represent a mutual adaptation between the demands of the commercial-industrial system and the variable social systems found in pre-modern and contemporary African societies.[36]

The position may have both theoretical and factual support. It seems quite clear that the literature on economic development has fairly consistently underplayed the organizational flexibility and adaptability of the commercial-industrial system. At the same time, at least some students of contemporary Africa argue that such systems as that of migratory labor represent stable adaptations between divergent systems.[37] The very considerable development of wage-labor patterns, whether seasonal or settled, in the commercialized agricultural undertakings established by native farmers lends some further support to the view that the "stabilized sector" may not only include agriculture, but include it in ways somewhat alien to "Western" conceptions. It remains true that there is a labor market more or less corresponding to industrial economic patterns. Its exact dimensions are difficult to assess, and the significance of the deviations and their stability are disputed.

For those large proportions of native workers who intermix subsistence farming, cash cropping, petty commerce, and wage labor, the concepts of "labor force," "gainfully occupied," "occupation," and "industry," in the sense of sector of economic activity, do not neatly differentiate persons,[38] but rather have at best a temporary cross-sectional utility.

As the lack of specialization in any one calling is a basic feature of the working population in Africa, employment statistics can only show the number of workers occupied at a given moment in definite occupations.[39]

[36] Balandier, G., 1958; Comhaire, J. L., 1956; Herskovits, M. J., 1956, 1960.
[37] Elkan, W., and Fallers, L. A., 1960.
[38] United Nations, Department of Economic Affairs, 1954.
[39] International Labour Office, *op. cit.*, p. 111.

Some approximate sense can be made of distributions of "workers" by major economic sector, distinguishing agriculture, "industry" (mining, manufacturing, construction) and "services" (commerce, professions, government, service and the like). Even with this crude classification, however, the agricultural sector fails to distinguish among subsistence agriculture, cash cropping and various forms of farm tenancy, and agricultural wage labor. Thus, among wage earners as such, agriculture may provide relatively minor employment in areas where subsistence farming and small proprietorship prevail, and account for 40 to 50 per cent of wage employment where commercial agriculture is on a larger scale, as in Southern Rhodesia, Kenya, Tanganyika, and South Africa.[40]

Mining accounts for almost one-fifth of the African wage-earners in South Africa, and a substantial proportion, from 8 to 13 per cent, in Ghana, the Republic of the Congo and the Rhodesias, but it must be noted that wage-earners in turn represent less than a fifth of the economically active males in Ghana, though nearly a half in the Rhodesias. Secondary industry, other than mining, is of small quantitative significance as an employer throughout Subsaharan Africa, ranging sharply downward from 20–25 per cent among wage earners in South Africa and the ex-Belgian Congo.[41]

"Services" of all sorts generally represent a larger proportion of the employed population than does secondary industrial production. The statistical materials, unreliable at best, here encounter a further difficulty in that reliance on distribution of wage-earners excludes the self-employed. This category is of considerable importance in petty trade, whether the traders be the Asians of eastern and southern Africa or the Africans in the West. It should also be noted that governments are substantial employers of African labor, running as high as almost 30 per cent of wage earners in former French West Africa, where, however, the total of all wage earners is very low, and over 20 per cent in Kenya, where wage earners are a substantial proportion of the gainfully occupied.[42]

However, except for a few detailed studies, occupational distributions strictly defined are essentially meaningless. The reason is that a majority of workers are unskilled, and accordingly have the widest possible transferability between occupations and between sectors of the economy. Various studies indicate that at least one-half to three-fourths of employed Africans are in this category.[43] Fawzi finds that even among

[40] United Nations, Department of Economic Affairs, 1954, pp. 24–25.
[41] International Labour Office, *op. cit.*, pp. 666–667.
[42] *Ibid., loc. cit.*
[43] Balandier, G., 1952b; Hauser, A., 1955, Xydias, Nelly, 1956a.

governmental employees in the Sudan, who might be thought to comprise an especially select group, fully one-half are in the lowest category of skills.[44] Moreover most of the employment and occupational data on African labor refer to males, for the rather simple reason that women are very little represented in the labor market. Women contribute an important and often even a major portion of the labor in subsistence agriculture and, in West Africa, in petty trade. With a few exceptions they are not commonly employed at wage labor.[45]

To the extent that a genuinely stable and committed African labor force develops, one would expect the appearance of occupational prestige patterns approximating those of older industrial countries. Two studies indicate that such is the case, though the inferential conclusions of their respective authors differ in one significant respect. Mitchell and Epstein[46] find little or no evidence of genuine class identification within the African group, the economic and political leaders tending to be spokesmen for Africans generally. Xydias, on the basis of some discontinuities in the prestige scale, concludes,

> Our theory is that social classes are coming into being and that their existence is already intuitively perceived by the Africans; although they are not yet sufficiently aware of these classes to speak of them or to classify them as we ourselves do.[47]

There is a remarkable paucity of descriptive materials relating to the organization of non-agricultural enterprises in Africa. The extensive *Survey of African Labour* by the International Labour Office says nothing on the subject apart from some comments on special problems of first-line labor supervision. One study of workers in Stanleyville contains a few data concerning the distribution of workers by size of enterprise. Approximately one-fourth of the wage-earners surveyed worked in undertakings employing 50 or fewer workers, about one-half in enterprises employing 51 to 300 workers, and one-fourth in "large" undertakings with over 300 workers, of which approximately one-tenth was in two enterprises employing over 1,000 workers each.[48] Except for large mining employers, the small to medium-sized enterprise seems most common.[49] The policies of mining employers have varied from those of the Copper Belt in Northern Rhodesia, with fairly impersonal management of unskilled, temporary employees, largely housed in bachelor barracks, to the more paternalistic management of the Com-

---

[44] *Op. cit.*, pp. 8–13. [45] Elkan, W., 1956.
[46] Mitchell, J. C., and Epstein, A. L., 1959, *passim*.
[47] Xydias, Nelly, 1956b, p. 468. [48] Xydias, Nelly, 1956a, pp. 287–288.
[49] University of Natal, 1950, *passim*.

pagnie de Haut-Kantanga, where it has been the policy to develop a stable labor force. Reports on fairly large-scale plantation and forestry projects indicate a variety of compromises between "modern" methods of organization, supervision, and remuneration, on the one hand, and an unskilled, uncommitted, and largely transitory labor force on the other.

Fairly pervasive organizational problems in African non-agricultural enterprises arise out of racial distinctions between workers and supervisors, with or without African "gang leaders" as intermediaries,[50] and the common tribal diversity of the African labor force itself, which may or may not be overriden by the new circumstances at the workplace.[51] Both the "color bar" and tribal diversity operate to maintain a distorted organization of the enterprises, and to provide a technically irrelevant complication in the modes of management and personnel administration. One of the most remarkable features of economic change in Africa is the increased employment of Africans by Africans in commercialized agriculture. Some of the arrangements of tenancy and personal dependency have a distinctly archaic flavor.[52] Others strongly resemble a fully developed labor market in the agricultural sector of the several economies.[53]

It is not surprising, in view of the small numerical importance of "stabilized" workers in Africa, that labor organizations are relatively weak or non-existent. The organizational weakness of unions of African workers, and their modest economic power, is complicated by two additional factors. The first circumstance, by no means uncommon in newly developing areas, is that unions tend to be highly political in their orientations and policies, partly as a consequence of the meager direct bargaining strength of unskilled and semi-skilled workers. The second circumstance, which has a special significance in Africa, has to do with the official and unofficial restrictions on freedom of association and collective bargaining on the part of native workers—a manifestation of the "color bar."[54] The extreme case here, again, is South Africa.

In situations where a high volume of employment by Africans has been coupled with the development of some stable workers and the emergence of some workers having more than minimum skills, unions of native workers have achieved some modest direct influence, as in Nigeria and Rhodesia. In Ghana unions have come under strong governmental control. But the "color bar" can discourage African unionization, and prevent the formation of multiracial unions. The

[50] Balandier, G., 1952a, *passim*.   [51] Sofer, C., 1954, *passim*.
[52] Richards, A. I., 1954, *passim*.   [53] McCulloch, M., 1957, *passim*.
[54] International Labour Office, *op. cit.*, pp. 271–278.

African workers themselves are not immune to considerations of "cultural" differences, as shown by unions formed on tribal lines.[55] And though there is ample room for difference of view as to whether the "color bar," primarily political unionism, and the persistence of tribalism are temporary phenomena, a reasoned guess is that organizations based on common interests based on status are likely to emerge, followed eventually by organizations deriving primarily from common occupational interests, as the occupational structure of the African labor force assumes a more "normal" shape.[56]

4

The rationale for the organization of this report up to this point has been a simple three-stage model of social and economic transition. A number of topics having a significant bearing on labor in Africa, however, do not fit this scheme.

Educational standards and achievements for African population are relatively low throughout Subsaharan Africa. Only in the ex-Belgian Congo is the estimated adult literacy rate as high as 35–40 per cent. The estimated literacy in Uganda is 25–30 per cent. Ghana, Kenya, Northern Rhodesia and Southern Rhodesia have literacy rates of 20–25 per cent. The 5–10 per cent category includes the Cameroons, Gambia, Liberia, Nyasaland, Ruanda-Urundi, Sierra Leone, Tanganyika, and Togoland. A census enumeration in Nigeria, 1952–1953, indicated a slightly higher rate of 11.5. Finally the large terrorities of former French Equatorial Africa and French West Africa, as well as Angola and Mozambique, have estimated adult literacy rates of 1–5 per cent.[57] Data for South Africa are not available, but African literacy is probably under 10 per cent.

The proportions of the total population in schools of any grade range from about 2 per cent in former French West Africa and Gambia to about 12 per cent in Ghana and Southern Rhodesia.[58] All of the countries and territories of Subsaharan Africa are in the lowest two categories of proportions of school-age children actually in school, those having 20 to 40 per cent and those under 20 per cent, with the single exception of Southern Rhodesia, where 40 to 60 per cent are so enrolled.[59]

This non-existent or meager education does not seriously affect the economic potential of African labor as long as it is confined to strictly unskilled jobs. But the experience of industrialized countries indicates

[55] Elkan, W., 1956, pp. 49–59.
[57] United Nations, 1956, pp. 80–81.
[59] *Ibid.*, p. 67.
[56] Moore, W. E., 1960, *passim.*
[58] *Ibid., loc. cit.*

that the increased productivity of an economy requires the upgrading of labor, a steady reduction in the number and proportion of unskilled jobs, and the training of technical, managerial, and professional personnel. Such advanced training is not totally unknown among Africans,[60] but the numbers so trained are extremely small.

The African situation is of course only a relatively extreme instance of a phenomenon common in economically underdeveloped areas—an acute undersupply of indigenous workers trained for responsible positions, possibly coupled with some oversupply of certain categories of educated persons, either in view of the absolute demand or of the actual accessibility of positions to natives. It has been particularly the experience of colonial territories that the civil service has been especially attractive as an employer. The phenomenon of the unemployed or underemployed "intellectual" is not unknown in Africa, although it is less common than in some other areas of the world.

Education is of course promoted by modern states for reasons outside the merely technical advantages of literacy and trained skills for labor productivity. Aside from considerations of political and social participation, an especially acute problem where emerging African nationalism faces a variety of tribal and local allegiances in the same territory, education is also looked to as a way of developing new economic wants and aspirations.[61] On the other hand, some observers have noted the limited impact of formal education as such, when set in a social environment providing strong negative or at least traditional pressures, such as the opposition between individualistic educational achievement and the strongly collectivistic values and norms of the tribal cultures.[62]

Another problem has to do with general or recurrent labor shortages, at the wages and under the conditions offered, coupled with extreme under-utilization of potential labor resources—that is, underemployment, of which Africa provides a classic case. Visible unemployment is relatively rare, and confined to certain cities where immigrant workers may exceed the labor demand. Nearby areas may at the same time have shortages of labor for agricultural work.[63] Subsistence agriculture of course had a chronic surplus of labor, in the sense of "full" utilization, as partly demonstrated by the maintenance or near-maintenance of production, despite the absence of large numbers of migratory laborers.

Estimates of underemployment or overstaffing in commercial farming,

[60] International Labour Office, *op. cit.*, pp. 34–39; United Nations and United Nations Educational, Scientific and Cultural Organization, 1961.

[61] Hoyt, E., 1954, *passim.*

[62] Hudson, W., 1955, *passim.*

[63] International Labour Office, *op. cit.*, pp. 118–122.

mining and manufacturing are non-existent. Such estimates would in any case require a stipulation of the technological level to be used as a base of calculations. Cheap, inefficient, and even "redundant" labor may still be less costly than a more advanced technology, which would require not only additional capitalization but probably also more highly skilled and highly paid workers. Nothing resembling precise studies of productivity is available with regard to African labor. This does not alter the unanimous conclusion that productivity is extremely low. The factors are not difficult to identify. They range from the environmental and physiological—climate, health, and nutrition—through inadequate technical organization and financial incentives, to the lack of coincidence in attitudes and values in the traditional and induced social systems. Climatic factors are probably less important than the prevalence of various endemic diseases and low standards of diet and nutrition.[64] Some employers have issued food rations to workers to assure the maintenance of adequate nutritional standards, although this is recognized as paternalistic and distrustful of the employees' capacity to make "sensible" budgetary decisions.

The most common assumption has been that African workers will be used at unskilled jobs, requiring and justifying very low wages, which in turn provide little incentive for conscientious productive effort. The utilization of cheap, unskilled labor also has implications for the technical organization of production, including types of supervision. Wage scales are generally determined on the basis of minimum subsistence for the bachelor worker, with or without additional family allowances.[65] Such low wage scales are maintained in part by the racial differences in opportunities, and in part by the fact that unskilled wage labor can always be displaced by other rural migrants. Indeed, there are some indications that wages can be kept below the effective urban subsistence level because of the assumption that the worker gets additional support from his claims upon the products of his native village. Adjustment to a migratory labor system has still another consequence for productivity. This is the extremely high rate of labor turnover, with its inevitable costs in recruitment, payroll record keeping, and instruction on the job. Changes of employers, which are also very frequent, have the same effect.[66]

Attempts to improve the productivity of African workers, apart from various incentive schemes, have centered on the development of criteria of selection, including psychological tests, and the provision of increased

[64] International Labour Office, *op. cit.*, pp. 147–150.
[65] *Ibid.*, pp. 274–294.
[66] United Kingdom Trade Commissioner, Board of Trade, 1954, *passim.*

training, both at the job and in technical schools. Some limited success has been reported, under generally adverse social conditions.[67]

"Cultural" impediments to productivity are also difficult to assess precisely. The common lack of an individualistic competitive orientation on the part of the African was noted with reference to educational problems. It can be assumed that this also operates to restrict levels of aspiration in employment. The ILO *Survey* observes:

> Whatever the circumstances, there can be no doubt that the African is ill-adapted to any conditioning that he has received through his economic and cultural background for assimilation as an effective element in a wage economy on the European pattern. It is equally certain, of course, that his aim in seeking wage-paid employment heavily influences his attitude to work and his response to incentives and makes it inevitable that his reactions will differ widely from those of the European worker, whose background and aims are so different.[68]

The social as well as economic security of the African may still largely depend upon his ties to the traditional social structure, as noted in the discussion of migratory labor. His feeling of insecurity in urban employment has been marked by observers in commenting on the lack of commitment and attendant productivity among wage earners.[69] The "feeling" of insecurity may very well be objectively justified.

The lack of commitment may stem in part from policies of employers, and even of governments, as they limit union organization and collective bargaining on the part of African workers. Apter emphasizes the positive attitudinal advantages to be gained from some participation in setting the terms and conditions of employment.[70]

Some factors related to low productivity of labor may now be summarized as a set of quasi-equations which may be metaphorically called "vicious circles."

Low wages, bad health and nutrition, poor performance.
Low wages, low incentives, poor performance.
Low wages, low skills, poor organization.

These "circles" require little further comment. They are not unique to Africa, although the system of migratory labor gives them an especially durable structural support there. When private and public discimination is added, the circle grows a little larger, so that to these equations starting from low wages a fourth may be added:

Low wages, low income, poor demand.

[67] International Labour Office, *op. cit.*, pp. 165–166, 212–215.
[68] *Ibid.*, p. 141. [69] DeBriey, P., 1955, *passim*. [70] Apter, D. E., 1954, *passim*.

Since the inconsistency of standards, attitudes, and values looms so large in problems of productivity, it is natural that attempts should be made to adjust policies and practices to take into account the workers' attitudes and experience. Thus a common practice in plantation agriculture has been task-payment rather than time-payment as more nearly fitting the experience of the subsistence farmer-turned-worker, including his lack of orientation to precision in matters involving time. Similarly, it is reported that with reference to the divergent tribal origins of workers, "The general consensus of opinion seems to be that on the whole, ... homogeneous working groups give the best results."[71] Considerations of ethnic origin and individual status within the traditional structure also affect the selection of "headmen." These adaptations may be more effective in the short run than in the long, for they may prove to be barriers to the acceptance of more rational organization and criteria of selection and efficiency.

The great range of regulations that may be comprised by the term "labor legislation" and the multitude of political entities to be considered in this report make impracticable a detailed compilation of labor codes. Some general comments must suffice. In common with many under-developed areas, African countries often have fairly "advanced" legislation regulating the terms and conditions of employment, union organizations, social security, and the like.[72] As is the case in other under-developed areas, those regulations may be poorly enforced, or in effect applicable to only a minority of workers, such as those employed in large enterprises.

The International Labour Organization, through its draft Conventions and Recommendations, has had considerable influence on the course of labor legislation in Africa. Some of the Conventions, such as those relating to forced labor, regulation of recruitment, and abolition of the "penal sanction" in labor contracts, have had a special or even unique applicability to African practices. The summary of the situation by the International Labour Office is cautiously optimistic:

> In the majority of African countries there is already a substantial body of basic labour legislation based in large measure on Conventions and Recommendations adopted by the International Labour Conference. Indeed the the extent to which such Conventions and Recommendations have already contributed . . . to the establishment of a framework of basic labour standards which are in force over extensive parts of the African Continent is one of the most striking features in the present situation. . . .[73]

[71] International Labour Office, *op. cit.*, p. 160.
[72] *Ibid.*, pp. 259–273, 322–441, 464–466.
[73] *Ibid.*, p. 521.

5

From the range of topics covered in this paper, a few major points and issues may be noted for final emphasis.

1. The subsistence, or perhaps more properly the "traditional," sector of the economies of Subsaharan Africa demonstrates hardy survival powers in the face of modern economic, political, and other social pressures. They are by no means untouched, however. Some productive processes have been reorganized as a consequence of the periodic withdrawal of male laborers who leave to work in industrial projects, while cash from both labor and agricultural products exerts a growing influence. The absence of men has affected family relationships, and has tended to alter the position of women and children.

2. An outstanding feature of African labor is found in its pattern of temporary migration, predominantly by males, who neither fully abandon traditional modes of social organization, nor fully accept the norms and values of "modern" economic organization. It may be anticipated that the subsistence sector will increasingly be incorporated into national economies, and that the migratory labor system must be viewed as transitional, though this view is by no means universally accepted.

3. A small and not precisely determinable number of African workers are more or less fully incorporated into urban labor markets. The commercialized and industrialized portion of African economies have been identified as the "stabilized" sector, but only by contrast with such transitional adaptations as temporary labor migration. Even those workers who remain permanently in the labor market may not be genuinely committed to an urban-industrial way of life. Such commitment is strongly discouraged in the multiracial territories in the degree to which the policy of *apartheid* is implemented, but may be expected to grow in importance in the future.

4. Distinctions by color have been common, but African homogeneity is based more on anti-colonial and racial grounds than on basic similarities in its highly diverse traditional cultures. The persistence of tribal, linguistic, and other cultural distinctions among Africans, even in the cities, impedes types of social organization adapted to new economic activities.

5. Though Africans must be assumed to be capable of learning the skills appropriate to a modern economy, given adequate incentive and opportunity, neither of these "givens" has been generally present. So rare indeed have been the opportunities for Africans to do skilled labor, except through governmental employment in British and French West

Africa and Uganda, that the restraints of tradition cannot be judged against the restraints of discrimination.

6. As long as low-cost labor is available for positions requiring minimal skill, public or private employers must count on continued high turnover, low productivity, restrained expansion in effective consumer demand, and perhaps exceptionally high costs for technical and managerial personnel.

7. The strains inherent in industrialized societies are probably heightened by the various adaptive mechanisms developed in Subsaharan Africa that permit the partial persistence of traditional forms. Future labor systems may not precisely resemble those of the oldest industrial economies, but they will not resemble present African forms, either.

14

The Movement Into the
World Economy

by William J. Barber
Wesleyan University

The movement into the world economy has unquestionably been one of the major spurs to dynamic economic change in African territories below the Sahara. What innovations has it produced and what adjustments have followed in their wake? These questions permit no simple answers. The process of economic change, complex in any society, is far more complicated in a situation in which external forms of economic organization have been brought into contact with traditional indigenous ones. Nor can we be certain that all of the contrast between modern Africa and the Subsaharan area of a century ago can be attributed to the inititation of organized international commerce on a large scale. Even had Africa been left untouched by external influences, some form of economic change would doubtless have occurred, although its nature and magnitude cannot possibly be known. Despite these qualifications it remains the case that the massive movement into the world economy is the most important single economic fact of Subsaharan economic life over the past century.

2

The introduction of European economic influence provides a useful point of departure for an examination of African movement into the world economy. Trade across what now would be regarded as international boundaries was not entirely absent from the African scene at earlier periods. West African gold is known to have moved in international commerce since at least the eighth century and, by the beginning of the eighteenth century, the value of these exports has been

estimated to have reached at least £200,000 sterling per annum.[1] Trade
in spices and other tropical products between East Africa and the Middle
East was also long established. In addition, some trading activity
developed within the continent. Such cases, however, should not
obscure the fact that before the middle of the nineteenth century, trade
in goods formed only a negligible part of total economic activity throughout Africa south of the Sahara. The single international economic
transaction with a wide impact was the form of trade "which destroys
all others"[2]—the slavers' trade in men.

External rule provided the main impetus for the movement into the
world economy for reasons that are not difficult to comprehend. All of
the early administrators of Africa in the era following massive European
intervention faced a common problem; each sought to make colonial
adventures pay for themselves. Political control by European powers
thus provided an imperative for the stimulation of export production.
This was clearly apparent in the practice of the chartered companies,
the administrative agents through which most European governments
found it convenient to assert imperial authority. Only in this fashion
could the companies aspire to obtain quick returns on their investments.
The colonial governments which eventually displaced company administration had equally forceful reasons for assigning high priority to the
stimulation of exports. Unlike the chartered companies, they were not
concerned with profits to be distributed to private shareholders, but
they did require resources from which to forge the apparatus of administration, as well as to provide rudimentary public services. Organized
government itself was not possible without an adequate transport and
communication system. Given the state of the Africa these colonial
governors found, the capital that was needed could only be obtained
from abroad. Insofar as metropolitan governments required their
dependencies to be self-financing, production for export was essential if
foreign exchange to service external debt was to be generated.

Stimulation of production for export had further attractions. Most
European powers saw the initiation of monetized production as part of
their "civilizing mission" in Africa. The indigenous peoples, in their
view, could only be advanced from their rude state by educating them to
new standards of taste and to higher levels of productive performance.
Moreover, it was thought that in some areas the final suppression of the

---

[1] Fage, J. D., 1959, esp. pp. 15 and 47. McPhee, Allan, 1926, p. 50, reports an even
higher total: "The estimated total export of gold from the Gold Coast from the date of
Portuguese discovery till the beginning of last century was £600,000,000, but between
1700 and 1800 the annual amount exported had fallen from nearly £3,500,000 to
between £360,000 and £400,000."

[2] Curtis, L., 1937, Vol. II, p. 257.

slave trade would not be complete unless an alternative "legitimate" trade could be created. Where the traffic had flourished earlier, commercial channels—both within Africa and overseas—were too well established to remain idle. If they could not be diverted to other transactions, clandestine slaving might well recur.[3] Mixed with these factors was a consideration of prudence. The *pax* in Africa, it was widely believed, depended on the provision of opportunities for Africans to earn money incomes. Otherwise, idleness among African men might well breed mischief and thereby expensive threats to the new order.

Impressive arguments could thus be marshalled for launching modern forms of export production that would both raise revenues and absorb the latent energies of Africans. But even in cases when overseas demand for tropical products was buoyant, exportable supplies could seldom be made available without heavy investment of external resources. These costs could be minimized when exploitable natural wealth was readily at hand. The early histories of French Equatorial Africa and of the Belgian Congo provide the most dramatic illustrations of what has since been described as the "era of despoliation."[4] In both territories, forest resources were subjected to ruthless treatment by pursuers of quick gains, with natural rubber, timbers, and the products of the wild palm as the particular targets. Even if the conscience of Europe had not been aroused by excessive exploitation, these practices could not long have survived. Little attention was given to the replacement of resources that had been destroyed. By 1910, the readily accessible areas of tropical forest wealth had been thoroughly bled and the volume of these exports had begun to decline. It could only have been sustained through substantial capital expenditures, which few of the original concessionaires were capable of financing. Despite the scars left south of the Sahara by the most aggressive of the chartered and concessionaire companies, these private organizations generally failed to realize the profits they had so vigorously sought. The French companies suffered severe capital losses, and the chartered companies in German territories died, largely for lack of adequate financial support. Even Rhodes' British South Africa Company—which had formidable capital supplies at its disposal—failed to pay a dividend during its tenure as a governing authority.

Building an export structure on more stable long-term foundations called for substantially different approaches. Either new techniques for the production and distribution of existing items of export had to be

---

[3] This factor had an important influence on early British policy toward West Africa. For a full discussion, see Hancock, W. K., 1942, Vol. II, pp. 158ff.

[4] For details, see Frankel, S. H., 1938, pp. 33ff.

developed or production of new commodities was necessary. In the simplest cases, improvements in transport which lowered costs were sufficient to produce the desired results. No innovation in the commodity pattern, but only a geographical widening of the market, accounts for the substantial increase in exports of groundnuts from Northern Nigeria as the railroad approached Kano in 1911; similar effects could be observed in the response of groundnut producers in Senegal to access to modern transport facilities. Examples such as these presumably moved Lugard to declare that "the material development of Africa may be summed up in one word—transport."[5] But the problem of stabilization was not always so easily solved. Opportunities to market their goods had little effect in inducing many West Africans to improve the quality or to expand the output of palm products. While they were prepared to pick the wild fruit, they were disinclined to add to their earnings by taking systematic care of the palm.

In the case of mineral products—the category of exports which has earned the largest share of subsaharan foreign exchange in the twentieth century—exploitation on any scale generally required the technical knowledge and capital that Europeans brought with them. In many cases, expansion in mineral exports during the colonial era was accomplished through the use of new techniques for working deposits that were already known to Africans. Many of the gold fields of West Africa and the tin deposits of Nigeria were mined by Africans before European intervention. In such a heavily mineralized area as Northern Rhodesia, European discoveries preceding the diamond-drill method of prospecting were sited on bodies of ore long known to Africans. Entirely new types of commodities, however, played a major role in swelling receipts from agricultural exports. Cocoa and coffee were unheard of in Africa before the colonial period and, in some parts of the continent, cultivation of cotton awaited European intervention.

Whatever the combination of devices used, the period of colonial rule can claim a substantial accomplishment in expanding the export economies of subsaharan territories. An impressive growth in export volume and value has been recorded in the twentieth century, the only serious interruption occurring during the years of the Great Depression. Particularly after World War II, earnings of foreign exchange increased rapidly, their rate of growth exceeding that of the value of total world trade. None the less, Subsaharan Africa continued to be a minor contributor to the aggregate volume of world trade. In 1958, exports from these territories accounted for only slightly more than four per cent of the world total of merchandise exports. However, the share of Africa in

[5] Lugard, Lord F., 1922, p. 5.

all trade is somewhat understated in these calculations because gold is excluded from the computation of merchandise exports.[6]

3

What innovations were produced below the Sahara by the stimulation of modern forms of international trade, and what was the impact of these developments on the economic life of the indigenous peoples? In an attempt to sketch an answer to this question, it will be convenient to draw an arbitrary line of demarcation between two types of effects; those which are the direct consequence of the organization of international commerce on modern lines and may be regarded as primary, and secondary effects, the by-products of successful launching of export industries. The dividing line between these forms of change cannot always be clearly drawn. It will nevertheless be useful to consider separately several of the more prominent primary and secondary effects of the movement into the world economy.

Reduced to its essentials, the primary process of economic change brought about by the inauguration of modern forms of export activity was one that juxtaposed two contrasting types of economic organization. One was a monetized exchange economy, largely introduced by outsiders, and the other, the traditional economic system of the indigenous peoples. Throughout the continent south of the Sahara, the initial phases of this contact had at least one common feature; everywhere the introduction of the new kind of exchange activity led to some disturbance of traditional forms of economic and social organization. Part of this disturbance was more a function of political than of economic change. The mere assertion of imperial authority, quite apart from the impetus to production for export that accompanied it, called for readjustments in indigenous institutions and practices. This was clearly apparent in the effects of the colonial *pax*. Law and order, to the extent that they could be enforced by European authority, stripped the adult African male, whose role in traditional society had included duties as a warrior and guardian, of part of his former functions. Further, the uprooting of the slave trade created additional slack in the indigenous systems.

But another aspect of the disruption of indigenous institutions rested more on purely economic factors. The new form, an exchange economy oriented toward export, imposed new demands upon Africans, and created new economic opportunities for them. In particular, it called upon them to increase their total productive activity and to narrow the

[6] Calculated from United Nations, 1959.

L

range of their individual activities, whether as laborers in European employ, as producers of marketable agricultural surpluses, or as self-employed artisans or tradesmen. To what extent, however, did these economic demands conflict with the indigenous economic system? In one sense, there was probably remarkably little economic clash between the two, although this point cannot be conclusively demonstrated. Quite apart from the immediate effect of European rule in increasing the slack within the traditional economies, a substantial underutilization of potentially available labor characterized them in their pristine form. The existence of such excess capacity meant that additional forms of economic activity could be undertaken without sacrifice in the conventional level of physical output in the traditional economy.

Competition between the old order and the new emerged forcefully, however, in another respect. Even if Africans could participate in the money economy without cost, in terms of measurable output, to the indigenous economy and thereby augment the real income of the family group, some adjustment in traditional society was inevitable. Participation in the money economy obliged Africans to adopt new roles and to alter certain patterns of behavior. Thus, despite the economic slack within traditional organization, the absorption of African energies in the exchange economy was neither automatic nor spontaneous. In the early days of these export economies, difficulties in inducing Africans to take up new kinds of work were almost universal. Throughout the continent, colonial administrations and their commercial predecessors found it expedient to use various forms of coercion in order to draw Africans into the money economy. Such tactics, however, were not always regarded as adequate. In several classic cases, relief from the "native labor shortage" was sought by importing indentured workers from Asia. Sugar planters in Natal, the builders of the Uganda railway, and mining firms in South Africa and the Belgian Congo adopted this practice. Their example was almost followed in the Rhodesias shortly after the turn of the century.

Generally speaking, after a period of acclimatization to goods that could only be procured with cash, much of the African population voluntarily chose to participate in the money economy. This change in attitude entailed a substantial modification in African tastes. Originally, the incentive to acquire money income, over and above the requirements of tax obligations, was partly directed to the satisfaction of traditional wants as well as to the gratification of new ones. In British Central Africa, for example, where rinderpest sharply reduced the cattle population shortly before the coming of the white man, cash was sought for the purpose of rebuilding herds. There and elsewhere plows, implements that could be readily fitted into the traditional agricultural pattern, were in heavy demand in the early stages of contact. In areas influenced by the teaching of Christian missionaries, a shift in tastes was often expressed in the form of active demand for textiles and European garments. But in some instances, the reaction to the white man and his ways was less tolerant; firearms, on occasion, served as a major incentive good. And, in West Africa particularly, the liquor trade, despite the constant concern of humanitarians about its consequences for vice and violence, was an important early lubricant of monetized exchange activity.

While adjustment to the direct impact of European economic and political contact had certain common features in Subsaharan Africa, there were also important differences which must now be noted. Such is the heterogeneity of Africa that the experience of each territory— indeed, of each ethnic entity—may be regarded as unique. There are thus severe limits to the validity of generalizations about large segments of the continent. Nevertheless, it is possible to identify two quite distinct patterns of contact between the imported money economy and the indigenous economic structure. For purposes of illustration, it will be instructive to consider the specific cases of two quite diverse sets of territories; one, Ghana and Nigeria, lying on what Hancock has described as the "traders' frontier"; the other, the Rhodesian territories, on the "settlers' frontier."[7]

On the *traders' frontier*, climate and the risks to health associated with it had an important influence on the terms of contact established between the indigenous economy and the Euroamerican exchange network. Until the twentieth century, much of the interior of West Africa still merited its reputation as the white man's grave, scarcely conducive to the attraction of a permanent community of white settlers. At the same time, the resource base of this part of the continent was not one that made European enterprise outstandingly profitable. While there were profits to be won from its natural wealth, they could not compete with the more richly mineralized parts of Africa for the favor of private investors.

The area encompassed by the present Ghana and Nigeria still had its attractions for European traders who sought two particular prizes: the acquisition of palm products for export and access to domestic markets in which imports could be sold. Several factors combined in the early days to shape the relationship between European tradesmen and the indigenous peoples. Initially, both economic considerations and risks to health deterred Europeans from extending their direct operations far

[7] Hancock, W. K., 1942, Vol. II, *passim*.

into the interior. Overhead costs in the West African trade were high, even when coastal outposts were the main setting of European activity; the employment of Europeans for the tasks of bulking petty quantities of export commodities from widely scattered producers and of distributing imports to dispersed inland markets would have made costs prohibitive. The fact that some Africans already had experience in trading simplified the process of establishing a division of labor in the distributional network, by which Africans became the middlemen who linked the interior with the wider international economy. It also added some complications that European political power was invoked to eliminate. In those cases, in which independent African traders were sufficiently well established to rival the control of European firms over export produce, the position of the former was reduced by the imposition of heavy license fees that were beyond their means to pay.[8] As arrangements were later worked out, European firms typically supplied imported consumer goods to be transported inland in the charge of African middlemen. There they would be sold on local markets in exchange for indigenous forms of money, most notably, cowrie shells, although manillas, the Maria Theresa dollar, brass rods and trade gin were also widely used. With such forms of cash at his disposal, the middleman could then proceed to purchase export commodities from individual producers. In this connection, it may be noted that the use of native money, which was still widely circulated at the time of the founding of the West African Currency Board in 1912, gave the African middleman a distinct advantage over potential European rivals. As long as traditional media of exchange were important in internal commerce, their bulk and inconvenience were enough to discourage European tradesmen from entering this sphere of trade.

Through time, the extension of the newer trading network affected increasing numbers of Africans, not only as traders and porters, but also as consumers and producers. Perhaps its most impressive consequence was the opening up of new opportunities for the production and sale of export commodities. But there was another impact on indigenous production which is often overlooked. At times, imported consumption articles competed with the outputs of native producers. The quantitative significance of this reflex on indigenous economic life is impossible to determine; certainly, however, the impact was far less severe in West Africa than in some Asian countries. In the instances in which traditional crafts were in fact put out of existence by competition, it would probably be inaccurate to attribute the outcome solely to policies that permitted the importation of cheap manufactured goods from metro-

[8] Cook, A. N., 1943, pp. 100–104.

politan countries and which afforded virtually no protection to indigenous artisans.

Another factor was also involved; a shift in tastes on the part of African recipients of money income, which had the effect of diverting their expenditure for consumption goods in favour of novel imported products. Nor was competition limited to consumer markets; at a later date, the more serious form was for raw materials. Hence when materials used by indigenous craftsmen were sought in export markets, handcraft workers risked the loss of their supplies. Nigerian tin workers, for example, were unable to compete with overseas buyers of ores after European firms took over the major mining fields.[9] In another case, however, domestic producers withstood competition from abroad more successfully. Before World War I, serious efforts were made to divert the cotton output of Nigeria's Northern region to the mills of Lancashire and to substitute textiles of British manufacture for native handloom products in Nigerian markets. The war and the high import prices that accompanied it gave the native industry a new lease on life by increasing the ability of local weavers to pay for raw cotton.[10]

In the aggregate, there can be little doubt that contact with the world economy provided a stimulus for expanded outputs of West African agricultural and sylvan products that far outweighed the contraction experienced by certain indigenous producers. But expansion in the output of export crops could have been accomplished by various means, each with characteristic effects on the indigenous population. African growers could have been encouraged to produce for export or, alternatively, European plantations organized. In the first years of British jurisdiction over what were to become Ghana and Nigeria, there was little practical choice between these options. As long as tropical diseases were still unconquered, few non-Africans were tempted to launch plantation enterprises. Most of the plantations that were started, notably the cocoa plantations begun in Nigeria in the 1890s, were financial failures and soon collapsed. Cocoa, the commodity which has come to be the most important agricultural foreign exchange earner in this part of the continent, thus came to be fitted into the scheme of production as an African crop. Once its merits had been clearly demonstrated, Africans took to cocoa growing with surprising speed. In Ghana and Nigeria, outputs expanded about tenfold in each of the two decades between 1900 and 1920.[11]

[9] Bower, P., 1948, pp. 4–5, notes that "in 1884 it was found that the tin used by the Hausa for tinning their brassware was mined by Nigerians ... and smelted in primitive clay furnaces, but by 1923 this indigenous industry had completely disappeared."

[10] McPhee, A., 1926, p. 49.

[11] Hancock, W. K., 1942, Appendix C, p. 338.

By the first decade in the twentieth century, advances in tropical medicine put a different complexion on the question of methods of organizing the production of export crops. Throughout British West Africa, requests for plantation privileges, particularly for the systematic cultivation of the palm, were repeated and insistent. All were denied in this period, save one grant in Sierra Leone which was so qualified that the successful applicant did not exercise his privileges.[12] It was demonstrated by the Unilever interests that plantations methods could be successfully pursued, however, when after numerous refusals from British administrators in West Africa, they ultimately received a concession in the Belgian Congo.[13] Palm oil output expanded there at a much more rapid rate than was recorded for Nigeria.

Economic factors were thus not left entirely on their own to work out the relationship between the indigenous population and the Western exchange economy in the production of export crops. In British West Africa, administrative policy provided free entry for Africans into these activities while it excluded most foreigners. This policy must be understood within the context of the philosophy of indirect rule, which called for the preservation and protection of indigenous society and institutions. But it was more than an application of a social theory that led colonial governors to doubt the wisdom of granting European planters access to West African land. There was also considerable basis for scepticism about the economic prospects of plantation methods in this part of the continent. Their costs would inevitably be high, and the results of early experiments were far from reassuring. Not only had the cocoa plantations in Nigeria proved to be abortive, but the venture of the Empire Cotton Growing Association had also soon failed. Prospects for success could, of course, be considerably brightened if governments were to assist in lowering costs through direct or indirect subsidies. British colonial authorities in West Africa anticipated that such requests would be forthcoming, and they preferred not to face them.

Their approach meant that a major avenue into the money economy and toward the acquisition of higher real incomes, in a form which meant minimal disturbance in the traditional structure of indigenous society, was left open to Africans. This is not to suggest that the injection of new export crops and expanded production of old ones did not lead to readjustments in familiar practices, both social and economic. The important point is rather that the adjustments in traditional rela-

[12] Subsequently, some minor plantations were developed for the production of rubber and palm oil in Nigeria and limes in Ghana.
[13] Wilson, C., 1954, Vol. I, *passim*.

tionships were far less severe than would have been the case if the cultivation of export crops had been organized on a plantation basis. This
alternative would have involved substantial upheavals, and would have
cast Africans primarily in the role of wage laborers.

In one field of export activity, however, the concession principle was
followed on the traders' frontier. Indeed there was little alternative if
significant increases in output were to be realized. The technical
requirements of mineral production in volume virtually demanded the
application of Western technologies and methods of organization. In
any event, the granting of concessions to mining firms in these territories was a matter largely resolved by parties other than governments.
In most cases, these concessions were negotiated directly by the agents
of foreign firms with native chiefs, the latter disposing of assets which,
within tribal custom, they were presumably charged to defend. Governments were not averse to the entry of outside firms to prospect, develop,
and work mineral deposits; they were, however, concerned about the
tendency of chiefs to treat all or most of the proceeds as their private
account. The development and operation of mining created a demand
for Africans as wage laborers but, in these territories, their claim on the
African labor force was always relatively small.

On the traders' frontier, the physical environment and the endowment
of natural resources, the pre-existing structure of indigenous society,
and colonial policy thus combined to give the terms of contact between
the money economy and indigenous economic organization their particular form. Together they assured that the major direct impact of
contact with the international economy would be felt through expansion
in output and income of African farmers, and through growth in the
number of African traders. A demand for wage laborers was also created,
but it was of minor significance in the aggregate. The striking qualitative feature of the relationship between the alien and the indigenous
forms of economic organization in these territories is the extent to which
induced forms of exchange activity were assimilated into the traditional economic structure.

Let us now turn attention to the direct impact of the injection of the
modern money economy, in this case in the Rhodesias on the *settlers'*
frontier. In important respects, the process of adjustment was less complex there than in Ghana and Nigeria. Broadly speaking, the indigenous
economic structure in Central Africa was much less differentiated than
the one that had developed in parts of West Africa in pre-colonial days.
Few of the tribal peoples in the Rhodesias had participated in substantial
exchange activity and there was no counterpart to the well established
trading networks which antedated European contact on parts of the

traders' frontier. One of the few exceptions was the trade between the Lozi and Tonga peoples; the former, it has been reported, supplied hoes and other iron goods in exchange for ivory and slaves.[14] But, by and large, the indigenous economic structure in Central Africa was built up around closed and self-contained economic groups with the family as the basic unit of production. Exposure to the Western money economy thus produced few complications of the sort that emerged elsewhere when indigenous craftsmen were competed out of existence.

Perhaps the most important difference between the two cases arose from the fact that in the Rhodesias no direct attempt was made to graft monetized production on to the indigenous economic structure. Instead the basic framework around which the money economy was organized was an imported one. The climate and geological resources of the area—both of which were attractive to prospective European settlers—made this possible. Initially, mining was the main base of the money economy beginning with the working of gold, manganese, asbestos, and chrome deposits in Southern Rhodesia, and culminating in copper mining in Northern Rhodesia. Europeans provided the capital and the skills required to build up these export industries, and the economic institutions they established were modelled on those of industrialized societies. Understandably, some contact with the indigenous economic structure was inescapable because Africans were required as wage laborers, but this was minimal. Problems in inducing them to take up wage employment, familiar in other parts of the continent, were encountered. The remedies sought meant that the bulk of the indigenous population observed the penetration of the money economy more through the activities of the labor recruiting agent and the tax collector than through those of traders.

In the Rhodesias, the importation of European forms of organization was not limited, however, to types of production primarily intended for export markets. European farmers were also attracted as settlers, and their major economic function, in the first decades of British control, was to satisfy the monetized demand for foodstuffs generated locally from the base provided by the mineral export industries. Generally, there was a surplus of their principal crop—maize—for export, but this was peripheral to their major task.

The presence of this group has had far reaching consequences. In the first place, it blunted much of the economic pressure that might otherwise have induced African farmers to produce surpluses for sale. Indigenous agriculturalists, in the first instance, were unprepared to

[14] Colson, E., and Gluckman, M., 1951, p. 107.

supply the varieties of output demanded in the new domestic market. In addition, they did not have unrestricted access to its opportunities. Policies of land segregation, in effect, meant that most of the farming area close to monetized markets was reserved for Europeans. Nor did governments in the Rhodesias offer aid to Africans in adapting their cropping patterns and techniques on a scale comparable to the assistance offered by British West African governments. Even so, some African farmers managed to produce crop surpluses and to sell them, although this device for earning money income was effectively open only to a minority of the indigenous population.

All this meant that the bulk of the African population had only one avenue into the money economy—wage employment. But even when Africans became wage earners, non-economic factors influenced the character of the jobs available to them. In the main, jobs requiring any degree of skill were open only to Europeans. When the export economies were first organized, there was no alternative but to call upon European immigrants to supply the technical and managerial skills required for rapid economic expansion, arrangements that left their mark on the subsequent terms of contact of African wage earners with the money economy. That few of them have risen above unskilled status is not, however, solely the result of the color bar in employment. Racial restrictions on the eligibility of Africans to acquire property in European areas—with the consequence that most African wage earners had to be separated from their families—reinforced a migratory pattern of employment. And, as long as high rates of turnover were anticipated, employers could not be expected to impart skills to a transient African labor force.[15]

The major direct impact of Western economic contact with the indigenous economic structure in the Rhodesias was thus cast in a different mold than in Ghana and Nigeria. In the former case, wage employment predominated, while in the latter, production of crops for export and trade held primary significance. The relations between the innovative and the traditional economic structures as concerns the nature of access to expanding economic opportunities in the two parts of the continent, affords a further contrast. With the exception of access to commanding positions in overseas trade, Africans in Ghana and Nigeria generally enjoyed freedom of entry into all parts of the money economy, while European access to land was restricted by non-economic considerations. In the Rhodesias, however, non-economic factors narrowed the range of economic opportunities open to Africans.

[15] For a fuller discussion of the complexities of this issue, see Barber, W. J., 1961, pp. 30-40.

4

What have been the secondary effects of the substantial expansion in the volume of exports and resulting increases in revenues of later decades? One school of economic thought, from which, however, there has been considerable dissent, has approached this question by viewing international trade as the "engine of growth." In this line of argument, income from exports is viewed as transmitting impulses throughout the economy, which induce expansions in production to serve domestic demand and lead in turn to rising levels of income, saving, and capital formation. In other words, the progressive immersion of the indigenous population in the money economy is expected to follow from the stimuli provided by contact with the world economy, although this process will admittedly take time.

In African economies several qualifications are necessary in this interpretation of the "contamination" or "spread" effects of trade. In the first place, not all of the money income generated by exports has been retained within Africa. As has long been emphasized, economies of the type that have developed south of the Sahara are notoriously vulnerable to leakages from their domestic income stream. Part of their net geographical income inevitably flows abroad, and has no stimulating effects on the domestic economy. The most prominent forms of leakage are transfers of earnings by expatriate enterprises and transfers by governments to service externally-held debt. In addition, in Africa, private remittances by extra-territorial workers and the provision of retirement funds, particularly for colonial officials, made some claim on the earnings of foreign exchange by most territories. Historically, another drain was a by-product of colonial monetary systems. Though the process differed in detail, it was necessary for almost all of the African dependencies to set aside a part of their foreign exchange receipts to back their domestic money supply. In addition, a substantial part of the reserves of the commercial banking system was generally held abroad.

These forms of leakage inevitably resulted from the manner in which African economies were drawn into the network of the international exchange economy. External capital was essential in order to establish modern lines of production in the first instance, and it had a legitimate claim on a share of the income stream. Moreover, the organization of international trade demanded monetary arrangements that guaranteed the convertibility of African currencies. Given the notorious price instability of most African primary exports, gold being the only significant exception, it was essential to accumulate internationally acceptable reserves. Africa was clearly lacking in assets of high liquidity that could serve this purpose. African governments typically held most of their own reserves abroad, as did such public agencies as the statutory marketing boards. Indeed, the monetary arrangements typically put the colonial dependencies in the anomalous position of being lenders of capital *vis-à-vis* the metropoles.

The essential point, for present purposes, is that these leakages from the domestic income stream, understandable though they may be, did reduce the potential secondary impact of the growth in income generated from international trade. It is noteworthy in this connection that some of the poorest territories have tended to show surpluses in their visible trade accounts, even in the earliest years in which official trade returns were kept.[16] Mozambique is one of the few exceptions; presumably, much of the consistent visible deficit recorded there has been offset through receipts from the provision of transport services to neighboring territories, from tourism, and from the remittances of migrant workers.

Perhaps the most important dampening influence on the potential spread of movement into the world economy has been the important restraint on economic expansion set by physical conditions within the continent. Inadequacies in the transport system and deficiencies in local supplies of skill continued to be obstinate bottlenecks. Through time, growth in the money economy partially lowered these barriers by placing at the disposal of governments resources that would not otherwise have been available. However, even though local receipts were supplemented by external loans and grants, no African territory yet had an adequate stock of the social facilities essential for sustained economic advance.

These limiting factors applied generally throughout the subsaharan continent. We may now consider whether there has been any significant difference in the magnitude and the direction of spread effects in different parts of it. In the consideration of this matter, it will be useful to recall the distinction drawn earlier between the organization of the export economies in Ghana and Nigeria, and in the Rhodesias.

On the traders' frontier, monetized economic activity continued to be concentrated in the primary industries. Over time, export earnings and export volume increased substantially. But the base of the export structure remained narrow, and little progress was made toward diversification in the commodity pattern. Several new items entered the export lists, but the fortunes of the money economy in Ghana continued to be closely linked to the cocoa market, while in Nigeria the four export

[16] Based on analysis of merchandise trade accounts of African territories reported by Frankel, S. H., 1938, and in United Nations Yearbooks.

items of long standing (palm products, cocoa, groundnuts and tin) contributed 70 to 80 per cent of aggregate export earnings. Expansion in the agricultural export industries, however, called for important internal readjustments. Shifts in the agricultural population occurred and, to a certain extent, customary rights to land were modified. In the early 1950s, for example, it was estimated that in Ghana more than half of the cocoa farmers were "immigrants" who had acquired land through cash purchase.[17] Cocoa production—which, by its nature, demands permanence in cultivation and tenure—led to more substantial changes in indigenous economic institutions than did the production of other export crops.

The expansion of money income arising from growth in the export sector also generated heavier demands for wage laborers. Hired workers, drawn mainly from the poorer agricultural districts, were employed in increasing number by producers of export crops, particularly by cocoa growers. Governments, enjoying rising revenues, became the major contributors to the growth in the wage labor force. Meanwhile, urbanization set in at accelerated rates and augmented the monetized demand for foodstuffs. Generally speaking, the major economic repercussions of this expansion in domestic demand have not spread far beyond the urban environs, in part because of the cost of transportation, and in part because domestic food production and consumption are unspecialized. In the mid-1950s, for example, it was estimated that the bulk of the staple foods supplied to Lagos was produced near the city, and that 80–85 per cent of the food supplies of Accra were grown within a radius of 75 miles.[18]

There are, however, cases in which commercialization of agricultural production for domestic consumption caused the movement of crops over much longer distances. Many of the commodities involved, such as kola nuts, dried fish and sun-dried meat, became items the demand for which was supported by internal migrations of people who retain tastes for foods produced in their native localities.[19] Although not of impressive quantitative significance, an active trade in cattle developed, most notably between Northern Nigeria and the coastal districts. Generally, however, the expanding money incomes of export crop producers were not accompanied by commensurate increases in demand for marketed foodstuffs. Only the cocoa growers in Nigeria's Western region appeared to rely on the market for most of their subsistence requirements.[20] Elsewhere producers of export crops supplied the major share of their staple foods for their own production.

[17] Mair, L. P., 1951, p. 58.
[18] Johnston, B. F., 1958, p. 15.
[19] Bauer, P. T., 1954, pp. 382–385.
[20] Johnston, B. F., op. cit., pp. 16–18.

Secondary development in manufacturing to serve rising domestic demand was even more limited. Although some increases in volume of manufacturing output occurred, they were still of minor significance. Deficiencies in capital and skill, as well as the small size of the domestic market, inhibited large scale advances in this direction. It is noteworthy that many of the remaining indigenous craftsmen transformed their roles by producing and servicing modern articles. However, these occupations, it would appear, soon became crowded and few of the participants were able to earn high incomes from their efforts.

Developments over the years also changed the role of the African in the distribution system. As the transport network into the interior improved, European firms found it profitable to take over retailing functions they had previously delegated to semi-independent African intermediaries. Erosion in the status of African traders was also hastened by the collapse in export prices in the early 1920's, a crisis that many of them could not weather.[21] In the 1950's, some of the larger European trading firms cut back direct operations in the interior, opening this field once more to Africans. While the division of labor in the organized trading system underwent change, unorganized petty trading became almost a universal pastime among Africans. The typical size of transactions might be insignificant, but the ubiquity of this practice was nevertheless symptomatic of the spread of monetized exchange, on the one hand, and of a dearth of more productive economic opportunities, on the other.

Perhaps the most serious deterrent to more widespread repercussions of the expansion of the money economy is a consequence of the structure of the export industries themselves. The strategic recipients of money incomes have been African producers of export crops and expatriate trading enterprises. Neither of these groups has had forceful incentives or impressive potential to accumulate capital for domestic investment. The diffusion of money income among agricultural producers, whatever its merits on welfare grounds, did not create ideal conditions for the generation of substantial savings, since the agriculturalist, however profitable his activities may be, usually does not have sufficient personal resources or sufficient access to capital markets to bear the risk of beginning a competing import enterprise. Nor were trading ventures disposed to invest heavily in local manufacturing for the domestic market, although they have given some support to the processing of export products. The prospects for profits were often far from bright, but there was in addition an understandable reluctance on the part of the larger firms to venture beyond their familiar fields of competence

[21] Mars, J., 1948, p. 120.

and to risk reductions in the turnover of standard import lines by creating competing domestic sources of supply.[22] Some of these obstacles to domestic investment were later minimized through the device of tapping surpluses from the statutory marketing boards to finance domestic capital formation.

While the stimuli generated by expansion in the export sector touched these economies in a variety of ways, they did not set off a self-sustaining process of economic expansion. With only a few exceptions, while the economic environment on the traders' frontier afforded Africans freedom of access to new economic opportunities, it did not succeed in expanding the aggregate number of attractive and productive opportunities at a sufficiently rapid rate.

In the Rhodesias, the main thrust of secondary economic expansion was substantially different. Export production continued to be dominated by the output of the mineral industries. But the growth in income that occurred there led to substantial increases in the volume of domestic savings. This result was facilitated by the concentration of the major taxpayers in a corporate form of organization, and by concentration of incomes in the hands of a resident, high-income group. While levels of both money income and saving fluctuated with the state of international demand for base metals, a marked advance in domestic capital accumulation nevertheless occurred. In the first post-war decade, investment was also supported by heavy inflows from abroad. By comparison with the situation in West Africa, the availability of investible funds was not a serious deterrent to expansion in the money economy.

The growth in aggregate money income in these territories stimulated shifts in the structure of monetized economic activity. Manufacturing outputs expanded markedly, particularly in Southern Rhodesia; much of this activity was supported by both capital and skills supplied from abroad. Apart from the food processing industries, the heaviest concentrations of secondary manufacturing activity fell into two categories; the manufacture of construction materials required in the domestic investment program, and the manufacture of light consumer articles for sale to Africans. While the European population has usually received in excess of 60 per cent of aggregate personal money incomes,[23] a large share of its consumption demand continued to be satisfied by imports. Nevertheless, it is noteworthy that the structure of the economy in the Rhodesias experienced a far more pronounced shift than occurred in the territories on the traders' frontier.

From this synoptic account of the course of events in the Rhodesian

---

[22] See Mars, J., *ibid.*, pp. 68–70, for further discussion of this point.
[23] Federation of Rhodesia and Nyasaland, *Annual Economic Reports*.

territories, it would appear that expansion in the export industries transmitted important stimuli to other parts of the economy. How did this process affect the terms of contact between Africans and the money economy? Initially, the significant form in which entry was open to them was largely confined to wage employment, and this continued to be the only avenue into the money economy that was universally available. Nevertheless, opportunities for Africans to earn money through the sale of cash crops increased noticeably. In part, expansion in the monetized demand for food contributed to this result, though perhaps the most significant factor underlying the improvement in economic prospects of African farmers was the rise of the European tobacco industry. Spurred by the United Kingdom's demand for non-dollar sources of supply, the European agricultural community in the Rhodesias shifted its major energies to the production of this crop after World War II, it thereby becoming an export sector rather than an import-competing sector. The adjustment in the production pattern of European agriculture meant that the increase in demand for foodstuffs accompanying the post-war expansion in money incomes was increasingly satisfied by African farmers, and governments, concerned about augmenting domestic food supplies, enlarged their supports for African agriculture.

Growth in the money economy and expansion in the demand for labor were also accompanied by some alteration in the conditions of wage employment for Africans. Historically, an important part of the effect of economic expansion on the labor market radiated abroad. The Rhodesias drew labor, both African and European, from beyond their boundaries. The inflow of extra-territorial African workers dates originally from the days when local people did not willingly take to wage employment, a situation which contributed to a widely-held view among employers that recruits from other territories were more reliable, more amenable to discipline, and obtainable at lower wages. The influx of Europeans, initially indispensable as a source of skills not available locally, came to be partially sustained by color bar restrictions. As the demand for labor in the money economy increased, the traditional color bar functioned as much to draw in Europeans to fill certain newly created posts as it did to keep Africans out of them.

After World War II, however, the conjunction of several factors meant that growth in the demand for labor had more forceful impact on the indigenous population of the Rhodesias. Increasingly, members of the local African population sought jobs as wage earners. Meanwhile, the relative contribution of extra-territorial workers to the employment aggregate diminished. While the absolute number of extra-territorial workers continued to increase, it did not keep pace with expansion in labor demand. Another important change was that some of the disabilities placed on African wage earners in the money economy were eased. Much remained to be done before access of Africans to the opportunities of the money economy was free of non-economic impediments, but amendments in the color bar in employment and in legislation on land segregation, although they affected no more than a small proportion of the African population, were still significant departures from institutional arrangments of the past.

It would thus appear that the secondary effects of subsequent growth in the Rhodesian money economy were considerable. Over time, both quantitative and qualitative changes in the economic opportunities available to Africans occurred, though the pace slackened considerably in the early 1960's. Monetized activity was still, however, concentrated in enclaves organized by Europeans. The indigenous economic structure, by making some of its labor slack available for wage employment, accommodated growth in the money economy without undergoing a radical transformation itself. Some substantial adjustments in traditional agricultural practice emerged in response to rising pressure on the land, to expanding demands for African-grown foodstuffs, to heavier claims of the money economy on the indigenous male labor supply, and to direct goverment intervention. Nevertheless, much that is familiar from the Africa of the past remained in this segment of the economic system.

5

The movement into the world economy during the period under review has produced some impressive economic changes and has swollen the values of many of the measurable indices of economic development. The pace of change has not been uniform throughout the continent, nor have the secondary effects of expansion in international trading activity been identical in all territories. In large measure, these differences in results are closely related to contrasts in the structural pattern to be found below the Sahara—contrasts that can be observed most clearly in the two types of cases considered above. As has been noted, the economic implications of monetized exchange for the indigenous population and for the subsequent extension of monetized economic activity are quite different when the primary base of export production is developed within the indigenous economic structure than is the case when it is organized around non-indigenous economic institutions.

Most of the period under review has been one in which economic life in Subsaharan Africa has been conducted within a framework of colonial rule. One of the consequences of the movement to political independence is that many of the formal constraints on domestic economic policy implied by colonial administration have been or are being removed. New governments in Africa now have a wider range of discretionary policy instruments at their disposal than were available to their colonial predecessors; they have a greater degree of autonomy in monetary and fiscal affairs and more maneuverability in trade and commercial policy. Thus, the terms on which African territories conduct their relationships with the international economy may differ from those of the past. Nevertheless, many of the basic problems of that period are likely to persist. New governments, no less than the ones they have replaced, will be obliged to come to grips with the problem of synthesizing modern modes of production and exchange with an indigenous economic structure which retains much that is traditional.

PART FIVE

Problems
of
Economic Growth

15

Independence and the Problem of Economic Growth

by P. N. C. Okigbo

Ministry of Economic Planning, Eastern Region, Nigeria

Emphasis laid on theories of "break-through" and "take-off," with their focus on raising the rate of investment, has distracted attention from other problems that economic growth as an objective posed for newly independent nations. It is generally taken for granted that once the rate of investment is sufficiently increased, either through domestic efforts or through international assistance, these countries will be on the road to the point at which growth becomes self-sustaining. Consequently, their leaders have tended to focus on the size of their investment plans, as if this factor alone will ensure rapid economic growth.

The problems, it should be recognized, have been political as well as economic. If they were to rely primarily on external assistance for their development plans, the leaders would face criticism at home for losing control of the economic destiny of their country. On the other hand, where the bulk of the population heavily discount the future in favor of the present, attempts by public authorities to raise investment to the rate warranted by the target rate of growth of income are bound to interfere seriously with the autonomy of individual preferences between present and future income. Even where adequate saving is forthcoming from domestic and external sources, it may be necessary to introduce changes in the techniques of production to increase the effectiveness of this investment. It is essential, therefore, to take fully into account these and similar problems that face the newly independent nations, which are at once jealous of their independence and anxious to achieve the maximum socially desirable rate of growth of per capita output. A discussion of economic growth in these nations must recognize two facts. The first is that time is a very scarce item. Nations newly constituted are impatient to achieve a number of objectives, some of which may be

323

mutually inconsistent. They are under pressure to accumulate capital quickly, but at the same time they are committed to raising the level of consumption out of current income; they want foreign investment while asserting economic nationalism; they want to maintain peace and tranquility in the countryside while they leap from an indigenous to a machine technology; they want to wipe out rural and urban unemployment quickly but, sometimes for reasons of prestige, wish to introduce the most modern capital-intensive techniques. If the societies are democratic, the leaders periodically have to justify their policies and achievements to the general public in order to continue in power.

The second fact is that the new nations without exception are dual economies. Alongside a predominant but primitive agricultural sector is a small but relatively modern sector. The process of economic growth requires that the sectors be transformed within a short period by telescoping and adopting the experience of centuries into a short span of years.

2

The value of time invariably enters as a significant factor. Every society has its own scale of valuation of present against future income. In a market economy free from interference by government, the social decision as to the fraction of potential consumption out of currently available income that should be foregone at any time in order to obtain a stream of income at a later time is made as a result of interaction between suppliers of saving, who decide how much private consumption to forego at various rates of interest on savings, and those who demand investment funds, whose demand at various interest rates is determined by their judgements as to the future product derivable from additional current investment. Given the future productivity of investment, the higher the valuation placed on current consumption relative to consumption in the future, the less willing the community to make the sacrifices essential to achieve a higher rate of income in the future. Given the current rate of return on the cost of investment, the course open to non-industrialized nations that wish to raise the rate of capital accumulation would be either to manipulate the conditions under which saving is forthcoming, or to manipulate productiveness of current investment through shifts in technology.

It is recognized that the longer the time horizon of investment plans and of future income streams, the less is the effective valuation placed on current consumption relative to consumption in the future, and the greater the sacrifices currently. The shorter the time horizon in the community, the higher is the expected future consumption needed to elicit a given proportion of saving out of current income, and the more difficult it is for the leaders in the society to persuade the community to make present sacrifices.

An example taken from Eastern Nigeria will illustrate the conflict that may arise between individual preferences between present and future income and the desire of the community to achieve a higher rate of aggregate saving out of current income. Farmers in Eastern Nigeria depend for their cash income almost entirely on the produce of wild palm trees. Experiment has established that the maximum yield is obtained where the density of palm trees is about sixty per acre, while the yield of trees in wild groves is notoriously low partly because of age and partly because of high density. In addition, improved varieties of seedlings have been developed that yield four times the average yield from wild groves.

The problem of increasing the output of palm produce and thereby the income of farmers can thus be attacked by persuading them to thin down the trees in over-crowded groves to the optimum density and, better still, to replant with improved varieties of seedlings.

However, it is essential to note that the benefits of replanting are to be realized only after six years. The public authorities, like the farmer, depend to a considerable extent on palm produce for revenue and are therefore understandably anxious to stimulate this development. But most farmers, preoccupied with problems of their present income, cling to their traditions. Hence the public authorities must either try various forms of persuasion or, as a last resort, interfere with the individual preferences by compelling compliance. In Eastern Nigeria the Government has, in fact, experimented with a number of incentive schemes aimed at inducing voluntary rehabilitation of palm groves by the peasant farmers.[1]

The possibility of conflict between individual preferences and the objectives of social policy is constantly brought home to economic planners. The magnitude of development plans for the public sector often imposes restraints on the private sector and impinges on the choices open to the private investor. The investment plans of government influence in large measure the types of assets which the private individual is likely to hold and thereby the rate and composition of private investment.

It should be evident that a difficult choice is thus offered to newly

---

[1] It is not without interest that the problem of land consolidation in Kenya, which plagued the Government for generations, could only be effectively attacked under the cloak of emergency regulations.

independent nations. To what degree should the autonomy of existing preferences between present and future income be respected? With the fear of social upheaval always lurking in the background, leaders in those nations having a parliamentary system of government must carry the community with them in adopting investment policies that conflict with existing consumption patterns. If this persuasion is difficult, there will be a tendency, as long as rapid economic growth remains an objective of policy having high priority, for the leaders to slip into varying degrees of authoritarianism.

This dilemma is not, however, inescapable. There is the alternative course of using external assistance to maintain a level of income in accordance with current preferences as expressed in markets. There is in addition, another alternative, possibly more painful but also possibly ultimately more rewarding, which seeks to influence the effectiveness of new investment by changing the techniques of production. This possibility is opened by technical advance. However, the clear division of the economies of new nations into two distinct sectors—a relatively primitive agricultural sector and a relatively modern industrial sector— may limit not only the scope but also the effectiveness of changes that can be introduced in the techniques of production.

3

These considerations bring us to the second fundamental problem facing newly independent nations, the dualism of their economies. This common characteristic is best described by what Hirschman calls the "prolonged coexistence and cohabitation of modern industry and of preindustrial, sometimes neolithic, techniques."[1] In most such nations there is a predominantly agricultural sector that produces food and most of the exports; there are, at the same time, small islands of modern industrial activity. The coexistence of two widely differing technologies has important consequences on the rate of capital accumulation, through its impact on the rate of technical advance, the allocation of resources, the balance in the growth of the two sectors, and the productivity of new investment. Leaders in such nations often refer to the technological gap that separates them from the older and more advanced countries.

Although the fund of technical knowledge that exists in the whole world is available to most countries, the application of this knowledge in the productive process varies from region to region. Within the newly independent nations themselves, a similar gap separates the indigenous agricultural sector from the exchange and industrial sector. In an

[2] Hirschman, A. O., 1958, p. 125.

attempt to narrow the gap between the two sectors and between their country and the industrialized economies, leaders often advocate the employment of the most up-to-date equipment, often adopting techniques that employ relatively large quantities of capital per unit of labor or land. Whatever the validity of this approach, it must be recognized that since the technologically backward agricultural sector is so predominant, the speed at which the level of applied technology in the economy can be raised depends in great measure on the speed at which the agricultural sector is being transformed.

We may here separate two elements that are involved in the process. The first is related to the fact that in the economic analysis of growth, technical advance is introduced from outside to explain changes in overall productivity of investment. Some forms of technical advance are likely to produce more of these changes than others. In the industrialized countries, attention has been focused on the role of investment in economic growth in such a way that the discussion of the forms of technical advance has usually been in terms of whether it has the effect of increasing or decreasing capital per worker for given levels of output and given wage and interest rates. The general state of the technological arts is taken for granted in the sense that inventions and innovations play a continuing and systematic role in the technical advancement of the economy. Hence the focus on the "capital-using" and "capital-saving" role of inventions. The problem of the application of new techniques in the productive process is obviously not as pressing as it is in nations that have to build from simpler technical foundations.

At any given time, any particular community has at its disposal a body of techniques of producing a given commodity. Some of these techniques may never have been tried at all, some may have been tried and discarded, and some may be currently in use. This body of techniques, whether or not currently in use, represents the current technology. The discovery of a new process widens the technological possibilities by adding a new combination for producing a given product. If the new process is found to be economical for some combination of resources, it may be adopted. Changes in techniques currently in use do not come merely through the discovery of a new process, but through its adoption by pace-setters or innovators, and its spread in the community by imitation.

In the economies that have had longer experience of industrialization, the existence of sufficient numbers of inventors, innovators, and imitators is taken for granted. The flow of information and knowledge from inventors and innovators to the imitators is presumed to be free and unencumbered. In the newly independent countries, however, there is a problem not only of finding these groups in adequate numbers, but of facilitating the flow of information to those capable of making use of it.

In such situations, difficulties arise more in relation to finding pace-setters and imitators than in discovering new processes. In agriculture it is still possible to raise output substantially by borrowing from the experience of other countries. Governments have tried to serve as inno-vators in this sector not only by re-establishing experimental stations, but also by instituting demonstration farms. However, the facilities for disseminating information and knowledge of new processes are poor, the models presented to the farmer are remote (and, frequently, in the view of the farmer, irrelevant), and the degree of receptivity manifested by the tradition-bound agriculturalist, to new ideas is low. A break in this chain is often sought either through compulsion, or through the slower but more rewarding process of improving the media whereby results of research are translated and transferred in intelligible and acceptable form to the farmers while allowing them to retain autonomy in their decisions as regards investment.

One of the major bottlenecks in the introduction and propagation of new ideas and techniques is the lack of trained manpower to work the models efficiently, and to explain the mechanism to the farmer in the field. Inventors and innovators may abound but they will be ineffective unless their efforts are widely copied by the community. As a result, technical training assumes for newly independent nations an importance assigned to inventions in the more advanced countries. Measures that widen the diffusion of technical knowledge may be more important for the economic growth of new nations than measures which deepen that knowledge.

One may ask what form technical advance would take in the pre-dominant agricultural sector. Among the leaders in newly independent nations, partly because of the obsession with the role of capital, there is generally the belief that the only form that can work is increased mechanization. Yet, if the objective is to maximize output per acre or per head, it may be that the measures that will transform agriculture will neither cost much money nor involve large-scale introduction of motive power. Such changes as improved strains of seedlings, improved systems of culture, use of the results of inventions abroad, such as fertilizers and pesticides, reorganization of land tenure, and soil classification, all these may involve less expenditure per unit of additional product than mechanization. Only in a few cases would expenditure on these items appear in estimates of net investment in the traditional framework of national accounting. Most of the suggested techniques depend more on the availability of knowledge than on the presence of machines. In other words, there may be more need for trained manpower as such than for machines and men to run them.

The second element relates to the effect for the growth of the economy as a whole of different rates of technical advance in the two major sectors. We have referred to the existence of a technological gap between the indigenous agricultural sector and the exchange industrial sector. This picture fits the Nigerian situation reasonably well, and should fit the situation in many new countries.

Important consequences follow from the fact that technical advance is relatively rapid in the industrial sector and stagnant in the agricultural sector. Changes in techniques for the production of export crops would enable newly independent countries to reduce their production costs and, given the state of foreign demand for their crops, to compete more effectively in the world market and thereby to increase their capacity to earn foreign exchange. Changes in techniques used to produce food for local consumption would help to reduce the real costs of labor in the industrial sector, and thereby pave the way for the adoption of capital-saving techniques in industry.

In practice we find that because it is relatively easier to import new techniques in industry, the technological gap between the industrial and the agricultural sector tends to widen; the industrial sector gets more and more modern, and leaders of new nations take great pride in showing off the plants that have the latest equipment in the belief that this enhances their prestige. At the same time they become more and more skeptical about the possibility of changes in agriculture, until the deterioration of production as a result of the combined pressure of population and unchanging methods of cultivation drive them to resort to compulsion.

4

The problem is compounded by the fact that while investment in industry on the whole tends to yield benefits in a relatively short time, investment in agriculture may take a relatively long time to mature. The temptation is therefore strong to look to industry as the only avenue to rapid economic growth. This attitude may lead to unwise allocation of resources if manufacturing industries are established without careful estimates of the level of costs. Economic planners in newly independent nations have a difficult problem of explaining to politicians who are in a hurry that, since an industry that has to be permanently subsidized, it is using up resources that would be more wisely applied elsewhere, the establishment of inefficient industries will retard the rate of economic growth.

In much of the literature on allocation of resources the problem of the optimal utilization of capital is viewed as subsuming all other problems. As a result, much of the discussion of allocation theory is focused on new investment. Should we not ask, however, whether the existing pattern of resource allocation is optimal, by reference to some norm of optimality and, if not, whether the mal-allocations represent irrevocable commitments?

An earlier misallocation of resources is often indicated by inflation, high interest rates on loans, foreign trade barriers, and poor tax and fiscal systems. A high rate of inflation indicates that more resources are applied to investment than is warranted by current saving, and that these resources are not being invested in the most productive channels. A high rate of interest on loans may indicate rigidities in the mobility of funds from surplus areas to deficit areas as well as a general shortage of loanable funds. Consequently, those in a position to use loans most effectively may have to pay more than their operations justify. Barriers to foreign trade are usually put up to protect inefficient operations; and while it is possible to justify some barriers where they are clearly temporary and are meant to protect an infant industry for a limited period of time, in the meantime, the consumer pays more for the product.

In some cases, such earlier misallocation can be corrected; thus, it may be wiser to dismantle a plant now than to continue to subsidize it indefinitely. However, we are led to the conclusion that corrections to past misallocation of resources may not contribute significantly to the rate of growth. In most cases, it is easier to correct for the past mistakes through future decisions as to investment.

The problem posed by allocation of new investment is, to repeat, to decide whether a new product should be produced at all, and, if it is to be produced, by what process. In most newly independent nations the principal factor that determines the answer to the first question is often the size of the domestic market, that is, the level of total income and the size of the import demand for the product. The second issue can be attacked, by an application of any of the investment criteria thought to be reasonable and relevant, though in this case the controversies that have been conducted in the learned journals have not made the choice any easier for the planner. In the final analysis, the prospective investor in industry usually looks at his prospective costs and returns, and the public authorities may, in addition, apply social benefit, balance of payments, or other considerations to determine whether and by how much they should subsidize the new activity.

Take for an example a case of a businessman considering the establishment of a brewery. He will examine the size of the market for his product reflected, as in most newly independent nations, by the data on imports of beer; he will examine his prospective costs of production, the availability of raw materials and labor; he will also look at the problem of distributing his finished product. If he satisfies himself that under the existing regulations in the country he can produce the commodity at prices competitive with those of imported beer and that he will earn a satisfactory rate of return on his investment, he may decide to proceed with his plans. In these calculations, he is guided by considerations of private profit.

The economic planner in these countries may then apply other considerations reflecting wider principles of social benefit. He may for instance, consider the extent to which the domestic production of beer will help to conserve scarce foreign exchange by weighing the gains from substitution of local manufactures for imports against the demand for imports of new equipment and additives used in production; he may also consider the social benefits arising from the establishment of this enterprise, such as employment opportunities in production, management and distribution, development of skills, and stimulation of related activities. He may find the project worthy of support on the ground of both private and social benefit.

The public authorities, however, may apply considerations quite at variance with those applied by the private businessman and the economic planner. They may decide to interfere with the location of the activity on the grounds of social justice, that is, in pursuit of the objective of an even distribution of activities to help depressed areas. A change of location in the light of this consideration may inflate costs beyond the point where it pays the businessman to proceed with the proposal. On the other hand, the public authorities may be quite ready to offer direct and indirect subsidies to achieve their objective.

This experience is not isolated; many examples of actual intervention by public authorities can be given. What is often lost sight of is that a permanent subsidy constitutes a permanent drain on resources that would be better applied elsewhere. Even worse is the situation in which, to buttress such mistakes, additional investment is required to save the public authorities from ridicule.

A further source of misallocation arises from the economic dualism in new nations. Processes of production that were earlier chosen but may be inappropriate at a later stage of economic development may compel the public authorities to adopt commercial policies that would sustain the misallocation. In an effort to demonstrate progress in some sectors of the economy, processes may be chosen that may be relatively more capital intensive than the economy would seem to warrant. Public policy may then artificially sustain these inefficient choices and thereby pave the way for future mal-allocations. For example, a tariff on an imported product may be raised to give a failing activity an appearance of success, new entry in the activity may be artificially restricted to limit competition; or outright subsidies may be granted to the inefficient establishment. The temptation to resort to these choices is greater where the public authorities themselves participate financially in the enterprise.

5

Reference is often made by leaders in newly independent nations to the need for maintaining a balance in the growth of the different sectors of the economy. This must be taken to mean that each sector grows at a rate consistent with the rate of growth of other sectors, so that there is no excess capacity. However, all models leading to the criterion of balanced growth assume ideal market conditions. Thus, if the market conditions are less than perfectly competitive, if labor and capital are not free to move between occupations, the maximal rate of growth cannot be achieved, and it may be justifiable to interfere with a view to correcting for market imperfections. Otherwise, the system will develop hiccups and bottlenecks.

The development of the agricultural sector that has to start from very low foundations makes it difficult to maintain a balance in the rate of growth of the different sectors of the economy. In practice, therefore, newly independent nations are prone to imbalances arising from any of four sets of phenomena. First, there are structural difficulties arising from flaws in the pricing mechanism that cause market forces and prices to reflect social choices inadequately. The existence of strong elements of monopoly in the economy may aggravate this tendency. In these nations, such elements exist in import and export trade, and may be encouraged by public policy in the industrial sector. Second, there may be technical difficulties and inefficiencies that cannot be rectified by market forces alone. Third, there are indivisibilities in the process of capital formation. Fourth, the creation of capacity in one field may necessitate creation of capacity in another, but complementary, field even though the demand for the second product is not high enough at the moment to justify the capacity created. As a result, investment policies are more likely to be shaped by reference to exposed shortages and bottlenecks than by reference to a pattern either of response of demand to increases in income, or of the internal rates of growth dictated by the system, however the latter might be determined.

The economic planner in these situations soon finds that it is extremely difficult to attain a balance between the growth of capacity in different branches of activity. In some cases, particularly in the industrial sector, it is possible to determine the requirements for additional capacity with some degree of accuracy. The planner, armed with input coefficients, cost and price data, demand elasticities and similar calculations, can offer a relatively informed guide to policy. However, in the agricultural sector, where action is most urgently needed, he is only a little less in the dark than other functionaries. And it is in this dark region that answers must be quickly found for policy makers who are not willing to wait for prolonged investigations. In the final analysis the limit to how much additional productive capacity should be created may be imposed by shortage of executive capacity—that is, the lack of trained manpower of the right quality and in adequate numbers.

The problems that face newly independent nations are in many ways similar to the problems that have been solved over the centuries in countries longer established, but with the difference that in the former the time element is more crucial. Most of the discussions in the learned journals treat the rate of growth of output as being made up of three components: the rates of growth of labor and capital, weighted by their respective marginal significance in the productive process, and the rate of technical advance.

A great deal has been written in the literature on technologically underdeveloped countries about the low productivity of labor. This is reinforced by the existence of underemployment in the agricultural sector. Since most newly independent nations are also under considerable population pressure, which tends to depress the growth of income per head, efforts directed toward improvements in the quality of labor would yield significant benefits even in the short run. This proposition is likely to be of great significance in the agricultural sector which, in Nigeria for example, accounts for just over 50 per cent of the national output, and in which the share of labor in the output of this sector is as high as 75 per cent.

The rate of growth of output in Nigeria in the decade 1950–1960 is of the order of 4 per cent per annum, while the rate of population growth is estimated at about 2.5 per cent. Thus the growth of output per head is about 1.5 per cent per annum. The proportion of income saved is between 10 and 12 per cent per annum. Analysis of the estimates of investment shows that public investment represents between 30 and 33 per cent of the total, and that about 70 per cent of this is concentrated in building and construction. The contribution of new investment to increases in the output of the economy as a whole is thus bound to be heavily influenced by the share of public investment in total investment, and by the proportion of Government investment represented by public buildings and construction.

Even where it is socially acceptable to raise the rate of investment above the current rate, the productivity of future investment will depend on how much of it is directed into "traditional" channels and how much into more productive forms. Additional saving effort may not contribute significantly to the rate of growth unless opportunities for investment taken up are more directly productive than the traditional channels. If we focus on the rate of saving as such, we may lose sight of the importance of the forms by which saving is turned into productive investment.

The conclusion to which we are led is that the major part in the development of newly independent nations may have to be played by technical advance and by wise allocation and reallocation of resources. The former improves the technique of production while the latter ensures minimal losses from misallocation. This analysis reinforces our earlier proposition that, for the economy to grow or, in some countries, to maintain the current rate of growth, technical advance must be relatively rapid in the dominant nonindustrial agricultural sector. It is in this branch of activity that we can expect the most substantial effects of the increase in productivity; further, such an increase in productivity will of itself make possible a reduction in real cost in the exchange sector and a higher rate of payment to labor.

6

Two aspects of the numerous problems that face newly independent nations seeking to increase their rate of economic growth have been treated here; the relatively short time horizon in such economies, and the dualism of the economic structure. The consequence of the former is seen in the difficulty of raising the rate of investment very much above what it is currently. These nations are obliged to move in two contrary directions: on the one hand, they desire to accumulate capital quickly; on the other hand, they want to raise the current level of living of the population. Faced with this dilemma, the way out appears to be to rely on external assistance, with the possibility of severe criticism at home, to seek measures that will improve their terms of trade, or to attack the problem of relatively low productivity by measures that will accelerate the rate of technical advance. One conclusion to be derived from our analysis is that the contribution of increased saving effort to the rate of economic growth must be supplemented by measures that increase the productivity of investment.

The second feature, the economic dualism in new nations, emphasizes the low level of applied technology in the economy as a whole, and in the agricultural sector in particular. The first point of emphasis is that rapid transformation of agricultural techniques holds the key to rapid economic development. The measures that can ensure this transformation may not cost much money, as they consist mainly in the dissemination and propagation of knowledge and practices. As regards the second point, a high rate of technical advance in the production of food relative to other sectors will stimulate industrial expansion; but domestic economic policy would have to be geared to shifting food consumption from imported to domestic products.

As we examine the consequences of economic dualism on policies of allocation and, in particular, on the policy of balanced growth, we may conclude that, first, current misallocations may engender commercial and industrial policies that would buttress existing inefficiencies; and secondly, that although balanced growth appears attractive, newly independent nations will, in practice, shape their investment policies in response to exposed imbalances and shortages.

An examination of the Nigerian situation suggests that as a result of the economic dualism in these countries, the public authorities have a key role to play in accelerating the rate of growth. Partly because of the relatively large share of public investments in total investment, and partly because, more than any other agency, governments have a better chance of influencing the course of technical advance in agriculture, they will increasingly depend on the public sector for rapid economic advance. This is not, of course, without its consequences; the larger the programs in the public sector, the more difficult it becomes for public authorities to respect the autonomy of individual preferences as expressed in markets.

It is therefore suggested that too much emphasis has hitherto been placed on the rate of capital accumulation as the key to the development of new nations. This emphasis must be complemented by a new emphasis on the forms by which available saving can be turned to productive investment, a facet of the problem that gains importance from the fact that it has been relatively neglected in the literature.

M

16

Trends in African Exports and Capital Inflows

by Walter A. Chudson*
United Nations

From 1950 to 1960, the value of exports from tropical Africa rose by about 70 per cent. This impressive performance was not far below the growth of world trade as a whole, and it is even more impressive when compared with the sluggish growth of exports from Asia except for Japan, and with the virtually stagnant condition of Latin America in export trade as a whole. Underlying the expansion of exports from Africa there was throughout the region a remarkably rapid growth of agricultural production, averaging about 3 per cent a year up to 1957. In certain countries this tendency was reinforced by a large expansion of mineral production.

The relatively high rate of expansion of African production and export of primary commodities during this decade continued a trend that can be observed since the late nineteen twenties. This growth was based, to be sure, on levels of output and exports that, except for a small number of commodities, represented a minor or negligible share of world trade. But the number of commodities in which African activity is important, particularly in world exports in contrast with world production, is appreciable. It is increased if we take into account different grades of commodities such as cotton and coffee, and also the fact that the African share in the statistics of world trade tends to be understated, owing to substantial re-exports of African produce from Europe.

The greater part of the growth in proceeds from African export trade during the nineteen fifties occurred in the early part of the decade, when an increase in quantity was reinforced by rising prices. After 1955, the

* The views expressed in this paper are those of the author and do not necessarily represent those of the United Nations Secretariat with which he is associated.

quantity of exports rose by over 25 per cent, but this was partly offset by a decline in export prices, with the result that the value of exports increased by only about 15 per cent. This phenomenon aroused apprehension over the potential contribution of export proceeds to the future development of Africa.

The expansion of mineral exports was limited to a few countries, whereas the growth of agricultural exports was widespread. Coffee recorded the most impressive gain, rising in volume by an average of 11 per cent per annum from 1950 to 1960. Cocoa exports were retarded by ecological factors, notably pests and disease, until about 1960, when the effects of disease control and of new plantings during the period of peak prices in the mid-1950s were felt. Large gains were recorded in the volume of exports of natural rubber, sisal, groundnuts and groundnut oil, timber and tobacco. The production of cotton and palm products lagged; a sharp increase in the quality of palm oil, however, compensated for the lesser output of palm products.

Practically all countries in tropical Africa participated significantly in the expansion of export proceeds, though at rates which varied both with increases in the volume of exports, and with disparate price trends. At the end of the decade, nevertheless, the relative position of most countries in regard to the share of total exports remained substantially the same as at the beginning. The chief mineral-producing countries of Subsaharan Africa—the former Belgian Congo, the Federation of Rhodesia and Nyasaland and the Republic of South Africa—still accounted for over half of the foreign trade of the region.

The post-war growth of exports was not accompanied by a significant increase in their diversification within particular countries. The cases of Tanganyika and to a smaller extent the Congo are perhaps the outstanding exceptions to this statement. At the end of the decade there were at least sixteen countries in which a single commodity accounted for over 30 per cent of exports, and this list would be considerably lengthened if all the independent French-speaking countries were taken separately. Improvement in the quality of product contributed to the increased value of exports of one or two products, but in general this factor was not of great importance. Nor can an increase in the proportion of processing carried on locally, also important in a few instances, be accorded a major role.

The expansion of African exports was favored by the relatively high rate of growth in the world import demand for tropical foodstuffs, and for some agricultural raw materials and minerals, in contrast with a lagging import demand for non-tropical foodstuffs. Thus, between 1928 and 1955 the volume of agricultural raw materials, tropical foodstuffs and minerals exported by primary-producing countries rose by 40 per cent, while non-tropical foodstuffs recorded a 15 per cent decline.[1] In Africa this factor was reinforced by various links with the markets of the several metropolitan countries. Perhaps the most significant example was the preferential treatment granted by France to exports from her African territories both through conventional commercial policy measures and through less orthodox methods of price-support. A more extreme case of subsidization was the preferential treatment of banana exports from Somaliland to Italy. Preferential treatment was of limited significance, however, in explaining the expansion of exports from the British territories, and did not enter at all in the case of the Belgian territories.

On the supply side, a significant part of the agricultural expansion can no doubt be attributed to the response of producers, both African and European, to the stimuli of rising prices and of various other factors tending to expand the scope of the monetary sector of agricultural production. These other factors also played a significant part in the large post-war investment in roads, railways, ports, warehouses and other marketing and processing facilities, and the application of technical assistance in a wide sense, embracing agricultural research, agricultural extension, and the like. The catalogue would also not be complete without reference to various forms of official compulsion on African producers, in some cases harking back to war-time or earlier measures.

The role of the State in the expansion of exports during the nineteen-fifties was largely limited to the indirect supporting action referred to above. The major exceptions were the successful Gezira Scheme in the Sudan, whose origins go back to the inter-war period, and the spectacularly unsuccessful Groundnut Scheme in Tanganyika, the leading example of a larger class of ill-fated ventures.

The specific effect on agricultural output of the Statutory Marketing Boards established during and after the war in certain African countries, notably Ghana, Nigeria and Uganda, is not easy to appraise. However, it is clear that, whatever disincentive effect may have resulted from actions by the Boards that prevented prices paid to producers from rising as much as world prices, output of many controlled crops did in fact increase sharply, though with the normal lag associated with tree crops in the case of cocoa and coffee. In any event, producers' prices were permitted to rise somewhat during the period, and the guarantee of a relatively stable figure appears to have acted to some extent as an incentive. These factors were reinforced by the positive effect on output of the technical and commercial functions performed on behalf of producers by the Boards. In the former French territories, price stabilization

[1] General Agreement on Tariffs and Trade, 1958, p. 4.

funds for major export crops began to operate only after 1955, and their effect on production was no doubt overshadowed by the effects of the relatively high prices obtained for these crops in the sheltered French market.

Some recognition should also be given to the circumstances and policies of certain competitive primary-producing countries outside Africa that tended to exercise restraint on their own exports. The African coffee-producing countries during the latter part of the period began to feel the pressure of the world coffee surplus, but their position would have been seriously worsened in the absence of restrictive action by the leading Latin American producers. A similar comment applies to short-staple cotton, the world price of which was supported by action of the United States during part of the period. The position of African sisal producers, under considerable pressure from Brazilian exports, would have been less favorable had the production of certain other countries, notably Indonesia, expanded as much as did that of Africa, and the same applies to oilseeds in relation to production in the Far East as a whole.

The appropriate framework for a consideration of Africa's export, prospects in the decade 1960–1970 would be, of course, a global projection of the prospective demand for and supply of particular primary commodities.[2] In the absence of the requisite information, we must fall back on certain global projections of demand for primary products that have been made in connection with efforts to estimate the import requirements associated with assumed rates of economic growth in under-developed countries and the means by which they might be financed.[3]

It is not necessary to examine here the specific assumptions and results of these projections. In broad terms they represent an extrapolation of trends during preceding decades, the main feature of which has been a rise in the import demand for primary products in industrial countries that is considerably less than the rise in their aggregate income. From the demand side, the basic explanation of this phenomenon has been the changing composition of consumption and the rising importance of services, but technological changes and commercial

[2] Considerable work is being done along those lines, particularly by various international organizations, but such comprehensive estimates are not available.

[3] The long-term market prospects for primary commodities were examined in considerable detail in GATT, 1957, pp. 17–35, and for exports of underdeveloped countries, including manufactures, in GATT, 1960, pp. 40–56. A similar projection is contained in United Nations, Economic Commission for Europe, 1958, Chapter V. A complementary analysis of projected "export requirements" of underdeveloped countries, based on assumed rates of economic growth and capital inflows is contained in *ibid.*, 1961, Chapter V.

policy in the importing countries have also played a part. From this tendency the conclusion is drawn that, for economically underdeveloped countries as a whole, the rate of growth in the demand for their exports of primary commodities, even on fairly optimistic assumptions, is not likely to satisfy the need for expanded imports associated with desired rates of economic growth that are assumed for this exercise to be considerably above those of the past decade.

Even if an increase in capital inflows were to occur, it seems that on most assumptions a substantial "import gap" would still remain. Hence the subsidiary conclusion is drawn that if the desired rates of growth are to be attained, a large increase in exports of manufactures would be necessary, both to the industrial countries and within the group of underdeveloped countries. It is obvious that tropical African countries in general are less well placed than other economically underdeveloped countries to expand exports of this nature. Thus, particular importance is attached in their case to the outlook for exports of primary commodities.

Quite apart from the margin of uncertainty which inevitably is attached to projections of this nature, it is clear that the position of individual countries and regions within the global estimates must be less certain than the estimates themselves. It seems useful, however, to note certain features of the demand projections referred to that are particularly relevant to the export prospects of African countries.

2

In general, on world markets, the export products characteristic of tropical Africa maintain their share in total expenditure, as expenditure rises better than do primary commodities as a whole. Among the minerals, aluminum is the outstanding example, but iron ore and certain non-ferrous metals also appear to hold considerable promise for some countries. Petroleum has not made its appearance in major quantities in Subsaharan Africa, but if we broaden the area under consideration to include Algeria and Libya, the recent developments in these countries strengthen the point just made. Also in the mineral category are the phosphate-producing areas and those areas which, with a large hydroelectric potential, may become significant producers of synthetic fertilizers for domestic consumption and export.

As noted above, the volume of international trade in tropical foodstuffs, including beverage crops, has tended to rise considerably more than that of non-tropical products. This tendency, which is likely to become stronger with a rise in world incomes, is relatively favorable for tropical Africa. If meat, potentially important for Tanganyika, Ruanda-

Urundi, Ethiopia, Somalia and perhaps other countries, could be added to the list the tendency would be reinforced, though this prospect is admittedly of negligible importance for the decade of the nineteen-sixties. Lumber and forest products may have strong possibilities, continuing their rising trend. Among other agricultural products, the only one of some importance that comes readily to mind is tea, for which the potential expansion is restricted by the limited amount of suitable land. The demand for industrial raw materials of agricultural origin, particularly fibers, is less promising than that for tropical foodstuffs.

An important unknown in the global projections for primary commodities, particularly as regards tropical products, is the demand of the Soviet Union and eastern Europe. According to estimates made by the United Nations, a rise in average per capita consumption of tropical fruits, coffee and cocoa in these countries to something like levels of consumption in the industrialized countries of western Europe in 1960 could raise the value of their imports from under-developed countries by some $2.5 billion a year by 1980, while some increase of other primary products might raise this increment to around $3 billion.[4] Should anything like this occur, the share of African countries as a whole in the expansion of primary exports to the Soviet bloc could not fail to be substantial under normal market conditions, and could perhaps be even greater if other considerations were to enter.

The question of the development of trade within Africa itself must also be considered. Tendencies may be noted toward movements in the direction of economic integration and, in a few cases, of actual or threatened disintegration of areas which have had formal or *de facto* customs unions and various common services.[5] Until structural changes are made in transport and communications and, more generally, until the size of the market increases through rising incomes within existing boundaries, it does not seem that the establishment of the institutional forms of a common market through lowering customs and fiscal barriers will make a major contribution to the development of African trade. In the decade 1960–1970, at least, African trade will no doubt continue to be dominated by the broader forces at work in world markets.

When we turn to the supply side of the export question it must be noted that many African countries became independent during a period of generally declining prices of primary commodities.[6] Apart from the

[4] United Nations, Economic Commission for Europe, 1961a, p. 8.

[5] For an exposition of the question in the context of British East Africa see United Kingdom, Colonial Office, 1961, and also International Bank for Reconstruction and Development, 1961, pp. 238–240.

[6] An analysis of the structural factors underlying this development is contained in United Nations, Economic and Social Council, 1961a, pp. 53–81.

repercussions on public revenue and on the financing of developmental expenditure, account must be taken of the response of individual African producers to declining prices. In a few countries, the impact on local prices was cushioned somewhat by price-support operations financed from the accumulated reserves of marketing boards and stabilization funds. Generally, however, a significant impact of weakening prices was felt in a number of countries. Since the cost of many African agricultural commodities is low compared with that of alternative products, and is likely to remain so for some time, it may be assumed that there will be little tendency for output to shrink in the face of price declines of the order so far experienced. Nor does it seem likely that the transition from subsistence to commercial production fostered by the earlier sustained rise in commodity prices will be easily reversed when consumption requirements become ingrained.

Price movements are only one of the factors that affect the supply of export commodities in African countries. For present purposes, these other factors may be grouped in two categories; those that are in some way related to the fact of newly acquired or emerging independence, which we may refer to as particular political factors, and those reflecting the characteristics of underdeveloped economies generally. It will be useful to give consideration to these factors as they relate to agricultural commodities, on the one hand, and minerals on the other.

The incidence of political factors on agricultural production may be felt in several ways. In some countries approaching independence during the latter part of the nineteen-fifties, the colonial administrations greatly reduced or abandoned their reliance on various measures of compulsion designed to foster increased agricultural output. Pressure was applied more frequently to the production of foodstuffs for domestic consumption than to export crops, but it also affected the latter. The shift from methods of compulsion to "friendly persuasion" has reflected the loosening of the strings of political authority accompanying the transition to independence. This development was paralleled by intensified agricultural extension, the provision of agricultural credit, the promotion of marketing and processing cooperatives, and the like. The newly independent countries thus were confronted with the need for maintaining or intensifying this effort, which, until independence, had been largely dependent on expatriate personnel. The other side of the coin is the potential capacity of the newly independent states to exert greater compulsion than the outgoing administrations. Two examples are the program adopted by Ghana to eradicate the "swollen shoot" disease in cocoa plants, and the mobilization of rural labor in Guinea.

Policies concerning land tenure and soil erosion may, in the long run, have important effects on output. It has often been observed that Africa is fortunate in not having to contend with the typical problems of land tenure associated with the *latifundia* of Latin America, or the landlord-tenant relationships of certain countries in Asia and the Middle East.[7] This favorable state of affairs is tempered, however, by the barrier to an increase in agricultural productivity that is represented by prevailing systems of communal tenure.

The understandable tendency on the part of the outgoing metropolitan administrations to move slowly in seeking a solution to the problem of land tenure will presumably yield to a more forthright approach. The situation has not been static, but it cannot be expected that the path will be smooth or that the effect on output will be rapidly felt. Some students expect the contrary during the period of transition. One basis for advocating the provision of "food-aid" to technologically underdeveloped countries has been its possible utilization to offset the negative effect on output during the transitional phase of land reform measures. In certain countries there is also, of course, the question of the effect on output of the future treatment of alienated lands now held by expatriate individuals and enterprises.

A similar issue that will in the long run perhaps have greater impact on agricultural output arises from the threat of soil erosion. A significant part of the agricultural effort made by certain outgoing colonial administrations was devoted to combatting erosion, often by measures involving various degrees of compulsion. Some assessments of the threat of erosion may be alarmist, but the thought has been expressed that newly acquired independence may provide a basis for the application of more effective measures to deal with the problem of erosion than were open to the departing régimes.[8]

Even where there is resistance to foreign economic penetration or the impairment of economic sovereignty, the development of minerals must depend heavily on foreign enterprise and hence on specific national policies in the recipient country. In independent African countries one can expect to see a wide variety of arrangements for mineral development, including the continuation of the traditional forms of foreign business investment, and experimentation with newly evolving forms of "partnership" between foreign and domestic capital and enterprise, both public and private. A trend towards separation of the pro-

[7] The exceptions that come to mind in Africa have been the quasi-feudal systems of Ruanda-Urundi and Ethiopia. The Bahutu uprising of 1958 radically altered the situation in Ruanda, which was in process of evolution, while the situation in Urundi was evolving fairly rapidly away from the traditional relationship.

[8] See L. P. Mair, 1960, pp. 447–456.

vision of technical knowledge and personnel from the provision of capital and entrepreneurial responsibility may also be observed. A number of independent African countries have adopted legislation for mineral development, or entered into specific agreements with foreign enterprises for this purpose, thus implying a positive attitude toward such arrangements. It may be that the least favorable period for new private foreign investment, particularly in minerals, is one of political and constitutional transition. As the political picture becomes clearer, the circumstances may be more conducive to positive investment decisions.

Few African countries have formulated an "integrated" development program, but a number have adopted more or less comprehensive sectoral programs for agricultural development.[9] These plans all include the objective of increasing agricultural output for export, and are focussed typically on the individual African farmer. The export operations of European farmers or expatriate plantations, of some importance in Tanganyika, the Republic of the Congo, Liberia and Somalia, are not explicitly included in most programs, and these producers are presumed to take care of their own interests without direct support or guidance from the State. The specific measures to be applied include research, agricultural extension, marketing facilities, provision of credit, irrigation projects—though these have been of limited scope, except for the Sudan—and a host of pre-investment and infrastructural programs, including topographical and soil surveys and the development of transportation and storage facilities, particularly feeder roads. There seems to be a growing consensus that, without denying the importance of fundamental agricultural research, the greatest potential gains are for the moment to be derived from effectively applying techniques already known. It is also held important that efforts to promote export crops be geared closely with market research, so that they reflect trends in world markets and the importance of local processing as well as of improving the quality of exported products.

As regards more long-run measures for the promotion of mineral production, African governments have generally displayed a strong awareness of the importance of geological surveys and related activities and have actively sought external assistance for this purpose. The full-scale exploitation of mineral deposits calls for large scale investment in power, transportation and communications, river development and other infrastructural projects, but this aspect of the problem has usually found its solution when other conditions are propitious.

[9] See United Nations, 1960c, Chapter B/II; also, Food and Agriculture Organization of the United Nations, 1958, Chapter III.

3

The concern of African countries with long-term trends in exports has been paralleled by the attention they have given the question of the impact of fluctuations in export proceeds arising from short-term instability in international commodity markets. The nature and extent of such fluctuations and their impact on economically underdeveloped countries have been studied at length.[10] Here the question may be narrowed by asking whether the degree of instability in export proceeds and its repercussions are significantly different in Africa than in economically underdeveloped territories generally.

The answer to this question has been provided in a 1960 study by the United Nations.[11] In the first place, as we have remarked, it should be noted that Africa plays a dominant or important part in world production and trade in a number of commodities including palm products, sisal, cocoa, and some non-ferrous metals. In common with other primary commodities, African exports, particularly those of agricultural and industrial raw materials, have been strongly influenced by demand in the industrial countries, especially those of western Europe, since about two-thirds of these exports are destined for that geographical area, as compared with about 40 per cent of the exports of all primary producing countries.[12] Thus the volume of demand for exports from Africa primarily depends on conditions in western Europe, though the prices received are also strongly influenced by demand conditions in the United States. For many tropical foodstuffs basic conditions of demand are relatively stable, and fluctuations of export volume and prices are heavily influenced by variations in supply, and by their attendant speculative effects.

As reflected in the year-to-year fluctuations of proceeds of foreign exchange derived from major export commodities, the annual variation experienced by African countries during the period 1946–1957 was 13 per cent, as compared with 12 per cent for primary producing countries as a whole; for Africa the degree of change in unit values, in fact, was larger than for the world as a whole, reflecting partly the fact that African exports are relatively concentrated in commodity groups such as beverage crops, which are subject to a relatively high degree of

---

[10] To cite only some of the recent literature, reference may be made to United Nations, Economic and Social Council, 1954; *ibid.*, 1959b, Chapter 2; *ibid.*, 1961b; General Agreement on Tariffs and Trade, 1958.

[11] United Nations, Economic Commission for Africa, 1960a.

[12] To the extent that certain commodities, such as diamonds, are re-exported from western Europe to other regions, this disparity is overstated. For the same reason, the share of Africa in world exports of these commodities is understated.

price fluctuation.[13] For a selected list of twenty African countries, the annual average variation in total proceeds from exports during 1948 to 1958 was 9.9 per cent. Since the countries of former French West Africa, former French Equatorial Africa and British East Africa were grouped, the degree of variation of individual countries may have been understated. Furthermore, countries with less diversification of exports were subject to a higher degree of fluctuation in proceeds from exports, as is indicated by the fact that during the period 1950 to 1958 the average fluctuation of African countries in this regard was about one-third less than that of the proceeds from the principal export commodity.

The application of measures to mitigate the impact of external instability in commodity markets is by no means unfamiliar to a number of African countries. The most common approach has been the operation of stabilization funds by statutory marketing boards or similar agencies. The taxation of exports has also varied with changing prices in world markets, in some cases through a sliding scale. The use of multiple exchange rates to accomplish the same result has been unknown, since the monetary arrangements of African colonial territories were generally characterized by the simplicity associated with currency boards or similar arrangements reflecting links with the monetary systems of the metropolitan countries.

Though marketing boards may carry out useful stabilization operations through the operation of buffer funds, which accumulate reserves during periods of relatively high prices, and draw upon them during periods of low prices, it would be inaccurate to picture the operations of the various African marketing boards in these relatively simple terms.

Certain important functions of a technical and commercial nature unrelated to the object of stabilization need not be further considered here. However, it appears that the chief object of the marketing boards during the phase of the post-war commodity boom was to combat the inflationary impact of increased export incomes during the period of shortages of imported manufactured goods. There was at the same time a desire to strengthen their capacity to offset any future price decline by increasing reserves. Both considerations led to a partial stabilization of prices received by African producers from season to season, but with producer prices at a considerably lower level than export prices. The reserves thus accumulated, notably in Ghana, Nigeria and Uganda, exceeded by far the requirements for year-to-year operations, and the

[13] The averages were obtained after eliminating trend. For all commodity groups analyzed, the average fluctuation in unit value was 16 per cent and in quantum, 7 per cent.

boards tended to support substantial expenditure for development, either on their own account or through loans and grants to support general public expenditure. At the same time export taxes, levied by government, were increased in order to avoid further accumulation of such reserves.

As weakness in international commodity prices developed during the second half of the nineteen-fifties, the remaining reserves were further reduced by expenditure in support of producers' prices and by further appropriations for development and even general budgetary support. The boards continued to follow a limited policy of stabilization of prices to producers from year to year, as well as within the growing season, but their function as a fiscal and developmental agency was sharply curtailed, a development resulting partly from the greater importance of variable export taxation in several countries.

The tendencies just mentioned refer to marketing boards in territories formerly under British administration. In the former French territories, a large number of national stabilization funds (*Caisses de Stabilisation des Prix*) were established in the mid-nineteen-fifties and continued to function after independence. Being established during a period of declining export prices they were partly assisted by loans from the French government. They were designed to operate on the principle of a revolving fund, and to provide a moderate degree of year-to-year stabilization of prices to producers of a given commodity, while not neglecting the trend of world prices. The function of stabilization of producer prices has been given predominant emphasis, but the funds, like their marketing board counterparts, can also serve to regulate the margins of middlemen.

Measures for direct stabilization of trade in individual commodities through formal international commodity agreements or less formal arrangements, are reasonably well known in many African countries, owing to their experience with this type of international action during the pre-independence period. The newly independent states manifested a strong element of continuity in their policies in this regard.

The Republic of the Congo and Nigeria participated in the First International Tin Agreement, and were also parties to the Second International Tin Agreement which entered provisionally into force in June, 1961. Membership of African countries in the one-year international coffee arrangement was broadened to include all significant producing areas except Ethiopia. In October 1960, representatives of twelve African countries producing *robusta*-type coffee agreed to establish an Inter-African Coffee Organization which adopted a resolution recommending that member countries take concerted measures to "defend" coffee prices. Ghana and Nigeria have been active in promoting an international agreement on cocoa, and there have been reports of informal discussions on sisal between Tanganyika and Brazil.

Perhaps the main issue confronting African countries in relation to international commodity arrangements, particularly those that may involve obligations to restrain exports or production, is, in the words of a United Nations study, "... the fact that African producers of many primary commodities are actually or potentially low-cost producers. ... There is thus a real dilemma in African policy toward certain commodity schemes which are primarily restrictionist." The most immediate problem arising is the question of African participation in an international coffee agreement. The burden of restriction of coffee exports by African countries under the several one-year agreements has been light compared with that of Latin American countries. Any short term projection of exports of African countries is heavily dependent on how this issue will be resolved.

4

There seems little doubt that the period since the second World War saw a larger inflow of capital into Subsaharan Africa, certainly if the Republic of South Africa is excluded, than any other comparable period. The character of the inflow changed radically from earlier periods; public funds largely financed investments of the type formerly supported by the flotation of securities in private capital markets, while private investment typically took the form of investment in foreign-controlled enterprises (so-called direct investment), a substantial part of the expansion of this category being accomplished through the reinvestment of profits.

The inflow of public capital vastly increased, rising steadily during the decade 1950–1960. In 1960, the aggregate amount of net public financial assistance received by African countries has been estimated to have reached the neighbourhood of $1,400 million.[14] This is the largest amount recorded in the decade, and represents an increase of over 80 per cent over the average of 1954–1956.

The importance of the combined inflow of public and private funds is indicated in the fact that for a representative group of African countries, over the period 1956–1960 the inflow equalled about one-fifth of the

[14] This figure is taken from United Nations 1960a, a report based on official estimates of capital-exporting countries. Estimated assistance from the Soviet Union and other centrally planned countries is excluded because of lack of information on actual disbursements.

foreign exchange receipts represented by commodity exports and capital inflow combined.[15] Among the areas in which capital inflows, including grants for budgetary support, represented a significantly larger share than the average was the French franc area, where the share of foreign funds in total foreign exchange receipts appears to have been about 47 per cent. Countries or territories fairly close to the average were British East Africa, Nigeria, and the Federation of Rhodesia and Nyasaland. At the lower end of the scale were the Republic of the Congo, the Sudan and Ghana.

A summary of public and private capital flows to African countries during the nineteen-fifties is given in Table 16.1, though its geographic coverage is limited, particularly for the period 1951–1955. It is important also to allow for conceptual differences when comparing statistics on private capital flows from various sources. For example, "official and banking" capital in the Table includes loans raised by governments in private capital markets abroad, and the treatment of reinvested profits is far from uniform. Nevertheless, the data indicate in a general way the geographic distribution of capital flows, the relative importance of public and private funds, and the changes for a number of countries over the period 1951 to 1959.

The lack of firm estimates of private long-term capital movements, particularly for earlier periods, makes analysis of the record of the past decade difficult. If South Africa is excluded from the comparison, however, it seems probable that over the decade in question the inflow of private capital, including reinvested earnings, was greater in the region as a whole than in earlier comparable periods. The aggregate net inflow, however, varied greatly from year to year and even more with respect to particular countries, and lacked the steady upward movement characterizing public capital inflows. In consequence the share of public capital in the total increased in the course of the decade.

As indicated in the Table, during the latter part of the decade investments in present or former French territories, including Algeria, are estimated to have amounted on the average to about $350 million a year, and in territories of English expression about $100 million a year.[16] United States capital accounted for most of the private investment by non-metropolitan countries, and was heavily concentrated in South Africa and the Federation of Rhodesia and Nyasaland. The outstanding value of such investments in Africa as a whole is estimated to have risen

[15] *Op. cit.*, p. 25.
[16] The estimate of French investments refers to business investments only and does not include outflows effected through transfers by individuals. The estimate is taken from Organization for European Economic Cooperation, 1961.

from $300 million in 1950 to $830 million at the end of 1959, $180 million having been added in 1958–1959 alone.

After 1957, the inflow was heavily supported by large investments in petroleum development in North Africa. Investment in mining and petroleum, in fact, absorbed the preponderant amount of funds throughout the decade. During the period 1956–1959 the bulk of the flow into Subsaharan Africa was concentrated in the French franc area, British East Africa, Nigeria, and the Federation of Rhodesia and Nyasaland. Had it not been for the large outflow from the Congo in 1959, this country would also have been included in the group. It is also reported that Portuguese private investments in the African territories of Portugal averaged about $40 million a year.[17]

Despite the uncertainty attaching to estimates of movements of private capital, it is clear that there was a sharp decline during 1950 to 1960 in the net flow of long-term capital to South Africa. In former British West Africa, a net outflow from Ghana was recorded during the period 1956–1959, but in the rest of the area a substantial inflow is indicated, mainly due to a rising level of petroleum development in Nigeria. While a considerable inflow into British East Africa is also indicated for the period, largely representing investment in Kenya, it should be noted that the rate of such inflow apparently declined during the period and in 1960 a substantial net outflow from British East Africa was recorded, probably reflecting political developments in Kenya and Uganda. A considerable rise in investments in the Federation of Rhodesia and Nyasaland is indicated, due both to mineral development and to expanding light industry producing for the domestic market. A similar expansion occurred in the then Belgian Congo, but, as noted above, was offset by a large movement of flight capital in 1959. An estimate of private foreign investment made in the French franc area during the early part of the decade is not available, but the figure shown in Table 16.1 for the period 1956–1959 appears to reflect mainly expanding investment in mineral development.

One feature of capital flows illustrated in our Table is the differing importance of public and private flows in particular countries and subregions. The inflow of private capital was considerably larger than that of foreign public funds in present and former British territories, taken as a whole, as well as in the Federation of Rhodesia and Nyasaland and in South Africa. The same would be true of the former Belgian Congo if official loans floated privately abroad were classified as private capital. In the territories of the French franc area, however, public funds were preponderant, despite the large inflow of private capital for mineral

[17] *Ibid.*, p. 12.

development in Algeria. In the Subsaharan portion of the French franc area the preponderance of public capital inflows was no doubt even greater.

Certain features of the post-war capital inflow have been typical of the general pattern of private foreign investment in economically under-developed countries during this period, but other aspects of this move-ment were transitory, reflecting the dependent status of the capital-importing territory. In the former category one may note the strong orientation of direct investment toward the extractive industries, with a consequent uneven territorial distribution, attributable in considerable measure to the reinvestment of profits earned in mineral investments. Foreign private investment in agriculture had been limited, although the difficulty of defining a "non-resident" in countries such as Somalia (banana plantations), Tanganyika (sisal plantations), Kenya, Uganda (Asian holdings), as well as in the Republic of the Congo, Angola, Mozambique, and the Federation of Rhodesia and Nyasaland compli-cates the problem of estimation. Africa has tended, however, to attract more foreign private capital into agriculture than have other economic-ally less developed regions, inflow being frequently combined with immigration. Finally, such foreign investment as has entered manu-facturing has been largely concerned with production for the domestic market and has gravitated toward a few areas, notably Southern Rhodesia, the Republic of the Congo, Kenya and to a small extent Nigeria, where the size of the market, reinforced by a substantial measure of protectionism in some cases, has warranted it.

An important transitory factor affecting the inflow of private capital has been the relative ease of floating government loans in the capital markets of the metropolitan country concerned. This was particularly important during the early nineteen-fifties for a number of countries and territories in the sterling area and for the former Belgian Congo. In the case of the Congo, such loans could be floated because of the formal guarantee of the Belgian government, while in the case of certain other dependent territories, of which Tanganyika is an example, the lenders may have considered that the securities carried an implicit guarantee of the metropolitan government. A large part of the expansion of external public debt was accounted for by South Africa and the Federation of Rhodesia and Nyasaland, whose positions as regards balance-of-payments during this period were strong. In general, both portfolio and direct investments in African countries were encouraged by the absence of exchange restrictions on transactions with the metropolitan country.

There can be little doubt that actions and objective conditions speak

louder than words in influencing the inflow of private capital to economically underdeveloped countries, whether the words be embodied in
slogans or in formal statutes. Nevertheless, words also count as symp-
toms of possible actions, and it is of interest, therefore, to note some
features of certain official policy statements and legislative measures
concerning foreign private investment in African countries.[18]

No fewer than twenty African countries have enacted special legislation or taken similar official action designed to encourage certain types
of foreign private investment, and numerous policy statements have
been made by these and other African countries to the same effect.
Generally, these countries have followed the well-established pattern
of tax concessions, relief from import duties, and other forms of assistance to approved enterprises. In addition, some of the protection against
imports has tended to encourage foreign investments in manufacturing.
There has also been much new legislation concerning mineral development, sometimes associated with a policy of encouraging more international competition in the development of minerals than had existed
in earlier years.

One aspect of government policy tending to limit private foreign
investment has been the attitude of governments toward the ownership
of agricultural land by non-Africans, whether residents or non-residents.[19] In several countries there has also been some evidence of a
negative attitude toward the continuation of commercial activities by
non-African residents or foreign residents, both individual and corporate.

During the nineteen-fifties, various measures were adopted by the
metropolitan countries, to encourage private investment by their
residents in their African territories, as well as in those of other areas.
These included the establishment of special financing institutions and
arrangements. The policies of capital-exporting countries concerning
the taxation of income earned abroad, combined with relatively low
rates of business income taxation in African territories, also served as an
incentive to direct investment. Official assistance to emigration by
Europeans to certain areas also contributed to capital outflow. In Subsaharan Africa, however, there was no far-reaching policy like that
adopted by France in Algeria under the so-called Constantine Plan,
which offered an extensive system of subsidies to new industries.
Several of the capital-exporting countries, however, adopted measures

[18] A list of laws and official texts concerning foreign private investment in underdeveloped countries is contained in United Nations, 1961, and earlier reports in the
same series.
[19] A survey of such measures is contained in United Nations, 1960d.

to guarantee private investments abroad against certain non-business risks, and to assure export credits.

It is important to bear in mind that the "investment climate" as reflected in government policies affecting private foreign investment is in itself not sufficient to determine the potential scope for such investment. Investment in manufacturing for the domestic market will depend, in the last analysis, on the size of the market. In view of the structure of African economies, it seems likely that such investment must for some time depend heavily on the growth of exports and of incomes in the agricultural sector generally. Even should there be a significant expansion of foreign investment in domestic manufacturing, the amounts of capital involved must remain small in relation to aggregate requirements for external capital. Investment in plantation-type agriculture by non-residents has always been of minor proportions, except in a few countries, and political and other factors are unlikely to favor its further development. Hence, any attempt to form a notion of the quantitative importance of the flow of private foreign capital into Africa must be based largely on the projected growth of mineral production and the related processing industries.

TABLE 16.1. *Subsaharan Africa: Net International Flow of Long-term Capital and Official Donations, by Country, 1951–1955 and 1956–1959 (millions of dollars, annual average)*

| Country or Territory | Total | | Net Official Donations | | Net Long-term Capital (d) | | | | | |
| | | | | | Total | | Official and Banking | | Private | |
	1951–1955	1956–1959	1951–1955	1956–1959	1951–1955	1956–1959	1951–1955	1956–1959	1951–1955	1956–1959
British East Africa (a)	...	94	...	24	...	70	...	26	...	44
British West Africa (b)	...	81	...	13	...	54	...	5	...	63
Congo (Leopoldville)	38	41	...	3	38	39	34	63	4	−24
Ghana	−37	−5	−1	1	−36	−5	−40	3	5	−3
Liberia	10	11	...	...	10	11	2	4	8	7
Rhodesia and Nyasaland	69	98	4	...	65	98	36	38	29	60
Sudan	−3	2	...	2	−4	−1	−3	...	−1	−1
Union of South Africa	129	2	...	...	129	2	36	6	93	−4
Franc Area (f)	(510)(c)	(639)(c)	(299)	(519)	(211)	(120)	(211)	(120)	...	(350)
Total of amounts shown (excluding British East and West Africa and private capital to franc area)	716	788	302	525	413	264	276	234	138	35
All Underdeveloped Countries	2,400	3,776	878	1,328	1,524	2,447	628	906	894	1,542 (e)

Source: United Nations, Economic Commission for Africa, *International Economic Assistance to Africa, 1960,* E/CN.14/152.

General Note: No sign indicates net inflow of funds; minus sign indicates net outflow; ... indicates not available; and (—) indicates less than $50,000.

Notes to Table:

(a) Kenya, Uganda, Tanganyika and Zanzibar.
(b) Including Nigeria.
(c) Excluding private capital.
(d) The terms "private" and "official and banking" in the balance-of-payments data compiled by the IMF refer to the sectors in the reporting country.
(e) Excluding franc area.
(f) Including assistance for current and capital expenditure.

17

International Organization and African Economic Growth*

by Lattee A. Fahm
Massachusetts Institute of Technology

Whatever its peculiar features and novelties, African economic growth represents a particular case of the classic economic problem of sustaining a maximum of wealth and welfare, given available resources. Prescribed solutions to the problem will differ, depending on whether it is regarded as a matter purely internal to Africa, or as an integral part of an international problem.

One method of approaching the problem as a purely internal matter would be to reorganize and coordinate plans for African economic development. The effect of the resulting changes in existing methods of production would be the same as that of expanded availability of resources; a more efficient allocation of resources and activities could result in increased possibilities for production on all fronts.

From the international point of view, the internal efforts could be supplemented by outside help in the form of additional resources. The net effect of outside aid is similar to that of an expansion of the power of the African countries to create wealth.

2

From the point of view of the economically underdeveloped nations of the world, the primary object of transfer of factors of production labor, technique, and capital by international organizations is to accelerate the pace with which the pre-conditions for self-sustained economic

---

* This paper is concerned mainly with those international organizations directly or indirectly concerned with African economic growth. IBRD, UNSF, UNTA, EPTA, UNICEF, and IFC, whose transfer of resources in loans, grants, and technical assistance have a *direct and measurable* effect on African economic growth. Cf. p. 362 for brief notes on these, and full names for the abbreviations given above.

growth in recipient countries can be established. Even if the twentieth-century international economy exhibited the idealized properties of pure competition in international exchange, flexibility in the prices of all traded goods and services, and general mobility of resources in time and space, the function of international organizations as institutions for creating and allocating resources would be indispensable in meeting the problem of providing those large "transfers of resources and technical facilities" that affect development and trade, but that cannot be provided directly through regular channels of trade and exchange.[1]

It is well known that the international market mechanism does not necessarily provide an efficient solution of the problem of allocating activities and resources among countries, and that, as a result, there tends to be a significant gap between the overall resources desired by countries in process of economic development and the resources provided for them. This has resulted in the creation of special international organizations, which can supplement the operations and correct the inadequacies of the customary international price mechanism as an instrument of global mobilization and allocation of resources. It follows from the preceding statement that contributions of international organizations to African economic growth—that is, contributions of labor, technique, and capital—have come to represent an essential part of the foreign resources needed to attain goals of growth.[2] Of itself, the normal international market mechanism may not be expected to provide them.

In addition to the inefficiency of international exchange for the allocation of resources, certain internal structural impediments to economic growth in Africa, such as high illiteracy, or high incidence of disease and deaths, pose formidable problems.[3] Meanwhile, an increased amount of outside capital will be required in the 1960s to maintain the level of economic development reached during the decade of the 1950s,[4] as will be indicated in more detail later.

Should international organizations, given the prevailing level of domestic resources plus private foreign contributions, fail to provide

[1] Ohlin, B., 1952, pp. 262, 263.
[2] For an expanded treatment of certain related problems in two West African countries, see Fahm, L. A., 1960.
[3] The focus of the present paper and its effective size do not permit a detailed discussion of such general problems. Readers interested in the discussion of such general problems may consult: Batten, T. R., 1956; Goldschmidt, W. (ed.), 1958; United Nations, 1959.
[4] The cumulative annual rates of growth (crude and undeflated) of selected African countries between 1950–1957 were: Ghana 5.8 per cent; Uganda 7.9 per cent; Kenya 10.9 per cent; Nigeria 5.7 per cent; Congo (Belgian) 8.6 per cent; Tanganyika 5.3 per cent. United Nations, 1959, p. 208.

the core of foreign resources necessary for maintaining a rate of economic development corresponding to the average of the nineteen-fifties, the pre-conditions for self-sustained growth will probably not be established. Such an event could have serious consequences. If development planning fails in key areas of Africa, the hopes engendered by rising expectations will be shattered. Hopelessness will give way to frustration; frustration may then call forth the use of desperate instruments designed to make the development effort a success at any cost, rather than an abject failure.

3

Before proceeding with a discussion of the role of international organizations in programs for the economic development of African countries, it may be useful to identify some of the key problems in African economic growth. Like all complex questions, that of African economic growth may be likened to an iceberg, only a portion of which is visible to the casual observer. Like an iceberg, the most important aspects of the problem—*quantitative* as well as *qualitative*—are submerged beneath the visible surface. It is no wonder, therefore, that, as we have seen in preceding chapters, some of the conscious efforts to deal with specific cases of the problem have failed,[5] partly because undue preoccupation with, and focus upon, the visible part of the iceberg led to errors in judgement, and hence to faulty prescriptions on the level of policy. Some of the very analytical and practical aspects of this problem that dictated the failure of these early experiments have continued to confront the students of African economic development. We shall concentrate on two of these; the problem of the interdependence of productive activities between countries in different regions of Africa, and the problem of foreign aid.

The difficulties arising from the first problem are due to the fact that activities in one part of the subcontinent react strongly enough on activities in other parts to necessitate joint evaluation of the worth of separate activities. For example, it is necessary to pay attention to such questions as the extent to which smelting bauxite and the production of aluminum in Ghana may affect the profitability of plans for expansion in Guinea; the effect of the expansion of rubber production in Nigeria on the correctness of similar plans in Liberia; and how the desire to expand cocoa production in French West Africa may influence similar

[5] Two instructive and prominent examples are the East African Groundnut Scheme, and the Niger Agricultural Project (in Nigeria). The failure of both projects has been a costly lesson in the history of specific development projects. For a full account, see Wood, A., 1950, also Frankel, S. H., 1953, and Baldwin, K., 1957.

proposals for Ghana. It is particularly important to consider interlocking programs such as the development of interstate transport, or the damming of a river flowing through more than one country. Radical as the suggestion may seem, all aspects of this problem point to a single answer. It is that, given the available resources and identifiable economic needs of a continent like Africa, the coordination of developmental programs on regional and interregional levels is as important as coordinating development projects within a single country.

The second problem, foreign aid, prompts many more questions. What is the minimum level of requirements for African economic growth in the way of foreign resources? How much outside aid must be provided by international organizations; in what form, and for how long? At the analytical level, we have no ready answers to these, and many other similar questions because a comprehensive survey of available resources and man-power and a unified or coordinated objective for the growth of economically developing countries in Africa are not available.[6] Only by setting the physical data of available resources against a well defined objective that also includes recognized political values and constraints, could the needed complementary foreign resources be determined, and the methods of financing them worked out.

The practical aspects of the problem, which are oriented toward policy, cannot be completely solved until the task of analyzing the data has been energetically and successfully undertaken. However, since the formulation of policies cannot await the complete solution of the analytical problem, a surrogate solution of the problem must be provided to facilitate decisions. It becomes not only expedient but necessary to employ a second best method; to formulate estimates based on all historical data available, and on informed guesses about needs from outside. At this point, however, a caveat must be added on the acceptability of projection of foreign aid. In the light of the structural impediments to direct and detailed measurement of resources and production possibilities that exist in virtually all African countries, the test of precision in measurement cannot be rigidly applied to a forecast; rather, the test of acceptability must be the degree of reliability and usefulness of the revealed magnitudes for formulations of general policy in areas requiring broad rather than precise dimensions of the relevant variables.

[6] Realizing the seriousness of this problem, the United Nations Special Fund has undertaken in several African countries (see Table 17.2; also p. 362, footnote 9) special explorations of resources and studies of feasibility for development projects. Furthermore, the Economic Commission for Africa is taking steps to initiate studies in selected areas affecting development planning.

4

The most important means by which international organizations and other agencies[7] contribute directly to African economic growth are their international programs of aid. During the nineteen-fifties, the components of planned development expenditures of selected African countries derived from foreign loans range from $\frac{1}{5}$ to $\frac{4}{5}$ of total outlays for development.[8] However, no amount of outside help can be substituted for firm

TABLE 17.1. *Financing of Development Plans of Selected African Countries— By Source of Funds*

| | Percentage of Total | | |
| | External Resources | | Local |
Country and Planning Period	Grants	Loans	Resources
Kenya (1957–1960)	10.4	75.4	14.0
Tanganyika (1957–1961)	14.8	74.0	11.0
Sierra Leone (1956–1959)	27.9	51.0	21.0
Nigeria (a) (1955–1962)	3.5	27.8	59.6
Belgian Congo (1950–1959)	6.4	39.6	53.8
Ghana (b) (1959)		32.0	68.0
Rhodesia and Nyasaland (1957–1961)		49.0	51.0
Angola (1953–1958)		5.0	95.0
Mozambique (1953–1958)		58.0	42.0

Source: United Nations, Department of Economic and Social Affairs, 1959, p. 246.

Notes to Table:
   (a) Only Federal Government figures.
   (b) Projects current as of 1959; external resources are a residual, as only local resources are listed in source.

determination and continuous effort by indigenous peoples in implementing a program of national economic development; foreign resources are needed because they render more productive additional effort made by the people, and because they help to accelerate the process of capital accumulation necessary for self-sustained growth. Thus the full significance of contributions from public international agencies lies not in the

   [7] Certain agencies whose operations are international, such as the Colonial Development Corporation (CDC) and the Colonial Development and Welfare Fund (CD and W) of the United Kingdom, the Agency for International Development (AID) and the Export-Import Bank (EXIM-BANK) of the United States of America; and Fonds des Investissements pour le Développement Economique et Sociale (FIDES), Caisse Centrale de la France d'Outre-Mer (CCFOM) and Fonds d'Aide et de Cooperation (FAC) of France, but which are instruments of foreign policy of the respective governments, are excluded from the category of international organizations. The contribution of such agencies is fully treated of under bilateral aid, and in Table 17.3.
   [8] See Table 17.1 for figures on specific countries.

relative proportions they bear to other sources which finance expenditures for economic development, but in their catalytic effect in inducing the nationals of various countries to make greater physical and material effort for the fulfilment of development programs.

There are at least seven international organizations that actively contributed aid in the form of loans, grants, and technical assistance to African economic growth.[9] All these, particularly the World Bank, have contributed toward financing and promoting general research, for the development of basic facilities such as communications, power, roads, and buildings, and for social services such as education, housing, water supply, and sewerage systems. As we have seen in an earlier chapter, the most important effect of such investment is not a direct increase in national income; rather its importance lies in the encouragement it

[9] The following are brief notes on participating organizations already identified on p. 357: see Table 17.2 for their contributions.

IBRD—The International Bank for Reconstruction and Development makes loans at fixed rates of interest to governments for developing basic and social facilities. The IBRD loans in Africa constitute the bulk of aid from all multilateral sources. Nevertheless, the Bank extended less than 15 per cent of its total outstanding loans to Africa from its inception to 1960.

UNSF—The United Nations Special Fund began operating in 1959. Its main activities, resource surveys, applied research, vocational and advanced technical training, and pilot projects—are to complement those of the EPTA. Its financial resources come from voluntary government contributions. African countries have received about $7.5 million of aid for exploration of resources and feasibility studies, among others.

UNTA—The United Nations Technical Assistance is administered by the United Nations and its Specialized Agencies, and financed through fixed contributions of United Nations members to the ordinary United Nation and Specialized Agency budgets.

EPTA—The Expanded United Nations Technical Assistance Program was started in 1950 as an addition to the regular programs. In the new program, the activities of the Specialized Agencies are tied closely to that of the World Bank and the International Monetary Fund. In contrast to the regular program, contributions to the Expanded Program are on a voluntary basis.

UNICEF—The United Nations Children Emergency Fund was originally established in 1946 to meet emergency needs for child care and welfare resulting from the second World War. Since 1950, its activities have been concentrated in the general promotion of child health. Contributions to the fund, public and private, are on a voluntary basis. Overall expenditure in Africa up to 1960 is estimated at about $17 million.

EEC—The European Economic Community established a Development Fund to promote social and economic development in the overseas countries and territories associated with the Community. From its inception to December, 1960 the Fund has made a commitment of $93 million and disbursed about $63 million in Africa. Contributions from the Fund are in the form of grants.

IFC—The International Finance Corporation was established in 1956 to promote private investment in economically underdeveloped countries by providing private finance for enterprises. Since International Finance Corporation loans are made to private enterprises, government guarantees are not required. The first loan in Africa, $2.8 million, was made in June, 1960 to a sugar producing enterprise in Tanganyika.

has given to directly productive investments by minimizing the risks and lessening the barriers that might otherwise deter potential investors.

Between 1954 and 1960, the less technologically developed countries in the whole African continent received not less than $4.8 billion in foreign aid. Over the same period of time, in all Subsaharan Africa, at least thirty-five territories and independent countries received only $2.8 billion, about 58 per cent of the total flow of aid. The remaining $2.0 billion was distributed among five countries in North Africa, namely, Morocco, Algeria and Sahara, Libya, Tunisia, and Mauritania. Each of the recipient countries in Africa south of the Sahara received a cumulative average of $80 million or an annual average of about $11.5 million in foreign aid, while each of the North African countries already mentioned received a cumulative average of $400 million or an annual average of a little less than $60 million. Thus for every dollar of aid spent or allocated to countries in Subsaharan Africa, five times as many were granted to other African countries, mainly in North Africa. The ratio of per capita dollar receipt of aid in North Africa to that in Africa south of the Sahara over the same period is also approximately 5 to 1.

It would thus appear, from the wide dispersion in regional and per capita receipts, that the overall allocation of aid among African countries for economic development has been unduly skewed, and perhaps less efficient than it might have been. The amount of aid which each country received, particularly in the form of bilateral assistance, was determined by the type of political and economic relations existing before and after independence between the various African countries and the metropolitan powers; the tests of potentials for development need and absorptive capacity[10] played a relatively less important role.

The history of international aid to Africa during the decade 1950–1960 reveals a preponderance of bilateral over multilateral contributions, such aid being largely tied to the foreign relations between the respective governments. It is significant to note that in Africa south of the Sahara, the various international organizations provided in loans, grants, and echnical assistance about $373 million[11] out of a total of $2,777 million, less than 14 per cent of the total. European governments and the United States, operating through bilateral channels, provided about $2,229 million, roughly 80 per cent of the total. Soviet Russia contributed $175 million, the remaining 6 per cent. The foregoing facts then make

[10] "Absorptive capacity" is defined as "the total amount of capital and technical assistance that a country can use in one year and still add to aggregate income during the period twenty to thirty years later."

[11] This figure includes a $2.8 million IFC loan extended to a sugar producing enterprise in Tanganyika, June, 1960.

TABLE 17.2. *Multilateral Assistance to Economically Less Developed Areas in Subsaharan Africa, 1954–1958; 1958–1960* (in $ million)

Receiving Country	Contributing Organization											
	IBRD Loans		SUNFED Grants		EEC Grants	UNTA Grants		EPTA Grants		UNICEF Grants	
	1954–1958	1958–1960	1958–1960	1959–1960	1959–1960	1954–1958	1959–1960	1954–1958	1959–1960	1954–1958	1959–1960
Angola	29.7					0.2	.055				
Belgian Congo		40.0			4.419	0.1	.014	.024		0.1	
British East Africa	15.6					1.2	.003	.136	.089	1.0	
Kenya		5.6		.313				.069	.055		.127
Uganda							.010	.097	.017		.083
Tanganyika							.058	.527	.095		.056
British South Africa						0.2	.012			0.1	
British West Africa						0.7	.004	.037	.006	1.3	
Gambia								.042			
Nigeria		28.0		.735			.066	.210	.119		
Sierre Leone							.006	.211	.051		.033
Cameroons (French)					7.332		.010		.036		.259
Ethiopia and Eritrea	3.1					2.3	.155	1.872	.439	0.4	
French Equatorial Africa		35.0		.930	15.946		.027		.003	0.5	.080
French West Africa	5.6				29.707	0.1		.117	.012		.467

Ghana	38.9	.345		0.4	.052	.467	.227	0.3	.297
Guinea		.425			.022			0.2	.131
Liberia				1.2	.149	1.029	.198	0.1	.035
Mozambique									
Rhodesia and Nyasaland	24.6		2.153		.037				
Ruanda-Urundi			1.125						
Somaliland	50.5			0.3	.058	.264	.018	0.3	
Sudan				1.2	.139	.930	.451	0.2	
Togo			.700		.004		.032		.048
Other				2.2	.629	.588	.318		
Total	92.9	3.448	60.682	10.1	1.537	6.602	2.166	7.4	1.740
All Africa: GRAND TOTAL	102.2	7.496	63.025	19.3	1.952	14.800	4.190	9.8	2.371

Sources: 1954–1958, United Nations, Economic Commission for Africa, 1959, *International Economic Assistance to Africa: A Review of Current Contributions*, Ref. No. E/CN.14/23, Appendix A; 1958–1960, International Bank for Reconstruction and Development, *Annual Reports*, 1958–1960; European Economic Community, *Bulletins*, 1959–1960; United Nations, EPTA, Annual Reports of the Technical Assistance Board, 1956–1960; United Nations, UNICEF, Annual Reports, 1958–1959

it clear that the international organizations participating in African economic development have played a comparatively weak role.

Endeavors by the World Bank to relax problems of international capital have been curtailed by the limitations set forth in the Bank's charter since it exists chiefly to "promote private foreign investment by means of guarantees, or participations in loans and other investments made by foreign investors, and when private capital is available on reasonable terms, to supplement private investment by providing, on suitable conditions, finance for productive purposes out of its own capital, funds raised by it and its other resources." This means that since only large private economic groups may actually have capital resources they can devote to direct international investment, the Bank has left this field almost completely to these groups. This position tends to perpetuate the growth of foreign economic power groups in the economically underdeveloped areas.

The provisions of the charter which define the rate at which the Bank must lend its funds limit its capacity to act as a source of long-term low-interest finance in Africa, since only the country which has developed some export trade can satisfy the requirements of the Bank regarding the repayment of loans; which means that countries which have a need for loans to finance less remunerative projects have great difficulty in obtaining them. Other circumstances also limit the Bank's lending operations. One is that many of the development plans presented to it have required major alteration, in part because adequate initial surveys were not carried out in the territories seeking aid. Most of all, there are the hindrances to its effectiveness which emanate from the policies of a public international financial institution functioning on strictly private banking principles.[12] The question is whether such principles should be applied in extending long-term development loans to African countries where business systems are not well developed.

To the extent that scarce outside resources must be provided through bilateral or multilateral channels, both help to satisfy overall African requirements. However, there are at least two strong considerations that point to the necessity for increasing the relative contributions of international multilateral organizations, in meeting the financial needs of African economic development. These matters involve the psychological response of the beneficiaries of aid, the politics of neo-colonialism, and the cold war, as well as the question of economic efficiency.

The psychological climate influencing the acceptability of Western aid offered under bilateral institutions is a mixture of mistrust and suspicion. In such an uneasy atmosphere, Africans become sensitive to

[12] Iliff, W. A., 1952, *passim*.

any gesture that may be interpreted as hampering or jeopardizing their overriding desire to preserve their political freedom and national pride. This feeling has been sharpened by the fear, especially in newly independent states of Africa, that unilateral aid by Western countries may play the classic role of the Trojan Horse by facilitating the triumph of neo-colonialism or involving them in the cold war. Political leaders in African countries have felt that because international organizations are multilateral sources of aid, there is only limited opportunity, if any, for exerting on a recipient political pressure calculated to force it to take sides in the cold war.

On purely economic grounds, the overriding consideration relates to efficient allocation of resources, in the long run, among developing African countries. Long-term aid is needed not only in sufficient quantity but, most importantly, in a stable and continuous flow over time. The characteristics of politically sensitive aid have given rise to serious discontinuities, that reduce their economic usefulness for long-term development. Furthermore, bilateral contributions from the metropolitan governments to their former or existing colonies have encouraged duplication of overhead capital projects within a region where a single large-scale project could supply the needs of the entire region. In the former British, French, and Belgian colonies in western and central Africa, there has been a wide array of duplications of projects, particularly in the development of hydro-electric power—the Inga power project in the ex-Belgian Congo and the Kouilou project in the neighboring Congo Republic, the Volta project in Ghana and the Souapiti power project in Guinea, the Volta project and the Niger power project in Nigeria. The problems of waste resulting from duplication of projects and of economic instability arising from the interdependence of vital productive activities within African continental regions of Africa have thus become crucial. Essential to their solution is that the governments under whose auspices projects have been initiated, and whose economic aid helps to implement them, coordinate their assistance. Lacking such coordination, grants in aid only constitute an additional obstacle to balanced African economic and technological development.

5

In some literature on economic development, the question of growth has been analysed in terms of the net effect of the interactions between two opposing social stimulants; the income-depressing stimulant, and the income-raising stimulant. In an economically underdeveloped country, the "income depressing factors may be more significant than

N

the income-raising factors. As a consequence, if the income-raising factors are stimulated beyond the maximum of the income-depressing factors, *the critical minimum* (level of effort) . . . (will be) . . . reached and the economy (will) be on the road to development."[13]

Some of the important variables stimulating growth are levels of income, investment, foreign trade, savings, and growth of population. The existing data on these variables for most of the African countries have been carefully studied with a view to getting some information on the level of supplementary outside resources required to satisfy the apparent economic imperatives of the "critical minimum" effort. Because of the fragmentary nature of relevant information, a firmly based projection of outside needs must be limited to a few countries. Such a projection, however, is too restricted, and does not provide a basis for valid generalization for most Subsaharan African countries. The problem of limited coverage, however, can be largely removed by the availability of Rosenstein-Rodan's study of the economic development potentials of many economically underdeveloped countries, and the ways of sharing the burden of foreign aid projected for those countries between 1961 and 1975.[14]

To preserve the internal consistency of original calculations and estimates, the published figures of Rosentein-Rodan may be abstracted to indicate the quantities of outside capital required to maintain economic growth in Africa south of the Sahara between 1961 and 1971.[15] The forecast must, however, be modified in one essential respect. This concerns the division of total foreign capital inflow between foreign aid and private foreign investment,[16] since the size of the flow of private investment projected by Rosenstein-Rodan for Africa south of the Sahara would seem to be too high. It appears that the most attractive forms of direct investment opportunities—in mining, oil explorations and development, and plantation agriculture—have become limited, because of energetic exploitation of these areas of enterprise in the past. With diminishing opportunities in such traditional areas, the flow of private funds into this sector must decelerate.

In the terms of his estimates, the forecast of capital inflow to Subsaharan Africa in the decade 1961–1971 is $3.4 billion; $1.5 billion for 1961–1965, and $1.9 billion for 1966–1971, giving an annual amount of $340 million. Taking the two five-year periods separately, the average annual amount of aid for the first is estimated to be $260 million; second,

[13] Leibenstein, H., 1957, p. 97. Parentheses inserted.
[14] Rosenstein-Rodan, P., 1961, pp. 107–138.
[15] See Tables 17.4 and 17.5.
[16] See Table 17.6.

$294 million. Of the estimated capital inflow of $3.4 billion, at least $2.8 billion is to be provided in economic aid; it is hoped that the balance of $0.6 billion will be covered by private foreign investment.

What percentage of the total aid can be expected from public international organizations now cooperating in African economic development? Because of psychological and political reasons, the minimum contribution from international organizations should ideally be above 50 per cent of the total. It has been pointed out repeatedly in previous chapters that investment in public transportation, power supplies, communication systems, and other basic installations that are preconditions to industry, have a long gestation period. Moreover, as we have seen, returns from these types of investment are most indirect because of the wide diffusion of their benefits through the economic system. On both counts, the risk involved in such large scale investment constitutes a strong disincentive to private foreign investors and consequently provide a strong argument for the provision of public investment or foreign aid.

During the nineteen-fifties, bilateral contributions constituted the great bulk of aid that went into public investment. There are, however, strong indications that bilateral contributions during 1961–1971 will not necessarily be maintained at the level reached in the second half of the nineteen-fifties. This is because the political and economic relationships that facilitated such an impressive outflow of aid to Africa from the metropolitan countries have been steadily eroded. Because they were continuously questioned and repudiated by Africans as a means of impeding the drive toward national freedom and political independence which swept across the continent, stoppage of aid to several African countries understandably followed.[17] Even where there was no abrupt discontinuation of direct aid, institutional policies were formulated that brought about the same result.[18] Thus the picture of foreign aid is marred by suspicion and uncertainty shared by both the contributing and the recipient countries.

6

Despite the fervent political nationalism found in many of the African states, Africa has not found a means to achieve economic nationalism.

[17] France cut off aid to Morocco, Tunisia, and particularly Guinea following independence. The failure of Belgium to provide adequate economic aid for Congo was one of the causes of the crisis there.
[18] The Colonial Welfare and Development Fund of the United Kingdom instituted a policy of not extending new grants or loans to independent former colonies, so that Ghana, Nigeria, and Sierra Leone were unable to continue to benefit from its funds.

It has been urged that for better allocation of foreign as well as domestic resources, and for an effective search for ways and means of achieving a development break-through, the various states will have to work together in designing economic development.

One approach to this, which would take into account the complexities of the internal problems militating against African economic growth, would be to create an Organization for African Economic Cooperation. The proposed organization could be charged with receiving and allocating all foreign aid given for purposes of African economic development. Some of the actual and potential waste of foreign resources caused by duplication of projects within regions could thereby be effectively controlled through the rationing of foreign aid among competing intra-regional projects. This would insure that outside resources provided for projects and communities could "have maximum catalytic effect in mobilizing additional national effort or preventing a fall in national effort."[19] In order to acquire all necessary information on resource availabilities and general needs, the proposed organization might commission an appropriate body to make a comprehensive exploration of Subsaharan African resources and man-power. The resulting technical information would provide data for solving some of the internal problems of interdependence and make for better coordination of programs for economic development.

The establishment of an Economic Commission for Africa under the auspices of the United Nations was a move in this direction. However, it cannot be an acceptable substitute for the proposed body for two reasons, the first being the character of its membership and the second, the kind of executive responsibility it has assumed. The Economic Commission for Africa is not, primarily, an African organization. It is an integral part of the United Nations, and seeks to operate only in areas in which that body has jurisdictional and organizational competence. In the second place, it is not a body empowered to make decisions. It is primarily an organ for the implementation of policy.

In different areas of the world, among countries that are situated on large land masses and confronted by common geopolitical problems, the necessity of independent thought and action, at the highest level, has long been recognized. After numerous experiments in Asia, the Americas, and Europe, it became realized that there was no other effective way to win wide-spread support for and to translate into far-reaching action all specific and general policies formulated for attaining better social, political, and economic life for all countries concerned. That is why the European countries established autonomous institutions, such as EEC,

[19] Rosenstein-Rodan, P., 1961.

outside the United Nations to deal with vital economic and social matters that are beyond the competence of the Economic Commission for Europe. In Latin America, for similar reasons, the existence of the Economic Commission for Latin America did not preclude the existence of the Organization of American States. The same reasons would seem to hold for establishing a body of restricted membership in contemporary Africa.

TABLE 17.3. *Bilateral Assistance to Less Developed Areas in Subsaharan Africa, 1954–1958; 1959–1960*
(in $ million)

Receiving Country	United Kingdom				U.S. America				France		USSR	Portugal		Italy	
	Loans	Grants	Loans	Grants	Loans	Grants	Loans	Grants	Loans	Grants	Loans	Loans	Grants	Loans	Grants
	1954–1958	1954–1958	1959–1960	1959–1960	1954–1958	1954–1958	1959–1960	1959–1960	1954–1958	1954–1958	1958–1960	1954–1958	1954–1958	1954–1958	1954–1958
Angola					0.2							−0.1			
Belgian Congo					−7.2	2.6									
British East Africa	53.4	90.3	21.0	17.9	0.2										
Kenya															
Uganda															
Tanganyika															
British South Africa	12.9	9.4	6.7	5.0											
British West Africa	3.7	49.1	5.0	15.4	−0.1										
Gambia															
Nigeria								1.8							
Sierra Leone															
Cameroons (French)					4.6	16.7	1.8	4.6	16.3	76.8					
Ethiopia and Eritrea					−0.9	0.2					100.0				
French Equatorial Africa					1.4	0.5			14.1	97.1					
French West Africa									62.4	191.0					
Ghana	1.6	8.2						0.9			40.0				
Guinea								2.1			35.0				
Liberia					5.8	8.2	0.3	5.1							
Mozambique					12.5							3.6	0.4		
Rhodesia and Nyasaland	20.1	15.8			31.5										
Ruanda-Urundi															
Somaliland					0.3	3.4		2.7							27.8
Sudan			11.6	0.6			17.8	13.0							
Other	−0.7	71.3			13.3	2.8		1.0	180.0	880.0					
Africa, South of Sahara, *Total*	91.7	172.8	152.6	115.1	61.3	34.7	19.9	31.2	272.8	1244.9	175.0	3.5	0.4	0.8	27.8
All Africa	91.8	297.2	152.6	124.3	71.6	195.0	66.4	122.5	1233.6	1941.0	450.0	3.5	0.4	0.8	27.8

Sources: 1954–1958, United Nations, Economic Commission for Africa, 1959, *International Economic Assistance to Africa: A Review of Current Contri-* (... Assistance for U.K. Overseas Territories), London, p. 17; United States

TABLE 17.4. *Gross National Product Projections of African Countries, South of the Sahara, 1961–1971 (in $ million)*

	1961 GNP	1961–1966 Rate of Growth per Annum (percentage)	1966 GNP	1966–1971 Rate of Growth per Annum (percentage)	1971 GNP
Angola	301.8	2.5	341.4	3	395.7
Belgian Congo	1482.0	1	1557.5	2	1719.6
British East Africa					
Kenya	624.2	3	723.6	3	838.8
Uganda	436.0	3	505.4	3.5	600.2
British South Africa	699.2	3	810.5	4	986.1
British West Africa					
Gambia	15.6	2	17.2	2	18.9
Nigeria	2920.4	3	3385.6	3.25	3967.9
Cameroons (French)	345.5	2	381.4	3	442.1
Ethiopia and Eritrea	1149.1	2	1268.7	3	1470.8
French Equatorial Africa	560.1	3	649.3	3	752.7
French West Africa	2159.1	3	2503.0	3	2901.7
Ghana	996.3	2.5	1093.2	3	1267.3
Guinea					
Liberia	113.7	2.5	128.6	2.5	145.4
Mozambique	491.0	2.5	555.5	3	643.9
Rhodesia and Nyasaland	1341.0	4	1631.5	4	1985.0
Ruanda-Urundi	351.0	2	387.5	3	449.2
Somaliland	77.4	2	85.4	2	94.2
Sudan	847.8	2.5	959.2	3	1112.3
Togo	63.0	2	69.5	3	80.5

Source: Rosenstein-Rodan, P. N., *op. cit.*, p. 40.

TABLE 17.5. *Foreign Capital Inflow Required for Underdeveloped African Countries, South of the Sahara, 1961–1971*

Country	Rate of Growth (per cent)	Average Savings Rate (per cent)	1961–1966 Marginal Savings Rate (per cent)	Capital Inflow 1961–66 ($ million)	Capital Inflow Per Annum ($ million)	Rate of Growth (per cent)	Average Savings Rate (per cent)	1966–1971 Marginal Savings Rate (per cent)	Capital Inflow 1966–71 ($ million)	Capital Inflow Per Annum ($ million)
Angola	2.5	4.5	8	44.9	9.0	3	4.9	12	66.8	13.3
Belgian Congo	1	1	5	148.4	29.7	2	6.5	11	no aid	no aid
British East Africa										
Kenya	3	7.5	12	41.4	8.3	3	8.1	15	20.0	4.0
Uganda	3	7.0	10	42.3	8.5	3.5	7.4	12	75.4	15.1
Tanganyika	3	7.0	10	67.8	13.6	4	7.5	15	171.8	34.4
British South Africa										
British West Africa										
Gambia	2	3.5	6	2.0	0.4	2	3.6	9	2.0	0.4
Nigeria	3	6.5	10	356.6	71.3	3.25	7.5	14	335.0	67.0
Sierra Leone										
Cameroons (French)	2	5.0	8	15.8	3.2	3	5.3	10	69.4	13.9
Ethiopia and Eritrea	2	5	9	50.6	10.1	3	5.4	12	217.3	43.5
French Equatorial Africa	2	6.5	9	70.0	14.0	3	6.9	12	62.0	12.4
French West Africa	3	5.5	9	377.8	75.6	3	6.0	12	353.6	70.7
Ghana	2.5	6	10	145.8	29.2	3	6.4	13	129.3	25.9
Liberia	2.5	6	9	8.2	1.6	2.5	6.3	13	6.3	1.3
Mozambique	2.5	5.5	8	48.5	9.7	3	5.8	12	83.9	16.8
Rhodesia and Nyasaland	4	12	20	no aid	no aid	4.0	13.4	20	no aid	no aid
Ruanda-Urundi	2	4	6	35.1	7.0	3	4.2	10	92.0	18.4
Somaliland	2	4	6	7.7	1.5	2	4.2	8	7.2	1.4
Sudan	2.5	5.5	8	75.3	15.0	3	5.8	12	145.3	29.0
Togo	2	4.0	6	6.3	1.3	3	4.2	8	16.5	3.3
Total				1,544.5	308.8				1,853.6	370.8

TABLE 17.6. Composition of Foreign Capital Inflow Per Annum ("AID" and Private Foreign Investment) ($ million)

	1961–1966			1966–1971		
	Capital Inflow	AID	Private Investment	Capital Inflow	AID	Private Investment
Angola	9.0	7.2	1.8	13.3	10.0	3.3
Belgian Congo	29.7	23.8	5.9	no aid	no aid	1.0
Kenya	8.3	6.7	1.6	4.0	3.0	1.6
Uganda	8.5	6.7	0.7	15.1	11.2	3.9
Tanganyika	13.6	10.9	2.7	34.4	25.8	8.6
Gambia	0.4	0.3	0.1	0.4	0.3	0.1
Nigeria	71.3	57.0	13.3	67.0	50.2	16.8
Cameroons	3.2	2.6	0.6	13.9	10.4	3.5
Ethiopia and Eritrea	10.1	8.1	2.0	43.5	32.6	10.9
French Equatorial Africa	14.0	11.2	2.8	12.4	9.3	3.1
French West Africa	75.6	60.5	15.1	70.7	53.0	17.0
Ghana	29.2	23.4	6.8	25.9	19.4	6.5
Liberia	1.6	1.3	0.3	1.3	1.0	0.3
Mozambique	9.7	7.8	1.9	16.8	12.6	4.2
Rhodesia and Nyasaland	no aid			no aid		
Ruanda–Urundi	7.0	5.6	2.4	18.4	13.8	4.6
Somaliland	1.5	1.2	0.3	1.4	1.0	0.4
Sudan	15.0	12.0	3.0	29.0	21.7	7.3
Togo	1.3	1.0	0.3	3.3	2.5	0.8
Total	308.0	260.2	48.6	370.8	293.6	74.2

18

Economic Growth and Political Reorientation

by James S. Coleman
University of California, Los Angeles

The central feature of the political map of independent Africa has been the continuation of the political fragmentation of the colonial period. In the main, African leaders have sought and attained separate sovereign statehood in each of the artificial administrative entities created by the European colonial powers. Exceptions have been the union of Eritrea and Ethiopia, the union of British Somaliland and Italian Somalia, the integration of British Togoland with the Gold Coast to form the independent state of Ghana, and the integration of northern British Cameroons into the Northern Region of Nigeria, each of which can be explained by very special circumstances. This is not, of course, a peculiarly African phenomenon, since the boundaries of the majority of sovereign entities in the contemporary state system derive from an imperial or colonial government. The remarkable feature of the process in Africa is that it occurred despite the extreme artificiality of those boundaries, the comparative brevity of colonial rule, and the explicit acknowledgment by most African leaders of the desirability of large-scale politico-economic units, a position underscored by their fairly general commitment to the ideal of African unity.

The reasons why virtually every one of Africa's colonial territories emerged as a separate sovereign unit need only be noted briefly here.[1] One set of considerations relate to the imperial legacy, which preserved and tended even to emphasize the separate existence of each artificial separate territory. The British treated each territory, large or small, as a world unto itself, destined to have its distinctive pace and pattern of political development. Although the main thrust of French policy during the colonial era was towards the creation of a monolithic unity throughout

[1] Apter, D. E. and Coleman, J. S., 1962.

Afrique Noire, each of the former fourteen territories emerged as a sovereign independent state, at least in part because of the French policy of "territorialization" after 1956.[2]

Another facet of the European colonial legacy must also be remarked, namely, that European rule in Africa enormously expanded the scale of political organization and economic intercourse. Large nascent nations, such as the Sudan, Nigeria, and Tanganyika, each embracing hundreds of traditional societies, are as much a part of the colonial legacy as are such fragments as Togo and the Gambia. Imperial rule in Africa, as elsewhere, provided the framework and introduced those integrative processes requisite for building larger-scale nation-states. In retrospect, therefore, the real criticism of European rule is that the colonial powers, while the situation was still malleable and their authority supreme, did not create or preserve larger and more viable entities.

The disinclination of the colonial powers to transcend their own fragmentation of Africa was reinforced by overwhelming practical considerations which confronted nationalist leaders of each territory. They were compelled to confine their agitation to the territorial political arena. Although African nationalism was, and to a considerable extent continued to be Pan-Africanist, the realities of the power structure of colonial Africa, as well as the variant colonial policies and practices of the different imperial countries, made it necessary for nationalism to become territorialized. In the post-independence period, new imperatives emerged—the need for "national" unity and a sense of "national" purpose, the need to legitimize new "national" governments and to inculcate "national" loyalties, and the need to protect newly discovered "national" interests. In short, strong pressures developed for leaders of the new states to solve the age-old problem of creating new nations out of the ensemble of disparate cultural groups situated by historical accident within the boundaries of the territories over which they inherited political power. Thus, one of the more significant consequences of African attainment of sovereign statehood has been a "balkanized" independent Africa, with all this implies for economic growth.

Foreign relations and defense have made up the major part of these new fiscal burdens, though their impact has not been the same in all states. Indeed, there have been wide differences in them, depending on the character of residual ties with the formal metropolitan powers, and the eagerness with which the leaders of the new states have sought to assert and to dramatize their new status in African and world affairs. In the immediate post-independence period the impact of this added

[2] For a discussion of the process of fragmentation in ex-*Afrique Noire* see Wallerstein, I., 1961, pp. 3ff, and Newbury, C., 1961, pp. 41ff.

burden was minimized by a variety of measures, including the utilization of consular and embassy facilities of the former metropolitan power,
the restriction of diplomatic representation to only a few major foreign
capitals, and sharing the costs of establishing and maintaining such
facilities with other new African states. The absence of technically
qualified foreign-service personnel, coupled with a realistic assessment
of benefits and costs, meant that initially, at least, the burden of diplomatic representation abroad had to be minimal.

As the new states became increasingly participant in international
affairs, the cost of external relations increased markedly. In the year of
its independence, the item for the external relations establishment in
the Federal budget of Nigeria (£670,240) constituted no more than
0.8 per cent of total recurrent expenditures, though this did not include
other substantial costs, such as those of the larger number of trade
missions and visiting delegations sent to various parts of the world.

Nowhere is the fiscal burden of sovereign statehood potentially
greater than in the field of defense.[3] Previously unified military forma-
tions developed on a regional basis during the colonial period dis-
integrated as a consequence of the political fragmentation of sovereign
statehood. The former Royal West African Frontier Force gave way to
the embryonic national armies of Ghana, Nigeria and Sierra Leone;
and the same tendency towards disintegration also became evident in
the case of the King's African Rifles of East Africa. Guinea's independence, followed by the breakup of the Mali Federation, and the final
collapse of the Franco-African Community, resulted in a dismantling
of the pan-African military formation created by France in *Afrique
Noire*.

The initial impact of the defense burden was heavier in the new states
of former French Africa than in those previously under British Administration. The main reason is that the latter, under British policy, were
partly or wholly responsible for the budgetary support of local forces.
In Nigeria, for example, there is little difference between the 4.2 per
cent of the Nigerian budget committed to military support in 1938–
1939, a year of pure colonialism, and the 4.4 per cent allocated in 1959–
1960, the year of independence.[4] For several years preceding Sudanese

[3] For a more detailed analysis see Coleman, J. S. and Brice, B., 1961.
[4] During the period 1939–1958 Nigeria did not carry the full burden of its military
establishment. Each year it made a "Contribution to His Majesty's Government on
account of Military Expenditures in Nigeria." The actual costs of Nigeria's military
forces during this period cannot be established, because of their integration with
the British Army in many ways. In 1958–1959, when Nigeria assumed full budgetary
responsibility for its forces, the estimates reflected an increase of more than £1.5
million.

independence, about 5 per cent of the Sudan's national budget was devoted to military expenditures. By contrast, in the former French territories, where there was conscription, African military units were considered an integral part of the French defense establishments, the costs of which were carried on the budget of metropolitan France.

But sovereignty also brought the opportunity to "think big" in internal affairs, in terms of social and economic development, and to ensure that priorities in the allocation of national resources would reflect popular aspirations. Indeed, one of the major nationalist arguments for the primacy of the "Political Kingdom," for complete African control of the machinery of the state, was that only through such control could any radical advance be made in the economic sphere. This was as much an argument against European conservatives, who contended that self-government would mean economic stagnation, as it was against European socialists who stressed the primacy of the class struggle and economic liberation. Most African leaders tended to regard the state as the indispensible instrument for the achievement of all other ends, particularly rapid economic growth.

National goals in Africa's new states reflected the strong determination to achieve rapid modernization. This is to be discerned in the recommendations of the Commission on Post-School Certificate and Higher Education in Nigeria:

> We believe it would be a grave disservice to Nigeria to make modest, cautious proposals, likely to fall within her budget, for such proposals would be totally inadequate to maintain even the present rate of economic growth in the country. Accordingly, we reject this approach. Our recommendations are massive, unconventional, and expensive; they will be practicable only if Nigerian education seeks outside aid and if the Nigerian people themselves are prepared to accord education first priority and to make sacrifices for it.[5]

To implement the Commission's recommendations the total capital expenditure for the period 1961–1970 was estimated at £75 million, with a total recurrent cost of the same order in 1970. The magnitude of this undertaking in the education field alone is illuminated by the fact that in 1959–1960 the total combined recurrent expenditures of the federal and the three regional governments of Nigeria was no more than £80½ million.

This predisposition to set national goals and to undertake massive programs irrespective of cost and strict balance sheet calculations of

[5] Nigeria, Federation of, Ministry of Education, 1960, p. 41.

direct and immediate returns is also reflected in the defense by Mamadou
Dia of such large-scale projects as the *Office du Niger*:

> Only projects of this scope can seriously contribute to the radical trans-
> formation of African agriculture. . . . Far from systematically denigrating
> such schemes, in the manner of certain economists who would have us, in
> the century of atomic energy, embark on an extended program of small-
> scale projects, we must therefore think in terms of developing them within
> a socialist perspective. Far from refusing to accept dimensions which some
> people, unable to transcend their own narrow outlook, considered mon-
> strous, we must adapt our conceptions to the immensity of Africa itself,
> multiply great projects for dams and irrigation, overcome hesitations, push
> aside petty calculations of immediate profitability, face the future with
> confidence and bring out of the files the plans for the rivers Senegal, Volta,
> Niari, etc. Without boldness in this field, we shall in the very near future
> face such serious difficulties resulting from the growth of population that
> no one can adequately envisage them.[6]

Statements such as the foregoing illuminate the spirit of impatience,
and the confidence, expressed by most African political leaders; they
also underscore the strong attraction the idea of the creative state held
for them.

The impulse to concentrate on dramatic large-scale projects has
sprung from a variety of factors. The desire of African leaders to bring
the material benefits of modernity to their people is, of course, to be
taken for granted. The passion to catch up with the more economically
advanced countries of the world, and thereby remove the stigma of
"backwardness," has been rooted partly at least, in the powerful
psychological craving for full acceptance. There has also been the strong
belief that political independence is only the beginning of "decolonization," and that the continued heavy economic dependence upon the
external world leaves Africa in bondage. This was dramatized in the
hostility of many African leaders toward association of their countries
with the European Economic Community, an arrangement which, they
felt, would perpetuate their status as producers of primary products for
advanced industrialized countries.

There have been two other related considerations of special significance in the African situation. One is that in rather marked contrast to
most of the rest of the ex-colonial world, most African countries during
their terminal colonial period had already been launched upon a multi-
dimensional process of modernization prior to independence. The
second is that in agitating for political independence, nationalist leaders

[6] Quoted in Hanson, A. H., 1960, p. 345.

made self-government the symbol not only for racial and individual dignity, but also the symbol of the opportunity to create their brave new world. The social mobilization of the terminal colonial period, and the political mobilization brought about by political agitation for independence, raised popular expectations in most African countries to a high level, resulting in strong political pressures for dramatic economic growth following independence. These pressures were stimulated and capitalized upon by political opposition, where it was allowed to exist. Thus, in the eyes of most African political leaders in power, large-scale projects and ambitious development plans were regarded as necessary not only for economic emancipation; they were also held to be imperative for continued popular support.

The highest priority was placed by African leaders upon educational development. One of the foremost nationalist indictments against alien rule was the charge of deliberate educational starvation as an imperial strategem to perpetuate the European presence. Beyond this was the recognition that lack of trained manpower, a prime requisite for economic growth, continued to be one of Africa's most serious weaknesses. Political leaders were also acutely conscious of the fact that the popular hunger for education, and the status and rewards it confers, comprised one of the most powerful social forces with which they must contend. Self-government provided the opportunity to respond to these intense popular aspirations.

Although there was a marked expansion in education during the terminal colonial period, most new African governments sought to dramatize the new era of independence by launching vast new programs of educational development. The introduction of universal primary education in Ghana and Western Nigeria, and the plans for the expansion of higher education in Nigeria as a whole, pursuant to the recommendations of the Commission previously cited, illustrate the general trend. Equally illuminating are the following figures:

Country	Percentage of National Budget Spent on Education		
	1939	*1950*	*1960*
Nigeria[7]	4.3	16.9	22.5
Ghana		9.0	15.0
Ivory Coast		11.0	20.0
Guinea		10.0	18.0

[7] The percentages for 1960 given in the table include both regional and federal expenditures. In the regions, education absorbed a much higher percentage of recurrent expenditures. For 1959–1960 these were: Western Region, 41.1 per cent; Eastern Region, 43.5 per cent.

It is ironical that this massive investment in education could in fact create one of the most serious social—and, in due course, political—problems which governing elites had to confront. Yet the economies of the new states were not expanding at a rate sufficient to provide meaningful career opportunities for the tidal wave of "school leavers" entering the job market. The situation was already becoming very acute in the two southern regions of Nigeria, where in 1960 the number of primary school leavers was more than 300,000, of whom only a small fraction would be able to go on to secondary school.[8] The same situation existed in varying degrees in other new African states.

There are varied political implications of this dilemma. In a competitive political system such as that of Nigeria, politicians soon began to recognize popular concern over the issue of "jobs for school leavers." The governments of Ghana and Guinea were forced to resort to compulsory service in "worker's brigades" in order to meet the growing problem of unemployed school leavers. As the latter flocked to the urban centers, they created a high potential for mob action, and became vulnerable to political manipulation. In the midst of a manifest need for trained manpower the new political elites have been confronted with the dilemma of balancing the imperative of responding to intense popular pressures for educational expansion against the dangers created by the imbalance between educational output and rate of economic growth over the next critical decade.

2

In most of the new African states the dominant impulse has been to consummate freedom in all sectors of the society. Sékou Touré affirmed this point most forcefully:

> . . . the anti-colonial struggle was not brought to an end on September 28, far from it! It has merely been taken up again, more powerfully than ever, under its double aspect of the struggle against the remnants of the colonial régime (through the adaptation of the means, of the structures, of the minds of men, to the new exigencies of a national life of freedom), and of the struggle against the colonial domination that still weighs on an important part of Africa.[9]

What are the economic implications of this inexorable drive for "integral decolonization"; for complete "re-Africanization," to use Touré's

---

[8] Callaway, A. C., 1961, noted the contradiction: "The more that is spent on education from Regional budgets, the less there is left to spend on recurrent costs of further capital outlay that could provide employment."

[9] Touré, S., 1959, p. 14.

phrases? It has its heavy costs, which African leaders seemed to be willing to pay as the price of what they regarded as freedom, despite the fact that such costs very materially affected prospects for economic growth, as well as the character of political systems.

The first and principal emphasis in this drive was "Africanization" of cadres, the substitution of indigenous persons for expatriates and resident aliens in the public and private sectors of the society. Pressure for Africanization of the bureaucracy was the more intense because most expatriate civil servants were nationals of the former imperial power. Despite their long experience, their familiarity with local administrative procedures and the distinctive problems and situations of the country concerned, and the fact that most who remain were prepared genuinely to serve the interests of the new nation, there were strong psychological reasons why their continued presence was at best reluctantly tolerated. Having served in high bureaucratic office, they knew most of the secrets. They were the former superior and tutors, and thus were in a better position than any to judge critically the errors or frailties of their former subordinates. Above all, their continued presence in numbers disproportionate to the numbers of expatriates of other nationalities made it difficult for the new governing elites to dramatize the break with the colonial past.

The determination to "Africanize" extended to all other aspects of national life, and particularly the educational and cultural spheres. Here again Sékou Touré put the point most forcefully:

> It is with regard to this cultural aspect that colonialism has had the most negative effect, because it has served to give complexes to most of those who underwent its influence in their cultural training. . . . Intellectualism itself is not under attack, but it is important to demonstrate the depersonalization of the African intellectual, a depersonalization for which no one holds him responsible, for it was the price at which the colonial régime gave him an education. The more he realizes the necessity of liberating himself intellectually from the complex of the colonized, the more he will rediscover original virtues and the more he will serve the African cause.

Hence, "the reform of Education in Guinea can set itself no other aim than the rehabilitation and free development of African civilization and culture."[10] Such statements reflected the fact that nowhere was the evidence of continued dependence upon, and hence resentment of the undue influence of, a foreign culture more striking than in the educational system, and particularly in the universities. As Hodgkin has pointed out:

[10] *Op. cit.*, p. 58.

Whatever the differences between . . . African universities, they share one common characteristic. They are striking examples of what has been called the "policy of identity"—the policy of exporting European, or Western, institutions to Africa. In general, African universities have been constructed on the basis of British, French, Belgian—and to a less extent North American—models, with the least possible modification. From the outset it has been assumed that this was desirable.[11]

What have been the costs of these post-independence measures aimed at "decolonization" and "re-Africanization"? Without reference to the high value placed on the "freedom" they bring, they clearly have had negative implications, during the short run at least, for economic growth. Whatever other ends have been achieved, the rapid departure of trained and experienced staff, and the sudden massive input and rapid promotion of largely untrained and inexperienced indigenous staff, unquestionably meant a drop in efficiency. To this must be added the psychology of resignation and withdrawal created by the climate of career uncertainty and insecurity.

In most former British territories, agreements were negotiated between the British government and the new African governments ensuring the legitimate retirement benefits and career interests of expatriate officers. Such agreements characteristically became part of that ensemble of legal arrangements comprising the independence compact, and provided for generous "lump sum" compensation for those officers whose careers were affected.[12] Provision was usually made for such officers to be re-engaged at full salary. Offers by the metropolitan country to assume part of the burden, as a form of technical assistance, were declined in certain instances on grounds of principle, namely that civil servants in the pay of a foreign government would be troubled by a conflict in loyalties. Although in most former French territories the transition was financially somewhat less burdensome, the general consequences of rapid Africanization were the same—a reduced capacity, at least initially, to provide the administrative competence requisite for development tasks, as well as further demands upon limited financial resources.

There was another perhaps more serious consequence, not so much

[11] Hodgkin, T., 1958, p. 5. He observes further, however, that in the late 1940's and early 1950's "African public opinion—opinion, that is to say, among the educated minorities who had agitated, in some cases for a generation, for African universities—was, on this issue at least, whole-heartedly in support of a policy of identity. What at all costs they wished to avoid was pseudo-universities, near misses, institutions which provided something less than a full university education as Europe understood it." There are, of course, many Africans who have continued to hold this view.

[12] For a more detailed analysis of such agreements see Coleman, J. S., 1961, pp. 477–493.

of the rate of Africanization, but of the terms under which the change has been made. As Africans were appointed, or promoted, to the "senior service" to replace expatriates, it was politically impossible, if not ethically intolerable, to deny them the same salary, perquisites, and allowances, or to insist upon longer hours of work or shorter vacations, than their European predecessors and their remaining European associates. The main thrust of nationalist agitation was equality; it was and has remained politically difficult in the extreme, except in such puritanical austerity régimes as those of Guinea and Mali, for African leaders to suggest, not to mention impose, reductions in salaries, allowances, and other perquisites more in keeping with the financial capacity of the country, and the relationship of the "senior service" to other occupational groups in the country.

Here two crucial points enter. One is that there has been perpetuated a standard of remuneration and reward, including subsidized housing, designed to attract and hold a relatively small European bureaucracy living abroad, having children in boarding schools of the metropole, and with a short working day, long leaves, and early retirement provided because of the alleged "unhealthy" climate. The financial burden of this alone has been substantial, particularly in view of the tremendous expansion in government activity and proliferation of government agencies incident to the change from a small administrative service concerned only with "law and order" to a leviathan charged with the dual function of managing a welfare state and stimulating an economy. The second point is that the assimilation of an Africanized public service to the same standards of salary, perquisites and allowances as those of its European predecessor has tended to preserve the wide socio-economic gap that always existed between the "senior," "European" sector and the "African" class of clerks, artisans, teachers, and so forth. The consequences have been obvious: inflation or discontent. Powerful political pressures were brought to bear upon the governments to close the gap by an upward revision of salary scales and allowances in all occupational categories, something that must inevitably affect all occupational groups. Yet if the gap is not narrowed, governments will be confronted with the same bitter resentment, disaffection, and political agitation that were generated by the "gap" during the colonial period.

Rapid Africanization had another important political consequence, the drastic curtailment in career opportunities in the public service for an ever increasing number of candidates. As has been indicated, there is considerable evidence of tensions between the new generation of secondary school and university graduates, and the veterans of nationalist movements who came to occupy most of the key political and bureaucratic positions in the new states. Members of the new generation are thus increasingly denied the opportunity the present generation has had to climb rapidly to positions of high responsibility, status, and affluence. Those obtaining appointments in the public service were more and more compelled to accept junior positions, in which they frequently had to serve under persons of limited training and education. Moreover, those African civil servants who benefitted from being on the spot during the period of extremely rapid upward mobility were in the main young, in most instances being no more than in mid-career; which means that a promotional freeze will increasingly set in, furthering the state of discontent in the junior ranks. Only a rapidly expanding economy, offering a progressive widening of career opportunities, could prevent this generational cleavage from becoming a serious political problem.

A concerted drive to Africanize and to secularize the educational system also had significant financial implications. Christian missionary enterprise has provided a major proportion of the costs of educational development. Whatever other judgment might be made of the contribution and role of missionary activity, there can be little question that it was a not unimportant source of what we now call technical assistance in both the educational and medical fields. The secularization of pre-university education inevitably added to the financial burden of the expanding educational system. The Africanization of universities, it became apparent, might lead to increasing difficulties in recruiting foreign scholars, partly because of the insecurities created by state intervention, and partly because of the severed ties with metropolitan institutions, which gave assurance that standards would be maintained, and that the new African institutions would command academic respect. Without qualified African academic staff to man these new universities, these difficulties could be overcome only by recruiting mediocrities, foreign or African—something that Africans were not willing to let happen—or by paying high salaries and offering special inducements for short-term foreign staff.

Once these likely consequences of rapid Africanization are noted, we come back to the inescapable fact that is was politically difficult, if not impossible, for governing elites to do otherwise than they did. The blame, if placed anywhere, had to be placed upon the lack of foresight in preparing Africans for the circumstances they confronted. Behind this, of course, lay the ensemble of discredited assumptions of the Euroamerican world regarding Africa and Africans.

Another trend to be noted among the new independent states was the formal declaration of a policy of "positive neutralism" or "non-alignment." The principal considerations that led African, like Asian,

leaders to take this position are fairly well known. Such considerations
as the enhanced security of this position, the opportunity to maximize
foreign aid through a diversification of foreign involvements, the
influence in world affairs they could exert, and the very genuine desire
to avoid African involvement in the Cold War, are fairly obvious. To
these must be added the strong urge to dramatize newly-won independence, to start with a clean slate unbiased by the prejudices of friends or
former masters.

There is another factor, however, that has special relevance in contemporary Africa. This is the political competition for mastery over
nationalist symbols among parties within competitive states, and for
leadership in the Pan-African movement among states within Africa.
Compared to other historic transformations in power relationships,
African States won their independence without much real struggle.
This left a profound sense of an uncompleted revolution, of the fact that
political independence really brought little change. Africa's continued
heavy dependence on the external world, and the absence of any visible
and dramatic progress, aggravated and deepened this sentiment. Given
this state of mind, the more radical, nationalist, Pan-Africanist elements
had a great advantage in the power struggle both within and among the
new states. As "neutralism" is essentially the external expression of
nationalism, any African leader that did not from time to time defy the
former imperial power on international issues, or warn of the ominous
threat of "neo-colonialism," laid himself open to the charge of selling
out the revolution or of being an "imperialist stooge."

What are the economic implications of this phenomenon, this fact
that the center of political gravity in Africa has seemed to lie in "pure"
neutralism? To the extent that neutralism brings greater security against
Cold War involvement, greater influence in contemporary world affairs,
and more aid from both sides of the Iron Curtain, one could argue that
it enhanced the capacity for economic growth, in addition to satisfying
a cherished craving for freedom of action. On the other hand, to the
extent that a sudden and dramatic shift to such a position meant the
sudden rupture of long-established economic ties with a particular
metropolitan country, the wholesale departure of experienced expatriate technicians and advisors willing to serve, just because they
were nationals of the former colonial power, and the abrupt cessation
of financial subsidies proferred by the former metropole for the transition period, it manifestly could have very serious consequences for
many of the new states. Except for Guinea, which deliberately and
precipitately opted for "pure" neutralism, all other African states to
varying degrees pursued a policy of gradualism in disentangling them-

selves from the network of ties that bound them to the former colonial country in an exclusive relationship of dependency.

The diversification of relationships of dependence on foreign countries is the logical consequence of a policy of neutralism. With the need of African states to draw heavily upon the external world, deliberate diversification is their only instrument for safeguarding themselves against being dominated by or under the influence of a single power. It makes it possible for them, despite their dependence, to feel completely independent. This is a factor of tremendous psychological importance. Moreover, it minimizes vulnerability in the many crosscutting power struggles that have developed within Africa itself.

3

Among the several currents of thought and political ideas found in contemporary Africa, at least two require brief analysis: Pan-Africanism and African Socialism. Pan-Africanism first emerged in the early part of this century as a movement for racial equality among American and West Indian Negroes. Following World War II, as Nkrumah has noted:

> Its ideology became African nationalism—a revolt by African nationalism against colonialism, racialism and imperialism in Africa—and it adopted Marxian socialism as its philosophy.[13]

During the agitation for national independence, pan-Africanism as an organized movement became moribund. African leaders in each territory and colonial system were fully occupied with the quest for self-government. During the period of agitation in the years of terminal colonialism, pan-Africanism was eclipsed by the ideology of territorial nationalism. With the attainment of independence by a large section of Africa, pan-Africanism emerged again as a dominant operative ideal. It continued to be a movement for "national" independence for areas of residual colonial or racial domination. For the African literati, especially as expressed in the concept of *négritude* developed by French-speaking Africans, it became a movement to vindicate African culture and to inculcate a consciousness of its essential dignity and equality with other cultures. For political leaders, with varying degrees of conviction and enthusiasm, it took its place as a movement for political unity.

Although virtually all politically conscious Africans have identified themselves as pan-Africanists, wide differences in meaning have been

[13] Nkrumah, Kwame, 1957, p. 53.

attached to the ideal. At least two types of contradiction or complications can be observed in the effort to realize the goals of pan-Africanism. One has been its entanglement with the personal or national aspirations of particular individuals or power systems. Given the pluralistic world power structure, in which sovereign states are the power units, the carriers must perforce be sovereign states. In contemporary Africa, the leaders of Ghana, Guinea and Mali have been the most articulate exponents of the ideal. Inevitably, it became difficult for other leaders in other states to distinguish between, let us say, the personal ambitions of President Nkrumah, the national interests of the state of Ghana, and the fact that he was merely using his prestige and the resources of his country to realize an ideal they all cherished.

The second contradiction in pan-Africanism is found in the lack of clarity as to whether it is a racial movement, or one for continental unity. Certainly in origin, it derived its main strength from the racial consciousness of persons of Subsaharan-African descent. There is very little evidence to suggest that it was not the memory of past indignities and inferior status, the craving for full acceptance, and the urge to vindicate African culture and the African past that provided the emotional enthusiasm for the pan-African ideal. If racial consciousness supplied the motive power, then the quest for continental unity, especially the effort to include the Arab North in the pan-African movement, must lack both substance and potential support. If, on the other hand, pan-Africanism was a revolutionary protest movement, then unity with all other protesting racial groups, both within and outside the African continent had a rationale. These two strands, with differing emphasis, are also found in the notion of *négritude*. This lack of clarity and agreement among pan-African spokesmen as to whether pan-Africanism is a pan-racial movement, like pan-Germanism or pan-Slavism, a pan-continental movement, like pan-Americanism or pan-Europeanism, or a pan-protestors movement, like pan-Asianism, has been one of the major obstacles to any serious advance being made to secure its goals. The fact that it incorporates multiple and contradictory goals illuminates at once its electicism and its inherent weaknesses.

Once this is stated, it is really quite remarkable how persistent and popular the pan-African ideal has remained among most politically-conscious Africans in the new states. This is explained partly by the fact that its core of strength, racial consciousness and assertiveness, has been undiminished, partly by the fact that the leading pan-Africanists have also been the most *avant-garde* in espousing "integral decolonization," and partly because of a growing awareness of both the crippling economic consequences of "balkanization" and the boundless opportunities for economic growth through unity. Whatever the explanation, it has come to be unquestionably the dominant ideology in post-colonial Africa.

If successful, the economic benefits of this vigorous quest for unity are so obvious they require no comment. If real political unity, the actual surrender of sovereignty, were achieved, the savings in government overhead resulting from "debalkanization" are equally obvious. Yet to these manifest advantages must be added two possibly negative consequences. One concerns Africa's association with associations of European states, the other relates to the internal power struggle within Africa. The reaction of Ghana and Nigeria to Britain's possible membership in the European Common Market, a case in point, was essentially negative. President Nkrumah stated the case in these words:

> A new threat has loomed up to the cause of African unity, no less ominous for being unobtrusive—the European Common Market. . . . We are most strongly opposed to an arrangement which uses the unification of Western Europe as a cloak for perpetuating colonial privileges in Africa. . . . The EEC, as at present conceived, will not only discriminate against Ghana and other independent States economically, but it will perpetuate by economic means the many artificial barriers imposed on Africa. Any form of economic union negotiated singly between the fully industrialized States of Europe and the newly emergent countries of Africa is bound to retard industrialization, and therefore prosperity and general development in these countries.[14]

There is here an admixture of special pleading for the Ghanaian economy, anti-colonialism, and fears regarding the unity of Africa, a relationship which is in itself illuminating. The relevant point is that insofar as the quest for African unity becomes a really significant factor leading to African opposition to association with groupings of ex-colonial powers, and if such opposition is sufficiently strong to persuade African states currently associated with them to withdraw, the crucial economic benefits enjoyed by such states would be lost. But given the fact that African economies are essentially competitive, it is doubtful whether the desire for unity in Africa, or the prospective economic rewards to be derived therefrom, have been thought to be sufficient to overcome the economic benefits of association.

Ironically, the quest for African unity could solidify certain cleavages that have appeared between African states. So long as there remained a common external "enemy," identified as "colonialism" or "neo-

[14] Nkrumah, K., 1961, p. 5.

colonialism," the impulse towards unity was understandably strong. Once the "enemy" no longer existed, a crucial element in pan-Africanism, the "revolutionary protest," and the "anti-colonial" strand ceased to be relevant. To the extent that African political unity thereafter continued to be a major ingredient in the foreign policy of certain African states, it could provoke resistance in other states. This factor has been undeniably present in the cleavage that occurred in 1961 between the "Casablanca" and the "Monrovia" powers. Unless manifest economic gains or other obvious rewards could be assured, the quest for unity, *qua* unity, was bound, as elsewhere, to generate tension between the doctrinaire unifiers and those leaders inclined towards a more pragmatic solution to their urgent national problems.

Here another factor enters. Most African leaders have called themselves "socialists," and have described their goal as the creation of a "socialist" society. This is not a distinctively African phenomenon; it has been common throughout the entire ex-colonial, indeed non-Euroamerican, world. The reasons are clear: the attractiveness of the Marxist-Leninist theory of imperialism as a simple clear-cut explanation of European colonialism, the intense exposure of colonials to left-wing groups in the metropolitan countries; the belief that socialism, or, better, "statism," is more appropriate for the conditions confronting economically underdeveloped countries than individualism and that it is a more effective means of rapid modernization; the justification of "elitism" which Marxist-Leninist theory provides, and even the fact that it was simply fashionable to be a socialist. We are not concerned here with this general phenomenon, but with two special facets of socialist ideology found in post-colonial Africa, namely, its eclecticism and its African character.

Hodgkin has rightly noted that "one marked characteristic of African national movements is their eclecticism—their habit of taking over ideas and terms which seem appropriate to their needs wherever they happen to find them."[15] The impact of Marxist ideas and language has been more marked among French-speaking than English-speaking Africans; the former having been influenced by the much more orthodox French Marxist parties, while the latter reflected the more pragmatic British Fabian tradition. Although African leaders from both traditions have used Marxist terms such as "vanguard" and "democratic centralism," nevertheless their concept of the "mass party," their insistence upon the primacy of Negro-African values as found in the notions of *négritude* and "African personality," their rejection of the class-struggle because it is nonexistent in African societies, and their nonacceptance

[15] Hodgkin, T., 1961, p. 29.

of many other Marxian presuppositions represented rather striking departures from, or at most adaptations of, orthodox Marxism.

The most marked feature of their socialist eclecticism has been their emphasis on the determinative importance of African values and the distinctiveness of African conditions. Indeed, the notion of "African Socialism" has seemed to command general acceptance, except among the few doctrinaire Marxists repelled by its racist implications. Nkrumah has put it this way:

> Our Party is great and strong because we aim for a socialist pattern of society. We are the Party of the workers, the farmers and all progressive elements in our community and we will remain faithful to the principles that guide us in *evolving our own Ghanaian* pattern of Socialist Society.[16]

Senghor, who developed the idea of an "African Socialism" more fully, has insisted that communal socialism was characteristic of traditional Negro-African societies, and that this provides the basis for a modern socialist society.[17] These examples make it clear how socialist ideology in contemporary Africa has been affected by the far more pervasive sense of racial consciousness, by a belief in the distinctiveness of African culture, and by the desire to exemplify neutrality through the refusal to borrow other systems indiscriminately. The implications of this eclecticism and Africanism have been that in actual practice, African socialism tends to be quite pragmatic, a characteristic that is a distinct asset in the efforts of African leaders to modernize their societies.

4

Two striking features have characterized the internal political organization of newly independent African states; the trend towards the emergence and consolidation of one-party systems, and bureaucratic centralism. With the exception of Nigeria, the Republic of the Congo and Cameroun Republic, all of the newly independent states became either single-party systems or were dominated by one party. In some cases, such as Guinea, Mali, and the Ivory Coast, the new state had a one-party system at the time it achieved independence; in other instances, as with Ghana, Togo, Dahomey, and Senegal, the majority party which inherited power progressively established what became in effect a one-party system. As a result of this general trend, an increasing body of African political theory rationalizing the one-party (*parti unique*, or *parti unifié*) system was propounded. Here we are concerned with the reasons for this trend, as well as the character of these systems.

[16] Nkrumah, K., *op. cit.*, p. 6.   [17] Senghor, L. S., 1959, p. 32.

There are several reasons for this general trend toward one-party systems. A major one was the extreme fragility of central institutions. These were the last to be created, to be Africanized, and to be endowed with legitimacy. Until shortly before self-government, they remained the preserve of the colonial bureaucracy and the ultimate symbol of alien control. Hence, it was the nationalist party leadership, functioning outside the formal structures of government, which commanded popular respect and allegiance. At the time of the transfer of power, indeed, the party was the only structure through which the new leadership was able to hold the new nation together. Sékou Touré has made this point quite emphatically:

> Behind the State there is something higher, which is the Party . . . if the Party does not function well, the State of Guinea cannot function well either, for it would be deprived of suitable control and direction of the masses. Consequently, as long as the Party remains solidly organized, the Government itself will always remain an efficient instrument in the service of the country.[18]

One is reminded of Nkrumah's admonition in this same vein, that "The Convention People's Party is Ghana and Ghana is the Convention People's Party."

Once it acquired power at the time of independence, the single party or the majority party, as the case may be, possessed the means either to prevent or to suppress opposition groups. In such monolithic one-party systems as Guinea and Mali, the very existence of an opposition party was made illegal. In other states where the majority party progressively consolidated its control, three types of strategies were used. One involved intimidation, prosecution on frivolous charges, nonauthorization of public meetings, and the like, all designed to make effective political action by opposition groups difficult if not impossible. The second strategy was to use patronage to "buy off" opposition leaders. The third was the distribution of such amenities as roads, piped water, hospitals, and schools in such a way that constituencies supporting the opposition were either deprived or less favorably treated.

Confronted with these disabilities, lacking resources to carry on meaningful political action, and weakened by the sense of the complete futility of either achieving power or obtaining benefits for supporters or constituencies, leaders of the opposition either joined the dominant mass party, or withdrew from political activity. This explains two other features of these party systems; the very substantial number of opposition leaders serving within the dominant party, and the fact that

[18] *Op. cit.*, p. 36.

most dominant parties came to embrace within their fold a wide spectrum of interests, associations, and ideological viewpoints.

African leaders have devoted considerable attention to rationalizing the existence of the one-party state, a major argument being that it is more appropriate to present circumstances than the multiple-party system. In the words of Madeira Keita:

> We realized that in the existing historical circumstances of Africa it was . . . extremely difficult with these coalition governments to assume the responsibility for the management of public affairs with any chance of success . . . there is no need to multiply parties, there is no need to give oneself the luxury of sterile and fratricidal opposition, there is no need to give ourselves a ministerial crisis every three months.[19]

This conviction that more than one party was unnecessary was buttressed by another argument, namely, that the differentiation of interests in Africa was either nonexistent or, at least, was not very sharp:

> Philosophical problems, religious problems, problems of ideology do not divide us. The only aspiration which animates us is the rapid march towards liberty. The only aspiration, the only determination which inspires us is that of being able to establish a State mechanism at the service of economic development, of social and cultural development.[20]

The crucial point here, as one African put it, is "that except for advocacy of sub-state nationalism, the 'outs' have no distinguishable platform to canvass; the 'ins' already canvass development and modernity."

To the foregoing has been added the argument that the idea of an official opposition was completely alien to the traditionally democratic African society. "There was open discussion and unanimity, not government by a majority." Even more significant is the proposition that democracy does not require inter-party competition; as Sékou Touré, Madeira Keita, and other African leaders have argued, within the party there can be discussion, self-criticism or, indeed, competition of ideas and talent. Moreover, they claim that maximum initiative devolves upon local and intermediate councils. Throughout their apologia has run the insistence that "African" one-party systems are democratic.

The second striking feature of the internal political organization of Africa's new states has been the heavy concentration of the power to make decisions within the central party executive or the bureaucracy,

---

[19] Keita, M., 1960, pp. 33ff.
[20] *Ibid.*, p. 36.

in many systems one and the same. This concentration has been much more marked in French-speaking Africa, partly because single parties in those states have tended to be more monolithic, but also because of the French legacy of centralism, statism, and the Napoleonic tradition of abhorring *"corps intermédiaire."* In contrast, the British effort to build up "native authorities," or local government bodies, endowed with a measure of local responsibility, was a restraint on this centralizing tendency; yet even here one finds that local councils have increasingly been subjected to firm central control.

What must be stressed here is that this bureaucratic centralism and "statist" mentality represents to a very considerable degree continuity rather than innovation. The brief experiment with parliamentary democracy in the terminal colonial period in most of the new states was just sufficient to politicize their cultural pluralism; it was certainly far from adequate to habituate even the politically relevant strata of the population to the process of reconciling interests and making public policy through an open democratic system. Colonialism in Africa was bureaucratic authoritarianism, controlled by an elite of the "elect." Government was regarded as "administration"; the people were the "administrés"; and politics, especially opposition politics, were barely tolerated until the terminal stages of colonial control.

PART SIX

Some Suggestions
for
Future Research

19

The Conference Discussions

by Melville J. Herskovits
Northwestern University

The discussions of the Conference were marked by a sense of the need to take full account of continuities in analyzing the economics of contemporary Africa. It became apparent that many values and mechanisms of the induced economic complex had their analogues in aboriginal practice, and that the factor of adjustment of older patterns through reinterpretation to fit new orientations could not be neglected. The comment of Jones about the treatment of the induced phenomena of contact, makes the point: "None of the papers offers evidence of the existence of Marshall's savages. . . . Far from being the conservative, unenterprising profligate men of fiction, the new Africans appear to be if anything, a little overly venturesome and overly profit-minded."

The gaps in the discussion of the economic picture of Africa in change that are to be found in the work of the Conference were perhaps inevitable, given the vastness of the field, and the implications for African modes of life of the responses that were made to the induced elements. On the other hand, many of the contributions, especially those found in the second and third Sections of this volume, take us to areas of activity that do not ordinarily enter into discussions of economics, but must be considered where economies based on a sparse technology and a concomitantly limited degree of specialization are under study. Succeeding chapters turn to more conventional economic problems, and put to one side consideration of their sociological and humanistic repercussions. This shift in focus is related to the fact that the newer African economies have become more specialized as they take on the characteristics of the impersonal, industrialized systems of world-wide scope into which Africa, like other technologically "underdeveloped" areas, is being ingested.

Though consensus is inevitably qualified in the discussion of specialists who come from different fields, and where formal agreement is not an objective, it was clear that in this Conference there were few who would dissent from the proposition that to understand the contemporary economies of Africa, the indigenous components must be accorded a larger place than they have been given. Certain facets of the problems that entered into the discussion would not change this conclusion, since they are tangential to the cross-disciplinary aspect of the approach. Thus, while the materials from that part of Subsaharan Africa which may be termed francophonic—that is, the countries that made up the former French West and Equatorial Africa, and the Republic of the Congo—were given less attention than they deserved, it is doubtful if economic adaptation in these countries sufficiently differs from those in the anglophonic territories to affect the over-all picture materially.

Some of the questions that arose out of the discussions suggest promising leads for future research. Resolution of particular ones, such as that regarding the nature of the pecuniary systems of pre-colonial Africa, is essential to an understanding of the transitions that took place during the colonial period. Thus, for example, the position of Schneider that, for the Turu of Kenya, livestock are a medium of exchange that can be equated with money has implications of considerable consequence when we seek to understand the adjustment of other cattle-keeping peoples to a system where currency is the primary medium of exchange. More research like that of Grévisse into the use of salt bars in the southeastern Congo[1] is needed to clarify the nature and functioning of pecuniary instruments in the aboriginal cultures of Africa. Quantitative data on money and trade found in the early travel literature about the western Sudan which were mentioned by Skinner in this discussion, may offer another lead. Above all, systematic study of the materials contained in ethnographic and travel literature, done on a broad comparative level, should not only clarify questions dealing with the adjustment of Africans to the new elements in their economies, but provide materials of prime theoretical significance.

Another problem that has been but lightly treated concerns the nature and the significance of internal trade in African countries. The chapter by Katzin indicates some of the implications of studies in this sector. She underscores the need for further study when she makes it clear that the field research which underlay her treatment of one aspect of this problem can be supported by reference to the work of but few other investigators. In terms of analysing the more monetized economies of the colonial and post-colonial period, the same need is made apparent in the chapters by Berg, Barber and Chudson. There is little question that the problem is one where field study is essential. As has been dis-

[1] Grévisse, F., 1950.

covered by historians who are concerned with the African past, the available documents do not provide the kind of data that the study of internal trade requires. Here, perhaps more than in any other aspect of African economics, the field methods of the anthropologist must be welded to the conceptual apparatus of the economist, both being utilized with sufficient flexibility to allow the student to profit from the contributions of each discipline without imposing elements from either that are not relevant to the particular situation under study.

There are some data, but not too many, on the nature of the internal trade grid. The relation of the petty trader to the supplier, and of this middleman to the European firms or African agricultural producers, has been described, more or less casually, for a number of countries. Perhaps one of the greatest opportunities for research into the dynamics of this exchange sector, on the local level, is to be found in eastern and southern Africa, where markets operating on a pecuniary base represent a distinct innovation. At the turn of the twentieth century, few if any such centers existed. Their later development was rapid. The nature of the transactions consummated in them, the aggregate amounts involved, the canons of business enterprise that developed, the reasons why traders go into the market, the degree of their commitment in terms of full or partial time given to trading, and the allocation of the market to men and women traders, are only a few of the areas for study in this newly developing aspect of economic activity.

The interrelations between political and economic change were given considerable attention. The validity of Fallers' formulation, that economic structures and processes in Africa are contained within political structures and processes, was apparent in the consideration of the larger aspects of economic growth, but its applicability to studies of internal operations did not enter. While it is obvious that the economic policies of the new African states regarding foreign trade and investment, taxation and economic controls are functions of the political scene, it is by no means understood how this relationship determines the details of government policy having to do with trade, or agriculture, or the encouragement of capital accumulation, and the effects of such policies and their implementation in various African countries. As in the case of the problems posed in the preceding paragraph, the question is one of initiating a shift in method. Field study is once more the only answer; field study which, if carried out in enough countries of Subsaharan Africa, can be aggregated to further our understanding of this important aspect of African economies.

Two further problem-areas may be mentioned here. One of these is the way in which the factor of multiracialism impinges on the economies, more especially, but not entirely, of the countries in eastern and southern Africa. The second concerns the relation between the size of a country, both in terms of its physical dimensions and demographic magnitude, and its viability.

This latter question is more discussed than studied and, except in extreme cases such as the Gambia, the existence of a relation between size and viability is taken more as an article of faith than as a problem for research. Admittedly the number of variables potentially involved makes the study of this relationship difficult; but the fact that it enters into so many discussions of African economies is sufficient reason for attempting to delimit and define the concept and detail its applicability.

Multiracialism entered only tangentially into Conference discussions, since it is customarily regarded as essentially a sociological problem. Yet this factor, which is ubiquitous in all countries of the eastern half of Africa from Kenya to South Africa, does have major impact on their economies. This is implicit, in the reiterated statements, usually made by non-Africans, that agitation by Africans for self-government, or for participation in the government of the countries in which they live, will frighten away foreign capital. The racial factor was the cause of the withdrawal of South Africa from the Commonwealth in 1960, a move whose economic repercussions were immediately apparent.

It is not on this level alone, however, that the racial factor has been a significant element in shaping the economies of these countries. It is particularly important in all questions touching on the work-force. A considerable literature exists concerning labor recruitment and labor migration, especially as this affects their economic repercussions. These are customarily considered in terms of the effect of the withdrawal of manpower from the rural areas on agricultural productivity, or, conversely, in terms of the contribution which remittances, gifts and the like have made to the rural economy. It would be very useful to carry out controlled research into problems that arise out of the organization of labor, the place of Africans and Europeans in the hierarchy of jobs, the limitations on geographical no less than job mobility, and above all, into the motivational aspect of African and European responses to this situation. Study of the rigid system of supervision of the African labor force in a city such as Johannesburg can not only throw light on other African situations subject to less control, but can be of value for the field of labor economics in general.

The comments of Kuznets in the final session of the Conference structured the problems to be faced in studying African economic growth in terms of their historical and functional dimensions. He suggested examination, first of the surviving indigenous elements in changing African economies, then of the responses of these economies to the impact of the impinging economic systems of the colonial powers, and finally, of the implications of the data for assessing future growth.

We may shape the study of African economic development along those lines, which correspond to the frame within which the discussions of the Conference were developed. The subject can thus be viewed as a series of phenomena resulting from the interaction of indigenous and induced elements that combined to make the African economies what they were at a given historical moment. It follows that if such analysis is to achieve significant results, both earlier and later components must be fully taken into account. Thus it is essential, in studying any aspect of African national economies, whether of independent countries or colonial territories, to assess the significance of the fact that all of them are made up of small tribal or ethnic elements, which in the pre-colonial period were autonomous, though under varying degrees of centralized control, and which have continued in some measure to retain the loyalties of their people. The fact that post-colonial Africa was subject to a process of political fragmentation, frequently called "balkanization," which represents a carryover of the arbitrary lines along which boundaries were drawn by the powers participating in the partition of Africa, cannot be neglected. Its importance is compounded when we see that the indigenous populations were, and in many cases have continued to be, small in relation to the areas they occupy and the natural resources they control.

An important indigenous element is the nature of the agricultural sector of African economies. That this was everywhere a major, if not the dominant, component in the earlier systems, is well recognized. What is most significant for us, however, is the economic structures on which these systems were based, particularly those that arose out of the relation between kinship and land tenure, or from the patterns of sex division of labor. More information is needed about the relatively sophisticated ways of effecting economic exchanges under the system of markets found in certain parts of the continent. Finally, it is necessary to take into account those forms of dominance in the aboriginal political structures whereby social differentiation bolstered the political power needed to manage the economy.

Following on the study of indigenous elements must come the analysis of existing orientations. Here colonial influences bulk large. What, we must ask, was the effect of colonial status on the indigenous economic systems and on the shape of those that took their place? What was the range of variation and the differing influence of the several systems under which Africans came to live? The changes involved in these transitions, it is clear, pervaded many aspects of the economy. To cite but one example, we may point to the imposition of new forms of land holding and of control over the ownership and use of land. The facts concerning the state of development of an infrastructure for the newer economy, and the extent to which planned projects in the fields of communication, transportation, education, power and the like were implemented, have yet to be brought together and analyzed.

Kuznets pointed out that our knowledge of African involvement in the network of foreign trade is in certain respects imperfect. Thus, for example, facts concerning the structure of foreign—that is, "expatriate"—producing agencies have not been aggregated, so that we only see a partial picture. Another question has to do with the theories of the relation between the state and economic growth that were developed concomitantly with the various nationalist movements. What, in the economic field, was the ideological influence of the European political movements with which the Africans came into contact? And in what ways have the newly constituted African governments moved after independence to implement the position taken as a result of these contacts? The role played in the formation of economic policy by the idea of "African socialism," a phrase so frequently heard on the lips of African politicians, is opened as an area of investigation in the chapter by Coleman.

The emergence of a trading class under the innovative economic system also has important implications. In western and central Africa, markets for intra-tribal exchanges were a fixture in the earlier economies, and the major induced elements were the fixed monetary standards to which the traders had to accommodate themselves and the intensification of specialization in the society, which gave traders new status by making many of them full-time businessmen. But in aboriginal eastern and southern Africa, among the herding peoples, specialization was rudimentary and trading minimal. Yet even here, the analogy between certain aspects of these little-specialized economies and some of the concepts of the intruding economic systems is patent. It obviously must have facilitated adjustment, and gives added reason for detailed study of this emerging trading class, found everywhere in Africa south of the Sahara.

As concerns questions having to do with future developments in the economies of Africa, Kuznets pointed out that it is important, because of the position of the agricultural sector of African economies, to assess its potential for economic growth; and, similarly, to examine the role which the increasing stress on small-scale industry will play. What requirements of the infrastructure must be met as African countries allocate resources to long-term projects? What are potentials for the development of large-scale industry, and the creation of export markets for its products? The relation between the political elite and the masses, particularly as this may be affected by the development of an urban proletariat under the impact of industrialization and urbanization, is also something to be anticipated. And finally, the various conceptions of what constitutes economic growth, and the ends that Africans seek as they promote it or are subject to it, must be expected to influence future patterns significantly.

These suggestions for research into the nature of African economic growth were supplemented by numerous suggestions arising from questions raised during Conference discussions. In considering the patterns of communalism that mark African life, and that have been of major importance in influencing the adaptation of Africans to the induced elements in their economies, Fallers, like Schneider in his chapter, suggested that on the level of microeconomic study, corporate kin groups could be considered as analogous to the firms of Euroamerican economies. Berg stressed the need to take into account intra-societal rates of change. Particularly in the study of indigenous market systems, such factors as the degree of competition, modes of entry into the market, and the effects of price-changes, merited greater attention by anthropologists than they have been given. On the other hand, Schneider pointed out the handicaps posed by an enthnocentrism that caused too close an application of Euroamerican economic concepts to the African scene, and suggested that there was need to recognize the rational character of the observed reactions of Africans to changes in their aboriginal economies.

This was somewhat along the line followed by Lorimer, who made the point that indigenous economies must not be thought of as static; that to describe a dichotomy between "static" aboriginal systems and "dynamic" induced ones was fallacious. In the African context, he contended, the function of the economist was to be concerned with existing economic institutions, and particularly to seek to understand the linkages between them, lest research be ordered by a distorted institutional framework. Chudson, carrying further Lorimer's caution, pointed out that the categories of indigenous and induced economic elements that framed the Conference discussions must not be taken to correspond to the more customary categories of underdeveloped and developed economies.

Much attention, especially in the concluding session, was paid to the methodological implications of a cross-disciplinary approach in studying the economies of Africa. Bohannan pointed out that social scientists tend to be constricted in their thinking by the ready-made categories of their disciplines, or those derived from related disciplines. He asserted that though the information in the studies anthropologists make in pursuit of their own problems is useful to those in other fields, anthropologists are not "information mongers" who can be used to search out data needed to pursue investigations in different fields. This was complementary to the position taken by Kuznets, that economists are not "suppliers of data" in the sense that they experience very real difficulties in obtaining the quantitative raw materials for their studies of African economic growth.

The question of interdisciplinary relationships was pursued farther. Schneider indicated that, in general, anthropologists have looked at their data in terms of equilibrium of roles and have tried to encompass within this framework the economic elements in the lives of the peoples they study, even where the dynamics of culture contact are in play. Harwitz introduced the concepts of macro- and microeconomics in this connection. Macroeconomies are to be thought of as an aggregation of microeconomies, with the entry of anthropology at the "micro" level. If we take the study of the market as an instance, we find that anthropological investigators tend to center on the equilibrium of roles played in the market rather than on the dynamics of the economic behaviour of participants, and thus handicap attempts to bring the resulting data into the realm of economic theory. Kuznets approached the question from a somewhat different point of view. What economists do in aggregating data from an indigenous society may involve bringing together materials that are not comparable. Anthropologists, and those in other relevant social science disciplines, can be of help in pointing out when this occurs. And Williamson introduced a further dimension when he urged the utility of employing the analytical tools of economic history in studying growth, development and change in African economies.

He also brought up a theme that had been implicit in the work of the Conference, but only was made explicit at the end. This had to do with the two ways in which the economic problems of Africa are approached; theoretical, wherein economists act as "philosophers," as he put it, and the practical, wherein the economist acts as planner. This was phrased by Moore in broader terms, as exemplifying the difficulty posed when the scholar is confronted with questions of policy that involve subjective evaluation, and thus move him from the area of analysis to that of action. Yet as Henry showed, these two are in many cases inextricably intertwined. This is to be seen in a project in Senegal, where micro-economic studies of villages were made in order to build a program of economic development. He brought the political factor back into the discussion by indicating its role in shaping aid programs, whether in the dimension of time or in that of practicality.

In this search for a broad base for approaches to the problems of African economic growth, both problems and methods of interdisciplinary attack were clarified. In essence, the question that was posed could be put in somewhat this way: How can a discipline, to which a holistic and cross-cultural point of view is basic, contribute comparative materials to the work of another which, because of world development, has had to cope with specialized data from industrialized societies; and *vice versa,* how can a specialized discipline, with techniques for conceptualizing one aspect of human activity, contribute insights to those who study culture in general, and in the process recognize the importance of the economic, or political, or demographic or historical components? It was apparent, in the final session in particular, that aside from the substantive data in the papers an approach to resolution of this issue may stand as the principal contribution of the Conference, not only to the study of African economies, but to the broader comparative effort to understand economic development in world-wide compass.

Bibliography

ADDAE, GLORIA, 1956: "The Retailing of Imported Textiles in Accra Market." *Proceedings*, 3rd Annual Conference, West African Institute of Social and Economic Research, pp. 5–57. Ibadan.

ADY, PETER, 1949: "Trends in Cocoa Production." *Bulletin of the Oxford University Institute of Statistics*, vol. 2, pp. 389–404.

—, 1953: "Fluctuations in Incomes of Primary Producers: A Comment." *The Economic Journal*, vol. 64, pp. 730–743.

—, 1960: "Cocoa Marketing in French West Africa." *West Africa*, nos. 2245–2247 (June 11, 18, 25).

Afrique Occidentale Française, 1950: *Annuaire Statistique de l'Afrique Occidentale Française* (Ed. 1949, vol. 1). Paris.

—, 1951: *Annuaire Statistique de l'Afrique Occidentale Francaise*, vol. 2. Paris.

—, Gouvernement-Generale de, Service de la Statistique Générale, n.d.: *Le Pouvoir d'Achat du Franc du Territoire à Diverses Epoques en A. O. F.* Dakar, mimeographed.

—, Haut-Commissariat de la Republique en, 1950: *Annuaire Statistique de l'Afrique Occidentale Française* (Ed. 1949, 2 vols.). Paris.

—, —, 1956: *Annuaire Statistique de l'Afrique Occidentale Française*, 1950–1954. Paris.

—, —, 1959: *AOF 1957: Tableaux Economiques*. Dakar.

ALBERT, ETHEL, 1960: "Une étude de valeurs en Urundi." *Cahiers d'Études Africaines*, vol. 2, pp. 147–160.

AMOGU, O. O., 1956: "Some Notes on Savings in an African Economy." *Social and Economic Studies*, vol. 5, pp. 202–209.

APTER, DAVID E., 1954: "Some Economic Factors in the Political Development of the Gold Coast." *Journal of Economic History*, vol. 14, pp. 409–427.

—, and Coleman, James S., 1962: "Pan-Africanism and Nationalism." Manuscript.

ARNOLD, ROSEMARY, 1957: "A Port of Trade: Whydah on the Guinea Coast," in *Trade and Market in the Early Empires* (Polanyi, Karl, Arensberg, C. M., and Pearson, Harry, eds.), pp. 154–176. New York.

AUBREY, H. C., 1951: "Small Industry in Economic Development." *Social Research*, vol. 18, pp. 269–312.

—, 1955: "Investment Decisions in Underdeveloped Countries," in *Capital Formation and Economic Growth*, National Bureau of Economic Research, pp. 397–440. Princeton.

BALANDIER, GEORGES, 1952a: "La Main d'Oeuvre chez Firestone-Libérie." *Présence Africaine*, vol. 13, pp. 347–354.

—, 1952b: "Le Developpement Industriel et la Proletarisation en Afrique Noire." *Afrique et Asie*, vol. 20, pp. 45–53.

—, 1958: "Problemes du Developpement Economique et Social de l'Afrique Noire." *Récherches et Débats du Centre Catholique des Intellectuels Français*, vol. 24, pp. 117–125.

BALDWIN, K. D. S., 1957: *The Niger Agricultural Project, An Experiment in African Development*. Oxford.

Banque Centrale des États de l'Afrique de l'Ouest, 1959: "La contribution financière du Royaume-Uni au developpement des autres pays du Commonwealth." *Note d'Information*, No. 57.

—, 1960 *Comptes Économiques du Mali: Études Économiques Ouest Africaines*, Fasc. 1.

—, 1961a: "L'évolution des dépenses publiques de 1950 à 1958 dans quelques pays Africains sous l'administration française." *Note de' Information*, No. 71.

—, 1961b: *Rapport d'Activité*, 1960.

BARBER, W. J., 1961: *The Economy of British Central Africa: A Case Study of Economic Development in a Dualistic Society*. Stanford.

BARTH, H., 1859: *Travels and Discoveries in North and Central Africa* (3 vols.). New York.

BASCOM, WM. R., 1952: "The Esusu: A Credit Institution of the Yoruba." *Journal of the Royal Anthropological Institute*, vol. 82, pp. 63–69.

—, 1959: "Urbanization as a Traditional African Pattern." *The Sociological Review*, n.s., vol. 7, pp. 29–43.

BATTEN, T. R., 1954: *Problems of African Development*. London.

BAUER, P. T., 1954a: "Statistics of Statutory Marketing in West Africa, 1939–1951." *Journal of the Royal Statistical Society*, Series A (General), vol. 117, pp. 1–30.

—, 1954b: *West African Trade*. London.

—, 1957: *Economic Analysis and Policy in Underdeveloped Countries*. London.

BAUMANN, HERMANN, 1928: "The Division of Work According to Sex in African Hoe Culture." *Africa*, vol. 1, pp. 289–319.

BERG, ELLIOT J., 1959: "French West Africa," in *Labor and Economic Development* (W. Galenson, ed.), pp. 186–259. New York.

—, 1960: "The Economic Basis of Political Choice in French West Africa." *The American Political Science Review*, vol. 54, pp. 391–405.

—, 1961: "Backward-Sloping Labor Supply Functions in Dual Economies —the African Case." *Quarterly Journal of Economics*, vol. 75, pp. 468–492.

BERREMAN, G. D., 1960: "Caste in India and the United States." *American Journal of Sociology*, vol. 66, pp. 120–127.

BERTRAND, R., 1956: "Construction et emploi d'un indice du rapport d'échange pour l'Afrique Occidentale Française." *Révue Économique*, vol. 7, pp. 280–307.

BEYRARD, N., 1960: *Étude sur la reform fiscale de la Côte d'Ivoire*. Abidjan, mimeographed.

BINGER, LOUIS G., 1892: *Du Niger au Golfe de Guinée* (2 vols.). Paris.

BIOBAKU, S. O., 1952: "Historical Sketch of Egba Traditional Authorities." *Africa*, vol. 22, pp. 35–49.

BIRMINGHAM, WALTER, 1960: "An Index of Real Wages of the Accra Labourer, 1939–1959." *Bulletin of the Economic Society of Ghana*, vol. 4, pp. 2–6.

BOHANNAN, LAURA AND PAUL, 1953: *The Tiv of Central Nigeria* (Ethnographic Survey of Africa, Western Africa, Part VIII). London.

BOHANNAN, PAUL J., 1954a: "Migration and Expansion of the Tiv." *Africa*, vol. 24, pp. 2–16.

—, 1954b: *Tiv Farm and Settlement*. London.

—, 1957: *Justice and Judgment among the Tiv*. London.

—, 1959: "The Impact of Money on an African Subsistence Economy." *The Journal of Economic History*, vol. 19, pp. 491–503.

BOVILL, E. W., 1958: *The Golden Trade of the Moors*. London.

BOWER, PENELOPE, 1948: "The Mining Industry," in *Economics of a Tropical Dependency*, Vol. II, *Mining, Commerce and Finance in Nigeria* (Margery Perham, ed.), pp. 1–42. London.

BRADBURY, R. E., 1957: *The Benin Kingdom*. London.

BRELSFORD, W. V., 1947: *Copperbelt Markets*. Lusaka.

BROZEN, YALE, 1954: "Determinants of Entrepreneurial Ability." *Social Research*, vol. 22, pp. 339–364.

BROWN, L. H., 1957: "Development and Farm Planning in the African Areas of Kenya." *East African Agricultural Journal*, vol. 23, pp. 67–73.

BURDEN, G. N., 1951: "Labour Migration in Africa." *Corona*, vol. 3, pp. 55–58, 100–102.

BUSIA, K. A., 1951: *The Position of the Chief in the Modern Political System of the Ashanti*. London.

BUTT, AUDREY, 1952: *The Nilotes of the Anglo-Egyptian Sudan and Uganda*. London.

CAILLE, RÈNE, 1830: *Travels through Central Africa to Timbuktu* (2 vols.). London.

CALLAWAY, ARCH C., 1961: "School Leavers in Nigeria." *West Africa*, Nos. 2886–2889.

CARREIRA, ANTONIO, 1948: "Problemas do Trabalho Indigena no Colonia da Guinéa." *Bolletim Geral das Côlonias*, vol. 24, pp. 35–62.

CHEVALIER, AUGUSTE, 1909: "Dans le nord de la Côte d'Ivoire." *La Geographie*, vol. 20, pp. 25–29.

CLAYTON, E. S., 1959: "Safeguarding Agrarian Development in Kenya." *Journal of African Administration*, vol. 11, pp. 144–150.

CLEMENCE, R. V. AND DOODY, F. S., 1950: *The Schumpeterian System*. Cambridge (Massachusetts).

COALE, A. J. AND HOOVER, E. M., 1958: *Population Growth and Economic Development in Low-Income Countries*. Princeton.

COLE, A. H., 1959: *Business Enterprise in its Social Setting*. Cambridge (Massachusetts).

COLEMAN, JAMES S., 1961: "The Legal Aspect of Staff Problems in Tropical and Subtropical Countries," in *Staff Problems in Tropical and Subtropical Countries* (International Institute of Differing Civilizations), pp. 477–493. Brussels.

—, and Brice, Belmont, 1961: "The Role of the Military in Sub-saharan Africa." Manuscript.

COLSON, ELIZABETH, 1951: "The Role of Cattle among the Plateau Tonga." *The Rhodes-Livingstone Journal*, No. 11, pp. 10–46.

—, 1954: "Ancestral Spirits and Social Structure among the Plateau Tonga." *International Archives of Ethnography*, vol. 47, pp. 21–68.

—, and Gluckman, Max (eds.), 1951: *Seven Tribes of British Central Africa*. London.

COMHAIRE, JEAN L., 1956: "Economic Change and the Extended Family." *Annals of the American Academy of Political and Social Science*, vol. 305, pp. 45–52.

COMHAIRE-SYLVAIN, S., 1951: "Le Travail des Femmes à Lagos, Nigeria." *Zaire*, vol. 5, pp. 169–187, 475–502.

COOK, ARTHUR N., 1943: *British Enterprise in Nigeria*. Philadelphia.

CORNEVIN, ROBERT, 1956: *Histoire de l'Afrique*. Paris.

Côte d'Ivoire, Gouverneur, 1958: *Rapport présenté à la session budgetaire 1957 de l'Assemblée Territoriale*. Abidjan.

—, Inspection Territoriale de Travail, 1947: *Rapport Annuel, 1946*. Abidjan, mimeographed.

—, —, 1952: *Rapport Annuel, 1951*. Abidjan, mimeographed.

—, Service de la Statistique, 1957–1962: *Bulletin Statistique Mensuel*. Abidjan (?)

—, —, 1958a: *Inventaire Économique de la Côte d'Ivoire, 1947–1956*. Abidjan.

—, —, 1958b: *Les budgets familiaux des salariés africaines en Abidjan (Août–Septembre 1956)*. Abidjan.

—, —, 1958c: *Enquête Nutrition—Niveau de Vie: Subdivision de Bongouanou 1955–1956*. Paris.

—, —, 1959(?): *Inventaire économique de la Côte d'Ivoire, 1947–1958*. Abidjan.

—, —, 1961: *La Situation Économique de la Côte d'Ivoire en 1960*. Abidjan.

COYAND, YVES, 1956: "La Culture du riz à l'Office du Niger." *Riz et riziculture*, 2e année, 4e trimestre.

CURTIS, L., 1937: *Civitas Dei*. London.

DALTON, GEORGE, 1961: "Economic Theory and Primitive Society." *American Anthropologist*, vol. 63, pp. 1–25.

DEAN, PHYLLIS, 1953: *Colonial Social Accounting*. Cambridge (England).

DE BRIEY, P., 1955: "The Productivity of African Labour." *International Labour Review*, vol. 72, pp. 119–139.

DELAROZIÈRE, R., 1950: "Étude de la stabilité de la population de la subdivision de Fefoussam pendant les années 1946 et 1947." *Études Camerounaises*, vol. 3, pp. 137–187.

DENHAM, D. AND CLAPPERTON, H., 1825: *Narrative of Travels and Discoveries in Northern and Central Africa in the Years 1822, 1823, and 1824.* New York.

DE SCHLIPPE, PIERRE, 1956: *Shifting Cultivation in Africa, the Zande System of Agriculture.* London.

DEYRUP, FELICIA J., 1957: "Limits of Government Activity in Underdeveloped Countries." *Social Research*, vol. 24, pp. 191–201.

DIKE, KENNETH ONWUKA, 1956: *Trade and Politics in the Niger Delta, 1830–1885.* Oxford.

DOUCY, ARTHUR, 1954: "Le Role des Influences coutumières sur les travailleurs indigènes du Congo Belge." *Révue de l'Institut de Sociologie*, vol. 4, pp. 817–830.

DUBOIS, FELIX, 1879: *Tombouctou, la mysterieuse.* Paris.

DUPIRE, MARGUERITE, 1956: "Organisation Sociale du Travail dans la Palmeraie Adioukrou (Basse Côte d'Ivoire)." *Revue de l'Institut de Sociologie*, vol. 2/3, pp. 271–292.

East African Royal Commission, 1955: *Report* (Cmd. 9475). London.

EASTERBROOK, W. T., 1949: "The Climate of Enterprise." *American Economic Review*, vol. 39, pp. 322–335.

ELKAN, WALTER, 1956: *An African Labour Force.* Kampala.

—, 1958: "The East African Trade in Wood Carvings." *Africa*, vol. 28, pp. 314–323.

—, and Fallers, Lloyd A., 1960: "The Mobility of Labor," in *Labor Commitment and Social Change in Developing Areas* (Moore, Wilbert E. and Feldmen, Arnold J., eds.), pp. 238–257. New York.

European Economic Community, Office Statistiques, 1961: *Informations Statistiques*, January–March, No. 1.

EVANS-PRITCHARD, E. E., 1953: "The Sacrificial Role of Cattle Among the Nuer." *Africa*, vol. 23, pp. 181–198.

EZEABASILI, A. N., 1960: "The Ibo in Town and Tribe." *African World* (April), pp. 8, 10, 12.

FAGE, J. D., 1959: *Ghana, A Historical Perspective.* Madison (Wisc.).

FAHM, L. A., 1962: "Capital Formation, Balance of Payments, and Absorption Capacity in Ghana and Nigeria," in *Pan-Africanism Reconsidered* (American Society of African Culture, ed.), pp. 169–187. Berkeley and Los Angeles.

FALLERS, LLOYD, 1959: "Despotism, Status Culture and Social Mobility in an African Kingdom." *Comparative Studies in Society and History*, vol. 2, pp. 11–32.

—, 1961: "Are African Cultivators to be Called 'Peasants'?" *Current Anthropology*, vol. 2, pp. 108–110.

FAWZI, SAAD EL DIN, 1957: *The Labour Movement in the Sudan, 1946–1955.* London.

FIRTH, RAYMOND, 1929: *Primitive Economics of the New Zealand Maori.* London.

FLEMING, R. I., 1961: "Africa's Challenge on the New Frontier," in *Activities of Private U.S. Organizations in Africa* (Hearings before the Subcommittee on Africa of the Committee on Foreign Affairs, House of Representatives, 87th Congress, First Session), pp. 237–246. Washington, D.C.

FLOYD, B. N., 1960: "Changing Patterns of African Land Use in Southern Rhodesia." (Paper presented at the Annual Meeting of The African Studies Association, Hartford, Connecticut.) Mimeographed.

Food and Agricultural Organization of the United Nations, 1958: *The State of Food and Agriculture in 1958*. Rome.

—, 1961: *FAO Africa Survey. Report on the Possibilities of African Rural Development in Relation to Economic and Social Growth*. Rome.

FORDE, DARYLL, 1951: "The Yoruba-Speaking Peoples of Southwestern Nigeria." *Ethnographic Survey of Africa, Western Africa, Part 4*. London.

— (ed.), 1956: *Efik Traders of Old Calabar*. London.

FORTES, MEYER, 1945: *The Dynamics of Clanship Among the Tallensi*. London.

—, 1948: "The Political System of the Tallensi of the Northern Territories of the Gold Coast," in *African Political Systems* (M. Fortes and E. E. Evans-Pritchard, eds.), pp. 239–271. London.

France, Republic of (Ministère d'Outre-Mer), 1957: *Inventaire Sociale et Economique des Territoires d'Outre-Mer, 1950 à 1955*. Paris.

—, (Ministère d'Outre-Mer, Service des Statistiques Outre-Mer), 1960: *Outre-Mer 1958; Table économique et social des états et territoires d'Outre-Mer*. Paris.

FRANKEL, S. H., 1938: *Capital Investment in Africa*. London.

—, 1953: *The Economic Impact on Underdeveloped Societies*. London.

GAITSKELL, ARTHUR, 1959: *Gezira, A Story of Development in the Sudan*. London.

GAMBLE, DAVID P., 1957: *The Wolof of Senegambia*. London.

GARLICK, P. C., 1959: *African Traders in Kumasi* (African Business Series No. 1). Accra.

GEERTZ, CLIFFORD, 1956: "Religious Belief and Economic Behavior in a Central Javanese Town: Some Preliminary Considerations." *Economic Development and Cultural Change*, vol. 4, pp. 138–158.

General Agreement on Tariffs and Trade, 1957: *International Trade, 1956*. Geneva.

—, 1958: *Trends in International Trade*. Geneva.

—, 1960: *International Trade, 1959*. Geneva.

Ghana (Gold Coast), Department of Labour, 1939–1948: *Annual Reports*. Accra.

—, Office of the Government Statistician, 1948–1961: *Quarterly Digest of Statistics*. Accra.

—, —, 1955: *1954 Akuse Survey of Household Budgets*. Accra.

—, —, 1956a: *Sekondi-Takoradi Survey of Population and Household Budgets, 1955*. Accra.

Ghana, Office of the Government Statistician, 1956b: *Kumasi Survey of Population and Household Budgets, 1955*. Accra.

—, —, 1957: *Accra Survey of Household Budgets, February 1953*. Accra.

—, —, 1958: *Survey of Population and Budgets of Cocoa Producing Families in the Oda-Swedru-Asamankese Area, 1955–1956*. Accra.

—, —, 1960a: *Economic Survey, 1959*. Accra.

—, —, 1960b: *Annual Report on External Trade of Ghana*. Accra.

GLUCKMAN, MAX, 1944: "Studies in African Land Tenure." *African Studies* vol. 3, pp. 14–21.

—, 1945: "African Land Tenure." *Human Problems in British Central Africa*, vol. 3, pp. 1–12.

—, 1959: "The Technical Vocabulary of Barotse Jurisprudence." *American Anthropologist*, vol. 61, pp. 43–53.

—, 1960: "The Rise of a Zulu Empire." *Scientific American*, vol. 202, pp. 157–167.

GOLDSCHMIDT, W. (ed.), 1958: *The United States and Africa* (report of The American Assembly on Africa). New York.

GOODFELLOW, D. M., 1939: *Principles of Economic Sociology*. London.

GOULDSBURY, V. S., 1896: "Report of his Journey into the Interior of the Gold Coast." Accra, 27 March, 1876. C.O.96.119, No. 5162/s, enclosed in Governor G. C. Strahan to Lord Carnarvon, 30 April, 1876 in the Public Record Office. Cited in Wolfson, Freda, 1958: *Pageant of Ghana*. London.

GRAY, ROBERT F., 1960: "Sonjo Bride-Price and the Question of African 'Wife Purchase'." *American Anthropologist*, vol. 62, pp. 34–57.

GREEN, M. M., 1947: *Ibo Village Affairs*. London.

GREEN, REGINALD H., 1960: "Ghana Cocoa Marketing Policy 1938–1960: A Study in Economic Policy and Performance." *Proceedings*, 1960 Conference of the Nigerian Institute of Social and Economic Research. Ibadan.

GRÉVISSE, F., 1950: "Salines et Salinières Indigènes du Haut-Katanga." *Bulletin du Centre d'Études des Problemes Sociaux Indigènes*, No. 11, pp. 7–85.

GRIAULE, MARCEL, 1954: "The Dogon of the French Sudan," in *African Worlds* (Forde, Daryll, ed.), pp. 83–110. London.

GUILLEMIN, R., 1956: "Évolution de l'agriculture dans les savannes de l'Oubangi." *Agronomie Tropical*, vol. 11, pp. 143–176 and 279–309.

GUILLOTEAU, J., 1950: "La degradation des sols tropicaux," in Record of the XXVth Meeting held in Brussels on the 28, 29 and 30th November 1949, International Institute of Political and Social Sciences (Comparative Civilizations), pp. 83–135. Brussels.

GULLIVER, P. H., 1951: *A Preliminary Survey of the Turkana*. Capetown.

—, 1955: *Labour Migration in a Rural Economy*. Kampala.

HAILEY, LORD MALCOLM, 1957: *An African Survey, Revised 1956*. London.

HAMILTON, ALEXANDER (see McKeever, S. (ed.)).

HAMMOND, PETER B., 1959: "Economic Change and Mossi Acculturation," in *Continuity and Change in African Cultures* (W. R. Bascom and M. J. Herskovits, eds.), pp. 283–356. Chicago.

P

HANCE, W. A., 1958: *African Economic Development*. New York.

HANCOCK, W. K., 1942: *Survey of British Commonwealth Affairs*, vol. 2. London.

HANSON, A. H., 1960: "Nile and Niger: Two Agricultural Projects." *Public Administration*, vol. 38, pp. 339–352.

HASSOUN, ISAM AHMAD, 1952: "Western Migration and Settlement in the Gezira." *Sudan Notes and Records*, vol. 33, pp. 60–112.

HAUSER, A., 1955: "Quelques rélations des travailleurs de l'industrie à leur travail en A. O. F." *Bulletin de l'Institut Français de l'Afrique Noire*, vol. 17, ser. B, pp. 129–141.

HAWKINS, E. K., 1958: *Road Transport in Nigeria*. Oxford.

HEARN, HUGH, 1956: "Marketing and Distribution." *East African Economic Review*, pp. 127–134.

HERSKOVITS, MELVILLE J., 1926: "The Cattle Complex in East Africa." *American Anthropologist*, vol. 28, pp. 230–272, 361–380, 494–528, 633–664.

—, 1936: "The Significance of West Africa for Negro Research." *The Journal of Negro History*, vol. 21, pp. 15–30.

—, 1938: *Dahomey, An Ancient West African Kingdom* (2 vols.). New York.

—, 1940: *The Economic Life of Primitive Peoples*. New York.

—, 1952a: *Economic Anthropology*. New York.

—, 1952b: "Adapting Societies to New Tasks," in *The Progress of Underdeveloped Areas* (B. M. Hoselitz, ed.). Chicago.

—, 1955: *Cultural Anthropology*. New York.

—, 1956: "African Economic Development in Cross-Cultural Perspective." *American Economic Review*, vol. 46, pp. 452–461.

—, 1960: "The Organization of Work," in *Labor Commitment and Social Change In Developing Areas* (Moore, Wilbert E. and Feldman, Arnold S., eds.), pp. 123–135. New York.

—, 1962: *The Human Factor in Changing Africa*. New York.

HILL, POLLY, 1956: *The Gold Coast Cocoa Farmer*. London.

—, 1961: "The Migrant Cocoa Farmer of Southern Ghana." *Africa*, vol. 31, pp. 209–230.

HIRSCHMAN, ALBERT O., 1958: *The Strategy of Economic Development*. New Haven.

HODGKIN, THOMAS, 1958: "The Idea of an African University." *Ibadan*, No. 4 (October).

—, 1961: "A Note on the Language of African Nationalism," in *African Affairs* (St. Anthony's Papers, No. 10, K. Kirkwood, ed.). London.

HOLAS, B., 1957: *Les Sénoufo*. Paris.

HOSELITZ, B. F., 1952: "Entrepreneurship and Economic Growth." *American Journal of Economics and Sociology*, vol. 12, pp. 97–110.

—, 1960: "The Market Matrix," in *Labor Commitment and Social Change in Developing Areas* (Moore, W. E. and Feldman, A. S., eds.), pp. 217–237. New York.

— (ed.), 1952: *The Progress of Underdeveloped Areas*. Chicago.

HOYT, ELIZABETH, 1952: "Economic Sense and the East African." *Africa*, vol. 22, pp. 165–170.

—, 1954: "Les dépenses du consummateurs sous l'influence du changement technique: quelques rémarques de politique sociale." *Zaïre*, vol. 8, pp. 115–122.

HUDSON, W., 1955: "Observations on African Labor in East, Central and West Africa." *Journal of the National Inst. of Personnel Research*, vol. 6, pp. 18–29.

HUNTER, T. AND DANSO, T. V., n.d.: "Notes on Food Farming at Ejura," in *Year Book, 1930* (Gold Coast, Department of Agriculture). Accra.

HUNTINGFORD, G. W. B., 1950: *Nandi Work and Culture*. London.

—, 1953: *The Southern Nilo-Hamites*. London.

ILLIF, W. A., 1952: "The World Bank as a Borrower." *The Financial Times* (April 8). London.

International Bank for Reconstruction and Development, 1955: *The Economic Development of Nigeria*. Baltimore.

—, 1961: *The Economic Development of Tanganyika*. Baltimore.

International Labour Office, 1958: *African Labour Survey*. Geneva.

JOHNSTON, B. F., 1958: *The Staple Food Economies of Western Tropical Africa*. Stanford.

—, and Mellor, J. W., 1961: "The Role of Agriculture in Economic Development." *American Economic Review*, vol. 51, pp. 566–593.

JOHNSTON, SIR HARRY H., 1906: *Liberia*. London.

JONES, E. H., 1960: "Busoga Farms Bunya," in *Symposium on Mechanical Cultivation in Uganda* (J. L. Joy, ed.), pp. 75–86. Kampala.

JONES, W. O., 1959: *Manioc in Africa*. Stanford.

—, 1961: "Food and Agricultural Economies of Tropical Africa." *Food Research Institute Studies*, vol. 2, pp. 3–20.

KABERRY, PHYLLIS, 1950: "Land Tenure Among the Nsaw of the British Cameroons." *Africa*, vol. 20, pp. 313–316.

—, 1952: *Woman of the Grasslands, a Study of the Economic Position of Women in Bamenda, British Cameroons* (Colonial Research Publication No. 14). London.

KEITA, MADEIRA, 1960: "The Single Party in Africa." *Présence Africaine* (English ed.), vol. 2, No. 30, pp. 33ff.

Kenya, Colony and Protectorate of, 1958: *Report of the Working Party on African Land Tenure, 1957–58*. Nairobi.

—, Department of Agriculture, 1954: *A Plan to Intensify the Development of African Agriculture in Kenya*. Nairobi.

—, —, 1961: *Annual Report*, 1960. Mimeographed.

—, Ministry of Agriculture, Animal Husbandry, and Water Resources, 1956: *African Land Development in Kenya 1946–1955*. Nairobi.

—, —, 1958: *Accelerated Development of African Agriculture 1958/63. Detailed proposals of the Ministry of Agriculture*. Mimeographed.

KENYATTA, JOMO, 1938: *Facing Mount Kenya, the Tribal Life of the Gikuyu.*

KÖBBEN, ANDRE, 1954: "Eigendom en Bezit van Land bÿ de Agni." *Tydschrift van het Koninklÿk Nederlandsch Aardrÿkskundig Gahootschap,* vol. 71, pp. 312–320.

KUCZINSKI, R. R., 1936: *Colonial Population.* Oxford.

LAWRENCE, J. C. D., 1957: *The Iteso.* London.

LEAKEY, L. S. B., 1952: *Mau Mau and the Kikuyu.* London.

—, 1956: "The Economics of Kikuyu Life." *East African Economic Review,* vol. 3, pp. 165–180.

LEITH-ROSS, SYLVIA, 1938: *African Women.* London.

LENGELLÉ, M., 1954: *Les Cahiers Économiques* (October).

LEUBUSCHER, CHARLOTTE, 1944: *Tanganyika Territory.* London.

LEVY, M. J., JR., 1952: *The Structure of Society.* Princeton.

—, 1955: "Some Social Obstacles to Capital Formation in Underdeveloped Areas." *Capital Formation and Economic Growth,* pp. 441–501. Princeton.

LEWIS, W. A., 1953: *Report on Industrialization and the Gold Coast.* Accra.

—, 1961: "Education and Economic Development." *Final Report,* Conference of African States on the Development of Education in Africa, Addis Ababa, 15–25 May. UNESCO/ED/181.

LIEBENSTEIN, H., 1957: *Economic Backwardness and Economic Growth.* New York.

LITTLE, KENNETH L., 1948: "Land and Labour Among the Mende." *African Affairs,* vol. 47, pp. 23–31.

—, 1951: *The Mende of Sierra Leone.* London.

LLOYD, P. C., 1954: "The Traditional Political System of the Yoruba." *Southwestern Journal of Anthropology,* vol. 10, pp. 366–384.

—, 1955: "The Yoruba Lineage." *Africa,* vol. 25, pp. 235–251.

—, 1959a: "Some Notes on the Yoruba Rules of Succession and on 'Family Property'." *Journal of African Law,* vol. 3, pp. 7–32.

—, 1959b: "Family Property among the Yoruba." *Journal of African Law,* vol. 3, pp. 105–115.

LONSDALE, CAPTAIN R. LA T., 1882: Parliamentary Papers 46, 1882 (C–3386) No. 42, enclosure 2. Cited in Wolfson, Freda, 1958: *Pageant of Ghana,* pp. 182–186. London.

LUGARD, LORD FREDERICK D., 1922: *The Dual Mandate in Tropical Africa.* Edinburgh.

MAIR, L. P., 1951: "Agrarian Policy in British African Colonies." Land Tenure Symposium. Leiden.

—, 1960: "Social Change in Africa." *International Affairs,* vol. 36, pp. 447–456.

MALINOWSKI, BRONISLAW, 1926: *Argonauts of the Western Pacific.* London.

—, 1938: *Coral Gardens and their Magic* (2 vols.). London.

MALCOLM, D. W., 1953: *Sukumaland.* London.

MANOUKIAN, MADELINE, 1950: *The Akan and Ga-Adangme Peoples of the Gold Coast*. London.

—, 1952: *The Ewe-Speaking Peoples of Togoland and the Gold Coast*. London.

MAQUET, JACQUES, 1961: *The Premise of Inequality in Ruanda*. London.

MAREES, PIETER DE, 1602: *A Description and Historical Declaration of the Golden Kingdom of Guinea, Otherwise called the Golden Coast of Myna*. . . . Translated from the Dutch. Purchas His Pilgrims, vol. 6, 1905. Cited in Wolfson, Freda, 1958: *Pageant of Ghana*, pp. 50–57. London.

MARRIOTT, MCKIM, 1960: *Caste Ranking and Community Structure in Five Regions of India and Pakistan* (Deccan College, Monograph Series, No. 23). Poona.

MARS, J., 1948: "Extra-Territorial Enterprises," in *Economics of a Tropical Dependency*, vol. II, *Mining, Commerce and Finance in Nigeria* (Margery Perham, ed.), pp. 43–136. London.

MARSHALL, LORNA, 1957: "The Kin Terminology of the !Kung Bushman." *Africa*, vol. 27, pp. 1–24 (1959).

—, 1959: "Marriage among the !Kung Bushmen." *Africa*, vol. 29, pp. 335–365.

—, 1960: "!Kung Bushmen Bands." *Africa*, vol. 30, pp. 325–355.

MAUSS, MARCEL, 1947: *Manuel d'Ethnographie*. Paris.

MAYER, PHILLIP, 1950: *Gusii Bridewealth Law and Custom*. London.

MCCALL, D. F., 1956: *Effect on Family Structure of Changing Economic Activities of Women in a Gold Coast Town*. Ph.D. Thesis, Columbia University.

MCCULLOCH, MERRAN, 1957: "The Social Impact of Economic Development on Rural Areas in East and Central Africa." *Information*, vol. 14, pp. 1–17.

MCKEEVER, S. (ed.), 1934: Alexander Hamilton, *Papers on Public Credit, Commerce and Finance*. New York.

MCPHEE, ALLAN, 1926: *The Economic Revolution in British West Africa*. London

MEEK, C. K., 1931: *A Sudanese Kingdom*. London.

MERSADIER, Y., 1957: *Budgets familiaux africains; étude chez 136 familles de salariés en trois centres urbains du Senegal*. Saint-Louis du Senegal.

MIDDLETON, J. F. M., 1953: *The Kikuyu and Kamba of Kenya* (Ethnographic Survey of Africa, East Central Africa, Part V). London.

MINER, HORACE, 1953: *The Primitive City of Timbuctoo* (Memoirs of the American Philosophical Society, No. 32). Princeton and Philadelphia.

MITCHELL, J. C., 1956: "Urbanization, Detribalization and Stabilization in Southern Africa," in UNESCO, *Social Implications of Industrialization and Urbanization in Africa South of the Sahara*, pp. 693–711. Paris.

—, and Epstein, A. L., 1959: "Occupational Prestige and Social Status among Urban Africans in Northern Rhodesia." *Africa*, vol. 29, pp. 22–40.

MONTEIL, P. L., 1894: *De Saint Louis à Tripoli par le Tchad*. Paris.

MOORE, WILBERT E., 1946: "The Migration of Native Laborers in South Africa." *Milbank Memorial Fund Quarterly*, vol. 24, pp. 401–419.

420   *Economic Transition in Africa*

MOORE, WILBERT E. 1951: *Industrialization and Labor*. Ithaca.
—, 1960: "Notes for a General Theory of Labor Organization." *Industrial and Labor Relations Review*, vol. 13, pp. 387–397.
—, and Feldman, A. S. (eds.), 1960: *Labor Commitment and Social Change in Developing Areas*. New York.
MURDOCK, G. P., 1959: *Africa, Its Peoples and Their Cultural History*. New York.

NADEL, S. R., 1942: *A Black Byzantium, the Kingdom of Nupe in Nigeria*. London.
NEWBURY, COLIN, 1961: "The Government General and Political Change in French West Africa," in *Africa Affairs* (St. Anthony's Papers No. 10, K. Kirkwood, ed.). London.
NICULESCU, BARBU, 1954: "Fluctuations in the Incomes of Primary Producers: Further Comment." *The Economic Journal*, vol. 64, pp. 730–743.
Nigeria, Federation of, 1955: *Report of the Fact-Finding Committee on the Minimum Wage Question*. Lagos.
—, 1959: *Laws of the Federation of Nigeria and Lagos in Force on the 1st day of June, 1958*. London.
—, 1961: *Digest of Statistics*, vol. 10, No. 1 (October).
—, Department of Labour, 1940–50: *Annual Reports*. Lagos.
—, Department of Statistics, 1948–60: *Digest of Statistics*. Lagos.
—, —, 1958: *Urban Consumer Surveys in Nigeria: Lagos, Ibadan, Enugu*. Lagos.
—, —, 1959: *Urban Consumer Surveys in Nigeria: Kaduna and Zaria*. Lagos.
—, —, 1960: *Annual Abstract of Statistics*. Lagos.
—, Ministry of Education, 1960: *The Report of the Commission on Post-School Certificate and Higher Education in Nigeria*. Lagos.
NKRUMAH, KWAME, 1957: *Ghana, the Autobiography of Kwame Nkrumah*. Edinburgh.
—, 1961: report of address in *Daily Times*, p. 5 (July 21). Lagos.
NOLL, NED, 1900: "Le Haut Dahomey, d'après le Lieut. Tilho." *La Géographie*, vol. 1, pp. 402–404.
Northwestern University, Program of African Studies, 1959: *Africa* (Studies of United States Foreign Policy, No. 4, Committee Print, Committee on Foreign Relations, United States Senate, 86th Congress, 1st Session.). Washington.
NURKSE, R., 1961: *Patterns of Trade and Development*. New York.
NYE, G. W., 1940: "Cotton-Breeding Organization," in *Agriculture in Uganda* (J. D. Tothill, ed.), pp. 207–216. Oxford.
—, and Hosking, H. R., 1960: "History and Development of the Cotton Industry in Uganda," in *Agriculture in Uganda* (J. D. Tothill, ed.), pp. 183–193. Oxford.
NYIRENDA, A. A., 1957: "African Market Vendors in Lusaka." *Rhodes-Livingstone Journal*, No. 22, pp. 31–63.

NYPAN, ASTRID, 1960a: "Market Trade in Accra." *The Economic Bulletin*, vol. 4, pp. 7–17. Accra.
—, 1960b: *Market Trade*. Accra.

OHLIN, B., 1952: *Interregional and International Trade*. Cambridge (Massachusetts).
OLLONE, CAPTAINE DE, 1901: *De la Côte d'Ivoire au Soudan et à la Guinée*. Paris.
OPPENHEIMER, H. F., 1956: "Industrial Relations in a Multi-Racial Society." *African Affairs*, vol. 55, pp. 313–319.
Organization for European Economic Cooperation, 1961: *The Flow of Financial Resources to Countries in the Course of Economic Development*. Paris.
OTTENBERG, PHOEBE, 1959: "The Changing Economic Position of Women Among the Afikpo Ibo," in *Continuity and Change in African Cultures* (W. R. Bascom and M. J. Herskovits, eds.), pp. 205–223. Chicago.
OTTENBERG, SIMON, 1956: "The Development of Village Meetings among the Afikpo People." *Proceedings*, Annual Conference of Sociology, West African Institute of Social and Economic Research, pp. 186–205. Ibadan.

PACQUES, VIVIANA, 1954: *Les Bambara*. Paris.
PALMER, H. R., 1908: "The Kano Chronicle." *Journal of the Royal Anthropological Institute*, vol. 38, pp. 62–65.
PARK, MUNGO, 1799: *Travels in the Interior Districts of Africa* (2 vols.). London.
PARSONS, TALCOTT, 1954: "An Analytic Approach to the Theory of Social Stratification," in *Essays in Sociological Theory* (revised edition), pp. 69–88. Glencoe (Illinois).
PAULME, DENISE, 1952: "La femme africaine au travail." *Présence Africaine*, vol. 13, pp. 116–123.
POLEMAN, T. T., 1961: "The Food Economies of Urban Middle Africa: The Case of Ghana." *Food Research Institute Studies*, vol. 2, pp. 121–174.
POQUIN, J. J., 1957: *Les relations économiques éxterieures des pays d'Afrique noire de l'Union Française, 1925–1955*. Paris.
PRAIN, R. L., 1956: "The Stabilization of Labour in the Rhodesian Copper Belt." *African Affairs*, vol. 55, pp. 305–312.
PRINS, A. H. J., 1952: *The Coastal Tribes of the North Eastern Bantu*. London.

REDFIELD, ROBERT, 1956: *Peasant Society and Culture*. Chicago.
REDLICH, FRITZ, 1949: "The Business Leader in Theory and Reality." *American Journal of Sociology*, vol. 8, pp. 223–230.
RICHARDS, AUDREY I., 1948: "The Political System of the Bemba Tribe, Northeastern Rhodesia," in *African Political Systems* (M. Fortes and E. E. Evans-Pritchard, eds.), pp. 83–120. London.
—, 1954: *Economic Development and Tribal Change: A Study of Immigrant Labour in Buganda*. Cambridge (England).
—, 1958: "A Changing Pattern of Agriculture in East Africa: The Bemba of Northern Rhodesia." *Geographical Journal*, vol. 124, pp. 302–313.

ROSENSTEIN-RODAN, P. R., 1961: "International Aid for Underdeveloped Countries." *Review of Economics and Statistics,* vol. 43, pp. 107–138.

ROUCH, JEAN, 1954: *Les Songhay.* Paris.

—, 1956: "Migrations au Ghana (Gold Coast) (Enquête 1953–1955)." *Journal de la Société des Africanistes,* vol. 26, pp. 33–196. (English translation by P. E. O. and J. B. Haigham, 1954, Accra, mimeographed.)

SAMPSON, H. (ed.), 1960: *World Railways 1960.* London.

SAMUELSON, PAUL A., 1951: *Economics.* New York.

SCHAPERA, I., 1937: *The Bantu-Speaking Tribes of South Africa.* London.

—, 1953: *The Tswana.* London.

—, 1955: *A Handbook of Tswana Law and Custom.* London.

SCHNEIDER, HAROLD K., 1953: *The Pakot (Suk) of Kenya, with Special Reference to the Role of Livestock in their Subsistence Economy.* Ann Arbor (University Microfilms).

SCHWAB, GEORGE, 1947: *Tribes of the Liberian Hinterland.* Cambridge (Massachusetts).

Sénégal, Service de la Statistique, 1953–1960: *Bulletin Statistique.* Saint-Louis du Sénégal.

SENGHOR, LEOPOLD-SEDAR, 1959: *African Socialism,* New York.

SHEDDICK, V. G. J., 1953: *The Southern Sotho.* London.

SINGER, H. W., 1953: "Obstacles to Economic Development." *Social Research,* vol. 20, pp. 19–30.

—, 1954: "Population and Economic Development." *Proceedings,* World Population Conference, vol. 5, pp. 737–761. Rome.

—, 1961: "Problems of Small Scale Industries in Tropical Africa." A paper presented to the Conference of the International Economic Association on the Development in Africa South of the Sahara, July 1961, at Addis Ababa. Mimeographed.

SKINNER, ELLIOTT P., 1960: "Labour Migration and its Relationship to Socio-Cultural Change in Mossi Society." *Africa,* vol. 30, pp. 375–401.

SLUITER, GREET, 1960: *Kikuyu Concepts of Land and Land Kin* (M.A. Thesis, University of Chicago). Manuscript.

SMITH, MARY F., 1959: *Baba of Karo.* New York.

SMITH, MICHAEL G., 1955: *The Economy of Hausa Communities of Zaria.* London.

SMYTHE, HUGH AND MABEL, 1960: *The New Nigerian Elite.* Stanford.

SOFER, CYRIL, 1954: "Working Groups in a Plural Society." *Industrial and Labour Relations Review,* vol. 8, pp. 68–78.

SOUTHALL, AIDEN W., 1953: *Alur Society.* Cambridge (England).

—, 1954: "Alur Migrants," in *Economic Development and Tribal Change: a Study of Immigrant Labour, in Baganda* (A. I. Richards, ed.), pp. 141–160. Cambridge (England).

Southern Rhodesia, 1955: *What the Native Land Husbandry Act Means to the Rural African and to Southern Rhodesia.* Salisbury.

STAMP, DUDLEY, 1953: *Africa: A Study in Tropical Development.* New York.

STEPHENS, RICHARD W., 1958: *Population Pressures in Africa South of the Sahara*. Washington.

TALBOT, P. AMAURY, 1926: *The Peoples of Southern Nigeria* (4 vols.). London.

TAX, SOL, 1953: *Penny Capitalism: a Guatemalan Indian Economy* (Smithsonian Institution, Institute of Social Anthropology, Publication No. 16). Washington.

THOMAS, E. M., 1959: *The Harmless People*. New York.

TOURÉ, SÉKOU, 1959: *Toward Full Re-Africanization*. Paris.

UDY, STANLEY H., JUN., 1959: *Organization of Work*. New Haven.

UGANDA GOVERNMENT, 1955: *The Advancement of Africans in Trade*. Kampala.

United African Company, Ltd., 1949: *Statistical and Economic Review*, No. 3, pp. 40–43.

—, 1959: *Statistical and Economic Review*, No. 22, pp. 56–58.

—, 1961: "The Coordination of Transport in Tropical Africa." *Statistical and Economic Review* (25 March).

United Kingdom, Colonial Office, 1946: *Enquiry into the Cost of Living and the Control of the Cost of Living in the Colony and Protectorate of Nigeria* (The Tudor-Davies Report) Colonial No. 204. London.

—, —, 1948: *Report of the Commission of Enquiry into Disturbances in the Gold Coast, 1948* (The Watson Commission Report) Colonial No. 231. London.

—, —, 1961: *East Africa. Report of the Economic and Fiscal Commission*. Cmnd. 1279. London.

—, Trade Commissioner, Board of Trade, 1954: *The African Native Market in the Federation of the Rhodesias and Nyasaland*. London.

United Nations, 1954: *Enlargement of the Exchange Economy in Tropical Africa*. Ref. No. E/2557, ST/ECA/23. New York.

—, 1957: *Report on the World Social Situation*. Ref. No. E/CN.5/324/Rev. 1, ST/SOA/33. New York.

—, 1959: *Yearbook of International Trade Statistics* (2 vols.). Ref. No. ST/STAT/SER.9/10. New York.

—, 1960a: *International Economic Assistance to Africa, 1960*. Ref. No. E/CN.14/152. New York.

—, 1960b: *International Action for Commodity Stabilization and the Role of Africa*. Ref. No. E/CN.14/68. New York.

—, 1960c: "Survey of Development Programmes and Policies in Selected African Countries and Territories." *Economic Bulletin for Africa*, vol. 1, chapter B/II. Ref. No. E/CN.14/67. New York.

—, 1960d: *The Status of Permanent Sovereignty Over Natural Wealth and Resources*. Ref. No. A/AC.97/5. Rev. 1. New York.

—, 1961: *The Promotion of the International Flow of Private Capital*. Ref. No. E/3492. New York.

United Nations, Department of Economic Affairs, 1951: *Economic Conditions in Africa: Supplement to World Economic Report, 1949–50.* Ref. Nos. E/1910/Add.1/ Rev.1, ST/ECA/9/Add.1. New York.

—, —, 1954: *Enlargement of the Exchange Economy in Tropical Africa* (Supplement to *World Economic Report, 1952–53*). Ref. No. ST/ECA/23. New York.

—, Department of Economic and Social Affairs, 1959a: *Economic Survey of Africa Since 1950.* Ref. No. E/CN.14/28. New York.

—, —, 1959b: *World Economic Survey 1958.* Ref. Nos. E/3244, ST/ECA/60. New York.

—, Department of Trusteeship and Non-Self-Governing Territories, 1955: *Special Study on Economic Conditions in Non-Self-Governing Territories, 1954.* Ref. No. ST/TRI/Ser.A/9/Add.1. New York.

—, —, 1958: *Special Study on Social Conditions in Non-Self-Governing Territories,* 1957–58. Ref. No. ST/TRI/SER.A/14. New York.

—, —, 1960a: *Special Study on Educational Conditions in Non-Self-Governing Territories.* Ref. No. ST/TRI/SER.A/16. New York.

—, —, 1960b: *Progress of the Non-Self-Governing Territories Under the Charter, Vol. 5, Territorial Surveys.* Ref. No. ST/TRI/SER.A/15/Vol. 5. New York.

—, Economic and Social Council, 1954: *Commodity Trade and Economic Development.* Ref. No. E/2519. New York.

—, —, 1961a: *Commodity Survey, 1960.* Ref. No. ST/ECA/67. New York.

—, —, 1961b: *International Compensations for Fluctuations in Commodity Trade.* Ref. No. E/3447. New York.

—, Economic Commission for Africa, 1956: *A Survey of Geological and Mineralogical Resources in Africa.* Ref. No. E/CN.14/30. New York.

—, —, 1960a: *International Action for Commodity Stabilization and the Role of Africa.* Ref. No. E/CN.14/68. New York.

—, —, 1960b: *Transport Problems in Relation to Economic Development in West Africa.* Ref. No. E/CN.14/63. New York.

—, —, 1961: *Economic Bulletin for Africa,* Vol. 1. New York.

—, —, Working Party on Economic and Social Development, 1961: *Demographic Factors Related to Social and Economic Development in Africa.* Ref. No. E/CN.14/ESD/12. Addis Ababa.

—, —, and United Nations, Educational, Scientific and Cultural Organization, 1961: *Final Report,* Conference of African States on the Development of Education in Africa, 12–15 May, 1961. Ref. No. UNESCO/ED/181.

—, Economic Commission for Europe, 1958: *Economic Survey of Europe in 1957.* Ref. No. E/ECE/317.

—, —, 1961: *Economic Survey of Europe in 1960.* Ref. No. E/ECE/419. Geneva.

—, Statistical Office, 1960: *Statistical Yearbook, 1960.* New York.

University of Natal, Department of Economics, 1950: *The African Factory Worker.* Capetown.

VAN DONGEN, IRENE S., 1954: *The British East African Transport Complex* (Research Paper No. 38, University of Chicago, Department of Geography). Chicago.

VON SICK, EBERHARD, 1916: "Die Waniaturu (Walimi)." *Baessler-Archiv,* vol. 5, pp. 1–62.

WAGNER, GÜNTHER, 1940: "The Political Organization of the Bantu Kavirondo," in *African Political Systems* (M. Fortes and E. E. Evans-Pritchard, eds.), pp. 197–236. London.

—, 1956: *The Bantu of North Kavirondo* (ed. Lucy Mair) (2 vols.). London.

WALLERSTEIN, IMMANUEL, 1961: "How Seven States were Born in Former French West Africa." *Africa Report,* pp. 3ff. (March).

WATSON, WM., 1958: *Tribal Cohesion in a Money Economy.* Manchester.

WHITE, CHARLES M., 1958: "Terminological Confusion in African Land Tenure." *Journal of African Administration,* vol. 10, pp. 124–130.

WILLIAMS, J. W., 1956: "The Finance and Development of Small Enterprise." *Annual Conference of Sociology,* West African Institute of Social and Economic Research, pp. 25–27. Ibadan.

WILSON, CHARLES, 1954: *The History of Unilever* (2 vols.). London.

WILSON, GODFREY, 1941–1942: *An Essay on the Economics of Detribalization in Northern Rhodesia* (Rhodes-Livingstone Papers No. 5). Livingstone.

WILSON, MONICA, 1951: *Good Company.* London.

WOLFSON, FREDA, 1958: *Pageant of Ghana.* London.

WOOD, ALAN, 1950: *The Groundnut Affair.* London.

World Railways, 1960 (see Sampson, H., ed.).

World Power Conference, 1960: *Statistical Yearbook, No. 9.* London.

WRIGLEY, CHRISTOPHER, 1961: "Economic Problems of Development." *Proceedings,* Conference on Research in West Africa, March 22–27. Ibadan.

WRIGHT, F. D., 1953: *African Consumers.* London.

XYDIAS, NELLY, 1956: "Labour Conditions, Aptitudes, Training," in UNESCO, *Social Implications of Industrialization and Urbanization in Africa South of the Sahara,* pp. 275–367. Paris.

ZIMBE, B. M., 1938: *Buganda ne Kabaka.* Kampala.

Index of Subjects

Acculturation (culture-contact), 7, 286–7, 303; economic, in E. Africa, 68; general economic, in Africa, 399–401, 403–5; see also Reinterpretation

Adioukron (Ivory Coast), 278

Afikpo-Ibo, landholding patterns among, 104

African personality, 392

Africanization, 383–5

Age-grading, 278

Agricultural production; see Production, agricultural

Agriculture, 277, 333–4, 352; African, 309; development of, 332; subsistence, 287; traditional, 246; see also Exports, Imports, Division of labor, Production, agricultural, Productivity, Technology

Aid; see Assistance

Akan, ranking of descent groups, 123

Allocation of aid, 363

Allocation of resources, 326, 330–2, 334, 357–8, 367, 369, 380

Aluminum, 341, 359

Ancestors, role of: among Kikuyu, 145–8; in landholding, 105–6, 109, 111; among Tiv, 135–9

Animal husbandry, in W. Africa, 79–80

Apartheid, 283

Ashanti, 82, 89; landholding among, 103, 109

Assistance, bilaterial, 361, 363, 372; international economic, 323, 359 ff.; technical, 362

Authoritarianism, 326

Authority, evaluation of roles of, 119; as principle governing exchange, 119; as principle of stratification, 120–7

Baganda; see Ganda

Balanced growth, 332–3

Balkanization, 378, 390

Banking, 312, 366

Bantu, inter-lacustrine and southern, 123

Bantu of N. Kavirondo: business enterprises, 184; exchange equivalents, 65

Bantustans, 283

Barter: in Mossi markets, 86; in Salaga, 94; in W. African trade, 86

Bemba (N. Rhodesia), landholding patterns among, 103, 109

Benin, 82–4, 86

Boundaries, 377–8

Bridewealth: among Bantu of N. Kavirondo, 65, Gusii, 66, Iteso, 66, Nandi, 65, Ndorobi, 147, Sonjo, 66, Suk of Kenya, 64, Sukuma, 67, and Turu, 55–6, 61, 64; in other E. African societies, 64

Buganda; see Ganda

Bureaucracy, 384

Burundi, as a caste society, 121

Business enterprises, 179, 183; limits to size of, 193–7

Caisses de Stabilisation des Prix; see Stabilization funds

Capital, 54, 265, 310; accumulation of, 190–3, 361; in business and trade, 180–3; determinants of, accumulation of, 21–2; human, 251; inflows, 24, 341, 349 ff., 358, 368; intensity, 324; overcoming lack of, 188; shortage of, 193–5; see also Infrastructure, Investment

Capsid, 166, 201

Career opportunities, 386–7

Cash, as medium of exchange, 67–8

Cash crops, 287, 317; in E. and W. Africa, 184; *see also* Production, agricultural

Caste, Indian and African, 122

Cattle, 304; as bridewealth, 56; in E. African markets, 73; economic functions of, among Turu, 54; and grain, 67, 69; among Iteso, Turkana, Gusii, and Duruma, 66; as money, 8, 12, 53; population of, 168; as sacrifice, 72; slaughter of, 68–9; as source of prestige, 62; among southern E. African tribes and Sukuma, 67; as symbols and facilities, 73, 125; in terms of trade, 54–5; trade in, 314; as wealth, 70–1; in W. African markets, 79

Census; *see* Population

Centralism, 395–6; bureaucratic, 393; democratic, 392

Chagga (Tanganyika), innovation in business, 185

Chiefs: and concessions, 309; as political officials, 119; prerogatives of, 125–6; recruitment of, 124; rights in land among Nsaw, 100, Nyanga, 102, Ashanti, 103, Tswana and Mwambe, 104, and S.E. African peoples, 103; rights in land recently, 110; role in Yoruba land tenure, 141

Cities, food imports into, 152; *see also* Urbanization

Civil servants, 386–7

Cocoa, 165, 184, 213, 218, 225, 302, 307, 313, 338–9, 342, 346, 349, 359; production of, 17–18; value of output of, 19

Coffee, 153, 156, 171, 185, 218, 225, 302, 337–40, 342, 348–9; in Uganda, 167

Cold war, 366–7, 388

Colonial administration, 343–4

Colonial period, 279, 377

Colonialism, 383–4, 389, 396

Colonies, government and economic growth in late 19th century of, 300

Color bar, 285, 311, 317

Commerce, petty, 287

Commercial policy, 340–1

Commercialization, of agriculture, 314

Commitment, 286; of labor, 294

Commodity agreements, 348–9

Communications, 270, 342, 362

Community, 405; improvement unions, 185, 192; local, and land, 134

Concessions, 309; tax, 353; *see also* Plantations

Conspicuous consumption: and capital shortage, 195; cattle as, 73

Construction, 334; industry, 316

Consumer goods, 54; domestic production of, 316

Consumption: of food, 152; of food per capita, 156; out of current income, 324

Contract: as basis of social system, 149; and land tenure in Africa, 148; and land tenure in Euroamerica, 139; as organizing principle, 134

Cooperative work groups, 279; in Dahomey, Jukun, and Mossi, 81

Cooperatives, 185, 343; in Africa, 185

Coordination of projects, 367

Copper, 310

Corvée, 125, 280; *see also* Labor

Cost of living, 201–3, 210, 214–15, 225, 227–8

Cotton, 185, 302, 307–8, 337–8, 340; in Gezira, 173; in Uganda, 166

Councils, local and intermediate, 395

Craft guilds, 83–5, 118; in W. Africa, 77

Craft specialization, 82–5; part-time, in Africa, 119; in W. Africa, 77

Credit, 345; agricultural, 343; given by merchants of Djenne, 95

Crop rotation, 246

Cultural: discontinuities and continuities in Africa, 127–30; dynamics, 7; evaluation of roles, 116, 120–1; factors in social stratification, 113–16; heterogeneity among African societies, 128–9; homogeneity of African societies, 122, 127, 130

Dahomey, 80–4, 87, 92

Data: lack of, 4; necessity for collection of, 74

Death rates; *see* Population
Debt, external, 312
Decolonization, 383, 385
Defense, 378; cost of, 379–80
Demography; *see* Population
Demonstration effect, 249, 381
Dependency, 250–1; *see also* Mortality, Population
Depersonalization, 384
Depression, Great, impact on African exports, 18
Detribalization, 286
Development plans, 275, 323
Development program, 361–2
Diamonds, in world trade, 15
Diplomatic representation; *see* External relations
Direct investment; *see* Investment
Discrimination: legislative or customary, 285; by race, and labor, 290
Disease; *see* Health, Population
Diversification, 338; of exports, lack of, 313; of external dependence, 388–9
Division of labor, 278–9, 403; in craft work, 278–9; related to technological complexity, 116; sexual, 116; sexual, and agricultural productivity, 154
Divorce, grounds for, in allocation of land, 106
Dual economies, 324, 326
Dualism, 331, 334; *see also* Dual economies

Earnings, 200–1
Economic behavior, nature of, 8, 486; behavior, social and cultural setting of, 74; dependence, 381; differentials, social stratification and, 10; factors in landholding, 99; factors in social stratification, 113; integration, 342; organization, 277; system in landholding patterns, 114; systems in Africa, 179, 182
Economic development, 380, 384–5; 391, 395; barriers to, 193–7; and new states, 129; potential for, 368; rate of, 323, 333; pre-conditions for, 357, 359

Economic processes: as dominated by political factors, 127, 129; in social stratification, 124
Economics, general theory of, in E. African societies, 54, 74
Economy (economies), 284; changes in, resulting from European contact, 97; market, in Turu, 61–2; monetary, 279; private and public sectors of, 325; relation of size and viability of, 402; social and cultural setting of, in E. Africa, 73; sources of change, 184
Edo, 86
Education, 229, 247, 252, 362, 382, 384, 387; cost of, in Nigeria, 380; and dependency, 250–1; as infrastructure, 26, 270–2; and labor, 291–2
Elite, 405; in African politics, 383; role of, in new states, 128–9; in social stratification, 122
Elitism, 392
Employment, 287; *see also* Labor, Productivity, Occupation
Enterprise, foreign, 344
Entrepreneur, 128, 272; definition of, 182; functions of, 9; functions of, as performed by states, 129; "innovating" and "imitating," 186–9; lack of, in Africa, 193–6; status of, 197
Equality, of pay and perquisites, 386
Erosion, 246, 344; in S. Rhodesia, 168
European, 310; commerce in Africa, 179–80; concepts regarding land as contrasted with African, 134, 148
Ewe, 87–8
Exchange economy, 303–4; equivalents among Bantu of N. Kavirondo, 65, Duruma, 66, Gusii, 66, Iteso, 66, Nandi, 65, Suk of Kenya, 64–5, Sukuma, 67, and Turkana, 66; equivalents, in terms of cattle, 54; equivalents in terms of goods other than cattle, 55; political factors controlling, 119; production for, 184; redistribution, 119; *see also* Markets, Media of exchange Money, Redistribution

Executives, shortage of, 333
Expatriates, 384–5
Experimental stations, 328
Exports, 310, 313, 329, 337; agricultural, 16, 151; and agricultural productivity, 156; connection with internal economic structure, 20; costs of production of, 154; demand for, 346; and domestic food production, 163; importance of, in African economy, 15; increase in value of, 1907–29, 17, 1935–55, 18; increase in volume of, 1935–55, 18; livestock, 61; markets for, as stimulus, 20; prices of, 226–7; production of, 300; and real incomes in W. Africa, 216–17; secondary effects of volume of, 312; taxes on, 227; trade in, 179–80, 185; trends in territorial shares, 19; world markets for, 25; *see also* World demand
Extended family: as economic unit in W. Africa, 80–1; obligations as impediment to economic growth, 195
Extension services, 165–6, 177, 273, 339, 343, 345; *see also* Infrastructure, Research, Technology
External relations, cost of, 379

Fabian socialism, 392
Family, primary, 277
Family heads, role of: in landholding, 105; in landholding among Nsaw, 100, Nyanga, 101–2, and S.E. African peoples, 103; in Yoruba land tenure, 142–3
Farm inputs; *see* Production, agricultural, Productivity
Farming; *see* Agriculture
Fertility: and exhaustion of soil, 155; of urban population, 248; *see also* Population
Fertilizers, 328, 341
Financing, 360; of infrastructure, 274–5; *see also* Capital, Investment
Fiscal systems, poor, 330
Food, 13, 314, 329; in E. Africa, 14; purchased, 162; staple, in Turu, 55
Foodstuffs, tropical, 338, 341

Forecasts, 368–9
Foreign aid, 359–60, 368, 388; *see also* Assistance
Foreign exchange, 302, 312, 331
Foreign relations, 378; *see also* External relations
Fulani, 79

Ganda (Baganda, Buganda): attitudes toward cattle, 125; business enterprises, 184; as centralized, stratified society, 127; landholding among, 105; social stratification among, 120
Geological surveys, 243, 345
Gezira Project, 164, 173, 339
Gold, 299–300, 310; fields, 302; production of, 18–19; in world trade, 15
"Gold-coasting," as business practice, 188
Goods and services: demand for new, 127; evaluation of, in social stratification, 113; preferences for, 323–6; in social stratification, 124–6
Government loans, 352
Grain, 54; relation between livestock and, 57; as staple food, 55; as trade for livestock in E. Africa, 57
Grants, 362
Groundnut Scheme, 174, 339, 359
Groundnuts, 314, 338; production of, 17
Guarantees, by World Bank, 366
Gusii, bridewealth and exchange equivalents, 66

Hausa, 83–4, 87–9, 91–2; merchants, 193
Head tax; *see* Tax
Headmen (village), role in landholding, among Bemba (Rhodesia), 103, Mambwe (N. Rhodesia), 104, Tonga (Rhodesia), 103, Tswana (S. Africa), 104, and other S.E. African peoples, 103
Health, 247–9; public, 246
Homestead, economy of: in production of goods and services, 117; in Turu, 56

Housing, 247, 362
Hut tax; *see* Tax
Hydro-electric power, 367

Ibo, 86, 88–9, 92; cooperatives, 186, 191; role of entrepreneurs among, 189
Illiteracy, 358; as impediment to economic growth, 195
Immigration, European, into Rhodesia, 311
Imperialism, 389
Import-competing industries: importance of, 23–4; as index of growth, 21; indigenous control of, 23; potential size of, 23; role of, 20; and size of markets, 25
Imports: barriers to, 330; demand for, in Turu, 62; food, 152; as incentive goods, 280; as index of size of market, 331; prices of, 210; as substitutes for local goods, 306–7; trade in, 179–80, 184, 186, 188–90; during World War II, 211–12
Incentive, for money income, 280, 304; goods, 305; in Turu, 60
Income, 368; and demand for food, 160; of farmers, 211; industrial origin of, 48; leakage, from domestic stream, 312; money, total and per capita, 200; real, 1949–59, 218; real, in W. Africa, 1939–60, 199–238; real, and World War II, 203; sources of, for Africans, 287; total, 330; *see also* Prices, Standards of living, Wages
Income distribution, 22; *see also* Technology
Indenture, 304; *see also* Labor
Indians (East), economic role of, in Africa, 179–80
Individuals: recent changes in landholding of, 111–12; rights in land of, 105–6
Industrial societies, 287; economic characteristics of, in social stratification, 117
Industrialization, 270, 391; and agricultural improvement, 177; and future growth, 23–6; and popula-

tion capacity, 244; and population growth, 252; and scale, 247
Industry, 404
Inequality, political and economic, 122
Inflation: in France, and income in W. Africa, 213; and marketing boards, 347; and real income in W. Africa, 211; as sign of misallocation, 330
Infrastructure, 197, 229, 263, 269, 313, 345, 362, 404–5; sources of capital for, 20–3; *see also* Communications, Education, Irrigation, Power, Railroads, Sewerage, Transportation, Water supply
Innovations, 303, 327; in African economies, 184–90
Interdependence, economic, 359 ff.
Interest rates, 324; high, 330; on loans of grain among Logoli, 71; on loans of millet in Turu, 57
Investment, 265, 269, 272, 323, 330–4, 344, 368; criteria, 330; direct, 349, 352; domestic, in Africa, 315; in education, 383; in exploitation, 301; foreign, 349 ff., 401; foreign, private, 366; foreign, and rate of interest, 324; guarantees, 354; in industry and agriculture, 329; patterns of, 190–3; public, 275; *see also* Capital
Iron ore, 341; deposits and transportation of, 266
Irrigation, 165, 345
Iteso: cattle as bridewealth, 66; sale of cattle, 66; table of exchange equivalents, 66

Kikuyu: beads as "currency," 65; business enterprises, 184–5; community improvement, 192; landholding among, 120, 144–8; livestock as standard of value, 65; trade with Masai, 65
King: economic prerogatives of, 126; as political official, 119; role of, in landholding among Rotse, 101, Ruanda, 103, and Yoruba, 141; role of, in trade, 127

Kinship, 277, 403; evaluation of, in social stratification, 117; and land tenure, among Tiv, 135–41, and Yoruba, 141–4; obligations as impediment to economic growth, 195; systems in land tenure and use, 134; systems in social stratification, 123–4

Kola nuts: in Djenne, 95; trade in, in Ghana and Ivory Coast, 93

Kongo, 108; principles of landholding, 99

Labor, 281, 402; commercialization of, 127; control of, 126; forced, 214, 216, 280; legislation, 295; male, in agriculture, 164; as means of acquiring land title, 104; migratory, 281–4; in mining and manufacturing, 310; seasonal, 284; shortage, 292; skilled, 272; skilled and unskilled, 288–9; skills, lack of, 313; supply of, and coercion, 304; systems, 279; wage, 287; wage, demand for, 314

Labor unions; see Trade unions

Land: commercialization of, 127; as factor of production, 126; limits of available, 26; sale of, in E. Africa, 65, Sukuma, 67, and Turu, 56; sale of, and transfer of, 69; as scarce resource, 175, 280; surveys of resources of, 243

Land Apportionment Act, in S. Rhodesia, 169

Land reform: consequences of, in Africa, 135, 148–9; among Kikuyu, 147–8, and Yoruba, 143–4

Land tenure, 314, 328, 344, 403; and agricultural improvement, 176; on paysannats, 168; political aspects of, in Africa, 10; problems of, in new states, 109–10; in Turu, 56; in W. Africa, 80; see also Chiefs, Headmen, Kinship, Lineage

Leaders, 380–1, 383; African, 377–8

Leather goods, trade in, 15

Leisure, and sexual division of labor, 154

Lending, international, 362, 366; of IBRD, 366

Levantines, economic role of, in W. Africa, 179–80

Light industry, 351

Lineage, and land tenure: as factor in landholding, 100–1, 103–5, 107–12; among Tiv, 135–41, and Yoruba, 141–4

Linguistic usage, in landholding, 100

Liquor, as incentive good, 305

Literacy; see Education

Livestock, 400; as bridewealth among Ndorobo, 147; see also Cattle

Loans; see Interest rates, Lending

Logoli, 65, 68–9, 71

Lozi (Rhodesia), landholding among, 107; trade with Tonga, 310

Lulua (Congo), landholding among, 110

Lunda, landholding among, 103, 109

Maize, 152, 165, 310; rust, 152

Malaria, 246

Management, 272; in African business, 182, 194–7

Manganese, 310

Manioc, 154

Manufacturing, 315, 329, 341, 354

Manure, 54, 57

Marketing boards, 316, 339, 347; see also Marketing policy

Marketing policy, 211–12, 215, 226–7, 339

Markets, 17, 25, 179–80, 182, 272, 346, 401, 404; in Bidu, 88, Dahomey, 87, Djenne, 94–5, Gold Coast in 1602, 92, Kikuyu, 65, Nupe, 88, Salaga, 93–4, Timbuktu, 95–6, and Tiv, 88; cycles, 85–6; feeder, 86; in grain and livestock, in E. Africa, 69, in pre-colonial W. Africa, 9, 81, and in Turu, 61; as integrating principle in capitalist society, 134; occurrence of, in W. Africa, 85; present, in W. African hinterland, 97; production for sale in, in W. Africa, 81–2; scramble for, by Europeans, 97; size of, 330, 342, 354; and transportation, 244–5, 264; volume of sales in Hausa, 91–2; see also Production

Marxian socialism, 392

Masai: trade with Bantu, 66, and Kikuyu, 65

Matrilineal peoples, recent problems of land inheritance among, 111

Mau Mau: as rooted in land controversies, 147; and Swynnerton Plan, 172

Mechanization, 174; of agriculture, 165; *see also* Production, Productivity

Media of exchange, 306, 400, 404; in E. Africa, 53, 64; in the Gold Coast, 93; after introduction of Euroamerican economy, 67; among the Kikuyu and Logoli, 65; in Salaga, 93; in Timbuktu, 95; among the Tswana, 67, and Turu, 63; in W. Africa, 77, 86, 88, 91

Men, 401; interest of, in cattle, 70; rights of, in land, 104, 106–8; role of, in Turu household, 56; traders of W. Africa, 181

Metals, non-ferrous, 341, 346

Metropolitan powers, 363, 378–9, 388

Middle class, commercial, in Africa, 179, 193

Middlemen, 401; Arab, in trans-Saharan trade, 78, and among Turu, 55; guilds of, in Nupe, 88; influx of, in Turu, 61; in markets of Dahomey, 81, Djenne, 95, Hausa, 89–90, Mossi, 94, and Salaga, 93–4; Somali, among Suk, 68; women as, in W. African markets, 87–8, 93; *see also* Traders

Migration, 249, 281–3, 311, 314, 317; conditions leading to, 22; internal, 241–2; inter-territorial, 242; of labor force, 24; seasonal and semipermanent, 17

Minerals, 247, 272, 302, 344, 351, 353–4; exports, 338; production, 17–19, 337; resources, 25, 243

Mining, 309–10, 368

Missionaries, 305

Mobilization, social and political, 382

Modernization, 381

Money, 54, 282; acquisition of, 304; backing of issue, 312; demand for, 127; *see also* Cash, Media of exchange

Money economy: impact of, on traditional economies, 12, 67; and market economy, 63; in Rhodesia, 317–18; among Wanyatura (Turu), 53

Moral ideas, as basis of social stratification, 113

Mortality, 247; and dependency, 251; *see also* Dependency, Population

Mossi, 80, 94; adjustment to new lands, 111

Multiracialism, 285–6, 402–3

Mwambe (N. Rhodesia), landholding patterns among, 104

National goals, 380

Nationalism, 369; economic, 324; political, 378

Native Land Husbandry Act, 168; in S. Rhodesia, 169

Ndorobo, in Kikuyu landholding patterns, 147

Negritude, 129, 389, 392

Neo-colonialism, 366–7, 388

Neutralism, 387

Niger, Office du, 164, 173–4, 381

Niger Agricultural Project, 174, 359

Non-alignment; *see* Neutralism

Nsaw (Cameroons), allocation of land among, 100–1; rights to land among, 106

Nupe, 80, 83, 88–9, 91–3; landholding patterns among, 108

Nyanga (Congo): alienation of land among, 108; land rights and linguistic usage, 101; landholding among, 101–2

Occupation, 293; of labor, 287–8; *see also* Labor, Underemployment

Oilseeds, 213, 340

Output per capita, 323

Palm oil, 278, 338

Palm products, 218, 302, 314, 325, 338, 346; in foreign trade, 15; on plantations, 308

Pan-Africanism, 388, 390

Paramount chiefs, role in landholding among Nsaw, 100

Partnership, 344; *see also* Investment

Party, political, 394–6

Pax (colonial), 301, 303

Paysannats indigènes, 165, 167

Peanuts, incomes of growers of, 210, 213; *see also* Groundnuts

Petroleum, 341, 351, 368

Planners, economic, 329, 331, 333

Plans, 357, 359–60; agricultural development, 345

Plantains, 152–3; and labor requirements for food production, 154

Plantations, 175, 307–9, 368

Plowing, 165, 173

Political: and economic change, interrelations between, 401, 403–5; factors essential to economic growth, 197–8; factors in future stratification, 129–30; factors in landholding, 99–101, 103–4, 106, 112; factors in trade, 126–7; fragmentation, 377; independence, 319, 323, 343, 367, 369, 381–2, 388; one-party system, 393–6; organization and land tenure, 133–4, among Africans generally, 148–9, Kikuyu, 144, and Yoruba, 141; persuasion, 326; roles, evaluation of, in social stratification, 119; systems, 384; *see also* Authority, Chiefs, Kings, Land tenure

Polygyny: conditions of, in Turu, 56; importance of, in production of grain, 71; in social stratification, 123

Population, 152, 280, 329; carrying capacity, 241; censuses of, 243; classed as wage-earners, 16; and demand for food, 156, 164; density, variations of, 241; economically active, 16; farm, 163; fertility and mortality, 248; growth, 247, 368, 381; growth and economic growth, 24, 250–2; growth and mortality, 249; in native reserves, 168; non-farm, 156–7, 163

Ports, 264–5, 267–8, 339

Power: electrical, 270, 362; electrical, and minerals, 247; utilities, 177

Power, political: as basis for social stratification, 126–7; importance of organization of, in Africa, 115

Prestige: attached to landholding, 107; cattle as measure of, 62; in rights over land, 101; in Turu, 62

Price system, 246, 332, 358

Prices, 339, 346–7, 403; in Bida, 88; in Dahomean markets, 87; declining, 342–3; of exports, 338; as measure of per capita income, 200; time series of, 230–8

Processing: facilities and supply, 339; local, 338

Production, 357; characteristics of indigenous systems of, 15; for domestic markets, 23; of food, 152; of goods and services as factor in social stratification, 124; land as factor of, 133; for money, 127; role of domestic and kinship units in, 117; site of, 117; for world markets, 1885–1905, 15

Production, agricultural, 151, 272, 337, 402, 404; changes in, 163–77; for cities, 314; for domestic consumption, 25; economics of, 155; in indigenous W. African economies, 77, 79–81; pattern of, among Tiv, 137–8; and purchased food, 162; as replacement for war, 154; stimulation of, 9; traditional, 279; volume and value of, 18; during World War II, 211–12

Productivity, 25–6, 152, 244, 252, 294–5; agricultural, 151, 164, 178, 343; agricultural, and transportation, 245; demand and measured agricultural, 156; increases in, 24; of investment, 335; of labor, 293, 333; measurement of, 163; of migrant labor, 24, 242; *see also* Education, Migration

Profit, 331, 381

Profit motive, 399; among E. African peoples, 71–2, 181

Public authorities, 331

Public debt, 351–2

Purchasing power, 201–2

Pyrethrum, 171, 175

Racialism, 389–90, 393

Railroads, 265–6, 339; building of, 1885–1905, 16; end of period of building of, in 1914, 17

Re-Africanization; *see* Africanization

Reciprocity, 278; in exchange in E. African economies, 74; and security, 283

Recruiting; *see* Labor

Redistribution, in African exchange, 119–20, 126

Reinterpretation, as essential process in cultural change, 399

Religious factors: in landholding, 99–100, 103, 105, 108–9, 112; in social stratification, 114–15

Research, 339, 345; agricultural, 274, 328; on economic development, 361; *see also* Assistance, Experimental stations, Extension services

Reserves: of African banking systems, 312–13; of marketing boards, 347

Resources, 357–8, 360, 370; control over non-labor, 20–1; potentials, 243; *see also* Capital, Land, Minerals

Rice, 173

Rights, in women among Kikuyu, 145; *see also* Kikuyu, Land, Land tenure, Tiv, Yoruba

Roads, 266–7, 339, 362

Roles: allocation of, 124; cultural evaluation of, 116, 120; development of new occupational, 128; differentiation of, in Africa, 116, 119–20; occupational, in Africa and in industrial societies, 120–2

Rotse (Barotse, N. Rhodesia), landholding among, 101

Rubber, 338, 359; wild, in world trade, 15; world market for, 156

Rwandi: as caste society, 121; cattle as status symbols among, 125

Salaga, role in trade, 93–4

Savings, 368; of cooperatives, 185–6, 190; and domestic income, 21–2; in Ghana and Nigeria, 315; patterns of, 190–3; as percentage of income, 333; in Rhodesia, 316

Scale, of nation-states, 377–8

School leavers, 383

Security, economic and social, 283

Seeds, improvement of, 328

Senufo, 85

Settler's frontier, 305, 309 ff.; and U.N. prototypes, 20

Sewerage, 270, 362

Shortages, as economic planning indices, 332

Silviculture, 21; and food production, 153; *see also* Cocoa, Coffee, Rubber

Sisal, 338, 340, 346

Slaves, 280, 301; abolition of, 97; in agriculture, 81; as cause of change, 279; in craft production, 85; of merchants in Djenne, 95; of nobles in Timbuktu, 95; trade in, 15, 96–7, 300

Social benefit, as economic criterion, 330–1

Social organization, 279; in Africa, 148; aspects of, in landholding, 99; and land tenure, among Kikuyu, 144–8, Tiv, 135–41, and Yoruba, 141–4; as related to land, 135; *see also* Ancestors, Kinship, Social stratification, Status

Social stratification, 403; cultural factors in, 113; justification for inequality in, 121; models of, 122–3; place of businessmen in, 197; political factors in, 115–16, 119–20; recent changes in systems of, 127–30; relations between economic differentials and, 10; secondary culture of, 121–2; secondary structural aspects of, 122; in W. Africa, 81; *see also* Cultural

Socialism, African, 389, 392–3

Societies, "peasant," 121–2

Songhoi, 84, 92

Sonjo, bridewealth, 66

Sovereignty, 391

Specialization, 404; of labor in Africa, 179; of labor in political offices, 119; lack of, in labor, 287; variation in economic, in African households, 117–19

Stabilization, 286; *see also* Detribalization, Urbanization

Stabilization funds, 347; in French Africa, 227

Standards of living, 203, 217–18, 226, 247

Standards of remuneration, 386; *see also* Wage policies, Wages, real

Standards of value, goats as: among Kikuyu, 64, and Sonjo, 66; systematic, in E. African economies, 64; *see also* Cattle, Media of exchange

Starchy staples, 152

State, 377, 380–1, 390, 394

Statism, 392, 395–6

Status, 403; achieved and ascribed in Buganda, 121; as central to social system, 148; goods and services as symbols of, 124; systems of, as effected by extended kinship system, 123–4; in systems of social stratification, 122; *see also* Social stratification

Storage, 339

Sub-cultures: in caste societies, 121; "folk" and "elite," 121; general absence of, in Africa, 122; as related to social stratification, 121

Subsidy, 329–30, 332

Subsistence economy, 277; transition from, 181–2

Supply, 346; of exports, 339

Survey, 360, 366; *see also* Geological surveys, Minerals, Resources

Swollen shoot disease, 217, 343

Swynnerton Plan, in Kenya, 170–2, 178

Taboos, and fertility, 248–9

Tallensi (N. Ghana): crafts, 82; landholding among, 107

Target worker; *see* Labor, Migration

Tariff, 332; relief from, 353

Tax, 348; on exports, 347; head or hut, 281; payment of, 281; systems, poor, 330; *see also* Marketing boards

Tea, 175, 342

Technical advance; *see* Technological change

Techniques; *see* Technology

Technological change, 334, 340, 357; different rates of, in dual sectors, 329

Technological gap, 326–7

Technology, 247, 277, 293, 301–2, 326; agricultural, 318; applied, 335; changes in, 163–77; as determinant of income distribution, 22; from indigenous to machine, 324; of sectors, 20; *see also* Income distribution, Labor

Terms of trade: income, 203; net barter, 202

Territorialization, 278; *see also* Africanization

Timber, 338, 342

Timbuktu, 77–8, 84; markets in, 95; as trading center, 96

Time: horizon, 334; preference, 323–6; as scarce item, 323

Tin, 302, 307, 314, 348

Title; *see* Land, Land tenure

Tiv, 82, 88; kinship and land tenure, 135–41; landholding among, 104; political authority among, 119

Tobacco, 317, 338

Tonga (N. Rhodesia): landholding among, 103–4; trade with Lozi, 310

Trade: barriers to foreign, 330; capital formation in, 190, 193; foreign, 368, 404–5; goods, 279; in grain, 70; innovations in, 9, 184–9; inter-African, 19; between Kikuyu, Masai, and other E. African tribes, 65; in livestock among Suk, 71; patterns of, 179–82; patterns of, 1885–1905, 15; practices as impediments to growth, 194–7; in pre-colonial W. Africa, 9; role of rulers in, 126–7; routes, 89–96; status of, as occupation, 124, 197; systems in W. Africa, 77–9, 85–9; among Turu households, 59; *see also* Exports, Imports

"Trade chiefs," role of, in W. African trade and markets, 87

Trade unions, 214–15, 217, 228, 285, 290–1

Trader's frontier, 305; and U.N. prototypes, 20

Traders, African, 306, 309; erosion of status of, 315; *see also* Exports, Imports, Middlemen, Trade

Training, managerial, 196; technical, 328; *see also* Education

Transformation, 329; of agriculture, 328; structural, 163

Transportation, 247, 302, 315, 342, 345, 360; absence of heavy, 17; and agriculture, 164; dampening of secondary effects of, 313; and economic structure, 244–5; and export supply, 339; of exports, 25; financing of, 274; importance of, in African economic development, 15; and infrastructure, 264–9; lack of mechanized, 15; spread of, 24; and urban growth, 26

Trypanosomiasis, 246, 264

Tsetse fly; *see* Trypanosomiasis

Tswana (S. Africa), landholding among, 104

Turkana, livestock in internal and external trade, 66

Turnover of labor, 293; *see also* Labor, Migration

Turu; *see* Wanyaturu

Underdeveloped economies, 280, 343

Underemployment, 292–3, 304, 333

Unemployment, 247, 292; rural and urban, 324; *see also* Labor, Productivity, Urbanization

Unity, African, 377, 389, 391

Universities, 385, 387

Urbanization, 160–1, 245–7, 270, 282, 286, 314; and demand for domestic food, 163; and domestic economic growth, 26; *see also* Detribalization, Stabilization

Usufruct, rights in, among Tiv, 139

Utilization, optimal, of capital, 330; *see also* Allocation of resources, Capital

Values: attached to land, 104; attached to political power and offices, 119; concerning stratification, 113–16; 120–1; in Modjokuto, 114–15

Villages, regrouping of, 246

Wage earners, 218; incomes of, 209–10

Wage earning, 161–2, 310–11, 317; population classed as, 16

Wage policies, 214, 228

Wages, real, 210, 225

Wanyaturu (Turu, Kenya), 400; economy of, 59–61; goals and operations of economy, 55–6

War, as traditional male occupation, 154; *see also* Production, agricultural

Water supply, 270, 362; *see also* Infrastructure

Wealth: as basis for social stratification, 122–3; as source of prestige in Turu, 62; among Sukuma, 67, 71; variations in, among Turu, 59–60

Women; *see* Kikuyu, Land, Land tenure, Production, Trade, Traders

Worker's brigades, in Ghana, 383

World demand: for primary products, 340–2; for tropical foodstuffs, 338

World War II, 211; effect of, on labor supply, 216; effect of, on real incomes, 203

Yams, 152–3

Yoruba, 81, 86–7, 89, 92; cooperatives, 185, 191; land tenure and kinship, 141–4; specialization of labor among, 118

Yumbe (Republic of Congo): alienation of land among, 108, 110; landholding among, 102

Zulu, as centralized, stratified society, 126

Index of Names and Places

Abidjan, 174, 210, 225, 268

Accra, 163, 210, 217, 225, 314

Addae, G., 181 (n. 2), 193 (n. 36)

Ady, P., 212, 227 (n. 26), 230, 234-5

Albert, E., 121 (n. 13)

Amogu, O. O., 185 (n. 22), 191 (n. 29), 192 (n. 31)

Angola, 175, 266, 291, 352

Apter, D. E., 294, 377 (n. 1)

Arnold, R., 127

Asia, 119, 122, 124, 340

Aubrey, H. C., 198 (nn. 49, 50)

Balandier, G., 287 (n. 36), 288 (n. 43), 290 (n. 50)

Baldwin, K. D. S., 174, 359 (n. 5)

Bamako, 80, 85, 93-4

Barber, W. F., 9, 20, 173 (n. 38), 311 (n. 15), 400

Barth, H., 84, 91, 96 (n. 81), 97

Bascom, W. R., 118 (n. 6), 185 (n. 22), 191 (n. 30)

Batten, T. R., 358 (n. 3)

Bauer, P. T., 184 (nn. 14, 15), 186 (n. 23), 188 (n. 24), 190, 192 (n. 34), 193 (n. 36), 199, 202, 212, 230, 234-5, 314 (n. 19)

Baumann, H., 154 (n. 6)

Belgian Congo, 16, 18, 21, 24, 26, 162-3, 165, 167, 304, 308, 338, 351-2, 358 (n. 4), 367, 369 (n. 17)

Benin, 82-4, 86, 94

Berg, E. J., 9, 16, 20, 215 (n. 16), 282 (n. 21), 400, 405

Berreman, G. D., 121 (n. 12)

Bertrand, R., 212 (n. 12), 237

Beyrard, N., 227 (n. 27)

Bida, 88, 93, 118

Biebuyck, D., 21, 168 (n. 25)

Binger, L. G., 93

Biobaku, S. B., 87 (n. 45)

Birmingham, W., 199 (n. 3)

Bohannan, L., 80 (n. 10), 88 (n. 49)

Bohannan, P. J., 10, 21, 80 (n. 10), 88 (n. 49), 104 (n. 14), 119 (n. 9), 135 (n. 1), 406

Bongouanou, 153-4

Bornu, 89, 266

Bovill, E. W., 77-8, 93 (n. 65)

Bower, P., 307 (n. 9)

Bradbury, R. E., 80 (n. 12), 83 (nn. 23, 24)

Brice, B., 379 (n. 3)

British Central Africa, 304

British East Africa, 347, 350-1

British territories, 18, 179, 181

British West Africa, 308, 351

Brown, L. H., 170 (n. 32)

Brozen, Y., 198 (n. 47)

Burden, G. N., 282 (n. 19)

Burundi, 24, 121; see also Ruanda-Urundi

Busia, K., 103 (n. 8), 109 (n. 35)

Butt, A., 71

Cailie, R., 95-7

Callaway, A. C., 383 (n. 8)

Cameroons, 100, 104, 291

Cameroun Republic, 393

Carriera, A., 281 (n. 14)

Central Africa, 181, 190, 278, 310

Central African Republic, 154, 241

Chevalier, A., 93

Chudson, W. A., 9, 25, 27, 400, 405

Clapperton, H., 84, 89, 97

Clayton, E. S., 170-1 (n. 36)

Clemence, R. V., 183 (n. 10)

Coale, A. J., 250 (n. 6)

Cole, A. H., 182 (n. 8), 198 (n. 48)

Coleman, J. S., 9-10, 377 (n. 1), 379 (n. 3), 385 (n. 12), 404

439

Colson, E., 67, 104 (n. 14), 115 (n. 5), 310 (n. 14)
Comhaire, J. L., 287 (n. 36)
Comhaire-Sylvain, S., 181 (n. 2)
Commonwealth East Africa, 20
Compagnie de Haut-Katanga, 288–9
Congo, 21–2, 99, 101, 103, 105, 108–11, 119, 175, 281, 291; *see also* Belgian Congo, Republic of the Congo
Congo Republic, 266, 367
Cook, A. N., 306 (n. 8)
Cornevin, R., 77
Coyand, Y., 173 (n. 40)
Crine, F., 103 (n. 9)
Curtis, L., 300 (n. 2)

Dahomey, 81–4, 87, 127, 268, 393
Dakar, 152, 174, 210, 225
Dalton, G., 63
Damongo; *see* Gonja
Danso, T. V., 165 (n. 20)
Deane, P., 5
De Briey, P., 155, 294 (n. 69)
Delarozière, R., 283 (n. 22)
Denham, D., 84 (n. 28), 89 (nn. 55, 56)
De Schlippe, P., 278 (n. 2)
Deyrup, F., 197 (n. 46)
Dia, Mamadou, 381
Diké, K. O., 86 (n. 40), 97 (n. 83), 184 (n. 16)
Djenne, 78, 80–1, 85, 93–5
Doody, F. S., 183 (n. 10)
Dubois, F., 85, 94–6 (nn. 80, 81)
Dupire, M., 278 (n. 5)

East Africa, 53, 63, 67–72, 74, 181, 190, 194, 266, 277
East African Royal Commission, 283–4 (n. 26)
Easterbrook, W. T., 198 (n. 47)
Elkan, W., 128 (n. 24), 184 (n. 18), 287 (n. 37), 289 (n. 45), 291 (n. 55)
Epstein, A. L., 289
Ethiopia, 128, 244, 249, 342, 344 (n. 7)
Europe, 78, 122, 124, 135, 139
Evans-Pritchard, E. E., 72
Ezeabasili, A. N., 185 (n. 22), 192 (n. 32)

Fage, J. D., 300 (n. 1)
Fahm, L. A., 9, 23, 358 (n. 2)
Fallers, L. A., 10, 121 (n. 11), 122 (n. 15), 128 (n. 24), 133, 287 (n. 37), 401, 405
FAO (Food and Agricultural Organization of the United Nations), 173 (n. 40), 174 (n. 41), 176 (n. 45), 345 (n. 9)
Fawzi, S. E. D., 284 (n. 29), 288
Federation of Rhodesia and Nyasaland, 18, 21–2, 24–5, 338, 350–2
Firth, R., 7 (n. 3)
Fleming, R. I., 195 (n. 40), 196, 197 (n. 43), 198 (n. 49)
Floyd, B. N., 155 (n. 10), 168 (n. 26)
Forde, D., 118 (n. 7), 127 (n. 23)
Fortes, M., 105 (n. 15), 107 (n. 22), 108 (nn. 26, 27), 109 (n. 34)
Frankel, S. H., 15 (n. 2), 17 (n. 8), 275, 301 (n. 4), 313 (n. 16), 359 (n. 5)
French Equatorial Africa, 291, 347, 400
French West Africa, 17, 21–2, 288, 291, 347, 359, 400

Gabon, 5, 241, 248
Gaitskell, A., 173
Gambia, 248, 281, 291, 378
Gamble, D. P., 85
Gao, 78, 94
Garlick, P. C., 181 (n. 3), 193 (n. 36)
Geertz, C., 114
Ghana, 18, 21–3, 26, 87, 93, 99, 107–9, 165–6, 173–4, 179, 185–6, 190, 193–4, 198–9, 214, 242, 244, 266–7, 275, 288, 290–1, 305, 307–8, 311, 313–14, 339, 343, 347, 349–50, 358 (n. 4), 359, 367, 369 (n. 18), 377, 379, 382–3, 390–1, 393–4; *see also* Gold Coast
Gluckman, M., 100 (n. 2), 101 (n. 5), 103, 106 (n. 17), 107 (n. 19), 126 (n. 20), 310 (n. 14)
Gold Coast, 18, 23, 93, 166, 184, 300 (n. 1); *see also* Ghana
Goldschmidt, W., 358 (n. 3)
Gonja, 91, 174
Goodfellow, D. M., 63, 67
Gouldsbury, V. S., 94 (n. 69)

Gray, R. F., 66, 70, 74
Green, M. M., 185 (n. 22), 191 (n. 30)
Green, R. H., 212 (n. 11), 215 (n. 17), 217 (n. 20), 226 (n. 25)
Grévisse, F., 400
Griaule, M., 115 (n. 5)
Guillemin, R., 154 (n. 7)
Guilloteau, J., 155
Guinea, 85, 95, 173, 242, 267, 343, 359, 367, 369 (n. 17), 379, 382–4, 386, 388, 390, 393–4
Guinea Coast, 82, 119, 123
Gulliver, P. H., 66, 278, 283 (n. 24)

Hailey, Lord M., 185 (n. 21)
Hamilton, Alexander, 23
Hammond, P. B., 112 (n. 41)
Hance, W. A., 173 (n. 39)
Hancock, W. K., 184 (n. 14), 301 (n. 3), 305, 307 (n. 11)
Hanson, A. H., 381 (n. 6)
Harwitz, M., 406
Hassoun, I. A., 284 (n. 29)
Hauser, A., 288 (n. 43)
Hearn, H., 182 (n. 6)
Henry, P., 406
Herskovits, M. J., 7 (n. 3), 53, 72–4, 80 (nn. 8, 9, 13), 81 (nn. 14, 17), 83 (n. 22), 87, 124 (n. 17), 125, 181 (n. 5), 193 (n. 35), 287 (n. 36)
Hill, P., 110 (n. 38), 184 (n. 17)
Hirschman, A. O., 326 (n. 2)
Hodgkin, T., 384–5 (n. 11), 392 (n. 15)
Holas, B., 85 (n. 36)
Homan, 110 (n. 37)
Hoover, E. M., 250 (n. 6)
Hoselitz, B. F., 6 (n. 2), 17 (n. 7), 182 (n. 8), 198 (n. 49)
Hosking, H. R., 166 (n. 23)
Hoyt, E., 184 (n. 19), 292 (n. 61)
Hudson, W., 292 (n. 62)
Hunter, T., 165 (n. 20)
Huntingford, G. W. B., 65 (n. 10), 66, 71

IBRD (International Bank for Reconstruction and Development), 183 (n. 13), 196–7 (n. 46), 362, 366
Iliff, W. A., 366 (n. 12)

ILO (International Labour Office), 278, 281 (n. 15), 283 (n. 22), 285–6, 287 (n. 39), 288 (n. 41), 289, 290 (n. 54), 292 (n. 63), 293 (nn. 64, 65), 294 (nn. 67, 68)
India, 25, 121, 128, 135, 241
INEAC (l'Institut National Pour l'Étude Agronomique du Congo Belge), 167–8
Ivory Coast, 24, 85, 93, 110–11, 152, 199, 203, 214, 227, 248, 268, 277, 382, 393

Java, 114–15
Johnston, B. F., 9–10, 16, 20, 25–7, 79 (n. 7), 152 (nn. 1, 2), 155 (n. 10), 162 (n. 17), 167 (n. 24), 173 (n. 38), 174 (n. 44), 177 (n. 46), 274 (n. 8), 314 (n. 18)
Johnston, Sir H. H., 16 (n. 5)
Jones, E. H., 165
Jones, W. O., 79 (n. 6), 114 (n. 3), 152 (n. 1), 155 (n. 11), 399

Kaberry, P., 100 (nn. 3, 4), 104 (n. 14), 107 (n. 20)
Kamarck, A. M., 11, 15, 22, 24, 26
Kampala, 118, 269
Kano, 77–8, 84, 86–7, 89, 91–4, 96, 302
Katanga, 22, 24, 242, 274
Katzin, M., 9, 13, 25, 400
Kavirondo, 65, 73, 184
Keita, Madeira, 395
Kenya, 17, 20–2, 24, 64, 68, 107, 120, 135, 148 (n. 10), 155, 170–2, 175, 178, 184, 192, 243, 266, 268–9, 275, 288, 291, 325 (n. 1), 351–2, 358 (n. 4), 400
Kenyatta, J., 120 (n. 10)
Köbben, A., 105 (n. 15), 110 (n. 39)
Kumasi, 87, 93, 165
Kuznets, S., 402, 404, 406

Lagos, 94, 188, 210, 217, 225, 267, 314
Lawrence, J. C. D., 66
Leakey, L. S. B., 144 (n. 7), 147, 184–5 (n. 20), 192 (n. 33)
Leibenstein, H., 368 (n. 13)

Leith-Ross, S., 181 (n. 2)
Lengellé, M., 237
Leubuscher, C., 181 (n. 3), 281 (n. 17)
Levy, M. J., Jun., 124 (n. 16), 198 (n. 48)
Lewis, W. A., 23, 196, 271
Liberia, 16, 21, 85, 93, 266–7, 291, 345, 359
Little, K. L., 109 (n. 32), 278 (n. 3)
Lloyd, P. C., 141–3
Lonsdale, R. L. T., 93 (n. 67), 94 (n. 70)
Lorimer, F., 405
Lugard, Lord F., 15, 302

McCall, D. F., 181 (n. 3), 197 (n. 44)
McCulloch, M., 290 (n. 53)
MacMaster, D., 154 (n. 8)
McPhee, A., 300 (n. 1), 307 (n. 10)
Maine, Sir H., 148
Mair, L. P., 344 (n. 8)
Malcolm, D. W., 67 (n. 17), 69
Mali, 78, 173–4 (n. 41), 379, 386, 390, 393; *see also* Sudan, French
Malinows, B., 7 (n. 3), 99
Manoukian, M., 82, 88 (n. 48)
Maquet, J., 125 (n. 19)
Marees, P. de, 93 (n. 61)
Marriott, M., 121 (n. 12)
Mars, J., 315 (n. 21), 316 (n. 22)
Marshall, L., 114
Marx, K., 117
Mauritania, 241, 266
Mauss, M., 99
Mayer, P., 66
Meek, C. K., 81 (n. 16)
Mellor, J. W., 177 (n. 46), 274 (n. 8)
Mersadier, Y., 238
Middleton, J. F. M., 65 (n. 9), 120 (n. 10), 144 (n. 7)
Miner, H., 85 (n. 33), 95 (n. 77), 96 (n. 78)
Mitchell, J. C., 286, 289
Mombasa, 267, 269
Monteil, P. L., 94 (n. 71), 97
Moore, W. E., 11–12, 280 (n. 10), 281 (n. 16), 282 (n. 19), 284 (n. 27), 291 (n. 56), 406
Mozambique, 243, 266–7, 313, 352
Murdock, G. P., 79 (n. 5), 154 (n. 6)

Nadel, S. F., 80 (n. 13), 81 (n. 15), 83, 86 (n. 41), 88–9, 105 (n. 16), 108 (n. 25), 119 (n. 8), 188
Natal, University of, 289 (n. 49)
Newbury, C., 378 (n. 2)
Nigeria, 17–18, 21–6, 84, 104, 108, 129, 135, 139–40, 174, 179, 185–6, 190, 194–5, 198–9, 214, 266–7, 275, 290–1, 305, 307–8, 311, 313, 333, 339, 347–52, 358 (n. 4), 359, 367, 369 (n. 18), 378–80, 382–3, 391, 393
Nigeria, Eastern, 184–5, 191, 197, 325, 382
Nigeria, Northern, 15, 83, 140, 173, 184 (n. 15), 302, 307, 314, 377
Nigeria, Western, 141, 143, 162, 185, 188, 191, 228, 314, 382
Nkrumah, Kwame, 389–91, 393–4
Noll, N., 92 (n. 60)
North Africa, 77–8
North Kavirondo, 65, 70
Nurkse, R., 16 (n. 4)
Nyasaland, 17, 108, 242, 291
Nye, G. W., 166 (n. 23)
Nyirenda, A. A., 182 (n. 7)
Nypan, A., 193 (n. 37)

Ohlin, B., 358 (n. 1)
Okigbo, P. N. C., 9, 25–6
Ollone, L. G., 93
Onitsha, 86, 181, 183, 186–90, 192–7
Oppenheimer, H. F., 285 (n. 31)
Ottenberg, P., 104 (n. 14)
Ottenberg, S., 192 (n. 32)
Oyo, 129, 141

Pacques, V., 80 (n. 11), 85 (n. 35)
Palmer, H. R., 84 (n. 27)
Park, Mungo, 97
Parsons, T., 113 (n. 1)
Poleman, T. T., 152 (n. 2), 161 (n. 15), 163 (n. 18)
Poquin, J. J., 213 (n. 14), 237
Prain, R. L., 285 (n. 32)
Prins, A. H. J., 66

RDA (Rassemblement Démocratique Africain), 217
Redfield, R., 121
Redlich, F., 182 (n. 8)

Republic of the Congo, 20, 22, 103, 151, 241, 243, 267, 274, 288, 345, 348, 350, 352, 393, 400

Republic of South Africa, 15, 24, 266, 270, 275, 283, 338

Rhodesia, Northern, 5, 18, 22, 24, 103–4, 109, 151, 162–3, 175, 242, 266, 285, 289, 290–1, 302, 304–5, 310–11, 316–17

Rhodesia, Southern, 5, 18, 22, 168–70, 173, 175, 242, 266, 285, 288, 290–1, 304–5, 310–11, 316–17, 352

Richards, A. I., 103 (n. 11), 109 (n. 33), 278 (n. 2), 283 (n. 24), 290 (n. 52)

Rosenstein-Rodan, P., 26, 368, 370 (n. 19)

Rouch, J., 84, 284 (n. 28)

Ruanda-Urundi, 241–2, 248, 281, 291, 341, 344 (n. 7)

Rwanda, 24, 121, 125; *see also* Ruanda-Urundi

Salaga, 92–4

Samuelson, P. A., 183 (n. 12)

Sansanne Mango, 87, 94

Schapera, I., 67, 73, 104 (n. 13), 108 (n. 24)

Schneider, H. K., 8, 12, 64, 400, 405–6

Schumpeter, J. A., 183 (n. 10)

Schwab, G., 85 (n. 38), 93 (n. 66)

Senegal, 85, 199, 214, 227, 242, 302, 393, 407

Senghor, L. S., 393

Sennar, 89, 173

Sheddick, U. G. J., 67

Sierra Leone, 85, 151, 174, 291, 308, 369 (n. 18), 379

Singer, H. W., 11, 16, 20, 24–6, 197 (n. 46), 247 (n. 3), 250 (n. 5)

Skinner, E. P., 9, 17, 80 (n. 12), 118, 400

Sluiter, G., 120 (n. 10), 144 (n. 7), 145

Smith, M. F., 89 (n. 54)

Smith, M. G., 193, 197 (n. 44)

Smythe, H. & M., 129

Sofer, C., 290 (n. 51)

Sokoto, 92, 94

Somalia (Somaliland), 17, 241, 248, 339, 342, 345, 352, 377

South Africa, 5, 16–25, 53, 104, 108, 285, 288, 304, 350–2; *see also* Republic of South Africa

South West Africa, 17, 241, 266

Southall, A. W., 278 (n. 2), 281 (n. 13), 282 (n. 20)

Soviet Union; *see* USSR

Spengler, J. J., 241, 250 (n. 6)

Stamp, D. S., 79 (n. 4)

Stephens, R. W., 282 (n. 19)

Subsaharan Africa, 18, 24, 77

Sudan, 5, 17, 22, 53, 78, 81–2, 85, 103, 115, 119, 128, 173, 266, 275, 339, 345, 350, 378, 380, 400

Sudan, French, 164, 173

Swynnerton, R. J. M., 171 (n. 34)

Talbot, P. A., 81, 83 (n. 23), 86 (nn. 39, 42, 43), 87 (n. 44)

Tanganyika, 67, 108, 174–5, 185, 266–7, 275, 281, 288, 291, 338–9, 341, 345, 349, 358 (n. 4), 378

Tax, S., 182 (n. 9)

Thomas, B. E., 148 (n. 11)

Thomas, E. M., 114 (n. 2)

Tilho, Lt., 92

Timbuktu, 77–8, 82, 84, 87, 93–6

Togo, 87, 92, 291, 378, 393

Touré, Sekou, 383–4, 394–5

UAC (United Africa Company), 235–6

Udy, S. H., 279

Uganda, 24, 105, 165–7, 185, 243–4, 248, 266, 269–70, 274–5, 281, 304, 339, 347, 351, 358 (n. 4)

Union Minière, 274

United Nations, 18, 20–1, 345–6, 353 (nn. 18, 19), 358 (nn. 3, 4)

United Nations, Economic Commission for Africa, 19 (n. 11), 25 (n. 26), 346 (nn. 10, 11), 355 (n.)

United States (of America), 121, 340, 350

Upper Volta, 111, 216, 242, 248

USSR (Union of Soviet Socialist Republics), 342

Van Dongen, I. S., 265 (n. 2)
Vansina, J., 107 (n. 18)
Von Sick, E., 55, 61, 63–4

Wagner, G., 65, 68, 71, 105, 107 (n. 21)
Wallerstein, I., 378 (n. 2)
Watson, W., 104 (n. 13), 181 (n. 3),
    278 (n. 2)
West Africa, 9, 13, 77–8, 99, 103, 152,
    179, 289, 311, 316
White, C. M., 103 (n. 10), 104 (n. 12)
Williams, J. W., 197

Williamson, H. F., 406
Wilson, C., 308 (n. 13)
Wilson, G., 286 (n. 34)
Wilson, M., 108 (n. 29), 110 (n. 37)
Wolfson, F., 93 (n. 67), 94 (n. 70)
Wood, A., 174 (n. 42)
Wright, F. D., 181 (n. 3)
Wrigley, C., 264 (n. 1)

Xydias, N., 288 (n. 43), 289

Zimbe, B. M., 127